Wei
Weinstein, Lewis.
The heretic
$ 24.95

P9-ARU-609

THE HERETIC

Lewis Weinstein

goodnewfiction.com
New York

Copyright © 2000 by Lewis M. Weinstein
All rights reserved.
This book may not be reproduced, in whole or in part, in any form (beyond
copyright permitted by Sections 107 and 108 of the U.S. Copyright Law and
except by reviewers for the public press), without written permission from
the publisher.

This is a work of fiction. Some of the characters and events are based on
historical persons and events, but in all cases these persons and events have been
used fictitiously. All other characters and events are wholly products of the
author's imagination.

Author photograph by Patricia Lenny
Cover and interior design by Mayapriya Long, www.bookwrights.com
Printed in the United States of America

Published by
goodnewfiction.com
30 W. 63rd St., Suite 31N
New York, NY 10023
www.goodnewfiction.com

goodnewfiction books are distributed by Midpoint Trade Books

Cataloging-in-Publication Data

Weinstein, Lewis,
    The Heretic / Lewis Weinstein
      p.   cm.
    Includes Foreword by Msgr. Thomas J. Hartman
    ISBN 0-9671348-0-3 (alk. paper)
    1. History—Fiction. 2. History—Inquisition—Spain—Fiction.
    3. Jews—Persecutions—Fiction. I. Title.

2000   99-95226

DEDICATED TO

Patricia
who is my life

and to

Benjamin
who lost his much too soon

FOREWORD

by Monsignor Thomas J. Hartman

Marc Gellman and I rarely disagree. We're best friends. There are many best friends in the world, but the fact that he is a rabbi and I am a priest has caused some people to sit up and take notice. People see us on *Good Morning America* or *Imus In The Morning* or our own *God Squad* show. We try to look out at our world and find a reason for hope which cuts across our respective religious faiths and gets to the heart of spiritually responding to God and our neighbor. We've been at this for thirteen years and our disagreements and tense moments have been few.

Marc and I had it out one evening at a local television station. We were talking about the convent at Auschwitz. I was incensed. A Jewish rabbi — Avi Weiss — and a group of his followers had jumped over the convent wall to pray in protest. This startled and frightened the group of contemplative nuns who had built the convent at Auschwitz to pray for the victims of the Holocaust. "How," I asked Marc "can you or any other Jew support such an action? If Jews knew anything about these sisters they would realize that they were selfless, holy, and prayerful. They were committed to redeeming the ugly face of mass murder and destruction."

Marc listened. His face told me that he was searching for a way to share something painful with me in a caring way. He turned, looked me in the eye, and said, "Tom, you don't realize what the Cross of Jesus means to us Jews. For you the Cross is a sign of hope and redemption. For us it's a sign of despair and destruction. It was during the Inquisition and the Crusades that Christians led with the Cross as they murdered thousands of Jews. They killed Jews and

Muslims in the name of the Cross. Pogroms raped and pillaged our people in the name of vengeance toward the Jews that killed Christ." Marc's own aunt had once been abused by people leaving a Holy Week service looking for a Jew to vent their anger toward for the death of Jesus.

I didn't realize the depth of his feelings on the subject until we did that show. It took me aback. That which was a sign of hope and redemptive love for me — the Cross — was a sign of destruction for him. Recognizing this for the first time, I could see why a Jew would be offended at the sight of the Cross at the scene of one of the greatest massacres of Jewish people in human history. I turned and said, "Marc, if that's what the Cross represents to Jews, maybe we ought to take it down." "No," said Marc, "maybe we ought to build a synagogue next to the convent and we could both pray together."

The Heretic, a book by Lewis Weinstein, was where I turned in order to understand the Inquisition. I knew the outline of Christian atrocities but Lew's book taught me about the painful positions many good people were put into in order to survive. It's not a pretty picture. Their lives were all scarred in one way or another. But *The Heretic* reminds us of a history that we should not forget.

PROLOGUE

"No. Don't go out there," she pleads.

"You stay inside," he orders.

She shouts to her son. "Run! Get your father. Hurry!" She follows her father-in-law to the door, horrified by what she fears will happen.

The old man reaches the street just as the first of them come around the corner. He walks straight at them — they shrink back — the crowd has not yet gained the courage to attack one who is not afraid. They shout.

"Jewish pig!"

"Christ killer!"

"Devil worshipper!"

He raises his hands, and surprisingly, the crowd quiets.

"Why do you call me Jew?" he says softly. "I'm baptized just as you."

"Liar! We know what you converso Jews do. You don't work on Saturday, and you don't eat pork. You just pretend to be Christian."

"That's not true. I gave up the Jewish religion long ago. I wet my head in your baptismal water and I've been a good Christian ever since."

He smiles, laughs almost, knowing they are not convinced, that nothing he says will ever change their minds. But he is not afraid. He stands taller. He is eerily calm.

"You say I'm a Jew. Why? I don't pray to the God of Israel. I go to church and take the sacraments. My son is not circumcised."

He turns away. They follow. He spins to face them. It is time, after so many years. Time to be a Jew.

"Is this what you want?" he thunders.

Deliberately, he places his high crowned hat on his head. He tugs under his cloak and removes a long white scarf, the Jewish prayer shawl, the tallit. He holds it solemnly in front of him, aged eyes straining to see faded words. He prays silently, in Hebrew: Blessed are You, O Lord our God, King of the Universe, who has sanctified us by Thy commandments, and has commanded us to wrap ourselves in tallit.

He raises and twists the tallit. The pure white fabric unfolds, soars majestically and lands gently on his shoulders. He lifts it to cover his head. His face is hidden. He closes his eyes tightly. He is in another place.

He prays, she thinks, for the years he has lost, and perhaps also for the years ahead, though not for him: O God of Israel Who desires repentance, allow me to repent for the foolishness of my baptism. O God of Israel Who forgives, forgive me for willfully discarding Your commandments. O God of Israel Who redeems His people, accept me, and allow me once again to walk in Your ways.

He raises his voice, knowing the effect the strange sounding Hebrew words will have.

שמע ישראל
Hear O Israel
יהוה אלהינו
the Lord our God,
יהוה אחד
the Lord is One.

The crowd gasps. Swords are raised.

"Jesus of Nazareth is not God!" he shouts. "There is only one God, and He is the God of Israel!"

The first sword explodes against the side of his head, knocking his hat to the ground. A second shining blade slices into his shoulder. Bloodied, he does not fall. He says the Hebrew words slowly, powerfully.

ברוך שם כבוד מלכותו לעולם ועד
Blessed is the Name
of His glorious Kingdom
for all eternity

The bloody sword flashes again, and he smiles, the last act of his life. Now they all find courage. They know how to stomp on a dead man. Clubs and stones obliterate his features. Stabs to his chest. His tunic dark red.

She hears the horses a split second before the mob looks up. Her husband runs into the square, six armed men behind him. The mob retreats, its anger spent. He wraps the body of his father in his cloak, cradles the corpse gently in his arms, walks slowly into the house.

The young boy bends to retrieve his grandfather's bloody tallit from where it has fallen.

THE HERETIC

1

Six years later

"Bless me, Father, for I have sinned."

"The Lord be in your heart and on your lips so that you may worthily confess your sins."

The penitent's huge hands nervously gripped the rail between himself and the priest.

"Is it you, Father?"

The priest parted the curtain so the sinner could see his intense dark eyes, framed by heavy black eyebrows and the white inner hood of his otherwise black Dominican habit. He let the curtain fall.

"Did you bring information useful for the Lord's mission?"

"*Conversos* will pray tonight in a room under the home of the tailor Yacov Ardit."

"You're sure?"

"Yes."

"Will you be there?"

"I'm not a fool, Father."

"Thank you for your assistance. Do you wish to confess?"

The penitent shifted uncomfortably. He started to speak, closed his lips with a sigh, then finally, in a hoarse voice, "Only the sin of informing on those who trust me."

"But you do this for their benefit," the priest protested in a smooth deep voice, "that their souls may be saved." Then, reverting to the formal confessional drone, "May Almighty God have mercy upon you, and may He forgive your sins, and bring you to life everlasting."

"Amen," the penitent whispered, anxious to bring the encounter to an end.

3

"By the authority of our Lord Jesus Christ, I absolve you from your sins in the name of the Father and the Son and the Holy Ghost."

"Amen."

"Go in peace," said the priest. "May you be well." He paused, then added, "and your sons." He rose to leave.

The large man remained, hood drawn around his bent head, sobbing silently.

"Don Alonso must see you now."

The goldsmith straightened and stretched his body, stiff from hours at the bench. Passing a file to his son working beside him, he removed the apron from his belt, straightened his loose tunic and dark hose, placed his red brimless cap firmly on his head, and reached for his cape. Rushing from the shop, he squinted in the bright afternoon sun. The messenger had already disappeared.

At forty, Gabriel Catalan was a successful man. Of medium height and trim build, his dark brown hair fell in curls to his shoulders, showing only traces of gray. Lines around his eyes sharpened the intelligent look of his clean shaven face. He was the most prosperous jeweler in Seville, well known to the nobility, the Church, and even to members of the royal family. The shop he had just left was also his home, which he shared with his wife Pilar and their only child Tomas. It was a substantial property, much enlarged and improved after it was partially burned six years before by rioting *converso* haters.

Immersed in the familiar bustle of a spring afternoon, Gabriel sidestepped two men as they hoisted bundles of goods onto the back of a small burro. He smiled to a woman carrying bread in her arms and a jug of water on her head. Brilliant white buildings, although only two or at most three stories high, seemed to tower over him as he wound through the narrow streets. He delighted in the smell of myrtle, the sound of small fountains gurgling in the squares, palm trees reaching above the tops of buildings. Entry ways revealed brightly colored tiles and gave a passing glimpse of cool interiors. Gabriel rushed ahead, skirting the massive wall of the old Moorish *Alcazar*, now one of the many palaces of King Enrique IV of Castile.

Don Alonso's home dominated the northern edge of the city, near the Carmona Gate. Gabriel knocked at the massive doorway and was recognized by a servant in the distinctive blue tunic of the Viterbo household staff. The servant unlocked the heavy gate and escorted him to a group of dark wooden benches in an open courtyard.

"Please wait here. Señor Viterbo will be with you shortly."

"Thank you, Miguel."

Gabriel carefully folded his cape and placed it, with his cap, on the bench next to him. He wondered why he had been summoned.

His friend Don Alonso de Viterbo was the most prominent and wealthy *converso* in Seville. The Viterbo trading interests reached across the Mediterranean Sea to Constantinople in the east and around the Atlantic Ocean north to Bruges, and there was hardly a profitable business in which he did not have a part. But his real wealth, the basis for everything else, came from his position as chief royal tax farmer for the southern portion of Castile known as *Andalusia*.

The *converso* community in Seville included some eight hundred families, all of them second and third generation descendants of Jews who had been forcibly converted by crusading Dominican priests who swept through Castile in 1391 and again in 1412. Duly baptized, these *conversos* had pursued paths to wealth and power that had been denied them as Jews. They were prominent in trade, in the army and the law, in universities, and most critically, in public office. They had replaced the Jews in the royal administration, and pushed their way into the municipal councils where they often supplanted Old Christians. They had even entered the Church. Descendants of Jews were bishops in Coria, Cordoba, Cartegena, and Burgos, and an archbishop in Toledo. They had intermarried widely with the nobility among the Old Christians, who were unable to resist the allure of their wealth.

But with it all, they remained outsiders, called "New Christians" to distinguish them from those whose bloodline was not tainted by Jewish ancestry. Hatred for them seethed just beneath the surface, tenuously held in check by the authority of the kings and archbishops who needed their services.

Gabriel and Don Alonso had grown close in recent years. Since the violent death of his father Isaac, Gabriel had sought his Jewish roots. He found an ally in Don Alonso and they were now among those very few *conversos* in Seville who still tried to practice the Jewish religion.

Gabriel's solitude was broken by the appearance of Don Alonso. Without a word, he led Gabriel to a more private indoor space, where sounds were muffled by Flemish tapestries on the walls and heavy Persian carpets on the floor. Several inches taller than Gabriel, Don

Alonso was, as always, elegantly attired. His deep red robe, edges embroidered in gold, opened in the front to display the rich folds of a floor length gray gown. Goat leather buskins padded softly on the marble floor. Don Alonso's shoulders were broad and muscular. He wore a lustrous turban of golden silk. A short clipped beard completed his commanding presence. Gabriel was proud of the way his friend looked, so different from his own unadorned appearance.

"Please forgive me for interrupting your work, but ... I must show you!"

Gabriel was surprised by the unusual excitement in his friend's voice and eyes. Don Alonso was always calm. Not today. He unlocked a cupboard and removed a plain wooden box, holding it with both hands like a priest setting the table of the mass.

"Thou shalt teach the words of God to thy children," said Don Alonso. "That is the fundamental obligation of every Jewish parent, and here is the means that will enable us to fulfill God's commandments."

He opened the box and unfolded a heavy fabric which protected its contents. Removing a rolled sheet, he loosened a wide blue ribbon, and reverently laid the page flat, holding it down with four heavy golden candlesticks. Gabriel saw two columns of Latin writing on fine quality paper. Don Alonso read aloud: *You shall be holy to Me, for I the Lord am holy, and I have set you apart from other peoples to be Mine.*

"Is this a copy of our Bible?" Gabriel asked.

"It's our Bible, but not a copy," said Don Alonso. "No pen has touched this paper." His voice quickened. "See! There are no lines to guide a scribe. These words were not written by a human hand."

Gabriel was surprised to see Don Alonso's hand shake as he pointed. "How was it written if not by hand?" he asked.

"By the new method of a man named Johann Gutenberg."

Don Alonso reached into the box and brought out several small pieces of metal.

"These are called type," he said. "With this type, Gutenberg can produce a complete page all at once ... many pages, each identical. And quickly, too, as if by magic."

Don Alonso paused.

"It's been a year since King Juan died," he said, "and King Enrique does not protect *conversos* as his father did. Without the crown's protection, we can't exist here. All of the hatred which exploded six years ago is still there. There's no future for New Christians in Spain."

"Maybe this is God's way of calling us back," said Gabriel with a smile.

"Well, if that's true, most *conversos* haven't heard the call," laughed Don Alonso.

Then he became serious again. "Some of us, or at least our children, will be real Jews again. I don't know where. Surely not in Spain. Nor England, or France, or Germany. Expelled from all! But wherever Jews are, we'll need our holy books, and they're disappearing rapidly. Dominicans have burned most of our *talmuds*. In all of Spain, only a few copies left. The great works of Maimonides, and Rabbi Nachmanides — almost gone. The poetry of Solomon ibn Gabirol and Jehudah Halevi — who will ever know it if we don't save it?

"It's up to us, the few of us among the *conversos* who are still Jews … and Gutenberg's given us a way." Don Alonso leaned closer, speaking quietly, "I need your help. Rodrigo and Francesco, too. Will you bring them with you tonight? Gutenberg is here, in my house, and he'll explain."

It was all too fast for Gabriel. He didn't understand how Gutenberg's bits of metal could save Hebrew manuscripts. But if Don Alonso said it was so, then it must be.

"Of course," he answered.

Gabriel glanced furtively in both directions before stepping into the small tailor shop. He had not intended to join in prayer this day, but the conversation with Don Alonso had directed his mind to Jewish matters and here he was.

"Good afternoon, Señor Catalan," said a young girl.

"Hello, Esther." Gabriel spotted her younger brother and added, "And hello to you too, Ruyo."

Their mother appeared, a short full bodied woman with a plump, kindly face. She wore a dark tunic of rather coarse construction, reaching almost to the floor, loose except where drawn at the waist with a cord of the same material. Her head was covered with a tight fitting turban, the end of which hung down on her shoulder. Both children were dressed in similar tunics, but their hair was uncovered. Esther's hair hung in a long braid which reached below her waist.

"They're growing," Gabriel said. "Esther's quite the young lady. And Ruyo, how big you are!"

Miriam Ardit beamed, but her smile faded quickly. "I fear for them."

Gabriel knew that her fear was not misplaced. Life in Seville was chaos since King Juan had died. Nobles fought each other, and when their soldiers were idle, they preyed on farmers and townspeople. Jews were often convenient targets. Enrique, the impotent king of Castile, did nothing.

"Have any others come?" he asked.

"Leone and Ruiz, about ten minutes ago. Yacov went to synagogue."

"I wish I could be with him," said Gabriel softly.

"He'd like that, too."

Gabriel followed Miriam through the small tailor shop, which also served as the Ardit's living room. The table had been cleared of Yacov's work and dishes were set for the evening meal.

As always when he came to pray, Gabriel thought how remarkable it was that the Ardit family helped them. Most of those who had remained Jews, who had never converted, disliked and distrusted the *conversos*, and would have nothing to do with people they considered traitors to God. But Don Alonso had made arrangements with Yacov Ardit, and their small group had prayed there, once or twice a week, for almost two years.

"How's Pilar?" Miriam asked.

"She's fine," said Gabriel, but feelings of reproach and guilt beset him at the mention of his wife's name. Pilar hated all of the secret Jewish activities he had undertaken in the last several years, but none so much as the use of the Ardit house. Pilar had been a friend of Miriam Ardit since childhood, and she was furious that Gabriel and the others put the Ardit family at such risk. When Gabriel had first told her about it, she didn't talk to him for weeks, and her anger flared every time he went there.

How much better it would be, he thought, if Pilar shared his Judaism. Her grandparents had been Jewish like his, and had, like his, converted under duress. But there had never been any Judaism in her family, and even her friendship with Miriam carefully avoided topics of religion. When his father's violent death led Gabriel to the conviction that he must become as much of a Jew as he could, Pilar protested that he was foolish and selfish to pursue a path that could so easily destroy their family and imperil the entire *converso* community, most of whom had no interest in anything Jewish. Knowing that she was right distressed him even more.

Miriam drew aside the large curtain that separated the sleeping area from the front room and Gabriel followed her. She moved several pillows and pulled the bed away from the wall, exposing the outline of a previously concealed doorway. Gabriel helped her loosen a wooden panel, bent down, and stepped through. Miriam replaced the panel behind him.

He descended a long stone stairway, barely lit by several thick candles, and joined five other men in the semi-darkness. This small group accounted for about half of those *conversos* in Seville who were secretly Jews. The room was small, and, with many candles burning, hot and stuffy. Whitewashed walls, a worn carpet on the earthen floor, no furniture. Nothing in it to betray its secret purpose, except the single prayer book which Yacov Ardit left for them and removed every evening after they had gone.

These unusual Jews did not insist on the required ten men for a *minyan*. They never wore *tefillin* or prayer shawls. They just prayed quickly and disappeared as surreptitiously as they had arrived.

There were three means of entry. One long passage began near the wall of the *Alcazar*. Another was hidden in an interior courtyard several blocks away. The third, the one Gabriel had just used, came from the Ardit house.

Francesco Romo rushed in from the *Alcazar* passage after the service had begun. The flowing multi-colored arms of his silk blouse, his tight fitting tunic and hose, and the long Moorish sword held with thongs to a leather belt presented a dramatic contrast to the plain garb of the others. He looked more Castilian than many Spaniards who claimed pure descent from the ancient Visigoths. His elegant clothes, however, fit his occupation. He was one of Seville's leading artists.

Francesco eased his way through the other men and stood next to Gabriel.

"*Maariv* already?" he said.

"Is it dark?" asked Gabriel.

"No."

The *Minchah*, or afternoon service, had been completed, and the unbroken transition to the *Maariv*, or evening service, had begun. The worshippers tried to reach this point just as darkness fell, but underground, they could only guess the time.

"You saved me a trip," Gabriel whispered. "Don Alonso wants to meet with us tonight."

Francesco nodded without asking why. There had been many such calls over the years and he always responded.

Gabriel repeated with the others those blessings he knew, sometimes adding his own words of praise and awe. For him, prayer brought both calm and discontent. The ancient Hebrew words were his recently found route to God's love. When he said them they promised order in his often discordant world, and he felt the oneness of eternity.

But he could never forget that he didn't keep most of the commandments. 'Are you impressed, God,' he thought, 'that I come here to worship even as I ignore most of Your laws? Which is the greater hypocrisy, praying here, or kneeling in church and eating what the Christians claim is the body of Jesus?'

He prayed quietly for several minutes until another thought came to him. 'You know, God, that I want to bring Tomas. Pilar won't allow it. My son doesn't even know he's a Jew.' Gabriel sobbed silently, closed his eyes, and mouthed his unutterable passion, 'Please, God, help me. Don't let me be the last Jew in the Catalan family.'

They reached the *Shema* prayer and Gabriel repeated what he knew to have been his father's last words: *Hear, O Israel, the Lord our God, the Lord is One. Blessed is the name of His glorious kingdom for ever and ever.*

'One God,' Gabriel thought angrily, 'not three.'

"Drag the Jews out! Stone them! Light the fires!"

Sound froze in mid-word. The room became silent. The men looked nervously at each other as shouting from the streets above reached them.

Gabriel whispered to Francesco. "We have to get out. Quickly. Before we're trapped. You check the courtyard entrance. I'll go upstairs."

Gabriel motioned for the others to prepare to leave. Someone blew out the candles. Holding the damp walls for support, Gabriel moved slowly up the stone stairway to the Ardit house, each timid step a triumph over his trembling legs. But his hemp-soled shoes slipped on the damp steps and his knee smacked down hard, his stifled groan a roar in the silence. He shivered in the cool air.

When he was but one step from the top, he heard a crash above him, and knew that he had not chosen a safe route. He thought to retreat, but, fearful he might stumble in the dark and betray them all, he stood still, scarcely breathing. He noticed a sliver of light and pressed his eye against the tiny crack where the secret panel met the wall. He could see between the pillows into the Ardit's bedroom. The curtain was drawn, so he had no view into the room beyond.

A harsh voice bellowed, "Where are they?"

"W-who are you l-looking for?" Yacov Ardit stammered.

"Don't lie to me, you filthy Jew! We know that *conversos* are here."

The mob screamed its incoherent violence and Gabriel shrunk from the sound but Yacov's voice grew stronger, "There's no one here but my family. We're Jews, not *conversos*. Look, I wear my yellow badge."

"Jewish scum! You dare speak to Hernando Talavero with such arrogance!"

Without warning, the curtain was ripped from its hooks, and a large soldier dressed totally in black burst into the bedroom and Gabriel's view.

Talavero slashed furiously. He threw over a table next to the bed, slammed a pitcher to the floor, kicked the chamber pot across the room. His knife cut viciously into the bedclothes. Feathers flew.

Gabriel saw Talavero's eyes, red and furious, looking directly at him. He tried to control his trembling body, but Talavero did not see the panel behind the pillows. He looked away and left the bedroom.

'Thank you, God,' Gabriel exhaled.

"No! Not my daughter!" screamed Miriam. Gabriel had relaxed too soon.

His eyes were fixed in horror as Talavero's soldiers threw Esther onto the table. Dishes crashed. They spread her legs and pawed at her exposed thighs.

Yacov Ardit tried to push past Talavero. Talavero slashed and Yacov howled in pain, but still moved toward the men attacking his daughter. Talavero's arm raised up, sharp steel poised over Yacov's head.

"Stop!"

The knife flashed down, halting just as the point touched Yacov's back.

In the stillness, Gabriel heard his own breathing.

"We don't make war on Jews and rape their daughters," the new voice said. "Let her go!"

Gabriel didn't recognize the voice, but he felt its power. Talavero's men backed away from Esther.

"Where are the *conversos* who say Jewish prayers?" Gabriel heard. "I was told they would be here." There was no answer.

The distinctive black habit of a Dominican monk came into Gabriel's line of sight, and he saw a young face covered by a thick black beard. Intelligent dark eyes flashed fiercely about the room.

Surely those eyes would see the passageway that Talavero had missed. The monk glared at Talavero, and slowly his gaze encompassed each of the Ardits. But he did not enter the bedroom.

"Leave. Leave at once," he ordered, his voice curdling with disgust.

The soldiers moved toward the front door, followed by Talavero and the monk. The pounding in Gabriel's head subsided.

Then every muscle flinched again as a voice whispered only inches behind him.

"Gabriel, I'm here. It's Francesco."

"It was terrible," Gabriel croaked.

"The courtyard entrance was clear," said Francesco. "The others have left."

"You go, too. I'll see you tonight."

"Come with me."

"It's all right. The trouble's over. I want to see if Yacov's hurt."

Romo squeezed Gabriel's shoulder and went back down the stairs. Gabriel removed the panel and stepped cautiously into the Ardit's bedroom.

In the front room, Miriam knelt with Esther among the broken dishes. Ruyo was huddled in a corner, forgotten. Yacov sat on the only chair still upright, dazed, his thin frame shivering.

"Your arm is bleeding," Gabriel said as he approached.

Yacov looked up, comprehension gradually returning. "It's nothing." But he shuddered and Gabriel knew he was in pain.

"He was brave," Miriam said, putting her arm around her husband.

"He saved us all," said Gabriel.

"It wasn't me. Friar Perez made them stop," said Yacov.

"That was Perez?" Gabriel said, his eyes narrowing. Friar Ricardo Perez, a Dominican monk, had come to Seville a few months before, and Don Alonso had warned that he would come after them. Perez had been sent to Seville to find secret Jews among the *conversos*. Now it had begun.

Gabriel shuddered as he recalled the monk's fierce look. Perez would be a formidable adversary.

Gabriel moved through the darkened streets. He had to reach Rodrigo de Muya, and it was late. He ran past the soaring Moorish tower which dominated the central square. As he set off toward the Rio Guadalquivir, he failed to notice the beggar hidden in the shadows of the tower. Seville was full of beggars.

It took only a few minutes to reach Rodrigo's home and deliver his message.

The beggar followed.

2

Tomas Catalan dashed out as soon as dinner was finished, headed to the annual trade fair which had just arrived in Seville.

Gabriel sat with his wife in the fluttering candlelight, tall windows open to the interior courtyard. Pilar's long hair lay unfettered on the soft woolen tunic drawn closely to the shape of her body. Gabriel ached to touch her, to draw comfort from her closeness, but he had no expectations for this night, not after she heard the dreadful events he was about to relate.

"There was an attack today at Yacov's house."

"You were praying there again!" she said, her head taught, fury in her eyes.

"Yacov was cut but he's all right."

"Were they looking for you?" she demanded.

Gabriel didn't answer. Pilar clenched her fists, waiting. Finally he nodded.

"They didn't find us, but they went after Esther."

"Did they ... ?"

"No. The new monk, Friar Perez, stopped them."

"What was he doing there?" she asked, each word crackling.

"He ordered the attack. He seemed to know we'd be praying."

"How could he know?"

"He must have an informer."

"This is your fault," she hissed, "You and Don Alonso. Why, Gabriel? Why? You're going to kill us all with this Jewish business!"

"We'll talk more ... when I get back," he said, anxious to escape.

"Where are you going?" she said sharply.

He reached for her hand, but she jerked it away.

"I have to see Don Alonso," he said.

"Why? What else are you doing?" she asked furiously.

'Not now,' he thought, cringing inside, and looking away, 'There could not be a worse time to tell her about the Hebrew books.'

"I want to talk with Don Alonso about the Ardits. They need his help."

At least that wasn't untrue. Gabriel put his arms around his wife, but Pilar stood stiffly, not responding.

"We'll talk more tonight," he said. "I must go now."

"Be careful," she whispered, and Gabriel took what scant encouragement he could from her concern.

Gabriel waited in Don Alonso's library, his mind and stomach churning. He loved Pilar. She was his whole life, she and their son Tomas. Why was God interfering with the peace of his family? How could he risk so much just to say a few words to a God he didn't understand? Of course, it was his father's fault, too. 'You've really made a mess for me, father,' he thought. 'Why did you have to put on a *tallit* and say a *Shema* before you died?' Yet just as quickly, he was ashamed to be unfaithful to his father's memory.

Francesco Romo burst into the room, a picture of vitality, apparently undaunted by the knowledge that his life had been threatened only a few hours before.

"This room is more spectacular each time I see it," he proclaimed. "Look at these new carpets! And I haven't seen this tapestry before either. From Flanders, I'm sure. There's gold woven through it. And Bruges satin! Even Jesus looks good."

Gabriel smiled, amused by his friend's enthusiasm. "It's the Garden of Gethsemane at the moment Jesus was betrayed by Judas." He couldn't resist adding, "Or so they say."

"You blaspheme!" Francesco shouted in mock horror.

"Of course. That's what a heretic's supposed to do."

"Be careful or I'll report you to Friar Perez."

"Maybe you already did," Gabriel said, raising his eyebrows. "He was the one who sent those men this afternoon. Somebody told him we'd be there."

"If it was me, would I have been there with you?"

"How long can we survive this double life?" Gabriel asked. "Especially you. You see the Archbishop all the time. Have you met Perez?"

"Several times. He's intense. Hates heretics, especially secret Jews. Did you hear them today? Screaming for *conversos*. Swine they call us. How appropriate," he said, raising his eyes. "Perez is smart, but he's also naïve ... he has no idea of the complexities of the church. The Archbishop doesn't like him, but since he's been sent by the Dominicans, Fonseca can't give him orders. Nevertheless, he gave us a warning we can't ignore. No more praying together for a while."

Gabriel nodded. At least that would make Pilar happy.

"Do you have any ideas about the informer?" Francesco asked.

"No," said Gabriel.

"What would we do if we find him?"

"You know that Jewish law says informers must die," Gabriel answered.

"Yes, but who'd do it?" asked Francesco. "In the old days, Jewish courts would turn a convicted informer over to the king to be executed. I don't think that's a choice today."

"Still," said Gabriel, "we've got to know who told Perez. We're not safe until we find out."

"Find out what? Are you talking about this afternoon?"

Don Alonso entered the library from the opposite side of the room. He wore the same red robe, but had removed the turban. Gray hair fell in a perfectly groomed diagonal line from his ears to his shoulders.

"I heard," he said.

Gabriel sighed, "How did Perez know where we'd be praying?"

Don Alonso shook his head silently. He walked to the northern end of the large room and closed the shutters. "It's terrible when you have to hide in your own home. We'll do without the breeze." Coming back toward the other men, he added, "Gabriel, how's Yacov?"

"Shaken. And he's afraid, although he'd never admit it. He knows Talavero and his men will come back, for him ... and for Esther."

Don Alonso looked down, his gray eyes sad. "I caused this problem and I'll take care of it. Are you familiar with the town of Arcos de la Frontera? It's not too far from here ... but far enough. I have a cousin there. They could make a new start."

Why should they have to leave Seville, their home for generations? This is what Pilar will ask tonight, thought Gabriel, and I have no answer.

"Did you tell Rodrigo about our meeting?" Don Alonso asked.

Just then, Rodrigo de Muya's huge frame filled the doorway. He appeared out of place in Don Alonso's elegant home. His days were absorbed in the rough and dirty process of making paper, which the de Muya family had pursued for generations, and the look and smell of his work was with him.

Physically imposing, Rodrigo was nevertheless a gentle man. He was totally devoted to his two young sons, and often took them on horseback trips to the plains outside of Seville. He was, like the others, a *converso*, but his situation was even more complicated than Gabriel's. Rodrigo had married an Old Christian, not a daughter of converted Jews, and he had to hide every aspect of his Jewish life from her.

"You missed it today," said Francesco. "We had a bad scare."

"Gabriel told me."

One of Don Alonso's servants entered the room, followed by a stocky man in his fifties.

"Ah, Gutenberg," said Don Alonso. He took his guest by the arm and introduced him to the others. Gutenberg bowed, rather pompously Gabriel thought, extending his hand like a noble to his subjects. But the hand was that of a workman, rough, and stubbornly dirty under the nails. His dress was plain. He wore a loose brown tunic, of coarse wool, held at his substantial waist by a wide leather belt, worn and scratched. His boots were heavy leather, not well cut, with traces of mud. His face was broad and fleshy, and he spoke in a deep guttural voice, in a language unfamiliar to Gabriel.

After the introductions, Don Alonso paced slowly around the room. He gathered excitement with each step.

"God has granted us an extraordinary opportunity," he said with a dramatic flourish. "We have a chance to assure that our glorious Jewish centuries in Spain are not forgotten."

Then, abruptly, he became more businesslike.

"Johann Gutenberg lives in the town of Mainz, in Germany. He's developed a remarkable new way to make books. However, it's taken many years, and he had to borrow heavily to buy materials and equipment. His creditors are pressuring him to repay their loans. He came to me at the suggestion of our banking partner in Bruges, who knows that I deal in books and that I'm also interested in new ideas. I've agreed to provide the funds he needs. In return, Herr Gutenberg will teach us his new method. I've explained our need for secrecy, and I'm confidant we can trust him."

Don Alonso placed on his desk the same box Gabriel had seen that afternoon. He turned to the stranger and said in German, "Johann, please tell us about your work. I'll translate for you."

Gutenberg spoke quickly and Don Alonso had to struggle to keep up. "Always, men have copied books by hand. It was the only way. Until me! I change everything. Thirty years it's taken me. The press - type - ink. Almost perfect. Soon I'll be ready. Ach! But they want me to print now. And they want so many lines on a page. Too many! Too crowded!"

Don Alonso interrupted. "But Herr Gutenberg has already succeeded gloriously. Let me show you." He unrolled the page from the Bible, laid out a collection of tools and small metal letters, and stepped back to assess their reaction.

Francesco Romo scrutinized the page. "Outstanding! It looks like the work of a very skilled scribe."

Gutenberg beamed.

"Yes! Yes! Don Alonso told me you're an artist. So you see! Others would be satisfied with less. Look! Perfect letters. No smudges!"

Gabriel examined one of the metal letters. "This wasn't carved," he said. "How did you make it?"

"Very observant," said Gutenberg. "It wasn't carved. It was formed from melted metal poured into a mold. But extremely accurate carving was needed to make the mold. It took an outstanding goldsmith. Me."

'I could do that,' Gabriel thought, but his growing excitement was immediately tempered by fear of Pilar's reaction. He did not look forward to telling Pilar about this.

"These letters are backwards," said Rodrigo, cupping a tiny piece of metal in his huge hand. "How do they work?"

"I'll show you."

Johann took the letter from Rodrigo. Grasping it in a small clamp, he brought it near the flame of an oil lamp. After a few seconds, he plunged it into the flame itself.

The men were riveted. Don Alonso crowded in and Gabriel could feel his intense enthusiasm.

Gutenberg let the metal cool and then touched it to a blank sheet of paper. The letter ℬ appeared sharp and clear.

Rodrigo pursued his questioning. "So I see a letter, but what's the use of it? What's to be done with it?"

"With one letter, not much," Gutenberg said. "But, with many letters, a whole page can be printed. All at once! And not just one! Page after page."

Gutenberg put the letter down and stepped back, hands at his sides, bouncing slightly on his toes. "Now I'll ask you a question. How long does it take to copy the Hebrew Bible?"

"At least twelve months," said Don Alonso, "maybe eighteen. How long does it take to make a Bible by your method?"

The printer gloated.

"I don't make one Bible. On each press, I print one hundred copies of a page in a single day. I have six presses. In eighteen months," he paused to calculate, "I could print five hundred Bibles, compared with your one."

Gabriel was astonished, and the men looked at each other in amazement.

"Do you have Hebrew letters?" Gabriel asked quietly, sensing that he was being drawn inextricably into Don Alonso's remarkable plan.

"No, but if you are as good a goldsmith as Don Alonso said you are, you could make them. I'll show you."

"How do the letters make this page?" asked Rodrigo.

Gutenberg explained carefully and slowly, wanting them to understand. "First, I place individual pieces of type, one after the other, to spell a line of words. I place this line in a rack to hold it tightly. More lines go into the rack until I have an entire page. I attach the rack of type to a sliding shelf on the press. I place a fresh sheet of paper into a form which is hinged to the shelf above the letters. I spread ink on the type and rotate the paper until it's just above the type, not quite touching. Then I slide the type and paper under a very heavy flat iron press. I turn the great screw to squeeze the press against the back of the paper. Ink from the whole page of type is transferred smoothly and evenly to the paper. Then I have - this!"

Triumphantly, he held up the printed page. The men clapped and Gutenberg made a little bow. Gabriel revised his initial impression. Gutenberg was entitled to be proud.

"I use presses to squeeze water from paper. Is your printing press like mine?" Rodrigo asked.

"Very similar."

Francesco Romo turned to Don Alonso. "I understand why Gabriel's here. And Rodrigo knows about presses. But why me? I paint pictures. What can I contribute?"

Don Alonso smiled knowingly. "Johann, explain about the inks."

"At first I used ink made with water. No good. Smeared. Then I heard about the artist van Eyck. He boiled his colors with linseed oils to make a heavy paint, very sticky. That's how I make my ink. Do you know about van Eyck's paints, Señor Romo?"

"Indeed! I've used them.."

All eyes went to Don Alonso. The only noise was a sputter from one of the candles.

"So now you understand," he said. "I want to build presses and make Hebrew books. I want to print hundreds of copies of our precious manuscripts before they're destroyed by the Dominicans."

His look of exhilaration faded and he became deadly serious. "We all know that this will be dangerous work," he said. "If we're discovered, we'll be arrested. We might be executed. Our families will suffer."

Don Alonso drew himself to his full height. His voice thickened.

"We're the only ones who can do it," he said. "The Jews don't have the resources, and most of the *conversos* don't care."

On the table next to him was an ancient leather-bound volume. Don Alonso turned the pages, squinting closely at the faded writing, until he found the passage he wanted. He read aloud in Hebrew:

אֲדוֹן עוֹלָם אֲשֶׁר מָלַךְ
Master of the universe,
It is You who was,
You who is,
and You who shall remain
in awesome splendor.

"What Jew will know these words of Shlomo ibn Gabirol if we don't make sure they're preserved?

Don Alonso narrowed his eyes, his gaze far in the past or future, perhaps both. Coming back to the present, he walked silently to Francesco, then Rodrigo and last to Gabriel.

"I think it's worth the risk," he said. "But you must each decide."

Gabriel wanted to be the first to answer, but he thought of Pilar, and while he hesitated, Rodrigo said quietly, "I'll build these new presses."

Gabriel struggled to order his thoughts. He ran a hand through his already tousled hair. He massaged the back of his neck. He squeezed his arms tightly across his chest. When he spoke, he paused between each disjointed thought.

"This afternoon, we were almost caught at prayer ... there must be an informer among us ... I saw Friar Perez today and he frightened me ... making Hebrew books will surely be dangerous."

After an even longer pause, Gabriel looked directly at Don Alonso and said softly, "I know we may not have much longer to be Jews, and I think we should make the most of this chance. I want to help you."

He turned away, unable to keep his friend's eye. "But I can't answer now," he said. "I need more time."

"I understand," said Don Alonso, but Gabriel knew he was disappointed, and that he would be impatient. This decision could not be postponed for long.

Francesco Romo sauntered across the large room and stopped by Don Alonso's desk. Suddenly he laughed and shrugged in a carefree manner.

"Whatever Gabriel does, so with me," he said.

Pilar was awake when Gabriel slid under the linen sheets. She moved away, a small movement, but clear enough.

Gabriel sat up, feet on the floor, head down, dreading what was to come. Where to begin? The printing? Don Alonso's plan for the Ardit family? Should he try yet again to tell her why he wanted to be a Jew? Worst choice of all. He was never able to explain what he didn't fully understand himself.

The moonlight cast a soft glow on her bare shoulders. A thrill passed through him as he imagined her warm body next to his.

"Your meeting took a long time," she said, and her angry voice drove the smile from his face.

She sat up and he caught his breath at the sight of her full breasts more revealed than covered by her thin nightgown.

"I love you," he said, sitting close but not daring to touch her. He waited, hoping, but she was silent.

"I want to talk about my father," he began.

"Don't blame your father. Sebastian's dead," she said, using Isaac Catalan's Christian name. "Be responsible for yourself."

"I have no choice," he said, averting his eyes.

"No choice?" she demanded. "You choose every time you go to Miriam's house and put her family in jeopardy. Who makes you go?"

'God makes me go,' Gabriel thought, 'but how can I tell her that.'

"If I don't pray for several days, I feel lost, as if ..." He stopped, losing the thought. "Today I ..."

"What? What today?" she demanded.

Gabriel couldn't tell her about his first visit with Don Alonso, and how talk of the Hebrew books had led him to pray. Not yet. He frowned and shook his head.

"Don Alonso will help them," he whispered.

"Could he refuse?" Pilar snorted.

"But it's risky for him," Gabriel blurted.

Pilar glared at him in the dim light, her fierce accusation needing no words.

"I know," Gabriel said, looking down, "Their risks were greater. But we didn't think this would ever happen."

"I did! How many times did I say it?"

"Many times," he acknowledged, shifting his hands in frustration. "Pilar, please try to understand. These arguments are agony for me. I love you so much. I don't want to fight with you."

"Then why do you do these things?"

Maybe I can say it better this time, he thought without conviction.

"My father was a Jew. It was the most important reason for his life, and his death."

"My parents were also *conversos*," Pilar said, "but after they converted, they didn't become Jews again. Sebastian was a Christian for sixty years. Then, for five minutes, he's Isaac the Jew, and your whole life changes."

"Do you ever think that maybe, sometime, you ..."

"No. Never!" Pilar answered, cutting him off.

"But can you allow it for me?" he asked.

"You won't give this up, will you?" she said.

Amazingly, Pilar's face had softened. She looked directly at him for the first time in the conversation and Gabriel's heart trembled with hope.

"I love you, too," she said, her eyes imploring him. "But I don't understand you. I know you don't want to hurt me, or Tomas."

Gabriel knew he could not find words to explain the power that the God of Israel exerted over him. He spoke instead of the Ardits, and Don Alonso's plan. "They'll have to leave Seville. It's too dangerous here. Talavero will come back. Don Alonso has a cousin in Arcos."

"That's not fair!" Pilar exploded. "All they want is to be left alone. This is your fault! You and Don Alonso."

"I know," said Gabriel. "Yacov is the only Jew in Seville who helps us. I feel as badly as you do."

"Must they really go? Arcos is far."

"There's no other way," said Gabriel.

"I'll miss them," Pilar said, suppressing a sob. "Miriam is my best friend."

Gabriel opened his arms to comfort her, and was surprised when she came to him. He held her tightly and felt her tears as their cheeks touched. Gradually, she became quiet, and Gabriel kissed her bare shoulder. She melted into him, and he caressed her back. His hands reached her hips. A small moan came from her lips. Her mouth covered his with fierce kisses. He lifted her gown and his own, and pulled her on top of him.

Much later, he lay back. Pilar slept peacefully, her naked body bathed in moonlight. He matched his own breathing to the rhythm of her breasts, stared at the curve of her belly where it flowed into the mass of dark hair, and shivered at the stirrings of another erection. But he was reluctant to wake her, and he began to drift off, his mind and body at peace.

Gutenberg's guttural voice intruded. The Hebrew books! He hadn't told her! And tomorrow, he thought, Don Alonso will want an answer.

"He went to the home of that rich Jew. There was three of 'em."

"What Jew? Who went there?" Friar Perez demanded, drawing his robe close around him, uncomfortable in the beggar's frank gaze.

"Oh, excuse me, your Excellency, I thought they told you," the beggar answered, dragging out each word derisively. He started to laugh, but choked and cleared his throat with a disgusting noise. "One was Gabriel Catalan," he continued, "you know, that goldsmith who's not supposed to be a Jew no more, since you friars put holy water on him. I tell you truly, I don't see any difference. All those *conversos* are still Jews to me."

"Who else?"

"That fancy artist. Francesco Romo. And one more I don't know. A big man."

"Where were they?"

"Like I said, they went to the house of this rich Jew, the one that's got more money than King Enrique hisself —Don Alonso de Viterbo. Fancy name for a Jew, eh?"

"Why do you think that they're Jews?" Perez asked, excited now, hoping that maybe his day would not be a total failure.

"Once a Jew, always a Jew. They're just pretending to be Christians so's they can be important at court and take our money."

"Do you have any evidence? Did you hear any Hebrew words? Did you see any Jewish things?"

"When Jews that don't want you to think they's Jews get together and close the shutters on a warm night so nobody can see 'em, then that's somethin' Dominican monks should know about. Ain't that why they sent you here?"

The beggar smiled wickedly and came closer. Perez recoiled from his unwashed smell.

"Do I get a reward? I spent all night followin' him, you know."

"You followed Catalan?"

"That's what I said. Don't you hear well?"

"Why did you follow him?"

"He was runnin'. It didn't look right to me."

"Where?"

"Near the tower."

"When?"

"Just after dark."

"Where did he go?"

"Across the river, then back to his own house - for dinner I guess. Then to Don Alonso's great palace. I chased that little red cap all over Seville."

Could it be, Perez thought, that Catalan had something to do with the tailor and the secret praying? The beggar's instincts might be right.

"Do you know what a heretic is?" Perez asked.

"It's not me," said the beggar. "I believe in Jesus Christ and the Blessed Mother and everything else just like you tell me. Exactly like you tell me. Besides, I got no money, unless you give me some, so who would profit by it if I was a heretic?"

Perez stiffened and his face flushed. "You filthy ... !" he exploded. "Money has nothing to do with the purity of the Church. Get out of here!"

The beggar didn't move and the two men eyed each other.

Perez raised his arms in frustration, then took two coins from his pocket and laid them on a table, unwilling to touch the beggar's hands. The beggar grabbed the money and rushed to the door.

"I don't s'poze you'd mind if I was to bring more news like this," he said.

Perez shook his head once in reluctant assent, but as soon as the beggar left, his knees weakened, and he almost collapsed.

'What am I doing?' he thought. 'This morning, I forced a man to inform on his friends. Then I almost caused the rape of an innocent girl. Now I pay this awful person and even ask him for more information. Is this serving the will of Jesus? Is this how I save the church?'

He was alone in the monastery's open courtyard.

Without any conscious intent, he found himself kneeling in the ancient Moorish prayer niche, reborn as an altar after the Christian reconquest. His arms were stretched before him, his head rested on the cold stone floor. Chilled, he raised his head slightly and drew his hood tight. He felt the darkness, and the warmth of his own breath. He felt the presence of the Lord.

Lifting his eyes, seeing the stars, he prayed aloud, "O Lord Jesus, give me guidance. These were Your Chosen People of the First Covenant. Why do we persecute them? We forced them to convert. First Martinez, then Ferrer. Baptize or die! Why are we surprised if some wish to return to the God of Israel?"

Perez was frightened by this unexpected turn of mind. The instructions of the Dominican Order did not encourage understanding, tolerance, or sympathy. There was only the cold truth of the militant Church. Accept. Don't question. Especially not about Jews. Such thoughts could lead to his downfall.

All of the other heretical sects had been beaten down. The Waldensians, Cathars, and Albigensians had all fallen under the relentless pressure of the Dominican monks. Only Jews dared dissent from the doctrine of the Church. Only the Jews stood in the way of perfect Christian unity. Thus, the efforts of Ferran Martinez and Vicente Ferrer to convert them.

Perez recalled the teaching of St. Thomas Aquinas: once a Jew was converted, even by force, he was a Christian, and there was no possibility of return. If converted Jews could leave the church at will, it would demean the faith and hold it to ridicule. So said the Popes, so said his teachers at the university in Salamanca, so said Prior Torquemada in Segovia.

He resumed his conversation with Jesus, desperate to suppress the compassion which had frightened him a few moments before. "These evil Jews who killed You continue to reject Your teaching. They refuse even now to accept Your New Covenant and they insist on observing the outdated Laws of Moses which you have nullified. Some pretend to be Your servants, but surreptitiously retain their Jewish ways. These false Christians are a grievous threat to Your Church. They introduce doubt where only certainty must reign."

He rose in a sudden violent movement. The cowl fell back and his tonsured head was bared to God.

"I will destroy these secret Jews who pretend to be Christians! I will annihilate this army of Satan which grows strong in our midst!"

Fairly singing now, he raised his arms and roared to heaven.

"I will seek out Your enemies, Lord, and I will drive them from Your path!"

Flushed from his exertions, he sank to his knees, calm in the peace of his resolve.

"Thank you, Jesus, for the strength to reject false and seductive sympathies."

A plan took shape in his mind, and the bells announcing Matins brought joy to his heart.

3

"I talked to a prostitute last night at the fair."

Gabriel glared at his son Tomas. They were standing in an alcove, just off the main square near the Cathedral.

"Didn't I tell you to stay away from women like that?"

"But I knew her. She said hello to me. It would've been rude to ignore her. You always tell me not to be rude."

An impish smile crept over Tomas' face, and Gabriel realized that his son was teasing him. He returned the smile and his anger faded as he studied his son with pride. Only seventeen, he was several inches taller than his father, lean and exceptionally strong, the muscles of his legs and across his shoulders accented by tight hose and a close fitting tunic. His face shared some of Gabriel's sharp features, particularly around the nose, but the soft lips and mischievous smile were clearly Pilar's. And his mind was quick. He questioned everything.

"All right," Gabriel said, "who was it?"

"Fatima. You know her mother. She has the leather shop on Calle Curtidor. Her husband died last year. It's been hard for them and Fatima decided to help with the family income."

"And ... ?" Gabriel asked.

"I told her to go home, that there were other ways to make money. I told her you'd help by buying from their store."

"So, you've taken on another cause for which I'll have to pay. At least you resisted her temptations."

"It wasn't hard. Fatima's not so pretty." Tomas laughed. "But you should have seen some of the others!"

Gabriel laughed with him. "What else did you see last night?"

"Horses, mules, camels. The smells were ferocious."

"Were there any goods at this fair, or just prostitutes and animals?"

"Cloth ... from Flanders, I think. And furs. But mostly spices." With a twinkle in his eyes, Tomas repeated the outlandish stories he had heard from the spice dealers, mimicking their foreign accents. "This saffron comes from the nests of rare birds in Arabia ... My precious cumin grows at the top of trees in the center of mountain lakes ... Cannel is harvested in nets of pure gold from the river called the Nile."

"Did you see Don Alonso?"

"Twice. He was near the weighing section, with men he had stationed there to see that his merchant friends weren't cheated. I also saw him at the bookselling booth. They had wonderful books! Can I go back tonight and buy one?"

"Of course," answered Gabriel, pleased.

"When does the procession start?" asked Tomas.

"It'll be a while yet. The King didn't arrive until well after dawn. Are you excited to see the new Queen?"

"I like the horses and knights better. Who's that?" Tomas asked, pointing across the road to a small boy, conspicuous in a turban and bright silk pantaloons, wriggling impatiently under the eye of four Moorish guards.

"The son of Prince Hasan. His grandfather's the king of *Al-Andulas*, or at least part of it."

Gabriel and Tomas were joined in the alcove by several of the king's courtiers. They listened to the court gossip.

> "If King Enrique doesn't have a son this time, his half-brother Alfonso will be the successor."
>
> "Is Alfonso still kept at the palace in Arevalo?"
>
> "Yes, with his sister Isabel."
>
> "Prince Hasan was held there too, until he was released to go to Cordoba for the wedding. He told me that Princess Isabel is quite a horsewoman."
>
> "Forget Isabel. She means nothing. Let's get back to what's important. Does anyone think 'Enrique the limp' will ever have children?"
>
> "How much did he pay for the annulment from Pope Nicholas?"

"A fortune."

"It's lucky for Enrique that he got the annulment before Nicholas died. The new Pope is no friend of his."

"Poor Blanca. Sent back in disgrace to Aragon. She takes all the blame."

"They claim she cast a spell over Enrique. Rendered him impotent! Did you ever hear anything so ridiculous? Two prostitutes testified that they laid with the King and he got it in them. Of course, no one believes them."

"Will Enrique even try to fuck his new Queen? Or is it true that he likes men?"

Gabriel glanced quickly at Tomas, who was covering his face and doing all he could not to laugh out loud.

"Be careful who hears you. You could be executed for talk like that!"

"Enrique will never fuck any woman with that deformed thing of his. He can drink a hundred silver chalices overflowing with the broth of bull's testicles. It won't help."

"What?"

"That's right. It's huge at the tip and skinny at the base. He'll never get that thing into a woman."

"Well, there was close attention to the sheets in Cordoba on the wedding night.

"And?"

"Nothing. No blood. The Queen left the room just as she entered, totally intact."

"See. I told you."

"What a shame, especially for her. She looks like she would enjoy a good fuck."

"Suppose she wasn't a virgin before the wedding? Then there wouldn't be any blood."

"Never! Her brother kept that maidenhead under lock and key until he was ready to bargain it away.

"Do you think you could make love with official inspectors at the door?"

"With Juana? I could do it with all Seville watching! She's some piece. In Cordoba her gowns were cut so low that even the Archbishop got to see the royal nipples."

> *"They must have thought they were in Rome, where all the Cardinals have mistresses and lots of bastard children who get all the benefices. I think it was better when the Pope was at Avignon."*
>
> *"Why was it better? You think there was no fucking at Avignon? Haven't you read Boccaccio's tales?"*
>
> *"How would I get such a book? It costs a fortune."*
>
> *"I'll loan you my copy. You'll love it! Everybody fucks. Monks. Nuns. Everybody. But be careful who sees you reading it. Your confessor won't approve."*

"That's the book I want," whispered Tomas, but before Gabriel could answer, he added, "Listen. The procession."

Two hundred drums beat the stately rhythm of the march. King Enrique's special guards appeared first, resplendent in uniforms of crimson and gold, six dozen white horses marching in precise formation.

The standard bearers of the noble houses of Castile rode next, flags proudly displaying their own coats of arms and the lion and castle of their king. Each noble was followed by his contingent of knights, armor clanking and shining in the midday sun.

Archbishop Alfonso de Fonseca, who had performed the wedding ceremony in Cordoba the week before, came past on a horse that looked a little more spirited than he might have liked, his ecclesiastical robes and mitred hat somewhat askew. The archbishop was followed by a group of merchants and financiers, including Don Alonso de Viterbo and Don Diego Arias de Avila, the King's secretary and auditor of the royal accounts. Those two were deep in conversation and Gabriel wondered if Don Alonso was being asked to finance the upcoming war against the Moors.

Next the Portuguese. King Alfonso had remained in Lisbon, and the delegation was headed by Prince Henry, uncle to both Alfonso and Juana. Henry was known as the "Navigator" from his explorations seeking an ocean route around Africa to India. Gabriel and Tomas had marveled at his sleek ship when it came into dock several days before. There was nothing like it in the Castilian fleet.

The mendicant friars followed, dozens of black robed Dominicans sweltering in the morning heat. Gabriel cringed and looked away when he saw Friar Perez, eyes straight ahead, oblivious to everything around him.

"Here comes the little boy's father," said Gabriel, and sure enough, Prince Hasan approached, wearing the chain-mail armor still favored by the Moors, led by twenty-four sword-waving horsemen on black Arabian stallions.

"The King and Queen are next," someone shouted.

Gabriel and Tomas peered down the street. They saw King Enrique angrily wave his long arms at a group of men responsible for several large carts blocking the way. The men frantically pushed the carts away, squeezing between the procession and the crowds lining the street.

In the central square, the Prince's son grabbed at the guard nearest to him.

"Where's my father? When will he be here?" the boy hollered.

"Soon. You'll see him soon." the guard answered.

The black stallions reached the square, and the guards cheered and waved to their Prince, who sat tall and handsome in his saddle.

Gabriel heard the child cry out, "Abah! Abah! Here I am!" He watched in horror as the little boy stepped toward his father … and directly into the path of the rapidly rolling carts. The lead cart was less than ten yards away and the men pushing it were totally unaware of the child.

In one glance, Hasan took in the whole awful scene: his son smiling and waving, the cart with its large iron-rimmed wheels bearing down on him. "No! Stop! Stop the cart!" he hollered, struggling to dismount.

Tomas dashed into the street. He sidestepped two of the prancing black horses, and threw himself at the child just as the huge wheel rose above them. They crashed together on the ground. The cart blocked Gabriel's view.

The Prince, half out of his saddle, strained to see.

A murmur went up from the crowd, and everything stopped.

Even the drums.

King Enrique squinted forward, the sun in his eyes. Prince Hasan's guards reached the cart, horrified at what they might find.

Tomas rose with the unharmed child in his arms. Prince Hasan collapsed onto his saddle.

Tomas walked calmly to the Moor and lifted the child to his father's arms.

"May Allah smile on you," the Prince said, "as He has favored me by bringing you here today. To the end of days, you have my gratitude, and that of King Abu Nasr Sa'd, my father. Please tell me your name."

"Tomas. Tomas Catalan." The son of Gabriel and Pilar Catalan looked up with composed assurance into the bearded face beaming down at him.

"It's a pleasure to meet you, your highness."

Pilar heard the commotion in the streets.

"The Prince's son was almost killed!"

"Tomas saved Prince Hasan's son!"

Then Tomas and Gabriel arrived, flushed with excitement, surrounded by a throng of well-wishers.

"It was amazing, Pilar," Gabriel yelled over the tumult.

Neighbors arrived. Merchants. Housewives. Friends. Strangers. The space in front of the Catalan house filled with happy people.

"Make way! Make way for the king's stewards."

Horns sounded. A procession of iron-wheeled carts laden with baskets of food and wine edged through the crowd. A herald stood stiffly and proclaimed, "King Enrique the Fourth, monarch of Castile, wishes to thank and honor Tomas Catalan and his family for the rescue of the son of Prince Abu' l-Hasan Ali."

A king's feast of cheeses, meats, chickens, breads, fish, mutton, pork, sauces, pies, sausages, nuts, and seven partridges was set out on every available bench. People packed the street, eating, drinking, and praising the daring of Tomas Catalan.

Gabriel saw Pilar deep in conversation with Miriam Ardit at the edge of the crowd. Pilar's embroidered cloak contrasted sharply with Miriam, who was dressed as Jews must in a plain black robe, unadorned by jewelry. Yet Miriam had a serene beauty that neither plain clothes nor her heavy figure could obscure.

'This is a sad day for them,' Gabriel thought. 'How strange they are together, a *converso* and a Jew. Two little girls who met at the well and became lifelong friends. It couldn't have been easy, but Pilar doesn't do as others, and Miriam is different too.' Then an awful realization came to him. 'It's because of that friendship that the Ardits agreed to help us pray! Pilar is not only angry with me. She's guilty at her own part!'

Gabriel called to Tomas, and they walked arm in arm to the Ardits.

"Congratulations to the hero," Yacov said as they approached. "Today, you're the most famous person in Seville."

"I only did what anyone would have done," said Tomas, looking embarrassed.

"Tomas was the only one who saw the danger," said Gabriel. "Everyone else was watching the Prince or looking for the King and Queen. I didn't even know he was gone until I saw him run in front of the cart."

"You did well," Esther Ardit said softly, and then quickly averted her eyes. A blush came to her cheeks, and she stepped demurely behind her mother.

Tomas stared at Esther, saying nothing. Gabriel glanced quickly at Pilar, sharing a look of surprise. In a flash, Tomas had gone from confident hero to tongue-tied boy. As if there were not enough complications between the Catalan and Ardit families!

Tomas was rescued by the disturbance of a huge black stallion pushing its way through the crowd. A Moorish warrior dressed from head to ankle in chain mail armor, with a brilliant crimson overtunic, ceremoniously dismounted. The warrior removed his helmet and looked from side to side, a smile on his darkly handsome Arab face. He waited until the crowd grew attentive.

"I come from his royal eminence Prince Abu' l-Hasan Ali, the son of King Abu Nasr Sa'd. The Prince wishes to express his gratitude. He has sent a present for the young man who saved the life of his son."

Tomas stepped forward. The Moor bowed deeply and reached to a scabbard at his waist. He extracted a large dagger, and with a flourish, presented it to Tomas.

Tomas held the leather-covered grip and stared wide-eyed at a profusion of emeralds and diamonds. He raised the dagger for all to see, and bowed his thanks to the Moor, who gave him the scabbard, leaped back into the saddle, and maneuvered his stallion through the crowd.

As Gabriel watched the retreating Moor, his eyes were drawn to a black hooded priest standing slightly apart from the crowd. A spasm of fear shot through him.

'No, not Perez!' he thought. 'Why is he here!'

Gabriel looked frantically for Yacov, but didn't see him. He hoped that the Ardits had left before Perez arrived.

Perez walked slowly to where Gabriel was rooted, his powerful physique apparent even under the loose robe.

"Congratulations, Señor Catalan," the monk said with a smile. "Everyone in Seville, even in the monastery, is talking about your son."

Gabriel almost called him by name, catching himself as he was about to commit a stupid mistake. He drew a sharp breath and exhaled slowly.

"Thank you, Friar, but I'm afraid I don't know your name."

"Ricardo Perez," he said, smiling in a friendly manner which terrified Gabriel all the more. "Is this the hero?"

"May I present my son Tomas Catalan."

Tomas bowed his head respectfully.

"You're new to Seville, Friar Perez?" Gabriel asked.

"I've been here for several months. It's odd that we haven't met at mass. I'm sure I would remember your face."

"Sometimes I go to the Cathedral, and other times to the Church of Santa Maria la Blanca. Perhaps we've just been in different places."

"Perhaps so," said the monk gently, but with an ominous undertone that made Gabriel shudder. But before it was necessary for Gabriel to respond, Friar Perez nodded politely and left as quickly as he had appeared.

It was only then that Gabriel wondered how the Friar had known *him*.

Later that afternoon, after the crowds had gone, another visitor arrived.

Don Alonso offered his congratulations to Tomas and then motioned Gabriel aside.

"Gutenberg will sail on my next ship to Bruges. It's scheduled to leave in less than two weeks. I need to know what you're going to do."

Although he had expected exactly this, Gabriel was upset with himself that he didn't yet have an answer, and he snapped, "I can't tell you yet." He regretted his outburst as soon as the words were out of his mouth.

"About the Ardits," said Don Alonso patiently, ignoring Gabriel's tantrum. "They'll need an escort for the trip to Arcos. I have two men to send with them, but it would be better if someone they knew went along." He hesitated before asking, "Do you think Tomas might go?"

Gabriel didn't answer, and a cloud passed over Don Alonso's face. "They'll leave in two days," he said firmly. "I'll need your answer tomorrow morning."

"Pilar! Tomas! We must talk. Now."

The Catalan family assembled around the heavy wooden table where they ate, and where all serious discussions took place. Tomas still basked in the glory of the day's events, shoulder length hair even more unruly than usual, long legs extended in grand repose. Pilar was more relaxed than Gabriel had dared to hope.

"Tomas, the Ardits were attacked at their home last night, for helping secret Jews pray."

"I know. Everyone one was talking about it. Esther ..."

"I was there," Gabriel interrupted. "Yacov Ardit saved my life."

Tomas was shocked. "You ... you were praying?"

Gabriel spoke rapidly. "You met Friar Perez today. He's the one who ordered the attack. The Ardits aren't safe in Seville anymore. Don Alonso has arranged for them to go to a small mountain town called Arcos de la Frontera. They'll leave in two days." He paused. "Someone has to go with them."

"I'll go," Tomas said, a bright smile lighting his face.

"That was Don Alonso's suggestion."

"No!" said Pilar, her voice swelling. "It's too dangerous."

"Don Alonso will send two men," Gabriel argued. "We owe it to them. Yacov saved our lives."

Tears welled in Pilar's eyes, but surprisingly her voice was controlled. "Miriam made me see things differently. I don't feel the same as I did last night.."

Gabriel waited, anxious.

"Miriam said I must not be angry with you. She and Yacov considered it an honor to help secret Jews pray. They always understood the risks. She said it would upset her greatly if their troubles caused hard feelings between us. She said she loves us both, and she made me promise not to be angry with you about this."

Gabriel saw the hand of God. "Miriam Ardit is a remarkable woman," he said.

"She's very special," said Pilar, "and I'd like her to be as comfortable as possible about this trip and their new life in Arcos. I'm sorry I objected. How long will Tomas be gone?"

"It takes three days each way, so perhaps a week. But he'll be safe. Don Alonso is sending two of his best men."

Gabriel sensed that there would never be a better time to tell Pilar about the Hebrew books.

"I didn't tell you everything that happened yesterday," he said quickly. "There's a new way to make books and Don Alonso wants to make Hebrew books."

"Hebrew books!" cried Pilar. Gathering her breath, she continued, "And this new monk, this Friar Perez, he'll permit such things?"

"We'll keep it secret."

"How? You couldn't keep your praying secret."

"I don't know," Gabriel admitted.

"But still you want to make books?" Pilar demanded. "Where will this end? "

"Don Alonso ... "

"Enough Don Alonso!" exclaimed Pilar. "If it wasn't for Don Alonso, none of this Jewish business would have started."

Gabriel wasn't sure where it would end, but he knew it had started the day his father was murdered. That was also the day he learned that Don Alonso was a secret Jew.

"Isaac's *tallit*," he said. "It started with Isaac's *tallit*. Tomas, you brought it to Don Alonso's house after grandfather was killed. Do you remember?"

Tomas nodded sadly.

He must know everything, thought Gabriel. I must tell him.

"That night," Gabriel said, "Don Alonso took me to a small room. Grandfather's *tallit* was there. Don Alonso removed his rich robes and put on a plain black gown." Deeply affected by the memory, Gabriel smiled pleadingly at his son and continued. "Before my eyes, Don Alonso changed from a powerful Christian to a simple Jew. I was stunned. He told me that since Isaac had chosen to die as a Jew, it was my obligation as Isaac's son to honor his memory by saying *kaddish*. He showed me how to wear the *tallit*, and the prayers to say when putting it on. He gave me a prayer cap, and drew his *tallit* over his head to create a private space to be with God. I did the same."

"What's *kaddish*?" asked Tomas, and Gabriel felt Isaac's presence in his son's intense expression.

"A prayer in praise of God," said Gabriel, "recited by those who mourn a loved one."

"I mourn for grandfather," said Tomas. "Could I say that prayer for him?"

Gabriel felt a surge of love and pride for his son, but Pilar's voice quickly broke the moment.

"What does your father have to do with Hebrew books?" she demanded.

Gabriel spoke to Tomas.

"Your grandfather was born a Jew. His name was Isaac Catalan. When he was eighteen years old, just a year older than you are now, he was baptized. His new name was Sebastian. From then until the last moments of his life, he lived as a Christian."

"Why was he baptized?" asked Tomas.

"He was given a terrible choice ... accept Jesus Christ or die."

"Who ... ?"

"It was Archdeacon Ferran Martinez. For years he had spewed hatred against the Jews, but he was restrained by the king and the Archbishop. Then both the king and the archbishop died and Martinez ran wild. He incited mobs to burn Jewish homes and shops, and to kill Jews. Isaac heard Martinez screaming, over and over again, 'Baptism or death!' Four thousand Jews were murdered in Seville that day! Grandfather's parents were killed by those mobs."

Tomas ran his hand fitfully through his hair, and Gabriel saw pain in his face.

"Isaac saw his father bludgeoned to death. He saw his mother stripped of her clothes and forced to parade naked with other Jewish women young and old." Gabriel's voice broke. He struggled to continue. "She was raped, and finally she was hacked to pieces by the mob."

"A priest did that?" whispered Tomas, fury in his eyes.

"Grandfather Isaac hid with his dearest friend, David Modena, in this very house. If they had been found, they would have been killed. Finally, the few Jewish leaders who were still alive decided to accept baptism. They weren't cowards and they weren't afraid to die. But they couldn't bear to see the whole community murdered.

"David Modena disagreed. 'Better to die as a martyr,' he said, 'than forsake our covenant with God.' Isaac argued that the way to serve God was to live. They separated. Isaac was baptized in the square. David became a Rabbi.

"Isaac and David Modena never spoke again. Only when Isaac died did Rabbi Modena return to this house. Do you remember? It was a week after grandfather was killed. Tears ran down the rabbi's cheeks, but even then he didn't speak to us. He prayed the mourner's *kaddish* and left without another word."

Gabriel stopped. Tomas was breathing heavily, his hands clenched in front of him. Gabriel turned to Pilar.

"Now I'll answer your question," he said, taking a deep breath. I believe that making Hebrew books will justify my father's decisions … both to live as a Christian … and to die as a Jew. These books will allow Judaism to live … and honor my father's memory."

Gabriel looked back to Tomas. "Will you help me?"

Tomas put his fist on the table and Gabriel covered it with both of his hands.

"Grandfather told me that I was a Jew," Tomas said softly. "I'll be proud to help."

Pilar shook her head, amazed, distressed. Neither she nor Gabriel had known of this secret between Tomas and Isaac.

Gabriel closed his eyes momentarily, holding one fist in an open palm, then faced Pilar.

"I won't let my father's sacrifices go for nothing," he said. "We're running out of time and we have an opportunity that may never come again. I must do this!"

Pilar Catalan was deeply frightened. Her husband had barely escaped torture and death. Her best friend had been attacked and now had to flee Seville. Her son was heading toward unknown dangers. And both husband and son were going to make Hebrew books, and whatever that meant, it wasn't good.

Life in Seville had been easier for Pilar than most. The daughter of prosperous Jews who had, like Gabriel's parents, been forcibly baptized by marauding Dominicans, Pilar had grown up as a Christian, never exposed to Judaism except through her friendship with Miriam Ardit.

When she fell in love with Gabriel, Pilar gave no thought to religion or politics. Her quite reasonable assumption was that Gabriel was and would remain a *converso*. In the years that Gabriel's father Isaac had lived with them, she had come to love the old man, never suspecting that he harbored Jewish inclinations. She was shocked by the actions which led to his death, and she was totally unprepared for the news that Tomas had just shared. Isaac had told Tomas he was a Jew! How dare he?

Not that she had strong feelings about being a Christian. But a Jew! What did that mean? And why? After Isaac's death, Don Alonso had insisted that Gabriel pray for his father. She thought it was just that once, but Gabriel had been drawn in. He began to pray regularly with Don Alonso, learning the Hebrew language and customs. Then they had the idea of finding others and joining together to pray. Gabriel said it was God's commandment. She thought it was crazy. When it became too risky for so many men to come to Don Alonso's home, and they sought more secluded places to pray, Yacov Ardit had offered the room under his home. She went berserk when Miriam told her, and had never forgiven Gabriel for putting her dear friend at risk. Even with Miriam's plea keeping her outwardly in check, resentment boiled beneath the surface and she knew it would explode sooner or later.

And books! More insanity. Worse, Tomas was part of it, both the books and, inevitably, the Jewish business as well. This thought drove her to the edge of distraction. Her precious son, foolishly led into danger by her husband. What did Tomas know? He was young and ignorant and brash. He had just saved Prince Hasan's son, and thought he could do anything. He laughed at danger. Fear for him permeated every fiber of Pilar's body.

She cried herself to sleep, happy that Gabriel had not come to her.

"Today we learn to make type."

Johann Gutenberg and Gonsalvo de Viterbo, Don Alonso's son, along with Gabriel and Tomas, were gathered in a spacious well-lit room adjacent to the courtyard of the Catalan home. Gutenberg spoke, Gonsalvo interpreted.

"It's very complicated. Carving the letters, if you're a skilled goldsmith, this you can do. But making every letter exactly the same height, so they print evenly —this took years to accomplish. You will learn my years in one day! It's a good bargain Don Alonso made for you."

Gutenberg removed a piece of metal from the leather pouch hanging over his shoulder and laid it on the counter. "The type. You saw this before. See, it's reversed. So when it's inked and pressed to a piece of paper, the printed letter is right."

Tomas picked up the little piece of metal and fiddled with it, fascinated. Gutenberg showed them a small copper block. "The *matrix*.

Matrix means mother. It gives birth to many letters. To make type, the *matrix* is set at the bottom of a mold. Melted lead is poured in. Look."

They came close. Gutenberg could not have been more intense, or shown greater pride, if he had been describing the creation of the world.

"Here's the punch which hammers the letter into the matrix."

Gabriel reached for the punch, but Tomas got it first. It was about five inches long, made from steel. At one end, the letter B was carved backwards in the steel. Gabriel raised the *matrix* and Tomas held the punch next to it. The letter which protruded from the end of the punch matched the depression made in the *matrix*. Gabriel put his other hand over their combined hands and squeezed gently. Father and son smiled.

"This is hammered into the *matrix*?" Gabriel asked.

"Yes."

"Then there's a separate punch and *matrix* for each letter?"

"Yes. You'll need a complete set of punches and *matrices* for each alphabet you use. If you want more than one size, you need punches and *matrices* for each letter in each size. The punches must be meticulously formed. That's the art! You use the same gravers and files as in your goldsmith work. I'll show you."

Tomas had the type, the punch, and the *matrix*. He fit them together, absorbing their relationship.

"This will take a long time," said Gabriel, considering the work needed to create several full sets of twenty-two Hebrew letters.

"The *matrix* is only for the tip," Tomas said. "How's the type formed?"

Gutenberg took a strange-looking device from his bag, about as big and thick as his two large hands held together, part metal and part wood. "This is the mold. The *matrix* fits into the bottom."

Gutenberg gave the mold to Tomas and showed him where to insert the *matrix*, and how the mold held it tightly.

"The wooden handles protect your hands from the hot lead."

Gutenberg demonstrated the technique of pouring lead, a quick shake of the mold to fill all the crevices, and then opening the mold to remove the newly formed piece of type.

Gabriel was terrified. How was he ever going to do all of this? He remembered the artistry of the page from Gutenberg's Bible. Now he knew what was needed to produce it. It would take years. Then he thought of something else that Gutenberg had not mentioned.

"We'll need models of the Hebrew letters," he mused, "and the only person in Seville who has Hebrew manuscripts is David Modena."

4

A small group of riders left Seville at dawn the next day. Don Alonso's men, Juan and Gaspar, rode on horseback, Tomas Catalan and the Ardit family on donkeys. Two additional donkeys carried the Ardit's possessions. Tomas saw Gaspar talking quietly with the guards at the city gate, a hand was extended, and they left without challenge.

Behind them, Talavero's spy waited long enough to observe their direction and then hurried back into the city.

They crossed the Rio Guadalquivir on a bridge of planks laid on small boats strung tightly together, just reinstalled after the departure the previous day of the great high ship of the Portuguese Prince Henry. Esther looked back at the high walls of Seville, her sad eyes barely visible under a wide brimmed hat. Tomas tried to imagine how she must feel about leaving the only home she had ever known. He wanted to talk to her about it, but didn't know what to say, and the moment was lost.

Soon they reached the flat surrounding countryside, where groves of olive trees now and then broke the monotony of the parched yellow-ochre soil. The Moors had once made this land fertile, but after the Christian reconquest, it had rapidly declined to its former arid state. Streams were still running from the spring rains, but in another few weeks the summer sun would bake the earth.

The route they followed was to the south and east of Seville. Occasionally, they saw flocks of sheep in the distance but not a single human being for the entire first day. Hawks flew lazily overhead.

Esther sat straight on her donkey, long black hair woven in a single braid reaching to her waist, strong legs gripping the animal, dark wool dress pulled tightly around her hips.

Tomas couldn't take his eyes from her. He had always seen her as a little girl until two days before when her eyes had tied his tongue. He imagined her pure, a maiden from a *jongleur's* song of chivalry, but when she turned in the saddle, her full breasts aroused him.

They made camp at the edge of a creek below a high rock wall, and built a small cooking fire. Juan and Gaspar took care of the animals. Miriam and Esther prepared a meal of boiled meat.

Tomas watched as Yacov Ardit and his son Ruyo began to pray. They opened two small leather bound prayer books, one a well-worn family treasure and the other a departing gift from Don Alonso. Tomas was intrigued by the strange sounding Hebrew words. He imagined his father saying those words. Yacov reminded him of his grandfather.

After praying, they washed their hands in the creek upstream from where the animals were drinking, then joined the women at the campfire. Juan and Gaspar were already on lookout for the night.

Esther brought Tomas his meal. He was entranced as she glided in and out of the firelight. He thought he would explode with joy when she spoke to him.

"What did Prince Hasan say to you when you saved his son?" she asked.

Tomas blushed but managed to find his voice.

"He said he would be eternally grateful. He sent me a present too, a dagger. But ... you were there."

"No, we left."

He slid the knife from its sheath inside his boot and held it up. Diamonds and emeralds gleamed as the handle caught the firelight. Her eyes widened.

"It's beautiful, Tomas! Do you know how to use it?"

"I could never stab anyone," he said. "But I'm glad to have it."

"You never know what you can do until the time comes. My father was very brave when those men came. He was ready to do anything to save us, no matter what. Like you, with the Prince's son."

Again, Tomas ached to express his sympathy for what the Ardits had suffered, but he didn't know how.

"Your father isn't wearing his yellow badge," he said instead.

"No," she answered. "While we travel, he doesn't have to. He'll put it back on when we get to Arcos."

"It must be very difficult to be a Jew, Esther." It was thrilling to say her name aloud.

"It is. But you're both Christian and Jew. How do you keep things straight?"

"I don't do anything Jewish. My father does, but not me."

"Maybe some day," she said.

"Can I tell you a secret?"

"What?"

"I have a Hebrew name. My grandfather told me. It was the name of his father."

Esther waited. Tomas stared silently at the most beautiful face he had ever seen, forgetting that he was about to tell her something important. Then, with a start, he said, "It's Benjamin. I'm Benjamin Catalan." He paused, a pensive look on his face. "I never said that before."

Esther reached her hand to him, but stopped short, her fingers lingering in the night air.

"It's a wonderful name," she said. "Some day ... I just know it ... you'll be Benjamin to me."

Dawn was still two hours away when Captain Talavero roused his men. They buckled their swords, mounted their horses, and resumed the chase. They had tracked their prey into a long valley that led in only one direction, and Talavero was confident they could move even before the tracks were visible. This time, Perez knew nothing of their whereabouts and they had their own objectives. Talavero sought revenge on Yacov Ardit who had humiliated him. His men wanted Esther.

Tomas spent a restless night. As the stars spread in their changing pattern from one horizon to the other, visions of Esther's face pervaded his thoughts. He dreamed that he reached his hand to hers to complete the touch she had suggested, and each time his fingers burned in the heat of his fantasy.

She slept only a few yards away, but it might as well have been miles. Even if custom had not forbidden contact, Tomas could not have traversed the distance.

The Ardit camp stirred an hour before dawn. Yacov put something strange on his left arm and head that he called *tefillin*, and he and Ruyo said their prayers. Then they moved out as the sun rose. Tomas rode next to Esther at the rear of the otherwise single file of donkeys. Don Alonso's horsemen rode far out to each flank. The country became more rugged as they climbed from the *meseta* into the hills.

Tomas and Esther talked.

He told her about the fair and the King's procession. She explained Jewish customs. Tomas described mass and confession. They talked about food. Tomas told of trips to Cordoba and Jerez. They spoke of Don Alonso. And often they spoke of Gabriel.

"I work next to my father every day," Tomas said. "His hands are magic; his jewelry is the most beautiful in Seville."

"He's a nice man," said Esther. "I only see him when he comes to pray." She stopped abruptly. There would be no more such occasions.

"He wants to be as Jewish as he can be," Tomas said. "He wants to make Hebrew books."

"Books?" Esther asked.

"Yes. A man named Johann Gutenberg came to our house yesterday to teach us a new way to make books. I've never seen my father so excited. I'm going to help him. But it must be a secret."

Late in the afternoon, as the sun was beginning to set, they were still talking.

"Do you know Rabbi Modena?" Tomas asked. "My father told me about him, and I've seen him, but we've never met."

"I know the rabbi very well. We go to synagogue ... " Esther looked down, and Tomas was sorry he had asked about the rabbi and the synagogue she would never see again.

"I'm sorry you have to leave Seville. I saw you looking back. My father is sorry, too. If it wasn't for the praying ..."

"I'm going to miss Seville," Esther said. "But it's not your father's fault. Don't think that."

A frown passed over her face and she became pale. "I know we had to leave. I saw one of those horrible men."

"What man? Where?"

"One who came with Captain Talavero and ... when I went to get water, the next morning. He was in the square, looking at me."

"Did he do anything?" asked Tomas, alarmed. "Say anything?"

"No. But he scared me."

Just then they heard a shout. Gaspar was galloping in from the western flank.

"Seven riders behind us!" he hollered. "Can't tell who they are. We'll ride back to meet them. You go on as fast as you can. Ride hard all night. Maybe you can get to Arcos before dawn. We'll join you if we can."

"You're only two," Yacov said, "They'll kill you!"

"If we stay here, we might all die."

He galloped back towards the approaching horsemen, now clearly visible across the flat plain. Juan joined him. Tomas thought how much they must love Don Alonso to risk their lives without hesitation. He and the Ardits rode off in the other direction, toward a large cliff. The setting sun behind them cast frightening shadows on the rocks.

Tomas glanced over his shoulder as he rode. It was harder to see as the distance widened, but it seemed that the men were speaking.

'Please, God, don't let Esther be hurt.' he prayed silently.

He looked back again and his hopes were dashed. Both of Don Alonso's men lay still on the ground, and five of the horsemen were galloping toward them.

The donkeys slowed to a walk, energy spent. Tomas rode near Esther. She looked back frantically at the men gaining on them, and then at him. He had never felt more helpless.

They neared the cliff and came into a natural amphitheater. The trail cut through the rock ahead of them. If they could reach it, perhaps there would be a place to hide. Tomas smacked his donkey and Esther's, but the animals were exhausted. They would never make it. Horses pounded past them, cutting off their way.

"It's them!" Esther said to Tomas. "The men from the house!"

"What do you want with us?" Yacov asked, trying to be belligerent even as his thin frame shook.

Five riders circled slowly and silently around them. Tomas slid off his donkey and edged closer to Esther. One of the men rode in and brusquely knocked Yacov to the ground. He dragged himself up and limped backwards toward Miriam. Ruyo began to cry.

"So, Jew," said Talavero, "now we have you. Perez won't save you or your precious daughter this time."

"Let's see what's under her dress," snarled one of the men, reaching for Esther.

Tomas jumped at the man, but he was tripped. Falling, Tomas tried to grab the man's leg. He was hit from behind and lay still on the hard ground.

Talavero directed his men to tie Tomas, Yacov and Ruyo. "We'll take care of them when we're done with the women."

Yacov and Ruyo were tied in a sitting position with their wrists pulled sharply behind them. Two men approached Tomas where he lay on the ground, face down, his hands under him. One kicked him in the side. He didn't move. They rolled him over and tied his wrists together in front of him. They wrapped a rope around his ankles and were about to tie it when Talavero bellowed impatiently.

"Fuck the mother first. Make the Jew watch while we fuck his wife. Then we'll have the young one." His laugh was ugly. "Save the virgin cunt for me. Tie her up for now."

The men left Tomas and went to Esther.

Yacov let out an unintelligible howl. Tomas lay still.

Talavero laughed again. "Let the little Jew holler. Who's going to hear?"

Four men surrounded Miriam. They threw her cape to the ground, reached roughly under her tunic and ripped it off.

"Look at those big Jewish tits."

Tomas looked away. 'She's a mother. Esther's mother. How can they do this?' He thought of his own mother and raged against the rope holding his wrists.

The men assaulted Miriam repeatedly.

"Hold her legs apart. I can't get my dick in."

"Her cunt is slippery now."

They spurted into her again and again. When they stood up, they turned to Yacov, clutched their wet private parts, and shook them in his face.

Talavero sat on his horse and watched.

And so did Tomas.

He saw half-naked men cackling undecipherable obscenities. His eyes were drawn to the woman on the ground, on her back, legs spread, not making a sound as one man after another mounted her. He saw Esther with her eyes squeezed shut, her body compressed into a tight ball.

He moved his legs and realized with a start that the rope around his ankles was not tied. He began to work it loose. Now he could bring his feet close to his hands, facing away so they couldn't see him. His fingers closed on the Prince's dagger inside his boot. He eased it out and slowly began to cut at the rope around his wrists.

Yacov's screaming stopped and the sudden quiet was unnerving. Tomas heard the men on Miriam, private sounds that made him cringe.

Talavero dismounted and walked over to Esther, who was tied in a sitting position. He loosened the belt of his tunic and pulled down his hose and underdrawers. He seized her head and shoved her face into his naked crotch. She pulled away violently and Talavero lost his grip.

Tomas frantically worked the knife harder, cutting his arm.

"Untie her. Hold her down," Talavero shouted to his men.

They left Miriam laying motionless and naked. Without bothering to raise their own breeches, four men, dripping obscenely, advanced on Esther. She struggled to resist, striking at them as soon as the ropes were loosened, but they beat at her and twisted her arms and legs until she cried out and was still. Talavero ripped open her dress and the lace ties of her chemise, and threw them forcibly aside. Tomas could not look away. Esther lay naked on the ground, two men holding her arms, two more spreading her legs.

Talavero dropped to his knees and plunged forward. His throbbing erection ripped into Esther and a scream burst from her lips. Talavero held her hips against him as he thrust forward and back. His fingers left huge red marks on her white skin.

Somewhere in the darkness behind him, Tomas heard hoofbeats. Then he was free. With the dagger in his right hand, he raced toward Talavero. Two men blocked his way. He stabbed at one but the other knocked him to the ground and he dropped the dagger. He looked up and saw a sword raised high above him. The sword started down.

What happened next was a glorious incredible blur that Tomas would remember for the rest of his life. The sword continued to come towards him, but the arm holding it was no longer attached to the man's body. Tomas' puzzled eyes stared as the sword and the arm, rotating slowly, fell together in the dust. A black stallion reared and a second vicious cutting swoop sent the man's head after his arm.

Hasan!

Talavero jumped up, dripping with Esther's blood and his own ejaculation.

"This is a mistake," he screamed. "We're with King Enrique's troop, and these are just some worthless Jews."

Hasan glared and motioned to his men. They drew their swords and herded Talavero and the others into a tight group. One bent over, bleeding from a knife wound in his belly.

The Prince dismounted, took blankets from his saddle pack, and gently handed one to Miriam, another to Esther. Yacov, cut loose by Hasan's men, rushed to his wife and wrapped her in the blanket. Tomas started to go to Esther, but she staggered to her parents, awkwardly wrapping herself in the blanket.

Hasan spoke to Tomas. "We saw the trails ahead of us when we left Seville. Then we found four dead men and heard the screams. What are you doing here?"

"I'm taking my friends to Arcos de la Frontera," Tomas said, his voice barely loud enough to be heard.

Talavero hollered at the Prince, "Why are you helping these despicable people?"

Hasan stared at Talavero coldly and the soldier's arrogance drained from his face. He dropped to his knees, clutching his hands between his naked legs.

"This boy saved my son's life," said the Prince, his eyes glinting with rage. "These others are important to him, and so to me."

To his men, he said, "Take these animals with us. If they're really with Enrique, they'll have use as hostages."

Tomas was aghast. Talavero would live! He started to object, but Hasan was already moving. Mounting his horse, he said, "My father needs my help in our war against King Muhammed. My men will see you safely to Arcos."

Riding to Tomas, he reached into his wide sash and removed the jeweled dagger. Leaning down with a broad smile, he said, "I think you lost this. Be well, my young friend, until it is Allah's pleasure for us to meet again."

Spurring his horse, he led his men through the cut in the rocks.

5

Gabriel entered the synagogue.

He wore his best tunic and a new gray cape.

He peered timidly through the rounded entry arch, eyes drawn to the awesome raised *bema*.

Echoes ... the lilting chant of the word of God, read joyously from His Holy Torah ... his father, Isaac Catalan, younger than Tomas, called to this very *bema* for his Bar Mitzvah. Before Ferran Martinez. Before forced conversions.

Not for me, he thought. Not for Tomas. Not yet.

His eyes darted, absorbing everything in one ravenous gulp ... the delicate Moorish architecture, high windows and long wooden benches, the women's section, the Star of David carved into creamy white stucco.

Oil lamps guarded the ark, glowing day and night, symbols of the eternal continuity of God's covenant with the Jews. Gabriel would soon help to preserve the record of that covenant, and he was comforted by his connection to eternity.

Feeling the presence of the Lord in His holy place, Gabriel spoke silently to God. "I'll do Your work, Lord, but I cannot do it alone. You must help. Please don't abandon me." Thus he made his personal covenant, utterly certain that the God of Israel heard and concurred.

He went toward an open door, and found himself at the entrance to Rabbi Modena's study. The old man sat at his desk, staring at him, his white beard untrimmed and disheveled, obedient to the laws of Castile. A few wisps of hair protruded on either side of a large cylindrical cap. A heavy black robe fought the perpetual chill of the aged.

Don Alonso had arranged the meeting at his request, but now, facing the rabbi, Gabriel was unsure how to begin. He spread and clenched his fingers nervously.

"Why was he so stubborn?" Modena shouted suddenly, startling him. "If Isaac had stayed with me, he could have remained a Jew."

Gabriel understood that Modena was referring to the time when he and Gabriel's father Isaac, still young boys, had hidden in the Catalan house while the mob led by Archdeacon Martinez rampaged through the *juderia*. How long had the Rabbi been sitting there, re-living ancient memories, feeding his emotions?

"My father didn't think any Jews would survive," Gabriel said. "If they hadn't converted, Martinez would have killed them." Gabriel's respect for the old man kept him from adding 'including you.'

"After the riots were over," Modena pleaded, "he could have re-turned to the synagogue."

"How?" said Gabriel from the doorway, gently. "The church wouldn't let him go. Even *forced* baptism is irreversible in the eyes of the Church. Did others come back?"

"No," Modena said, shaking his head.

His frail body slumped, the belligerent tone gone. "I know it's non-sense. In my heart, I know. But I can't say the truth. For sixty four years, I can't say the truth!"

Gabriel moved close, gripped the old man's chair. Modena's face contorted, witness to the terrible struggle within him ... eyes closed ... lips moving soundlessly. A faint whisper.

"I failed your father. He was my friend, and I turned my back on him. I didn't have the decency to appreciate his sacrifice. When Isaac Catalan knelt in church and ate the body of Christ, it was repugnant to me. But who am I to judge? Was not Moses a secret Jew in the house of Pharaoh?"

Modena, head still bowed, spoke in a normal voice.

"Your father was a good man, as Jewish as he could be. Surely he died a Jew. Now he's gone and it's too late."

He rose, intense, imploring. "Can you ever forgive me?"

Gabriel was shaken by this unexpected turn. At best, he had hoped for reluctant cooperation. The old man's torment was painful to wit-ness.

"There's nothing to forgive, Rabbi," he said softly. "My father un-derstood. He was sad that you were so stubborn, but he didn't blame you, and he didn't hate you. Isaac always considered you his friend."

Rabbi Modena opened his arms and the men hugged. "I'm embracing Isaac. After all these years."

Their joy was short-lived.

An old man in a dark caftan appeared in the rabbi's doorway. "A monk is here," he said. "Friar Ricardo Perez."

Gabriel was trapped! What excuse could he give for being where he did not belong? But Modena motioned to him and he followed the rabbi into the sanctuary. Perez stood there, hands on hips, eyes raised, arrogantly surveying the synagogue.

Rabbi Modena walked straight toward Perez, arms extended in greeting.

"Welcome to our synagogue, Father," he said, and then, indicating Gabriel, "Do you know Señor Catalan? But of course. He does more work for the Church than he does for us. He's going to repair some of our silver pieces. We're just negotiating a commission. The pointer for our Torah is bent, the *tapuhim* are badly dented, and both of the Torah crowns need work."

The friar's dark face revealed nothing, "We've met. It's good to see you again so soon, Señor Catalan."

Perez walked deliberately toward the center of the synagogue. He's going to stand on the *bema*, Gabriel thought in horror, but Perez stopped short and spun to face them.

"Rabbi, I've come to talk with you about a serious matter. There are supposed Christians in Seville who practice the Jewish ritual and secretly observe Jewish holidays and customs. The Church cannot allow this heresy to continue. We must root out these judaizing *conversos* and bring them back to Jesus. You agree, don't you, Señor Catalan?"

"If it's true," said Gabriel, his heart pounding. "Have you evidence?"

Perez smiled, "Not yet, but perhaps you will help me. Do you know of any Christians who keep the Jewish Sabbath … or perhaps go to secret prayer meetings?"

"No," said Gabriel, looking straight at Perez and straining to hide his panic.

"And you, Rabbi?"

"I'm not aware of such things," said Modena, just the hint of a smile crossing his lips.

Perez glared at Gabriel. Of course it was more than coincidence that Perez had arrived at the synagogue just after him. Perez had followed him! Perez was speaking and Gabriel forced himself to listen.

"... perhaps you can help me translate. We Dominicans study Hebrew in order to read Scripture, but some of the words aren't clear to me. I'm interested in Isaiah's prophecies ... those which predict the appearance of our Lord Jesus as the Messiah. You're familiar with such references, Señor Catalan?"

"I've heard Isaiah read in Church," Gabriel answered.

"We'll discuss it some day," said Perez, "but now I must leave. Remember what I said about the *conversos.*"

He placed his hand on the goldsmith's shoulder. "I'm sure you'll negotiate a good arrangement, Señor Catalan. Don't let yourself be cheated."

Gabriel could not stop trembling; he could barely speak.

"Perez didn't believe your story," he gulped. "He was following me. He has an informer. He knew about the praying the other day. Maybe he knows I was there."

"Don't worry about him." Modena answered calmly. "The Archbishop hates him. Fonseca knows how valuable *conversos* are. Neither the king nor the church could exist without the money collected by *conversos*. Perez won't be a problem."

"I hope you're right, but he came close the other day," said Gabriel. "If we'd been caught at prayer, Perez would have all the evidence he needs, and Fonseca would have no choice but to help him."

"But he didn't," said Modena, walking back to his study.

"Now, tell me about this Gutenberg that Don Alonso is so excited about?"

Gabriel loosened a small bag which had been tied to his belt. He showed the rabbi the punch, *matrix* and letters, briefly explaining their use.

"I need models of Hebrew letters to carve into type."

The Rabbi's study was packed with books, some bound in leather and others in the form of scrolls. It was the most important repository of such treasures in all of southern Castile.

"I have many Hebrew letters," said Modena with a smile, pointing at the books. "Here's a Bible written just a few years before Martinez' riots made such activities impossible. Twenty-four volumes. The blue books are the Torah, the Prophets are in red, and the Writings are in brown."

Rabbi Modena opened one of the brown volumes and read: *Happy is the man who finds wisdom, Her value in trade is better than silver. The man who attains understanding, Her yield, greater than gold.*

"The Book of Proverbs, by King Solomon. So, we can pick letters and learn at the same time. Look."

Gabriel saw an interwoven pattern of white intersecting ribbons set against a rose colored background. The words were written around the borders. Other pages contained small paintings in brilliant reds and blues and yellows.

"It's beautiful!" he said. "I never dreamed that there were Hebrew books like this."

Modena took down another volume and laid it on the table. "This is a *Haggadah*. It tells the story of how God brought us out from slavery in Egypt." Next he showed Gabriel a long row of books he called the *Mishneh Torah*. "The legal code of Rabbi Moses Maimonides, summarizing three thousand years of Jewish laws. Are there enough Hebrew letters for you?"

"Plenty. But now I want to read the books, not just copy the letters."

Gabriel paused, balancing his obligation as a Jewish parent against the objections of his wife.

"And I want my son to learn, too," he said, his eyes pleading. "Will you help us, Rabbi?"

"It's dangerous for you," Modena said.

"I know. And for you too, if Friar Perez catches us."

"I'm an old man. What is my risk compared with the great *mitzvah* of teaching the ways of God to the son and grandson of Isaac Catalan."

On the return trip from Arcos, Tomas rode a horse for the first time. The Moors laughed at his awkwardness as they flew over the plains, but they taught him how to ride as they did, legs drawn up high in the stirrups. At night, by the campfire, they showed him how to use the Prince's dagger.

"Stay low. Feint one way. Turn. Move. Snap your wrist."

These activities kept his mind from the horrors he had seen.

He rode with the Moors until he could see the walls of Seville, and then he said goodbye to his new friends.

Leading one of Don Alonso's horses while riding the other, Tomas approached the city. He entered at the Carmona gate, purposely far from the Jerez gate he had left six days before, avoiding both questions and memories. He rode lethargically through the narrow streets in the hot midday sun. Eyes unfocused, he plodded on to Don Alonso's house. With each step, his mood darkened.

Don Alonso's welcoming smile turned ashen when he saw the horses without his men. Silently, he led Tomas to a private room on the second floor of the mansion and sent a messenger to bring the boy's parents. He gave Tomas food and drink while they waited.

Gabriel and Pilar burst joyfully into the room but stopped abruptly when they saw the distress on their son's face. They turned to Don Alonso.

"We've not yet spoken," he said. "But clearly something terrible has happened."

Tomas took a deep breath.

"It was Talavero and his men. They followed us. On the second night, they attacked. Juan and Gaspar were brave, Don Alonso. They did their best to give us time to get away." He paused. "They were killed."

He fought to compose himself. "They would have killed us all. But a miracle happened. Prince Hasan saved us. The Prince left some men to take us to Arcos, and they rode with me back to Seville."

"Juan and Gaspar are dead," said Don Alonso hoarsely. "They've been with me for over twenty years."

"We buried them on the way back. Their belongings are in the saddle bags."

"Thank you, Tomas. Their wives and children will appreciate that. I'll provide for them, of course." He paused. "Did you bury Talavero and his men?"

"Three of them. Hasan took Talavero and the other three men as hostages."

"That's a problem," said Don Alonso, frowning and shaking his head. "You say that the Ardits got to Arcos? You saw my cousin Isidro? He'll care for them?"

"Yes, he's found them a house. He also ... Señora Ardit ... Esther ... "

Tomas' voice failed him, and he struggled to contain his sobs. Pilar went to him and held him in her arms.

"What happened?" Gabriel asked. Pilar glared at Gabriel as she comforted her son, but Tomas disengaged himself and tried to continue.

"After they caught us ... they tied everyone ... except Señora Ardit."

Don Alonso put his hand on Tomas' shoulder and spoke softly to Gabriel, "Take him home. He'll be more comfortable with just the two of you. I'll talk with him later."

He turned to Pilar. "I'm so sorry."

"They raped them. Both of them. The señora and Esther."

The Catalan family sat on stone benches in their enclosed courtyard. Even in the shade, the heat was intense.

"Señora Ardit never made a sound. She just lay there. They didn't even cover her."

Pilar cringed and covered her face with her hands. "Hasan should have killed them all!" she said without looking up.

Tomas went on as if he was in a dream, "He swung his sword and the man's head was on the ground. He was still standing. Then he fell."

"O Gabriel, why did we let him go?" said Pilar, shaking her head.

"I stabbed one of them. I used the Prince's dagger. But I couldn't get to Talavero ... he was ... with Esther."

Opening his eyes, a look of bewilderment on his face, Tomas broke down, and his sobs echoed around the courtyard. Pilar hugged him and they cried together.

Perez has unleashed this violence, Gabriel thought. The horrible days are back.

"I'll kill him!" Tomas cried out.

"And Perez, too," said Gabriel quietly.

"There was blood ... on her ... and him." Tomas spoke from a distant blur. "She screamed ... I wanted to help ... she wouldn't let me. Before those men came, we talked ... And then after, she wouldn't look at me. I have to go back to Arcos. I want to be with Esther."

Tomas and Pilar went into the house, but Gabriel sat in the courtyard, numbed by the monstrosity of Tomas' story. Elbows on knees, head in his hands, he closed his eyes and rocked slowly from side to side.

Things were happening too fast, he reflected. For two decades, life had been peaceful and prosperous. Now, all at once, an unknown informer, Perez, Talavero, Gutenberg, Hasan, Rabbi Modena, Esther. He shook his head. Is this a test, God? What do you want of me?

He went to Pilar, needing the comfort of her presence. She was sitting on their bed, legs drawn tightly against her body, crying softly.

"Miriam Ardit is a modest woman," she said. "I'm sure even Yacov has never seen her naked, let alone her children, and, God forbid, in front of strangers. How will she face Yacov? How will she ever make love again?" She sighed, her body tense, fists clenched. "Esther ... Tomas can't possibly understand. And you ... you want to make Hebrew books?"

Tomas walked sluggishly into the shop. He looked exhausted, although he had slept much later than usual. Gabriel hugged him, trying to convey feelings he could not put to words.

"Herr Gutenberg will be here soon," said Gabriel.

"I'm ready," said Tomas without enthusiasm.

"Let me show you what I've done while you were away," said Gabriel, hoping to spark his son's attention.

"I copied these letters from Rabbi Modena's books. There's a page for each letter in the Hebrew alphabet, twenty-two pages." Gabriel identified each letter for Tomas, and they discussed the merits of the different styles. Some were bold, others were delicate.

"This letter ש is graceful, but it requires a very narrow cut. Maybe we should choose one that would be easier to carve," said Gabriel.

"I can carve it," Tomas said quickly. "Let's just choose the letters we like the best."

Father and son bent over the pages and soon, the models for the first printed Hebrew alphabet stared back at them from the table.

"I like these," Gabriel said.

"Which letters spell Esther?" Tomas asked, eyes suddenly alive.

Gabriel held his tongue. This was not the time. He selected four pages and placed them in their proper sequence on the table. Tomas took a clean sheet of paper, dipped a pen in black ink, and wrote, from right to left, the single word אסתר.

Gutenberg arrived by himself, although Gabriel had expected Gonsalvo de Viterbo to be with him. Now they would have to communicate with the few words each had learned of the other's language.

Gabriel led them to the same room they had used before, now outfitted for making type. It contained a workbench and all the tools and supplies Gabriel thought they would need.

Gutenberg took a metal gauge from his bag, and showed that the vertical height of his letters was precisely equal to the opening in the gauge.

Gabriel selected a steel rod and, directed by Gutenberg, filed two opposing sides at one end so that it fit exactly into the gauge. Filing the sides distorted the flat smoothness of the end, but after several attempts Gabriel achieved both a perfectly smooth face and the precise dimensions required.

Next, Gabriel drew a large א copying from the model he and Tomas had selected. Gutenberg produced a clamp from his bag and set the prepared steel rod into it, standing the clamp in front of a mirror so it could be seen in reverse. Gabriel sharpened a piece of charcoal and outlined the reversed letter on the end of the steel rod.

"Tomas, you try," he said.

Tomas selected a graver and began to scoop away tiny slivers of metal. He alternated between interior and exterior spaces, using different gravers and files, working around all sides of the letter. He seemed to know intuitively what to do, although once Gutenberg took the graver from his hand and showed how to accomplish a particularly difficult cut. Gabriel frequently refreshed the image when the cuts obliterated the outline.

Two hours passed; the only sound was of tools scraping delicately against metal. Finally, the letter א protruded from the end of the steel rod.

Gutenberg held the rod in the flame of a candle until it was covered with soot, and pressed it against a piece of paper. They looked closely at the image on the paper. There were several flaws.

Gabriel placed the carved steel punch into the sizing tool. It was too small—too much metal had been carved away. But even this did not lessen his joy.

"It's a good beginning," he said.

Gutenberg took the punch and hammered it into a copper block. The result was a *matrix* with the letter א sharply punched into it.

Gabriel tried to duplicate the German's work, but his hammering distorted the copper, and he failed to match Gutenberg's meticulous work. He shook his head in frustration. His appreciation for Gutenberg's skill was growing rapidly.

Gutenberg melted a mixture of lead and tin in a small pot. He quickly assembled a mold, choosing the *matrix* he had just punched, then poured in the liquid metal. He waited a few seconds, then popped out the hardened type.

As he repeated the process several times, Gabriel became increasingly disturbed, realizing that he and Tomas would have to do all this without Gutenberg to help them.

6

After fifty years of construction on the site previously occupied
by the grand mosque of Seville, the central nave of the huge Cathedral was all that was usable. Curved arches soared above rows of
white marble columns. Paintings, including several by Francesco
Romo, hung in every available space, and statues stood before each
column.

On the occasion of the Holy Feast of *Corpus Christi*, Archbishop
Fonseca, magnificent in the layers of his vestment, made his way to
the foot of the black marble altar. His chasuble of pure white linen
hung to the floor, a blue stole with fringed ends reached almost as
far. He wore a pallium of white lamb's wool around his neck, a woolen
robe of rich blue with gold fringe along the edges, plain sandals, and
a mitre with blue piping. In his arms was the cross-staff of his office.
The archbishop bowed, made the sign of the Cross, and intoned the
opening words of High Mass.

Ascending the altar, Fonseca began the Lesson from the first Epistle
of Saint Paul to the Corinthians: *Lord Jesus, on the night he was betrayed, took bread, and giving thanks, broke the bread and gave it to his
disciples, saying: take this and eat it; this is My Body which will be given
up for you. When supper was ended, he took the cup. Again giving thanks
and praise, He passed the cup to his disciples, saying: take this and drink
from it. This is the cup of My Blood, the blood of a new and everlasting
covenant. It will be shed for you and for all men so that sins may be
forgiven.*

Gabriel heard the Latin Mass, but his mind echoed with Jewish
blessings over bread and wine. Jesus was giving thanks to the God of

Israel, no doubt in Hebrew. Yet if Gabriel repeated those same prayers in Hebrew, the church of Jesus would burn him at the stake.

Hear what the holy Church maintaineth, that the bread its substance changeth into flesh, the wine to Blood.

Gabriel had always been intrigued with the idea of the living Jesus Christ embodied in the bread and the wine. For him it was a fiction. 'That's not really Christ's body,' he thought. 'Not for me. But suppose it *is* true for Christians who believe it?'

The Archbishop kissed the altar and began the offering. He took a small piece of bread become the Body of Christ and put it into the wine become Blood. Again he made the Sign of the Cross. He raised the Chalice high above his head, brought the cup to his lips, and drank.

Gabriel sensed his terrifying presence before he actually saw Friar Perez advance to assist Archbishop Fonseca in the distribution of the Host. He watched, horrified, as the congregants, including Don Alonso and Francesco Romo, received communion from Perez, dreading his own inevitable turn. Then Pilar and Tomas moved and he had to follow.

Gabriel opened his mouth, afraid he would gag when the Friar placed the host on his tongue. Perez smiled benevolently and it was over.

The Body of our Lord Jesus Christ preserve thy soul unto life everlasting.

After the congregants had received communion, Archbishop Fonseca came down from the altar and led the faithful through the streets of Seville. As they walked, Gabriel was again aware that Perez was near him. He forced himself to smile.

"Good morning, Friar," he said, certain that his voice betrayed the fear in his heart.

"Good morning, Señor Catalan," said Perez, smiling. "How goes the silver work for the Jews?"

"It goes well, Father," Gabriel started to say more, but Perez moved away. Gabriel noticed Francesco looking at him strangely.

Walking home later, Gabriel spoke quietly with Tomas.

"The meal where Jesus gave bread and wine to the Apostles was a Passover seder. And the thanks Jesus gave when breaking bread was the very same *beracha* that Jews say. Jesus must have said it in Hebrew, too."

"How could that be?" Tomas asked.

"Because Jesus was a Jew," Gabriel told him, "and so were all of his Apostles."

That same afternoon, a smaller conclave of the devout gathered at the paper mill of Rodrigo de Muya where Gutenberg was to show Rodrigo how to modify his paper presses for printing.

Francesco drew Gabriel aside, "What was all that with Perez this morning? You two seemed quite friendly."

Gabriel had the awful feeling that Francesco might think he was in league with Perez. Maybe he thinks I'm the informer!

"He saw me at the synagogue, and asked me ... "

"He saw you *where*? What were you doing at the synagogue?"

Gabriel explained about the manuscripts and the silver work. Francesco shook his head. "This life's too dangerous," he said. "We stand on the edge of a cliff and dare them to push us off."

"Let's try to do something useful before that happens," Gabriel answered with a smile, and they went inside.

"How long has your family made paper, Rodrigo?" Gutenberg asked.

"For almost three hundred years, ever since the Moors brought the first paper mills to Spain."

Rodrigo was standing near one of his vile-smelling vats where linen, cotton, and wood were boiled into the creamy pulp which was his raw material. He dipped a wooden tray into the vat. A thin layer of wet fibers clung to the fine wires which criss-crossed the tray. He waited a few seconds, then flipped the tray and dropped a new sheet of paper onto a piece of felt, at the top of a huge pile of interspersed paper and felt. Rodrigo easily lifted the heavy wet mound and placed it under the powerful screw press. Muscles rippling, he turned the handle, squeezing water from the paper.

"This press is good," said Gutenberg. "Let me show you how to change it for printing."

The two men bent over a table and Gutenberg sketched the press as it was, then added a table with rails extending forward under the press. He showed how a tray filled with type could be fixed tightly to the rails.

Rodrigo made careful notes and sketches as Gutenberg spoke. His thick brown eyebrows were drawn together, and his brow was wrinkled in intense concentration. He sharpened his charcoal frequently.

The hinged form on which the paper was held and then rotated close to the type was difficult to illustrate, especially with the lack of a common language, but they went over it several times, and finally seemed satisfied. Rodrigo stood straight and stretched his large body.

"I can do this," he said. "I can make a printing press."

Then, addressing Gabriel, he asked, "But where will we use it?"

"Rodrigo, can we speak?"

The two men stayed behind as the others left.

"The other night, at Don Alonso's house, you seemed troubled," Gabriel said. "Is something wrong?"

The huge man shuffled his feet. Gabriel waited, anxious.

"It's difficult at home," Rodrigo said. "Maria isn't the same as Pilar. It's different when your wife doesn't know about your secret life."

"I'm sorry," said Gabriel, ashamed that he had been suspicious of one of his oldest and dearest friends. A few minutes ago, he thought, I was worried that Francesco thought I was an informer, and now I think the same of Rodrigo. Perez is driving wedges between us.

"How are your boys?" he asked. "It's been at least a month since I've seen them."

Rodrigo beamed. "They're fine," he said. "They mean everything to me."

Two days later, the penitent arrived for his weekly confession.

"You're late."

"I'm sorry, father."

"I have an assignment for you. I want you to keep a close eye on your friends Gabriel Catalan and Francesco Romo, and tell me anything suspicious."

"Why, father?"

"Because you love your sons."

The old horse slowly picked its way up one of the many hills on the road to Segovia. In the hot summer sun, drenched with sweat, Friar Ricardo Perez' thoughts drifted to his life as a student at the university in Salamanca.

He saw himself sitting in a large room, studying Hebrew texts. It was hot and stuffy.

Suddenly, another hot, stuffy room came to his mind and he sat bolt upright in the saddle, startling the horse. His grandmother was dying. He had rushed to her side.

"I've been waiting for you, Ricardo. It's time for you to know."

"Know what, abuelita?"

"You're a priest now? A Dominican?"

"Yes."

"You're going to burn heretics?"

"They're enemies of the Church."

"Then start here, Ricardo!" She beckoned him to bend his ear to her lips, and hissed in his ear, "Shema Yisroel Adonai Elohenu."

He recoiled in horror and she laughed a vicious cackle. He couldn't breathe.

"I'm your first heretic! Your career is begun!"

He stood in shock.

"Your great-grandfather was a fool, a gambler. He lost everything. The ten year old daughter of a rich converso was a great catch for his son."

"I never knew."

"I never saw my papa again. They promised, but they lied." She coughed. "I lived a lie for fifty-eight years. Now you live with it, my grandson Hebrew priest!"

As he got closer to Segovia, he thought about the Prior of the monastery of Santa Cruz, a monk not much older than himself but far more certain in his convictions. It was this monk, his mentor, whom he had ridden twelve days to see. Yet drawn as he was to Tomas Torquemada, Perez became more nervous with each passing mile.

Torquemada had a single overriding obsession in a life otherwise devoted to the simple service of the Lord. Torquemada believed that Jews and *conversos* were plotting with the Devil to destroy his beloved church, and he vowed to see them crushed.

He was not, however, a man of action. He remained secluded in his monastery, where there were certainly no heretics of any kind, preferring to work through others. Perez feared that Torquemada was going to be disappointed in the agent he had trained for Seville.

It wasn't just that Perez had failed to unearth any judaizing *conversos*. Far more serious, he knew, was the weakening of his moral purpose. Even as he diligently sought to trap and expose Gabriel Catalan and the others, he was tormented by the idea that Jews might not be as serious a threat to the church as Torquemada thought. And as for the *conversos*, who could expect people baptized under a threat of death to be sincere Christians? Torquemada, he knew, would be crazed by any mention of these thoughts.

His heart beat faster as the walls of Segovia rose above the horizon. It had been almost a year. The slopes of the Sierra de Guadarramas appeared behind the ramparts and he remembered the bizarre menagerie at Enrique's favorite hunting lodge on the outskirts of the town ... a rare white bull, huge boars and bears, leopards, deer. Perez looked forward to the nightly roar of the lions, but after the charm and wealth of Seville, the streets of Segovia looked dirty and ill-kempt.

Deep in thought, Perez was almost upon the great *alcazar* of Segovia before he noticed its ship-like appearance guarding the confluence of the Eresme and Clamores rivers. Both prow and stern were graced by huge towers, although scaffolding surrounded the one nearest him. Weathervanes rose above each turret, but the pennants which signaled Enrique's presence were not flying.

Passing the royal castle, Perez rode through well tended fields and approached a small, noticeably clean village. Here lived the lay populace which served the monks. Ahead of him, a short traverse from the village, was the familiar water-filled moat and battlemented walls of the monastery of Santa Cruz, and the pointed spire of the abbey church.

The clopping of his horse on the drawbridge broke the midday silence. He passed through the open gate and entered the isolated world within, nodding silently to the taciturn monk who approved his entry. Dormitories, refectory, barns, storehouses, workhouses, and of course the cloistered walks – all the same. Gardens in their place, tannery and slaughterhouse off in the distance. He rode to the stable, left his mount, and walked along the arcade to the prior's house.

Torquemada answered his knock. He too was unchanged ... pale, deep sunken eyes, intense, polite but not friendly. Under his black habit Perez could see the ever-present hair shirt.

"Walk with me," Torquemada said bluntly, "I'm taking my afternoon exercise."

They strolled in the shaded passageways. Several monks crossed their path, silent and unacknowledged.

"Tell me about your work in Seville," said Torquemada.

"I'm afraid my progress is limited."

"Tell me."

"I've recruited an informer."

"Good."

"He told me about a secret prayer session, and I sent men to make arrests, but they didn't find anything."

"Did you go yourself?"

"Later."

"What did you see?"

Perez had a vision of the Ardit's back room, ripped apart by Talavero.

"Nothing," he said, and after a pause, "There was a problem."

"A problem?"

"When I arrived, the men I had sent were about to rape the tailor's daughter. Her father was trying to fight them. He would have been killed."

"And?"

"I stopped them."

"And?"

"I never went into the back room where the secret passage was supposed to be."

"Then perhaps your informer was not wrong."

It had taken less than a minute. Torquemada's questioning had quickly reduced him to nothing, revealing how inadequate he was for his task. It wasn't the informer and it wasn't Talavero who was at fault. It was he, Friar Ricardo Perez, who was responsible for the failed raid at the Ardit home.

"Your humanitarian instincts diverted you," Torquemada said gently.

Perez was surprised at what he interpreted as words of forgiveness.

"Good Christian humanitarian instincts, just as Jesus taught," Torquemada added. This time Perez caught the sarcasm.

"But the people you were protecting were not Christians," said Torquemada. "They were not real people, like us. They were Jews."

Jews breathe God's air, Perez thought. They eat and work and have children and die, just like us. Of course it was unthinkable to challenge Torquemada, who was still speaking, softly, but with terrifying intensity.

"Worse than Jews," he said. "They were Jews hiding *conversos*. That Jewish tailor was protecting enemies of the Church! *Converso* filth who pretend to worship Jesus Christ while they laugh at true Christians and defile His name! And you, Ricardo, didn't find them because you were worried about some Jewish slut!"

Perez ate a cold meal in silence. He was led to a small cell, sparsely furnished with a low wooden pallet and a thin blanket. The gloomy darkness was pierced by a small opening high in the wall, and the tiny glow of a single thick candle.

Torquemada ignored him. Night fell, and daylight, and the cycle repeated. He lived in total silence.

On the fifth day, Torquemada called him aside.

"You're a failure, Ricardo" he said. "You can't find judaizing *conversos* when they're under your nose. You feel sorry for Jews." Torquemada's eyes bore into him. "Why have you come to me?"

Unnerved by the days of silence and Torquemada's blunt question, Perez blurted out what he had desperately planned to avoid. "We forced the Jews to be baptized," he said. "Even St. Thomas Aquinas said it's wrong to compel Faith. How can *conversos* be heretics if they were never really Christians?"

Torquemada exploded.

"Jews desecrate the body of our Lord Jesus and you excuse them! Jews ridicule the glory of His birth and resurrection and you forgive them! Why do I waste my time with you? Go away from me!"

Perez, terrified by what he had done, fell to his knees. "Give me another chance," he pleaded. "I'll never weaken again."

Torquemada stormed off.

The next morning there was a leather folder on the table outside Perez' door containing five pages written in Latin on vellum. It was the official report of a debate held long ago in Barcelona before King James of Aragon. The disputants were Pablo Christiani, a converted Jew who had become a Dominican priest, and Rabbi Moses ben Nachman, the leading Jewish spokesman of his time, known as the *Ramban*. They had debated whether the Jewish Bible and Talmud proved that Jesus was the Messiah.

Perez read how Rabbi Nachman's futile arguments were easily turned aside by Father Christiani. Finally the Rabbi gave up and left Barcelona, neither daring nor able to further defend his erroneous creed.

Barely an hour later, a second, larger manuscript appeared. Perez, eager to please Torquemada, plunged into it. The Hebrew letters surprised and frightened him. He read the first page. It was the hidden report of Rabbi Nachman himself!

Immediately, he understood Torquemada's test. He was to read and reject this obviously false and pernicious record. He leaped to the task. But the straightforward style of the Rabbi's writing drew him in, and before he knew what was happening, it seemed to make sense.

The *Ramban* quoted the Hebrew prophet Isaiah, referring to the end of days when the Messiah would come: *And they shall beat their swords into ploughshares, and their spears into pruning hooks; nation shall not lift up sword against nation, neither shall they learn war any more.*

Ramban commented, "From the days of the Nazarene until now, the entire world has been full of violence, and the Christian nations spill more blood than all the rest. Isaiah wrote that the Jewish Messiah is to bring peace. Jesus did not bring peace. Thus Jesus is not the Messiah of whom Isaiah wrote."

The *Ramban* continued. "Our Bible says *'upon the Messiah will fall the task of gathering the banished of Israel.'* But the Nazarene gathered no one.

"Our Bible says *'the Messiah will build the temple in Jerusalem.'* But the Nazarene built no temple.

"Our Bible says *'the Messiah will rule over all peoples.'* But the Nazarene ruled over no one.

"Whoever he was, your Nazarene was not the Messiah foretold by Isaiah and the other Hebrew prophets. The Messiah of the Jews has yet to come, but all Jews await that day with great anticipation."

The *Ramban's* arguments were devastating. Perez put them aside. He knew exactly what he must do.

The next morning, after a choir of monks had sung Prime, Perez approached Torquemada.

"Thank you, Prior," he said brightly. "Rabbi Nachman's report proved conclusively how ridiculous it is for the Jews to deny that Christ is the Jewish Messiah."

"I'm pleased that you think so," said Torquemada. "What passages did you particularly note?"

"Nachman twisted the plain meaning of his own sacred texts."

Perez would have said more, but Torquemada showed no further interest. Torquemada must know he was lying, and that was exactly what he wanted him to do. He had passed the test!

" ... so, of course you must use torture," he heard Torquemada say.

"Torture? I must use torture?" Perez reeled. What was Torquemada talking about?

"Heretics often deny their sins. They must repent. Every Inquisition has used torture to save the souls of heretics. But don't be concerned. The pain their bodies suffer here on earth is nothing compared with what their souls avoid after death. You do them a great service."

"I don't know if ..."

"First," said Torquemada, "you threaten. Give the heretic time to think."

Torquemada spoke in a quiet, matter-of-fact manner. "If the threats don't work, take him to a dark room, far underground, lit by candles and the glow of burning coals. Let him see others in pain."

'Where will I get others?' Perez thought.

"Remove his clothes and strap him tightly to the rack. Again, give him time to think. It's especially effective if he can hear others screaming."

Perez was aghast. Torquemada described abject unthinkable horror in mild unemotional speech. What sort of monster was this man? Yet he felt himself drawn by Torquemada's hellish vision. He knew he should be repulsed, but his skin tingled as he awaited further details.

"If he still won't confess, you have no choice. Remember it's not you who makes this decision. The heretic brings it on himself by refusing every opportunity offered by the compassionate Church."

Torquemada lifted his arms and looked toward heaven, his face shining. "Raise the pulley. Turn the rack. Put the question to him."

"The question?" Perez whispered.

"Physical torture," answered Torquemada as if repeating the obvious. "Listen carefully, Ricardo. This is very important. The 'question' can be put only once. The Church does not allow torture to be repeated. But suppose the prisoner passes out before you have your confession? You must not stop! Do not conclude the proceedings! *Suspend* them until the heretic regains consciousness and can again feel pain. Do you understand?"

Perez nodded. The tide of Torquemada's demonic passion was unstoppable.

"Do you have a suitable place?" Torquemada asked.

"Underneath the monastery," said Perez, now truly enthusiastic. "Will the Archbishop permit this?"

"Keep that fool Fonseca out of this! Bishops have nothing to say about Dominican matters!"

"And the Sevillian authorities?"

"Only if you need them. The church cannot have blood on its hands. If the heretic won't confess, you must turn him over to the secular authorities to burn him for you according to the rule of Pope Gregory ... *the unrepentant heretic must be burned alive at the stake.*"

"Some day we'll have a real Inquisition in Spain," he said more calmly. "Then Jews and *conversos* will burn by the thousands. Enrique is weak but there will come a time when we have a proper king and these despicable Jews will be gone from our midst. For now, we must carry on alone."

"I'm ready, Prior," said Perez, anticipating the glory if he was the one who brought the Holy Inquisition to Castile.

"I know," said Torquemada. "God speed."

7

King Abu Nasr Sa'd, ruler of the western part of the kingdom of *Al-Andulas*, and father of Prince Hasan, had brought regal splendor to his remote wilderness camp high in the mountains near the Christian town of Ronda. Cool breezes dispelled the summer heat rising from the plains below. A waterfall sparkled in the distance.

Sa'd's warriors stood silent in the late afternoon sun, at rigid attention behind their king, armor glistening. There had been two months of curious delay, but now the moment had come. A steady beat of drums accompanied the measured tapping of Prince Hasan's horses as they climbed the rocky mountain path.

A single knight emerged from the tree lined path and rode solemnly into the grassy clearing. Then another. Fifty men were soon assembled. Horses stamped and snorted, armor clanked. The warriors dismounted. The king's signal silenced the drums.

Prince Hasan's huge black stallion appeared at the edge of the clearing, and reared, nervous from the long climb. In a single flashing motion, his men drew their swords and knelt before him, blades pointed down. The Prince looked neither right nor left. His strong arms strained to hold the skittish mount steady.

Hasan's face revealed none of the concerns churning within him. Why had this meeting been postponed? Did his father realize that he had changed during his years of exile? Would he treat him as an equal partner? Would he fear him as a rival? The history of the royal families of *Al-Andulas* included many examples of internecine murder. The fierce fighters accompanying him were loyal, and he was confident of their protection, but one never slept completely at ease, even in the house of one's father.

Two horse lengths from the King, Hasan reined to a halt. Raising up on the stirrups, he stood clear of the saddle, looked down at his father from the imposing height. King Sa'd nodded his permission, and the Prince dismounted.

He bowed and knelt. The king extended his hand and Hasan rose, smiling broadly.

"I'm here to help you, father," he said, his deep voice audible to the entire assembly. "I am at your service."

"And I welcome you back to the kingdom of our ancestors, my son," said Sa'd, his voice and demeanor immediately communicating the respect that Hasan had so ardently wished for. "Together, we'll conquer the pretender Muhammed and unite all of *Al-Andulas* under a single crown."

Sa'd embraced his son and the warriors roared. "Sa'd ... Hasan ... Sa'd ... Hasan." Lances and swords were thrust upward to match the rhythm of the shouts.

Father and son entered the king's white tent.

"Be seated, my son," said the king, pointing to pillows piled high on the Persian carpets. "First we'll eat."

The large tent was divided by hangings of richly brocaded fabric and the air was thick with incense. Young girls from the king's harem brought an array of dishes. Their silk gowns swirled as they turned and bent—thighs, buttocks and breasts gloriously displayed. Some were fair skinned, from the north. Others black, from Africa.

A tall negress offered the Prince a dish of chopped nuts covered with thick syrup and powdered sugar. She knelt before him. Her knees spread and the lustrous silk fabric parted, releasing an intoxicating mixture of perfume and her own exotic scent.

"I've been away too long," Hasan said.

Though he addressed his father, it was the woman who responded, opening her legs wider and stroking herself with the silk fabric.

"Your generosity is great, father," Hasan said, catching his breath.

"Perhaps we should postpone our talk just a little longer." King Sa'd smiled and rose to leave.

Hasan reached for the woman.

"We could have met before today."

Hasan was still enveloped by a warm sexual glow. He wondered if his father had watched. Perhaps, he thought, he'll enjoy her himself later tonight.

"I've been in *Al-Andulas* for almost eight weeks," Hasan said, sensing that this mild rebuke was not unexpected.

"It's been useful for me to keep Muhammed uncertain of our intentions," the King said. "As a result, he sought an alliance with Enrique, but he conceded too much. Now many of the leading families have turned against him."

"Is he still in the *Alhambra*?"

"Yes."

"When do we attack?"

"We'll leave tomorrow and attack two days later."

"I'm ready."

Instantly, Sa'd changed the subject. "I heard that my grandson was almost killed in Seville."

"His guards were negligent. They've been executed."

"A young boy saved him?"

"Yes, a remarkable boy. Tomas Catalan. It's odd, but we met again on the plain near Arcos."

The King's eyebrows raised, and Hasan told him the story.

"Why was the boy escorting Jews to Arcos?"

"I don't know. Perhaps they were persecuted in Seville. Many are. The Christians are such fools. We know how helpful Jews can be. Certainly our family owes much to our friendships with them."

"Christians hate the Jews," the king responded, "because they refuse to accept Jesus as God."

"But we also deny Christ's divinity," said Hasan.

The king laughed. "Yes, but we have swords. In time they'll come after us too. Jews and Muslims are both a blemish on 'Christian purity.' When the Christians stop fighting among themselves, we'll have our hands full."

"I've got four new hostages. One of them says he's a captain in Enrique's guard, a man named Talavero. Perhaps he'll be useful, after we're done with Muhammed, and have Enrique to deal with."

A guard entered. "Abdul has arrived from Granada."

"With what news?" said the king.

"King Muhammed has left the *Alhambra*. He's fleeing toward the Christians."

"Is it a trap?" Hasan asked, when the guard had left.

His father seemed pleased by his question. "Abdul is one of the most trusted men I have. I'll send others to verify his report, but I believe him."

"Then you should occupy the *Alhambra* as quickly as you can. Let me take my men and some of yours and follow Muhammed. I'll bring him to you."

"Bring him alive. I want to kill him myself."

Two nights after leaving Segovia, Friar Perez reached the village of Navas de Zarzuela. There was no monastery, and Perez was content to spend the night by himself in a field outside the village. He tethered his horse, ate a simple meal of dark bread and water, and lay under the stars.

He did not rest easily.

It had been so simple those last days with Torquemada. He had lied, of course, about the *Ramban*, and at first he was reluctant about the torture, but by the time he left, he was again a willing partner in the holy mission to exterminate backsliding *conversos* and their Jewish brethren. But now, with only a few miles between him and Torquemada, he was already unsure.

He dozed off, and when he opened his eyes, it was light. He jumped up, angry that he had wasted the early morning, and was blinded by a light brighter than a hundred suns. He squeezed his eyes closed, peered through a slit in the shielding lids.

He was surrounded by shadowy figures moving slowly past him. Gradually they took shape, a procession of men in pure white garments, carrying torches that lit the fields as far as he could see. There was singing, like that of monks chanting, but the voices had an ethereal quality, neither male nor female. It was the singing that frightened him.

The men faced inward, in a circle; there must have been a thousand. In the center, a light burned incomparably brighter than the torches. The light ascended. It was a hawthorn tree, like the burning bush from which God spoke to Moses. Above the tree, floating on the fire, was a lady so brilliant he could not look directly at her.

One thousand men turned. A path opened from where he stood to the tree. The singing subsided. The lady beckoned, but fear kept him rooted. Two men appeared at his sides and took his elbows. His feet did not move, yet he went forward. He neared the tree and it receded into the ground so that the lady was but slightly higher than him.

"My Son has sent me."

As soon as she spoke he found that he could look directly at her. Her face was round and white, and her hair was raven. She wore a gown of white and a golden crown. Her slippers were silver. She was of surpassing beauty, but her look was troubled.

"The Church of Peter is not pleasing to Him. Many, baptized in His name, are not true believers."

'What am I to do?' he thought, and this unspoken thought was heard and answered.

"You, Friar Ricardo Perez, are to purify the congregation of those who accept the Son. To you will be given powers of discernment beyond those of others who fail to act."

'But how will I know what to do?' Perez thought.

"You must follow your instincts, even when you are opposed. Rid the Church of those who would destroy it! Do His work on earth, and He will be pleased."

'I will,' he thought.

The lady smiled, and the tree rose majestically from the ground and its light illuminated the clouds. Once again he heard the singing, softly now, as the crowds followed the tree into the sky.

The light and the sound faded, it was dark, and he was alone in the field.

Each time Pilar Catalan tried to imagine herself in Miriam's place, the horror of it overwhelmed her. She had never known any man but Gabriel. The idea of strangers forcing themselves on her body was inconceivably vile.

A caravan was leaving Seville, and Don Alonso had offered to have letters delivered to the Ardits in Arcos. Pilar had debated whether to tell Tomas he could write to Esther. Perhaps it was best not to encourage the impossible. 'But why should that be,' she thought angrily. 'Love is not so easy to find.'

She wrote carefully, not wanting to embarrass her friend.

Dearest Miriam,

Seville is not the same without you. I miss our conversations. I often walk near your house, and even though it is now a leather shop, I feel close to you. Are you settled in your new home?

Tomas told us of your difficulties on the trip. It is surely a sign from God that Prince Hasan came along when he did.

Tomas also had much to say about Esther. Their lives are so different, and difficult, but it is good that they have found friendship in each other.

There is much more I want to say, but it is hard in a letter. I will come to see you, as soon as Gabriel can arrange a trip.

Please know that I think of you often and love you deeply.

Your friend,
Pilar Catalan

Tomas had never written a letter, and he was afraid. But he was bursting with feelings, and determined to do his best.

Esther Ardit,

It was good when we talked. I said things so easily to you that I never said to anyone else. I want to see you again, and I will come to Arcos soon. I have written your name in Hebrew. Do you like it?

Your friend,
Tomas Catalan

He reached into his pocket and touched the paper he had treasured since the day he and his father first made type. He held it to his lips and folded it with the letter.

"What are these?"

A smile creased Francesco Romo's face, "Why do you ask?"

"These sketches are different," Gabriel said. "I've never seen anything like them. They look so ... real."

"When I was in Florence last year," said Francesco, "I met an artist named Andrea del Castagna. He took me to the Church of the Carmelites, where I saw the most astonishing paintings. Not flat, like the art of Byzantium, but full and solid like real people. I was stunned. I sat on a bench looking at those paintings for hours. Then I took my pen and copied."

Gabriel looked in awe as Francesco explained. "This is St. Peter with the tax collectors at Capernaum."

"The robe looks real," said Gabriel. "His knee under the robe. His hand."

"This is the expulsion from the Garden of Eden."

Gabriel saw in Francesco's sketch the pain of our first parents as they knew God's wrath. "Did you meet the artist?" he asked.

"No. He died twenty five years ago."

"What was his name?"

"He was called Masaccio. It means 'clumsy Tomas' in Italian, but he was far from clumsy in his work. When I saw Adam and Eve leaving the garden, I cried, for them and for us. No one ever painted like Masaccio. My sketches are only copies. They don't have nearly the movement and power of Masaccio's paintings."

"Even so, they're exciting. Remarkable."

"Thank you."

"Are you going to use his methods in your painting?"

"I already have."

Francesco led Gabriel to a corner of his studio where the light was particularly good. A large canvas, tall as a man, was set on an easel. Francesco pulled back a covering.

Gabriel gasped.

"It's Moses, receiving the Ten Commandments."

"He looks alive!"

"It's almost done. I'm going to give it to Archbishop Fonseca."

"This will be the talk of Seville. Nothing like this has ever been painted in Spain." Gabriel looked admiringly at his friend. "You're a genius."

"No. I copied a genius."

Francesco walked to a table containing a variety of terra cotta jugs and containers. Nearby, a small fire of coals in a flat pan was held aloft by three chains attached to a hook in the ceiling.

"We mix. We heat. We hope the whole thing doesn't explode and kill us. Then we allow it to cool and store it in these jugs."

Gabriel took a cautious step back as Francesco began to work.

"The mixture can vary," he said. "We'll make it thin, with a little less linseed oil than I would normally use, since it'll be sitting for awhile. It will thicken in the jug."

When they finished, there were four large jugs of black ink, sticky enough to adhere to metal type.

"Why do you think the *Ramban* said that to King James of Aragon? It really wasn't very smart."

"So now you've become a Jewish sage?" Gabriel said, smiling broadly at his son. "You're just learning to read Hebrew and already you criticize one of our greatest rabbis."

"Just because Rabbi Nachman was famous doesn't mean everything he did was right," Tomas argued. "It was enough to prove that Jesus wasn't the Jewish Messiah. He didn't have to insult the king. He's lucky he wasn't executed on the spot."

"Maybe Rabbi Modena will have an explanation." He put his arm around his son's shoulder, pleased that Tomas was becoming a thoughtful Jew. It hadn't been easy, and both of them were careful not to flaunt their enthusiasm before Pilar, who remained opposed. But he was teaching the words of God to his son!

"Remember, in case Friar Perez shows up again, we're here returning the Torah shield we repaired last week."

Gabriel and Tomas entered the synagogue, walked through the darkened sanctuary lit only by the two oil lamps, and knocked at the door to the rabbi's study.

"My class has arrived," Modena said, laughing.

"Today we have questions you might not want to hear," Gabriel said as they took their usual seats around the Rabbi's table. "We've been reading the *Ramban's* report of the debate in Barcelona."

Tomas, impatient, looked to his father, received permission, and began, "I know that Rabbi Nachman was an outstanding scholar," he said. "And it certainly took great courage to defend Judaism before all the great men of Aragon. And I know that King James gave him complete freedom to speak his mind." Tomas paused. "But Rabbi Nachman also promised to stay within the bounds of good taste."

The twinkle in Modena's eyes gave him away. There were not so many young, questioning Jews to challenge him anymore.

"And what did the *Ramban* say that you find so objectionable?" the rabbi asked.

"He told King James that no intelligent man could possibly believe the story of Christ's birth, or His death and resurrection."

"Do you believe those stories?" asked Modena.

"No," said Tomas. "But Christians do. And I don't find their ideas any less believable than ours. We say that God personally wrote the Ten Commandments. And that He spoke to Moses from a burning bush. God can do anything He wants to do, including coming to earth in the form of a man, or being born to a virgin."

Modena thought for awhile. "God chose us to be His people, to keep His laws, and to love and honor Him. There is only one God. Jesus Christ is not God."

"Does it hurt our beliefs if others think he is?"

'Modena struggled with his answer. "Not if they don't insist that we believe it, too. Unfortunately, we can ignore them, but they can't ignore us. It is the foundation of their religion that the Nazarene is the Jewish Messiah. For them to be right, we must be wrong. Their religion requires a belief that God has rejected the Jews and accepted the followers of Christ as his new chosen people."

Modena turned to Gabriel. "You've been very quiet. What do you think?"

"I think Judaism is a very difficult religion," Gabriel said. "Christianity is easier. Christians don't read the Bible and they're not allowed to interpret its meaning. They must unthinkingly accept what their priests tell them. All they have to do is proclaim their faith in Jesus Christ, and their sins are forgiven. It's simple. They don't have to worry about hundreds of complicated commandments. Maybe God saw that most Jews don't keep His laws, so He sent Jesus with an easier way."

"You've learned strange things while you've been pretending to be a Christian. I've never heard such thoughts from Jews."

"We're Jews, too!" Gabriel retorted, raising his voice.

"Yes," Modena said. "You are Jews. But you think differently from any other Jews I've ever known. You know less, but you think more clearly."

King Muhammed fled due west from the *Alhambra*. With minimal supplies and only two hundred men, he raced west and north across the kingdom of Granada. On the third day, he crossed the border into Castile, on the plains near the mountain town of Jaen.

Muhammed felt safe. Soon he would link up with Enrique's troops. He would re-group to return to Granada in force and destroy his rival King Sa'd. He never dreamed that he would be pursued into Castile.

But Hasan never stopped. This would be his first battle as commander, and he would not be denied. He rode only at night, as quickly as the rugged terrain would permit. His forces remained quiet in the daytime. No fires were lit in his camp.

On his second night in Castile, the Prince and his men found Muhammed's camp. The guards were sleeping. Hasan organized his forces brilliantly. His own troops were assigned the middle charge, his father's to either flank, and a line of archers was stationed around the perimeter.

They roared into action just before dawn. Howling shrieks pierced the silence. Kettle drums boomed and trumpets blared. Muhammed's troops panicked. Hasan and his best men surrounded King Muhammed's tent, pinning them in, while the main body of fighters attacked. It was a complete massacre. Flashing swords found victim after victim. Severed heads lay grotesquely next to headless bodies still pumping their final blood. Horses slipped in the mess. Sounds of moaning and terror rose and quickly fell. The few who tried to run were brought down by the silent cross-bows.

The carnage lasted but fifteen minutes. Muhammed's entire force lay dead on the field.

The Prince gathered the abject King Muhammed and several members of his family, the only ones left alive, and began his triumphal march back to Granada.

After the Mass of the Immaculate Conception, celebrating the nativity of the Blessed Virgin Mary, many of the worshippers, including Gabriel Catalan, went from the Cathedral to join a large crowd already assembled in the square. A special platform had been constructed.

Friar Perez strode purposefully from the Cathedral and mounted the steps until he towered over the crowd. He was a tall man, still youthful at thirty-one, and powerfully built ... fierce eyes, tonsured hair, black beard, black habit of the Dominican Order

His deep voice boomed.

"A great honor has come to Spain and to our Dominican Order. The Holy Father Calixtus III has ordered the canonization of Friar Vicente Ferrer."

He paused while the crowd reacted, murmuring excitedly to each other.

"Much of St. Vicente's work was done in Castile where his sermons convinced six thousand Jews to convert. This was in the year of our Lord fourteen hundred and twelve. Perhaps some of you, or your parents, heard him speak."

Gabriel knew that many Jews did indeed convert in the wake of

Ferrer's preaching, but not from the power of his words. They were terrified by the mobs of flagellants and thugs Ferrer brought with him. They remembered the murderers led by Archdeacon Martinez in 1391, and they were intimidated by the new anti-Jewish laws, instigated by Ferrer, laws which left them virtually no means of feeding their families if they remained Jews.

Perez thundered on.

"But Jews are not the major problem we face today. It is among the *conversos* that the true threat to the Church resides. Many supposed converts actually despise Jesus and continue to practice their infidel Jewish rites.

Friar Perez' voice rose.

"We have judaizing heretics in our very midst today! *Conversos* who go by Christian names in public, but at home they're Abraham and Isaac and Jacob. Rich Jews who pretend to be Christians. And why are they rich? Because they steal our money! They prosper as our nobles and knights are impoverished. And all the while they practice their vile Jewish rites.

"It is unfortunate, but we have no Holy Order of Inquisition here in Castile to find these heretics and bring them to trial. So we, you and I, must reach into the impious souls of these secret Jews and drag them into the light of Christian Faith.

"The penalty for heresy is death by fire!

"You find them for me and ... I ... will ... see ... justice ... done!"

Gabriel trembled. He imagined that everyone in the crowd was looking at him. Perez' dark eyes flashed, his powerful arms reached to heaven, and his voice was awesome as he instructed the crowd.

"Tomorrow is *Yom Kippur,* the Hebrew Day of Atonement, the most sacred day in the Jew's obscene religion. *Conversos* who are really secret Jews will try to observe this holiday. As you pass through the streets, look for those who don't work ... who don't eat ... who stay at home all day. Those are the secret Jews who profane our Holy Church! I will join you, and we will find these judaizers.

"And then we will see them burn!"

His arms fell to his side and he was still before them, exhausted.

Gabriel stood dumbfounded while angry people milled about him in the square, looking for Judaizing *conversos.* Looking for him!

He was astonished to see Don Alonso walk directly to Perez. What was he doing? He must be congratulating the friar on his speech! Francesco Romo looked at him. Gabriel averted his eyes, not wanting Perez to see them together, but Francesco was walking toward him. Then Friar Perez left Don Alonso and also came towards him.

"Señor Catalan," Perez said, arriving first. "We meet again. At synagogue, at church, now here. It's actually a fortunate coincidence. I'd like to ask for your help."

"How can I help you?" mumbled Gabriel, dreading the answer.

"Tomorrow, I'm going to walk through Seville, looking for evidence of secret Jews. Your ancestors once were Jewish, so you may have a better instinct than mine to spot them. Will you walk with me?"

Perez smiled at Francesco as he waited for an answer. Gabriel remembered that Perez had spoken to him in Francesco's presence at the Corpus Christi procession. As before, he worried that his best friend would be suspicious of him. But surely Francesco would know it was impossible to refuse the friar's request.

"Of course," Gabriel said.

A strong wind whipped across the sunless plains. Marguerita Sanchez pulled her cloak tightly around her neck and rode on. The birthing had gone well, although the knight's lady had been bad-tempered. Now she was returning home to Arcos. Two men, sent by the knight to accompany her, rode twenty yards ahead. They were crude and vulgar, they smelled badly, and she was pleased they were no closer.

The riders ahead of her stopped. When she reached them, she saw a man lying face down, unconscious. He had no cloak against the cold and his tunic was badly ripped. There was blood on the ground under him.

"Let's go," growled the larger man. "If he's not dead, he soon will be."

"If we leave him, he'll surely die," said Marguerita, dismounting to take a closer look. She felt his strong neck and found a pulse. He was alive.

"Help me turn him over," she said. The riders laughed and didn't move.

"All right," she said angrily, "I'll do it myself."

The man was large, and Marguerita struggled. She placed her hands under his right shoulder and lifted until he rolled heavily onto his back. She went to her horse and took two blankets from behind the saddle. Returning, she covered him, tucking one blanket around him to get warmth back into his body. She folded the other blanket and put it under his head.

It was then that she saw his face. Holy Mother of God! It's him! She looked more closely. Age had taken its toll, but there could be no doubt.

A room in Seville. She was a young girl. A dashing young *caballero* pranced through her memory. The other prostitutes said she was a fool. But he brought her flowers and she loved him. They made wonderful passionate love and she couldn't wait for him to be inside her again. Then he left. She heard stories about him as he rose in the king's service. Then he disappeared completely. Now here he was, alone and dying on the cold desolate plain.

"Don't go," she called to the men who were already starting off.

"We're not staying," the smaller one responded. "Our orders are to return by sundown. We're not going to be nursing nobody who's going to croak anyways. We'll take you to Arcos if you're goin', but we ain't campin' out here with you."

"Then go," she yelled. "And good riddance!"

Marguerita was glad to be rid of them. She often traveled alone, and had spent many nights alone on the plains. In truth she was more leery of her guards than she was of any unknown danger.

She turned to her former lover. His breathing was steady, a good sign. It appeared that he had been struck in the head. She raised the blanket to look for other wounds. It must have been several hours and the bleeding had stopped, but there was damp blood on his legs. She raised his tunic and ripped off his hose and underdrawers. There was a knife wound in his thigh, but it didn't look too bad. She washed the cut with material she ripped from her dress, and wrapped it with his own hose. Her urgent work done, she paused to look at his naked body.

'You old whore,' she laughed to herself. 'You still love to look at that big cock.' Reluctantly she covered him. She felt him stir and was startled to see his eyes looking at her. He showed no recognition.

"What happened?" she asked.

"Bandits. They took everything."

"Where were you going?"

"To Seville."

Marguerita was one to make up her mind in a hurry.

"I'll take you with me to Arcos. You can stay until you get better."

"No. I can't," he said, avoiding her eyes.

"Why not?" Marguerita was puzzled. He would die if left out here. Why didn't he want to come to Arcos? Is he hiding? Then the answer came to her and, in characteristic fashion, she threw it right at him.

"You're a liar, Hernando Talavero," she said.

At the sound of his name, he bolted upright, squeezing his eyes against the pain. "Who are you? How do you know me?"

"You don't remember, do you? I should leave you to die, you faithless whore-fucker. But once you were kind to me, even if it meant nothing to you. Think, Hernando, think! Marguerita. The little room near the Triana fortress."

"Marguerita," he mumbled, "I remember. The girl in Seville."

"I'm a respectable midwife now. Knights and nobles call me to attend their snivelly wives. But you're not telling the truth. You weren't attacked by bandits. You *are* the bandit, aren't you? And one of your victims proved too much for you."

He did not deny her. "Thank you for stopping," he said with genuine emotion, and it was enough to make her feel like a young girl again.

She stayed with him for several days. She found an abandoned hut nearby and helped him struggle to it. She built fires against the cold nights and wandering wolves. She went into Arcos and returned with food and clothes, and a second horse. His wound healed and he said he had to go. He promised he would come to Arcos to see her, but she didn't believe him.

He also told her an incredible story.

"Prince Hasan took me prisoner. Then there was a war between two Arab kings, Hasan's father King Sa'd, and King Muhammed. Hasan captured Muhammed and brought him to the *Alhambra*. Sa'd and Hasan slaughtered Muhammed and his family. They cut off their heads and threw them in a fountain. The water was red with their blood. Everyone got drunk and I escaped."

Marguerita didn't believe a word of it.

8

Gabriel began his fast at sundown. The next morning, *Yom Kippur* morning, he waited for Friar Perez in the square by the synagogue. He was terrified to be with the Dominican, but he had never seen Jews praying in a real synagogue and it satisfied his sense of irony that the Jew-hating priest would help him accomplish this previously unattainable wish.

An old Jewish couple shuffled into view from one of the narrow side streets. Gabriel's heart went out to them, furious that the Church of Jesus Christ could be so cruel to these persecuted people. For even on this Day of Days, when Jews for centuries had dressed in their finest clothes, they wore coarse tattered clothing, and the hateful yellow badge, as required by the laws of St. Vicente Ferrer. The old couple ignored his smile. He was a *converso,* a traitor, and they wanted nothing to do with his kind on this sacred morning.

"I see you arrived early," said a deep voice, practically in his ear. Gabriel jumped and Perez laughed.

How does that man appear? Gabriel thought. I never see him coming. Do they teach that in the monasteries?

"Shall we go in? I don't expect to find any secret Jews at the synagogue, but it will help us set the proper mood for our search."

Gabriel followed Perez into the sanctuary, scarcely able to contain his excitement. A hundred large candles glowed on ledges around the walls and on tables near the *bema*. The smell of scented wax filled the room, companion to the lilting sound of Hebrew prayers chanted by men wearing pure white *tallesim*.

Gabriel was moved by sights and sounds he had only dreamed

85

about. My father Isaac prayed in this room, he thought. Probably with David Modena by his side. Isaac sacrificed his Jewish life for me. I would never have been born if he had been murdered that day in 1391. The memory of his father stiffened his resolve. I must get through this day!

Every eye turned to the Dominican monk and his *converso* accomplice. The praying stopped, replaced by looks of fear and hatred.

Rabbi Modena, who had been sitting quietly near the *bema*, rose deliberately, allowing his heavy cloak to fall to the floor. He faced the intruders without expression, then pointedly looked away. He walked to the *bema* and up the steps. Facing his frightened congregation, Modena raised his arms and sang in a voice that gave Gabriel chills.

שמע ישראל יהוה אלהינו יהוה אחד
Hear, O Israel, the Lord our God, the Lord is One

Modena waited. Haltingly, the congregation answered.

ברוך שם כבוד מלכותו לעולם ועד
*Blessed be His Name, whose glorious kingdom
is for ever and ever.*

Tears welled in Gabriel's eyes. The congregation gained strength until a hundred voices soared in unison: *And thou shalt love the Lord your God with all thy heart, and with all thy soul, and with all thy might.*

"They deny the Trinity," Perez hissed furiously to Gabriel. "Every day, they deny that Christ is God! Why do we permit this?"

"What are they saying?" asked Gabriel, aware of the trap. "Do you speak Hebrew, father?"

"Of course I speak Hebrew. I studied it for eleven years."

Our Father who art in heaven, deal kindly with us.

"They've stolen the Lord's Prayer," said Perez, his voice rising. "The Jews have copied Jesus' prayer on the Mount."

Gabriel knew that it was the other way around. Jesus, a knowledgeable Jew, had naturally incorporated already ancient Jewish expressions and prayers in his sermons. He watched Perez' face redden and heard the friar's breathing quicken. Perez' discomfort pleased him.

Finally, the friar stormed from the synagogue. Gabriel followed, but was unable to resist a last, longing look over his shoulder. He caught Modena's eye. Was there the flicker of a smile on the old man's face?

They walked to the street where the Ardit family had lived, and Perez headed straight to where Yacov's tailor shop had been. He appeared surprised to see someone working there, since every Jew would of course be in the synagogue. Leather straps and saddles hung in the opening.

"Isn't this the shop of the Jewish tailor?" he said, addressing the occupant.

"It was, Friar. But now it's a leather shop."

"Who are you?" Perez asked.

"My name is Pedro Fernandez," the man said proudly, standing tall.

"Where is Yacov Ardit?"

"He left before I bought the shop."

"Do you know where he went?"

"No. He just disappeared. No one talks about him."

Perez turned to Gabriel, "Do you know the Jew who used to live here?"

Gabriel pretended not to hear ... frantic thoughts ... did he see me talking to Yacov on the day Tomas saved Prince Hasan's son? ... does he know Tomas went with the Ardits? It's no accident we're here!

"Did you know this Jew?" Perez repeated, irritated.

"No," Gabriel decided.

"This tailor shop was an entrance to a secret synagogue," said Perez. Gabriel's mind raced ... one slip and he's got me!

"I think they were here," Perez brooded. "But we didn't find them. Now the tailor's gone. It's odd. The captain I sent here to look for the *conversos* is also gone."

Gabriel forced himself to remain silent. Perez walked on without pursuing the matter further.

"You know Francesco Romo, don't you?" Perez asked.

"We've been friends for many years."

"I saw you talking with him yesterday." A sinister smile edged its way onto Perez' face. "I think he's a judaizer."

"Impossible," said Gabriel. "I know him too well."

"Is that so?" sneered Perez, walking away.

For the next thirty minutes they strode silently through the empty streets, Perez always a little ahead.

There was a crowd outside the house of Don Alonso.

"This one's a good catch," Gabriel overheard someone saying as he and Perez drew near. "We'll be well rewarded if we find *him* mumbling Jewish prayers."

The mob was blocked by a troop of armed horsemen, however, and could not approach the Viterbo palace. They soon left.

"Do you know Don Alonso de Viterbo?" Perez asked.

"Yes," Gabriel responded, "Everyone does."

"How well do you know him? Have you ever been inside this home?"

"Yes, Father. He's a customer of mine."

"Have you been there at any other times, for dinner, or a social occasion?"

"No, Father. I'm just a goldsmith, hardly in the same social class as Don Alonso."

Gabriel was sure that these questions, like those which preceded them, were not thoughts of the moment. Perez had planned this day carefully, and the object was to catch him. Had he slipped?

They ranged into other neighborhoods of Seville, passing shops and taverns, sidestepping animals and carts, ignoring numerous prostitutes.

"Let's eat," Perez said suddenly.

"There's a tavern near here," Gabriel responded immediately. He had expected this test, and had resigned himself to the fact that there could be no *Yom Kippur* fast for him this year. They ate a simple meal of cabbage soup and bread. Gabriel paid for the meal, and they resumed their walk.

As the day went on, Perez' anger seemed to cool.

"I'm beginning to like Seville," he said, to Gabriel's surprise. "Have you lived here all your life?"

"Yes. And my family for generations."

"Was your father a goldsmith too?"

"Yes, and his father before him."

"When did you become a Christian?"

Gabriel had almost relaxed.

"I was born in the church."

"And your father?"

"He was baptized as a young man."

"When?"

"I'm not sure, exactly."

"Was it in 1391?" Perez asked.

Another test. Gabriel suppressed his rising emotions and answered flatly, "I don't know."

"Or don't want to talk about it?"

"I don't know," Gabriel insisted.

Their walk took them to a market area near the river. Perez' silence was ominous. Gabriel felt that he had to say something.

"Where you were born, Friar?" he asked.

Perez seemed startled to be questioned, but he answered. "In a small village north of here, past Cordoba. It's called Andujar."

"What does your father do?"

"He's a farmer."

"And his father?"

"I didn't know my grandparents," Perez snapped, looking quickly away.

Was Perez hiding something? Gabriel pressed.

"Brothers and sisters?"

"Five older brothers. That's why I'm a priest. The land went to the others."

"Where did you study?"

"At the parish school. Then, when I showed promise, off to the monastery. I was eight years old. The university at Salamanca, and lastly Segovia."

Gabriel took a deep breath. Did he dare ask? He must know. "What would you do if we found any secret Jews?"

"Ask them to repent."

"And if they did?"

"They would be accepted back into the church." Friar Perez thought for a moment. "Of course, they'd be punished first."

"And if they didn't repent?" Gabriel asked.

"Unrepentant heretics are burned at the stake," Perez said with a smile.

It was twilight when Gabriel got home. He drew Pilar and Tomas to him.

"It was awful," he said. "Perez tried all day to trap me. I hope I didn't act as terrified as I felt."

"You didn't look frightened," said Tomas.

"How do you know how I looked?"

"I followed you."

Gabriel shook his head, not sure whether to scold his son or hug him.

"We should leave this dreadful place," said Pilar.

Leaving Castile was an idea that Gabriel had often considered. He had enough money. They could go to the Orient. The Ottomans had taken Constantinople two years before and the Sultan openly welcomed Jews. But Gabriel didn't want to leave Seville. Even with the troubles, it was the land of his fathers, and he loved it. Jews had lived in Castile for over a thousand years. Maybe things would get better. In his heart he knew they never would, but still he could not leave!

"We have only a few minutes until *Yom Kippur* is over," he said. "Let's pray."

Gabriel watched sadly as Pilar rose hurriedly and left the room. She had never joined them in Jewish prayer. Gabriel and Tomas quietly recited the prayer of atonement that Rabbi Modena had taught them.

Our God and God of our fathers, we have been faithless, We have turned aside from thy commandments, and it hath profited us naught.

But thou art a God slow to anger and ready to forgive. May it be thy will, O Lord our God and God of our fathers, that we may sin no more, and as to the sins we have committed, purge them away.

Remember us unto life, O King, and seal us in the book of life, for thine own sake, O living God.

From the synagogue many streets away, the haunting sound of the *shofar* reached their ears. *Yom Kippur* was over. The Book of Life was sealed for another year.

Esther Ardit walked from the tailor shop back to the living quarters. "Mama," she said, "someone's here to see you... from Don Alonso."

Miriam, making breakfast, wiped her hands, and went forward to greet her guest.

"Good morning, señora," a tall dignified man said pleasantly as Miriam emerged into the shop.

"Good morning, señor. My daughter says you come from Don Alonso."

"Yes. I'm here to deliver these."

The messenger handed two letters to Miriam. Her heart jumped. This was the first communication from Seville since the Ardits had left. She recognized the familiar hand of Pilar Catalan. The second letter had Esther's name on it. Tomas!

"I'll be in Arcos for several days," the tall man said. "If you want to answer, I'll take your letters back with me."

"That's very kind of you."

"Then I'll see you tomorrow, señora, toward the end of the afternoon." He bowed and left.

"What did the man want?" asked Esther.

"He brought a letter from Señora Catalan."

"And ... ?"

With the first look of joy that Miriam had seen since they arrived in Arcos, Esther seized her letter and ran to her room.

Miriam broke the seal on Pilar's letter. She read that Tomas had told Pilar about the attack, and she was glad her friend knew about it and could share her anguish. She read that Tomas *seems to be quite taken* with Esther and it made her cry. But what she read next terrified her. *I want to come see you.*

'No! She mustn't. Not now.'

She heard Yacov and quickly stuffed the letter in her pocket. She rubbed her cheeks dry. Miriam had not spoken to Yacov more than absolutely necessary since that unimaginable night. She wanted to reach her hand to him, but it wouldn't move from her side. He looked at her, pleading, but she turned away, unable to respond to his pain.

"Here's your breakfast," she said flatly.

Esther stared at her name on the outside of the folded paper. She kissed where Tomas' fingers had touched. She had thought of him constantly, dreamed of him, hoped that he cared for her. She was certain he never would. He had seen her raped and he would never want her after that. She was surprised that he had written. Probably his mother had told him to.

She broke the seal and unfolded the page. Another paper, folded even more tightly, fell to the floor. She opened it.

אסתר

Chills cascaded through her body.

It was good when we talked, she read, and her mind shimmered with visions of the days on the plains, the fire at night, the sweet sound of his voice.

I said things to you so easily ... , and she whispered aloud, "and I to you, dearest Tomas."

I want to see you again ... I will come to Arcos soon.

She dropped the letter to the floor. Reaching for it, she saw her mother standing in the doorway.

"Señora Catalan wants to come to Arcos," Miriam said.

"Tomas, too," said Esther.

"We can't let them."

"What are we going to do, mama?"

"I don't know."

Miriam laid her hands on her daughter's growing belly, and they cried together in each other's arms.

"Remember I told you about that Romo fella? When he went to that meeting at Don Alonso's house? Well, I followed him again. He came into the *juderia*, like he always does, and he goes down this alley. The guard thinks he's looking for a whore, but I followed him. It's not whores he's lookin' for."

Perez recoiled from the beggar's smell of stale sweat, urine, and excrement. "Where did he go?"

"He went to pray, in one of them secret synagogue rooms you asked me to look out for."

"How do you know what it was?"

"I went up real close, next to some kind a' air hole, and I heard them funny words. It was Jew prayers all right."

Perez gave the beggar three small coins and asked him to keep on the lookout. This was the evidence he had been waiting for. Was it time to act?

He recalled his visit with Torquemada, and then, the glaring white image of the Virgin. The Virgin knew his name and talked to him!

This image was so powerful that he usually pushed it from his mind, afraid to consider its awesome implications.

Perez had learned that he was not the only one who had seen the Virgin. Two boys had been awakened on that very same night. Their story had been recorded in explicit detail by the local priest ... the white light ... the hawthorn tree. It was the hawthorn tree that convinced Perez it was real. He had told no one, and he had not heard of the boys' experience until several months after his own. So, just when he thought it was all a dream, that the Virgin would never appear on earth to speak with someone as unworthy as he, he knew that she had done just that.

When he learned of the boys' story, he sat alone for three days, without food or water, but still failed to achieve the clear resolve he sought.

What did the Virgin mean?

He is not pleased with the Church of Peter. Too many have been baptized in His name who are not true believers, but use the Church for their own earthly purposes.

Did She mean secret Jews? Or was it Christians, priests and even Popes, whose corruption and carnal behavior were a disgrace to the name of Jesus?

You are to purify the congregation of those who accept the Son. Follow your instincts, even when others oppose you.

The Mother of God said he was to follow his instincts. But those instincts were never clear. He was always changing his mind. He longed for someone to share his thoughts, but there was not a single person in Seville he could trust.

Now he must decide. Francesco Romo was a prominent *converso* and a friend of the troublesome Archbishop Fonseca. If Romo confessed that he was a secret Jew, Perez could do as he wished. No one would oppose him!

The idea of torture was still repugnant to him. It was the accepted method of the Church for dealing with suspected heretics, but it was an awful thought that a man of God would purposely cause pain to another human being.

Were Jews human? Rejecting Christ, had they not descended to a lower order of creatures? Was it not the Church's view that they were to be hated and kept in servitude forever? Who first taught this? Chrysostom? Augustine?

Of course it didn't matter. If he once again allowed human sympathy to interfere with his Holy mission, Torquemada would see that he was banished forever in some obscure monastery. His brilliant career would be over. He knew what he had to do, but disturbingly, the questions remained.

He was prepared, having modified the monastery for its new role. Underground rooms had been closed off. New locks had been installed in ancient jail cells. A rack and a hoist had been built, and a special platform for the water torture. Chains and hooks were installed. All he needed was a victim.

Torquemada had emphasized that the accused should disappear suddenly and quietly, and stay hidden until he confessed.

Perez knocked on Romo's door just after midnight, accompanied by four armed men. Francesco answered, still dressed. He was quickly overpowered, gagged, and blindfolded. A few minutes later, Romo was lying naked on a cold, damp floor, not knowing where or why.

"Father, Señora Romo is here to see you," called Tomas, peering into the back room where Gabriel was busy making type. Gabriel wiped his hands, stretched his aching back, and went to greet his guest. One glance told him that something was very wrong.

"He's gone!" she cried. "My Francesco is gone! I woke and went to breakfast. He never came down. His bed wasn't slept in. I don't know what to do."

"Tomas, call your mother. Señora Romo needs her."

Gabriel went to the window, concerned that the Señora had been followed, but he saw no one. He intercepted Pilar. "Francesco is gone," he whispered. "The Señora knows nothing."

"Has anyone come to see you?" he asked Señora Romo.

"No."

"Maybe he took a trip?"

"He would tell me. Something terrible has happened. He would send word if he could."

"Señora, my wife Pilar will help you now. I'll make inquiries."

"Francesco has vanished."

They sat in Don Alonso's garden. The smell of roses and orange blossoms, the soft whisper of the wind in the palms, normally so delightful, were an unwelcome intrusion on Gabriel's anger and fear.

"Do you think it's Perez?" Don Alonso asked.

"It must be. He suspected Francesco was a judaizer."

"He told you that? When? Why didn't you tell me?"

"I should have. It was on *Yom Kippur*, when Perez made me walk with him."

"Perez did what? Gabriel, you must tell me these things." His voice quieted and he added, "I'll ask Archbishop Fonseca."

"And I'll find out my own way."

"What do you mean?" said Don Alonso, alarmed.

"I'll look around. I've got to know what's happening."

Don Alonso looked at the ceiling. "It's far too dangerous. You're a goldsmith, not a spy. You know what it would mean to Pilar and Tomas if you got caught. And it would jeopardize the printing."

"Damn the printing!" Gabriel exploded. "That's probably what caused Francesco's arrest. It's not worth it."

"Not worth it? Seven hundred years of Jewish culture is not worth the life of one man?"

"Not this man! Francesco Romo is my best friend. I don't care if we ever print anything!"

Sometimes she saw him watching her, and she turned away. He had seen her being raped. He knew that her body was dirty and used.

She missed their talks as much as the other, the love-making. Quiet times between dinner and bed. Memories of passion. She ached for him constantly, but she was sure he found her repulsive.

Now she had no choice but to talk with him. Esther was starting to get big.

For the first time since they had been in Arcos, Miriam went into the bedroom after dinner. Yacov's startled, hopeful look brought tears to her eyes.

"Esther is with child," she said quickly.

Yacov's face twisted in agony and he buried his head in his hands. Miriam had never seen her husband cry, and it made her ashamed of how selfish she had been, never thinking of him.

She touched his shoulder and the impossible became natural again. Their sudden embrace was fierce. His fingers tore into her shoulders. She squeezed him until her arms hurt, and still she wouldn't let go.

"That bastard is the father?" he asked, still holding her tight.

"Yes."

Yacov breathed deeply. He pulled back, every muscle in his thin body tense.

"Why does God permit such atrocities?"

He faced the wall, arms raised. He didn't move for such a long time that she was frightened. His face, when he did turn, was even worse.

"I'll kill him!" He spoke softly, to himself as much as to her.

"I don't care about him," she said. "Think about Esther! Her life is ruined. She'll never marry."

Tears poured down her plump face. He came to her and they held each other for a long time. When they separated, he was amazingly calm.

"We'll hide her," he said with a nod.

"For now," she said, "but when the baby comes? What then?"

She was shocked to see him smile.

"What's wrong with you," Miriam said. "How can you smile?"

Yacov ran his hands along Miriam's sides, lingering at her heavy hips.

"Stop that. What are you doing? Not now."

Yacov's hands covered her belly. His mischievous look puzzled her.

"Why, Miriam," he said, "I think you're going to have a baby."

"You're crazy!"

Then she understood.

"We could fool them, couldn't we?" she said.

"It's up to you. Could you do it?"

He stroked her neck, her back, her arms. Months of tension were released. Peace spread blissfully through her body, followed by pounding sexual passion.

"Thank you," she said, grasping his body. "I don't deserve you."

She began to cry again, and his finger gently wiped away a tear.

"Yacov?"

"I've waited a long time, too," he said.

It was the first time they had ever seen each other naked.

9

Francesco Romo shivered uncontrollably. He hadn't eaten or slept for days. He was too weak to ward off the rats that ran freely over his naked body, ripping at his skin. He clutched his only possession, a thin tattered sheet, although it provided scant warmth against the bitter cold.

The cell door clanged. Rough hands roused him, pushed him along a dark hallway. A guard with a torch walked ahead.

"Down there," the guard pointed. He stumbled and fell, crashing down the unlit stairway, each blow bruising his weakened body. Falling into the deep. A landing, a small blessing. His hip throbbed. Was it broken? More stairs. Down. Down.

He started to sob, but immediately clenched his teeth. I will be strong! Later, when I'm dead, I can cry with God.

"Bring him in," he heard, recognizing Perez' powerful voice.

A large room. Pitch dark. Damp. Bone-chilling cold. Toes and fingers numb sticks. A table. The meager light of two thin candles. He was pushed toward it. Perez seated there, and behind him, another table. A young monk, a scribe. Two more monks hovering half seen in the gloom.

"Welcome, my son," Perez said, his tone honeyed and comforting, as if greeting one of his flock into church. "Soon you can go home. Simply confess your sins and Jesus will forgive you."

Francesco trembled, unable to comprehend. What did Perez want?

"You're tired, aren't you?" Perez continued. "You must be cold. I'm here to help you."

Then give me a blanket, you bastard, Francesco thought.

"I've ordered a hot dinner. Clean clothes. A dry cell. A real bed."

Francesco looked at him blankly. Perez seemed flustered.

"But first, my son, you must confess. Talk to me, and through me, to our gentle Lord Jesus."

"I ..." Sharp pain in his throat, his voice raspy, disembodied. A single word torn from the depths of his despair. "I don't know ..." Words forced out, his constricted throat throbbing.

Perez raised his hand. A monk appeared out of the darkness and gave Romo a bowl. Francesco held it stiffly with both hands, slurped greedily, the warm soup soothing.

"What don't you know?" Perez asked gently when Francesco had finished.

"I don't know what I'm accused of," Francesco said, his voice almost normal. "How can I confess when I don't know the charges?"

"Your soul must speak with God."

Frantic, Francesco cried out, "Who accuses me?"

"Who would know your sins?" Perez asked, ever so softly.

Francesco regained control. He made his lips tight, defiant. You have me, you Dominican bastard, but I won't give you anyone else. Hands on hips, he let the sheet fall. Stark naked, he stared insolently at Perez.

"Never!" he said boldly, confident now, proud of his found courage.

Perez leaped at Romo and struck the bowl from his hands.

"You stupid fool!" Perez hollered. "You'll learn not to fight me!"

Perez swept toward the door, two monks following. Over his shoulder he snapped, "Back to his cell. No clothes! No bed!"

Gabriel circled the monastery of San Pablo. He wore old clothes and walked with feigned difficulty, not sure if his disguise was adequate.

As Gabriel turned the last corner and began to retrace his steps, Friar Perez burst from a side door and strode briskly past him. Too late, Gabriel pulled his shawl tightly round his face. Perez did not appear to have recognized him.

When the friar was out of sight, Gabriel slumped to the ground at a nearby fountain, his back against a tree, pretending to sleep, but alert for Perez' return.

Two ancient monks came out of the monastery and struggled toward the fountain, shuffling their swollen feet slowly forward.

"What's happening underground?" one said, speaking loudly, as if to the hard of hearing.

"Hush!" said the other.

"Who's he got there?" the first monk bellowed.

"You talk too much."

"Does anyone know?"

"No. And you shouldn't either. Gossip is a sin."

"I'm old enough to know."

"Old enough to prepare for your Judgment Day. You should start with the virtue of silence."

"Perez has a prisoner at San Pablo. It must be Francesco," said Gabriel. "Have you any word from the Archbishop?"

"Fonseca knows nothing," said Don Alonso. "How do you know about a prisoner?"

"Never mind how I know." Gabriel was furious. "What are you going to do?"

Don Alonso stared at him. "I'll try to contact the king. But you know it's a great risk."

"What do I care for your risk?" Gabriel snapped. "Francesco will die if he doesn't get out of there."

"My risk is also yours and Francesco's," Don Alonso said patiently. "When one of us is in trouble, we're all in danger. Think what will happen to the *converso* community if I'm revealed to be a secret Jew. Who will approach the Archbishop, or the king? Who'll support the Jews in Seville? Who'll be here to arrange for the Ardits to get to Arcos?"

"I'm sorry," said Gabriel. "I'm not myself."

"I know," said Don Alonso, offering a sad smile. "We're all on edge, and for good reason. I'll do what I can, but you know that Enrique is not in Seville. He's probably in Segovia with those awful creatures of his. I'll send Gonsalvo tomorrow."

"You won't go yourself?"

Don Alonso sighed, "I can't."

Gabriel stood to leave.

"Wait," said Don Alonso. "I have letters for Pilar and Tomas from Arcos."

Don Alonso retrieved the letters and gave them to Gabriel.

"There's also news from Gutenberg," he said. "Unfortunately, not good."

Gabriel was not interested in anything except Francesco, but he made himself listen.

"By the time Gutenberg returned to Mainz," Don Alonso began, "his creditor had already filed a law suit. The trial was over before the Medici banker could get my funds to him from Bruges. He lost everything. Presses, type, everything."

"That's terrible!"

"Worse yet, the creditor hired Gutenberg's foreman and they're going to publish his Bible without him. Thirty years of work and someone else will get the credit. But my money finally arrived, and he's going to start up again. He's actually excited because now he can print a Bible with only thirty-six lines to a page. You remember that his creditor was insisting on forty-two lines in order to save paper."

"Persistent, isn't he?" Gabriel said admiringly, the edge gone from his voice. "Let's get Francesco back. Then we can do our own printing here."

"We know what you've been doing."

"At your age, you should keep your legs together."

A group of women were drawing water from the well in the square, sheltered by the high wall of the Duke's castle. Miriam Ardit's growing belly was the topic of their conversation.

"Miriam," said one of the women, laughing, as another woman approached, "here's Marguerita the midwife. It looks like you're going to be needing her soon."

"Did I hear someone say midwife?" Miriam saw a woman striding confidently toward her, wearing a luxurious woolen cape and what looked like a man's knee high leather riding boots. She did not look like the other women of Arcos.

Marguerita spotted Miriam's big belly. "It must be you," she said. "Let me introduce myself." She bowed, laughing. "Presenting Marguerita Sanchez, whose services have satisfied both princes and farmers, or at least their wives, for many miles around."

"It's a pleasure to meet you," said Miriam politely. "I will surely call on you if I need help, although my first two births were without difficulty."

She paused to make sure everyone was listening.

"Now this!" she said, pointing to her belly. "Ten years without a child, now this present from God. And, of course, from Yacov."

She rolled her eyes and the women laughed. None of them could have imagined the courage it took for Miriam Ardit to act so casually, or to speak so crudely about her husband.

Of course, none of them knew what had happened on the plains outside Arcos.

"It should be about this long and this wide. And not too thick. Her neck is quite delicate."

Pilar was certain the pendant was not for the customer's wife.

"What sort of design would you like?" she asked.

"I want to see the poetry of the Moors, the sensual feel of their language. I want her to fall into my arms every time she wears it."

Pilar was even more pleased than usual to see Gabriel striding purposefully toward the shop. She liked to watch him when he didn't know she was looking. His handsome face, hair curling onto his shoulders, and still trim body never failed to excite her.

"Gabriel, the Señor wants a special pendant for his lovely wife," she said pointedly.

"I'll help him. Here are two letters from Arcos. Don Alonso gave them to me."

Was there a flicker of interest on the customer's face at the mention of Arcos and Don Alonso? She wished that Gabriel had been more discreet.

Alone in the house, she opened the letter from Miriam.

> *Dear Pilar,*
>
> *I was so happy to get your letter. Seville seems far away, but you made it closer. I miss you. Arcos is very different. The good thing is that we are not persecuted here. Yacov has opened a tailor shop and has many customers. Ruyo has friends, but Esther not yet.*

'Poor Esther,' Pilar thought, 'trying to grow to a woman in a strange new place, without friends.'

> *She thinks often of Tomas, who was so brave and so helpful to us all. Of course for them it is not possible, not now. Although I regret to say this, please don't come to Arcos just yet.*

'I don't understand,' Pilar thought. 'Not now ... don't come just yet.' Why?

*Wait until we are more settled. Then you can come, and I
will welcome you with love and affection.*
                            Your friend,
                            Miriam Ardit

"Anything for me?"
She handed Tomas the letter and he was gone before she could
say a word.

Tomas could scarcely breathe. He didn't so much as read the
letter as inhale it.

Dear Tomas,
   *I too enjoyed our talks. But it is not a good idea for you to
come to Arcos now. There is too much danger. The Moors are
near the town all the time. Yesterday, two shepherds were killed.*
   *I want to call you by the special name you told me, but it is
our secret. It is beautiful that you wrote my name. I will cherish it.*
                            Your friend,
                            Esther Ardit

He was crushed. 'She doesn't want to see me,' he thought, and
then, 'She doesn't love me.' He sat for several minutes, head bowed,
then went gloomily to find his mother.
"She doesn't want me to come back to Arcos," he said, slumping
down next to her.
"That's odd," said Pilar, "Miriam said the same thing. I don't believe
them. There's something they're not telling us. May I see your letter?"
Tomas gave her the letter. Pilar read it quickly and looked back at
her son with a soft look that puzzled him.
"O, Tomas," she said, touching his hand, "This letter is full of
caring. What name did you tell her?"
"Benjamin."
"Because she's Jewish?"
"No, because I'm Jewish."
He saw her frown. "I'm sorry, mother," he said. Then, after a pause,
"I want to go to Arcos."
"So do I," she said, hugging him.

It was time.

The pains had begun, and the birth water had broken. A fire struggled to warm the room, but the March wind howled, and bursts of cold air penetrated cracks in the walls.

"I know it hurts," Miriam said, holding her daughter's hand. "I remember when you were born. The pain seems to go on forever, and you think it'll never stop. But finally the baby comes and it's over."

Esther writhed, her mouth twisted in a silent scream. "I hope you're right, Mama," she said. "I'm scared."

"You'll be fine, darling. Don't worry," she said, patting her forehead with a towel.

In fact, Miriam was more frightened than Esther. Something was wrong. The pains had gone on for sixteen hours, and the time between them was not decreasing. Perhaps the baby was turned the wrong way. Miriam had seen such a baby born to a friend of hers in Seville, and it had been a gruesome, bloody sight. Both mother and baby had died.

Yacov hovered at the door. She motioned to him. "I can't do this myself," she said. "We need the midwife. Go to Marguerita Sanchez. Remind her that we spoke at the well."

"But she'll know whose baby it is," Yacov protested. "After all we've done to keep it a secret."

"Don't argue with me!" Miriam hissed, trying to keep her voice low. "If you don't go now, Esther will die!"

Yacov put on his heavy cape and left.

Miriam returned to Esther, feeling helpless. She asked God to help Yacov find the midwife, and to keep Esther alive until she arrived.

The wait seemed endless. Where was Yacov? If Marguerita was away ... there was no one else. Miriam could do nothing but sit and wait, listening to Esther's moans. Finally, the front door opened.

"Blessed be the Name of the Lord," she said in Hebrew when she heard Marguerita's voice. She stepped aside as the midwife entered the little room.

Marguerita looked quickly at Esther, then stared at Miriam. "What's her name?"

"Esther," said Miriam. "I'll explain later."

"Bring a table for my things," Marguerita said to Yacov, who was again in his spot just outside the door.

"Will this do?" he said, returning almost immediately.

"What's happening," Esther said in a weak voice.

"That's what I'll ask you in just a minute," said Marguerita. "Esther, I'm going to help you have your baby."

"Will it be all right? It hurts so much."

"Yes. Don't worry. Just do what I tell you."

Cork-stoppered bottles and leather pouches came out of Marguerita's bag. She arranged them carefully on the table, explaining to Miriam, who comprehended nothing, about herbs, potions, and plasters. When she took out a long thin knife, Miriam's heart jumped. This was not a knife to cut the cord.

"Your husband can help. Give him this to mix with boiling water. Tell him to make a thick paste."

When Miriam returned, Marguerita had pulled back the covers and was feeling Esther's belly. Esther clenched her teeth in silence.

"The baby isn't turned the wrong way," Marguerita said, "but the opening is small. She's young, and her hips are narrow."

Marguerita walked a few steps from Esther. "This is going to be difficult," she told Miriam. "It may be necessary to choose between the baby and the mother."

"Jewish law is clear. The mother must live. She can have other babies."

"I can't promise anything about other babies. This one may do a lot of damage."

Yacov returned with a pot containing grayish paste.

"Is this what you wanted," he asked Marguerita.

"It's fine," the midwife answered. "Now warm this oil in another pot. Don't make it too hot."

She took a handful of the thick steaming paste and smeared it on Esther's belly, below the navel. Esther shuddered. Marguerita spread the plaster downwards, adding more from the pot, stopping just short of the birth opening.

She spoke softly to Esther. "The plaster will draw the baby down ... try to relax ... soon you'll have to work ... I can feel it starting to move ... it won't be much longer. When the baby's down, I'm going to widen the opening with my hands. It's going to hurt but I'll be as gentle as I can. Is the oil warm?"

Marguerita took the oil from Yacov and turned back to Esther.

Three fingers, then a tiny hand protruded from Esther's birth opening.

"Oh no! The baby turned. I have to get that hand back in and the arms below the head."

"You can do that?" Miriam whispered.

Marguerita pulled at the plaster, ripping hairs from Esther's belly. She covered her right hand with the warm oil and rubbed the slippery substance around and into the birth opening.

The baby's bloody fingers joined grotesquely with Marguerita's. Both hands disappeared inside Esther's womb.

"I'm moving the arm along the side of the baby's body," she described. "The other arm's where it belongs. The head is down."

And then, with a sigh of relief, she said, "It's going to be all right."

Marguerita removed her hand from Esther's womb, and the top of the baby's head was immediately visible.

"Now it's your turn, Esther. Are you ready?"

Esther responded with a wan smile.

Everything happened in a rush.

"Now, Esther!" Marguerita hollered. "Push! Push now! Do it! The baby's coming! Push! Here it comes. You're doing fine. Miriam, hold Esther's head. Keep pushing. Here it comes."

The head emerged. A shoulder. Another. Marguerita held the baby aloft and Miriam heard the first cry. Tears poured down Esther's cheeks.

"Thank you, Marguerita," Miriam said. "Bless you. You saved her life."

"And his too," said Marguerita, smiling for the first time and pointing to the proof as she cut the umbilical cord. "Here, wrap him in these towels."

Miriam took her infant grandson. 'It doesn't matter who the father is,' she thought. 'He doesn't know. He'll never know. The baby is beautiful. Esther's baby is beautiful.'

Miriam sat on a hard wooden bench while Marguerita packed her bag. Esther slept behind them.

"We pretended it was mine," Miriam said. "Esther's so young, and she has no husband."

"There are many like that," said Marguerita casually.

"Not among our people. It would be a terrible thing. She could never marry."

"Sometimes girls make mistakes," Marguerita said. "I made plenty."

"This was not like that," said Miriam. "We used to live in Seville, where Jews are treated much worse than here. A priest sent men to our house, looking for *conversos*, which they didn't find. But they found Esther, and almost raped her then. We left Seville, but these men followed us."

Miriam looked at Marguerita, trying to judge her response. She heard the desperation in her voice. Her whole family was at Marguerita's mercy. She decided. Only the brutal truth would convince her to keep their secret.

"Three men raped me over and over again while they made my husband and children watch."

Miriam saw the horror on Marguerita's face. She continued, "Then the leader of these awful men went to Esther. He forced himself into her. The baby is his."

"How did you survive?"

"It was a miracle. Prince Hasan saved us."

A puzzled look crossed Marguerita's face at the mention of Prince Hasan. Miriam expected more questions, but instead the midwife said gently, "I often know more than I tell. Your secret will be safe with me."

Relief flowed through Miriam's body. She rushed to the next room to tell Yacov.

"She'll keep our secret!"

To her surprise, Yacov was fuming. His arms were wrapped tightly across his chest and he was breathing heavily.

"What's wrong?" she said, alarmed. "Esther's going to live. The baby is beautiful. What's the matter with you?"

"That bastard!" he hollered, his body shaking with rage. "I'll find you some day, Hernando Talavero, and may God forgive me, I'll kill you!"

Miriam flinched at Yacov's intense hatred. Such feelings no longer served any purpose.

Marguerita stood in the doorway, looking wide-eyed at Yacov. Was she shocked at Yacov's outburst? Or was there something more? Miriam didn't dare to ask.

10

Gabriel was fuming. "So much for King Enrique's help! Francesco was arrested in December. Now it's April."

"I can't get to him," Don Alonso answered. "He's at Segovia, doing whatever he does with his dwarfs and eunuchs and young boys. Gonsalvo has tried. Don Diego de Avila has tried. I myself stood in vain before his gate. He won't see anyone. It's no use."

"Then we give up? How long can Francesco hold out?"

"I appealed to Archbishop Fonseca ... again. He's heard rumors that Perez has a prisoner, and he suspects it's Francesco."

"He suspects! Even an idiot would know. Why doesn't he do something?"

"He can't act without specific authority. Dominicans are responsible directly to the Pope, not to the archbishop. He wrote to Rome, and he expects an answer soon. It's all we can do."

"It's not enough," Gabriel groaned. "He's going to die!"

Friar Ricardo Perez paced impatiently. This was the fourth session, and he was frantic that his efforts had brought no confession, no accusation of others.

The supreme confidence which had led Perez to arrest Romo was a thing of the past. The Mother of Christ had urged him to trust his instincts, but so far he had failed, and the frightening consequences of that mistake were looming ahead. He had surely exceeded his authority and unless the results justified his action, he would be severely punished. For a brief moment, he considered letting Romo go, but the moment passed. There was no turning back. He could not allow himself to believe that the Blessed Virgin had led him astray! He could not allow that defiant, despicable Jew to humiliate him!

Candles glowed near the torture machines. Eerie mixtures of light, heat and smoke hovered over braziers of hot coals. The young scribe, as always, waited quietly at his small table.

Despite the fires of Hell within, and the balmy spring night outside, the underground room was bitterly cold. Francesco Romo was dragged in, bloody feet scraping on the rough floor, naked, shivering, denied even the thin sheet to which he had previously clung. His hands trembled in front of his groin.

Perez fought for control as he coolly studied the emaciated, sore-covered wreckage in front of him. This was no human being, no child of God whom Jesus had come to save. This was a Jew, less than human, who mocked the Lord and deserved any pain he could be made to suffer.

"Are you ready to confess?" Perez asked brusquely, without any pretence of the concern he had displayed on the prior occasions.

Silence.

Two black hooded guards took the prisoner to the hoist. Perez described the gruesome device as if it were a work of art.

"This harness is made from the finest leather. No matter how hard you fall, from whatever height, it won't break. Your bones will crack, your tendons will rip, but the ropes will hold. We shall demonstrate."

Francesco's thin arms were pulled roughly behind him. His wrists were tied tightly in straps joined together in a gleaming buckle, from which a heavy rope rose and passed over a pulley so high it could not have been seen but for the candles in the rafters. From the pulley, the rope descended into the hands of a guard.

The friar raised a finger and the guard stepped back, tensing the rope. Francesco's arms snapped upwards; his fleshless shoulders contorted. Protruding bones threatened to burst through his skin.

Perez made a final appeal. "I will grant you one last charity by helping you understand what you must tell me. Do you recall, Señor Romo, the sins you have committed by secretly practicing your heinous Jewish rites?"

No answer.

Perez screaming, "Tell me the Hebrew words! Say the words! Say *Shema Yisroel*!"

Francesco silent, his body stiff against the pain.

Perez, out of control, raving. "Who says these prayers with you? Where do you pray? Tell me! You must accept the mercy of the Church! I must save your soul! Please let me save you!"

Francesco glared at Perez, so directly and with such unexpected force that a chill coursed through the friar's body and he began to tremble.

Perez raised a shaking finger. The guard took another step, wrenching Francesco's arms, lifting him into the air.

Feet firmly planted, the guard pulled the rope hand over hand. Francesco rose higher and higher, just short of the rafter. A second guard took the loose end of the rope and fitted a large knot at its end into a ring bolted to the floor. The intervening length, reaching to the hands of the first guard, lay curled on the ground.

Perez hesitated, but he made himself think of the Virgin in the blazing light and his courage was restored. He gave the signal. Francesco plummeted downward, jolting to a stop at the end of the slack. His shoulders ripped from their sockets. Bone broke through the skin. Blood spurted.

Francesco gasped, retching, silent.

Perez hissed, "See what your friend Gabriel Catalan has brought upon you."

A smile spread across the prisoner's face.

Blind with rage, Perez waved violently and Francesco was jerked upwards. Again he plunged downward and snapped to a vicious halt. Both arms ripped completely from his body. Blood poured from the sockets.

Perez fled from the ghastly sight.

Perez ignored the padding of feet in the hallway.

A monk stood patiently by the door, awaiting permission to speak. Perez, gripped with fear, didn't want to hear. Finally, he nodded.

"The prisoner is dead."

Rodrigo de Muyo's huge frame cast a dark shadow over the front of Gabriel's shop. Gabriel saw the awful look in his friend's face and braced himself.

"Francesco is dead."

Gabriel slammed his hammer to the bench, shattering a delicate pendant he had worked on for weeks. His breath came in short bursts. Pain shot through his neck and erupted into his eyes.

Don Alonso looked old and withered. Deep lines dug into his cheeks. His elegant cloak lay rumpled on the floor.

"We tried to do too much," he said. "When Gutenberg came to Seville, I was sure he was bringing a miracle. It turned out to be a curse."

Don Alonso's head fell, forlorn chin brushing his chest.

"You were right, Gabriel. The printing wasn't worth it. It must have been that. Still, I should have been able to help him. It shows how little influence I have with King Enrique."

"It's not just you," said Gabriel. "Nobody can reach the king. He doesn't care. He plays with his animals and queers in that cursed refuge in Segovia while Castile falls into anarchy."

"Have Rodrigo dismantle the press," said Don Alonso. "Melt the type. Our printing adventure is over."

"No!" Pilar exploded.

Gabriel was shocked. Pilar had opposed the printing from the first day. Now, when he was ready to quit, she insisted they go on.

"Don't you see how dangerous it is?" he said. "You were right."

"Of course it's dangerous. But how do you know it was the printing that caused Perez to arrest Francesco?"

"What else? We haven't prayed together even once since the attack at Yacov's home."

"But you can't be certain. Perhaps it was something else."

She came close, intense. "You can't give it up. Too much depends on it."

"What are you saying? You don't care about Hebrew books."

"It's not the books. It's Tomas."

"What does this have to do with Tomas?"

"You and I are never going to leave this awful country," she said, "but the printing will take Tomas to a new life. Once Tomas learns to print, he can make books anywhere."

Gabriel was stunned. No matter how well he thought he knew her, his wife could still surprise him.

"You must do it!" she said, fiercely digging her fingers into his arms.

Gabriel pulled back, exasperated. "We can't," he said. "If we try to print in Seville we'll be caught. We'll all die ... like Francesco."

"There can be no printing in Seville," Pilar declared.

"But I thought you said ..."

"Yes. But not here."

"Where?"

"Take the press to Arcos. Assemble it there. Tomas will go."

"Tomas will go to Arcos?" he asked weakly.

"He can do it. You'll help him. It's better than sitting here waiting for Perez to put *us* beneath San Pablo."

"Does this have anything to do with Esther?"

Pilar answered with her first smile in days.

Gabriel was overwhelmed with Pilar's strength and insight. Her parents were simple people. She had little education. Yet she was a lioness! How fortunate to be her husband. A man must reach far to be worthy of such a woman.

"I'll talk to Don Alonso," he said with a sigh.

They followed the same trail as Tomas' first trip to Arcos almost a year before. There were hundreds of pack animals, horses, mules, and even cattle, which would be eaten as the journey progressed. The caravan carried silks, woolens, armor, weapons, pottery, furs, spices, and books, all received by ship in Seville, and destined for inland cities in Castile and Aragon.

Don Alonso's men would set up small fairs, stay for a few days, then move on. Don Alonso himself would accompany them only as far as Cordoba, after which he would return to Seville. The bulk of the wagons and men would not return for at least three months, and only then if everything went well. The stop in Arcos was mainly a diversion for the delivery of the press.

Tomas rode silently next to Rodrigo de Muyo, who would assemble the press in Arcos. When they passed the stream where he had camped with the Ardits, Tomas felt an intense longing. He closed his eyes. Esther moved in the light of the fire.

Several hours later they neared the place where Talavero had attacked. A rider came to Tomas from the front of the caravan. Don Alonso wanted to speak with him.

He kicked his horse into a gallop and rode quickly forward.

"You've become quite a horseman," Don Alonso said as Tomas reined in beside him.

"I had good teachers. Prince Hasan's men, on the way back to Seville."

They rode in silence until the familiar rockbound amphitheater rose up ahead of them. It was filled with wild spring flowers, an incongruous golden sea. Tomas looked away.

"Is this the place?" Don Alonso asked gently.

"Yes," said Tomas, moved by his concern.

"I thought so. I didn't want you be alone here."

Don Alonso extended an arm through the opening in his leather cloak and placed his hand on Tomas' shoulder. "Violence has been our companion for the past year and I suspect we're not done with it yet. This is a dangerous mission you're undertaking."

"Señor Romo died a horrible death, didn't he?" asked Tomas. "My father wouldn't talk about it. What happened?"

"Archbishop Fonseca found torture machines in the cellars underneath San Pablo."

Tomas cringed. "Will they do anything to Perez?"

"I don't know. Fonseca is furious. There'll be a hearing, and he asked me to participate. That's why I'm returning to Seville."

They rode past the spot where the rapes had taken place. Tomas was ashamed that he was excited by the thought of Esther's naked body.

"Are you afraid?"

Don Alonso's question jolted Tomas from his memories.

"Yes, but I try not to think of it."

"But you must! Never forget the nearness of danger! Never let your guard down!" He gazed sadly at Tomas. "Don't ever think you're safe. That's when it happens."

It was the largest trading caravan ever seen in Arcos de la Frontera. Residents lined up along the high cliff, from the Cathedral to the Duke's palace, jostling to see the huge assembly of men and animals and the renowned merchant prince who led them.

Tomas and Rodrigo were deep within the ranks, near the two covered carts which contained the press, Hebrew type, tools, lead, lampblack and linseed oil for printer's ink, and one thousand sheets of the highest quality paper Rodrigo's mill could produce.

They drew up below the sandstone cliffs of Arcos, on the far side of the Guadalete River. Isidro Lucero, Don Alonso's cousin, was among those who rode down to greet them. A fast rider had alerted him, and he had already procured a ramshackle old building for Tomas and Rodrigo towards the back end of town.

Late that afternoon, carts loaded with the goods purchased by residents of Arcos were hauled up the hills behind the cliff. Two additional carts, pulled by four oxen each, went to the site designated by Señor Lucero.

After dark, Tomas and Rodrigo closed the shutters and lit a single oil lamp. Rodrigo unloaded the heavy pieces of the disassembled press. Tomas stacked the bundles of paper, fifty sheets each, carefully wrapped, on a raised platform. When they were done, they spread their blankets on the floor.

"Are you excited?" Rodrigo asked.

"For many reasons," Tomas said. "I'm glad you came. I couldn't even budge those beams and you lifted them by yourself. How long will it take you to put it back together?"

"Six days," Rodrigo said.

"Exactly six days?" Tomas asked.

"I have a precise schedule for each day. I took it apart. I'll put it together."

This was a long speech for the normally taciturn Rodrigo. Although they had spoken little, Tomas had developed a liking for him. He was glad to have company in the strange house.

When they lay down to sleep, Tomas tried to remember every word he and Esther had spoken on that wonderful day, riding side by side on the vast plain. He heard her voice, playful, serious. He saw her smooth face and flashing smile. But suddenly, violent hands gripped her! She was naked on the ground. With enormous effort, he forced the image he should never have seen from his mind, but the night was no longer peaceful. He stared unseeing in the darkness, and sometime, much later, perhaps he slept.

"Good morning, Señor Ardit. Good morning, Ruyo."

"Tomas!" said Yacov, looking healthier than he had ever seen him. "Welcome. Don Lucero said you were here. I'll call Miriam and Esther."

Esther came into the shop and Tomas' breath was sucked away. Her body was full and sensual. Her long black hair hung loose. It was the first time he had seen her without a braid. Her cheeks were rosy, but, disturbingly, her eyes were timid and sad. Before he could say a word, Señora Ardit appeared behind her with a tiny baby wrapped in cotton blankets.

"Meet Judah," Señora Ardit said hastily. "Esther and Ruyo have a little brother. Judah is two months old today."

Tomas wanted only to talk to Esther, but they thrust the baby in his arms. He was astonished. Why hadn't they mentioned a baby in their letters? He gave it back as quickly as he could.

Esther stood off to the side. She looked pale and seemed frightened. He smiled to her, but she looked away and his heart sank. She said in her letter that she wanted to see him. Why was she acting like this?

The conversation about the baby went on endlessly. Tomas clenched his teeth. Esther did not talk to him. She said a few words to her parents, always about the baby, but nothing to him, not even a smile.

Miriam asked about his parents.

Yacov asked why he had come to Arcos.

Esther asked nothing.

Tomas was crushed.

Rodrigo arranged the beams that comprised the main pieces of the printing press. Once assembled, the press would be too heavy for six men to move.

Tomas remembered details Gutenberg had told him about his workshop in Mainz. He put the type near a window, where the letters could be seen in a good light. He strung ropes at the other end of the room where printed pages could be hung to dry. The press would go in the middle.

Just as Rodrigo had said, it took six days. Rodrigo set the timbers in place and Tomas fastened the long bolts that held them together. The tray for the type beds was last. Rodrigo's part was almost over. In another few days, he would return to Seville.

Tomas was building a case to hold the type, with a separate compartment for each letter. He worked in a sleeveless brown tunic, belted at the waist over a loosefitting linen shirt, and black hose with soft boots. Rodrigo had gone out for a walk, and it was one of the few occasions since they had arrived that Tomas was by himself.

He missed his father. He wanted to talk about the press, and what they would print first. He knew that Gabriel had only reluctantly agreed to his mother's idea of relocating the press, and he wondered if his father would ever regain his original enthusiasm about the printing. After Señor Romo's death, he had hardly talked at all, about printing or anything else. He wanted to hear his father's calm voice, feel his hand on his shoulder, see the love in his eyes.

Suddenly, he sensed he was not alone. His heart quickened. He reached to his boot for the Prince's dagger.

Then he saw her.

She had stayed out of his sight since that first day. Several times he had gone to her house, but she was never there. He was sure she was avoiding him. Now here she was, green eyes looking straight at him, hair hanging loose and full. His knees weakened. He started to speak but she raised a finger to her lips and the words remained locked in his throat.

Esther walked slowly across the room to him. The tiny sound of each step pounded in his heart. She didn't speak. She didn't smile. She came next to him and he smelled her intoxicating fragrance. She raised her hand and stroked his hair. She touched his forehead, and he stopped breathing. He felt her full breasts against him. She lifted herself high on her toes and kissed his cheek. His skin burned.

He touched her shoulders, but she was already backing away, her gaze fixed on his. He wanted to speak but again she raised her finger to her lips.

When she reached the door, the barest trace of a smile passed across her face. She stepped into the darkness.

11

Tap ... Tap ... Tap ...

The lethargic rhythm reflected Gabriel's despondent mood. He had no interest in his work. He grieved over his friend Francesco, and worried about Tomas, away in Arcos with a press which, for him, had lost all of its earlier luster. He was lonely without his son next to him at his bench.

He had grown distant from Pilar. She had her way with the press, and then it seemed that there was nothing more to say between them. He missed their conversations. He missed their lovemaking.

Someone was looking at him! There was no one in the shop. His eyes flickered to the street. A slight movement. Perez!

When he realized that Gabriel had seen him, the friar at first turned and started to walk away. Then he stopped, squared his shoulders, and came back to the shop. He stood motionless only a few feet from the bench where Gabriel worked.

Gabriel heard Pilar behind him. He felt her firm touch on his shoulder. "Stay calm," she said, but he could not be controlled.

"You ... killed ... my ... friend!" he screamed.

Perez stared at Gabriel, his coal black eyes beacons of hate. "Francesco Romo was a Jew," he said, smiling maliciously, his words a stream of venom, "and he died believing you were the one who informed on him."

Gabriel leaped, arms flailing for Perez' throat. Pilar screamed. His fingers closed on the startled friar's throat. Pilar clawed at his shoulders and he lost his grip.

Perez sneered and strode off.

He wandered aimlessly for hours. His cape was gone and his tunic was badly stained. He must have walked through puddles because his shoes were soaked.

I'm sure Francesco didn't confess, he thought, or Perez would have thrown that too in my face, or he would have arrested me. But did Francesco believe I betrayed him? How can I ever know? Why, God, do you test me so?

Perez is a vicious human being. Why does the Church, which preached love, permit him to do these things? How can a just God allow him to exist? Well, that will be Your problem from now on. I'm done. No more Hebrew books. No more prayers to a God who doesn't care. Tomas will come back from Arcos and we'll go back to our old life.

But then Perez will win. Can I let Perez crush my father's hopes? Brave Isaac who lived a lie for sixty years so I could know the truth. Was he really so brave? Why didn't he say something before? He taught me so little about being a Jew. Even when he died, I only know his words from Pilar.

Pilar. The thought of her luscious body depressed him. Will I ever feel her next to me again? I shouldn't have let her talk me into sending the press to Arcos. Now Tomas is gone too. Hebrew books. Who's going to read them? Does God care if we make them?

He wandered into the *barrio* Triano. Maybe I'll be attacked and killed, he thought, and it will all be over. He saw the infamous Taverna Lucas, a hangout for thieves and prostitutes. He went in and it wasn't long before he was approached. The negotiations were brief, and he followed the woman to her room. They were barely inside when she removed her clothes. He stared, not knowing what to do next.

"You ain't seen tits before?" she asked, and when he didn't answer, she said flatly, "Pay before we start."

He pulled a few coins from his purse and handed them to the woman.

"How you goin' to do it if you don't take your clothes off?"

The next few minutes were a fog. He took off his filthy clothes. The whore lay down and opened her legs. When he thought about it later, he had no memory of reaching a climax, or even entering her. His next clear recollection was that he was completely dressed, looking down at the woman, wishing she would close her legs.

"You *conversos* are very strange," she said.

"What makes you think I'm a *converso*?"

"You don't work our business without knowin' things like that. It's easy to tell. You look like a Jew, with your sharp nose. And you didn't hit me. But don't worry. I been doin' it with your kind for years. I like *conversos*. Especially that big one. He's not afraid like most of you. You think whores don't like it? Let me tell you, when Rodrigo de Muyo fucks me, I get crazy. It's not just his shoulders which are big. What a cock he has! But he's got trouble too, just like you. Some things he tells me, but the worst he saves for his monk priest."

Sharp stabs hit between his eyes. His head was crashing. Don't frighten her. Be calm.

"What monk priest?" he asked as calmly as he could.

"The one from San Pablo. Friar Perez. Señor de Muyo always comes to me right after he confesses."

The retching would not end. Vomit covered the side of the building, his hose and his shoes. He pounded the wall, bloodying his hands. Disgust with himself, love for Pilar whom he had betrayed, and fear, primal fear, boiled deliriously in his mind. It was a witches brew. He wanted to run away and die.

But he knew that now, of all times in his life, he could not run. Everything depended on him. If Rodrigo ever returned to Seville, Tomas would die in Perez' torture rooms, or worse, at the stake. Tomas, Don Alonso, Pilar, and himself. All dead.

I've got to go to Arcos, he thought. I must go now. Nothing else matters.

Pilar had cried constantly while Gabriel was gone. She was terrified that she had lost him. Now he was back, filthy, disheveled, smelling from vomit, and avoiding her eyes.

"It's Rodrigo," he said. "Rodrigo's the informer. I'm sure of it."

She waited, unsure.

"I should have realized before. He's been acting strangely for a long time. Tonight, I learned that he confesses to Friar Perez at San Pablo. No one goes to Dominicans to confess. He goes to inform!"

Pilar stifled her questions.

"I've got to go to Arcos," he said. "Rodrigo must never come back to Seville."

She decided to help, not confront.

"We'll ask Gonsalvo for men to accompany us," she said. We can leave by noon tomorrow."

"You're coming?"

"Yes."

She touched his shoulder. The look in his eyes told her that she had made the right decision. He would never leave again.

"The punishment for informing is death," Rabbi Modena confirmed. "But it requires a trial, and two independent witnesses. Who will hold the trial? Who will carry out the penalty?"

Modena's questions had the opposite effect from what the rabbi seemed to intend. Gabriel was not discouraged. Instead, he saw a way to return from his personal abyss. He would go to Arcos. And what he would do there would bring meaning to Francesco's death, and to that of his father Isaac.

It was Pilar who made everything possible. She had accepted him back without question. He vowed not to waste his undeserved second chance.

The steep cliffs of Arcos appeared on the horizon, but a howling thunderstorm immediately hid them from view. Two hours later they pushed their tired mounts across the Rio Guadalete and up the hill into town.

They found Isidro Lucero and he took them to the ramshackle house. The doctor bowed and left, inviting them to visit him when they were settled. The escort of armed men provided by Gonsalvo de Viterbo waited a short distance away. The ground was still wet from the storm. The fresh smell of rain permeated the late afternoon air.

"Tomas," shouted Gabriel as he neared the house.

"Father! Mother!" Tomas ran to them, trying to hug both at once. "What are you doing here? I'm so glad you've come."

"Is Señor de Muyo still here?" Gabriel asked, stepping back.

Tomas dropped his arms, puzzled, and Gabriel realized how abrupt he had been. "It's good to see you," he said. "But Rodrigo. Where is he?"

"He went for a walk, but he'll be back soon," said Tomas, wrinkling his brow. "He's packed, though, and planning to leave tomorrow. What's the matter?"

"I have bad news," said Gabriel. "Let's go into the house."

Tomas looked back and forth at his parents, alarmed. Pilar took his hand and they walked inside. Gabriel spoke quickly.

"Rodrigo informed on us when we prayed last year. And he's the one who led Friar Perez to Señor Romo."

"But he's one of us! He's my friend." Tomas said. His eyes swept the room. "Look what we've done here. I could never have done this by myself. Señor de Muyo would never hurt us."

Gabriel followed his son's gaze and saw a shop organized for printing.

"This is wonderful," he said, "and it's good that Rodrigo helped. But it won't be good if he tells Perez everything that's here and what we intend to do with it."

"What's going to happen?" Tomas asked fearfully.

"He can't be allowed to return to Seville."

"Where will he go?"

"He'll go nowhere," said Gabriel. "The penalty in Jewish law for informing on your fellow Jews is quite clear. Rodrigo must die."

"Gabriel! Pilar! What a pleasant surprise!"

Rodrigo ran excitedly into the room. He was followed closely by the captain of the Viterbo guard, but Gabriel motioned him back.

"Hello, Rodrigo," Gabriel said flatly.

Rodrigo stiffened. "What's the matter?" he asked wary. "Did you see the press? We're ready to print. It's wonderful that you're here." His confusion turned to alarm when Gabriel did not respond. "Why are you looking at me like that?"

"Don't you know?" Gabriel said bitterly. "Don't you grieve for Francesco? You and your Dominican confessor!"

"What's this about?" Rodrigo demanded, looking from Gabriel to Pilar to Tomas. Gabriel exploded. "I know you confess to Friar Perez!" he hollered, barely able to say the words. "Were you at San Pablo when Francesco was being tortured? Did Perez tell you every detail?"

Pilar took Gabriel's arm and he stopped. He knew that Rodrigo was Francesco's friend. Whatever Rodrigo had done, he could not have been a participant in Francesco's death.

"If he had told me that, I would have killed him," Rodrigo said. "I would have ripped him apart. I never knew. I swear it."

"And was it you who brought Francesco to Perez' attention. Did you tell Perez we were secret Jews?"

Rodrigo looked down without answering. His huge body sagged.

"I pray to God that I'm not responsible," Rodrigo said, barely audible.

"But you're not sure?"

"No. He learns things. He has the powers of the devil."

"You went to San Pablo?"

"Yes."

"Tell me," Gabriel said softly, seeing his friend's despair and knowing that he would never have done such a thing willingly.

Rodrigo took a deep breath, "Maria overheard me saying prayers in Hebrew. She asked what they were. I didn't tell her, but she must have guessed. Soon I had a visit from Perez. I thought he would arrest me, but instead he wanted me to help him find more secret Jews. He named Don Alonso." Rodrigo closed his eyes and hesitated. "Perez said if I didn't cooperate, my sons would be taken to a monastery and I'd never see them again. I thought I could trick him, and never really give him any good information, but he caught on." Rodrigo stifled a sob and continued. "One day, my boys disappeared. I was frantic. Six hours later, a monk brought them back."

Rodrigo paused. Gabriel said nothing, but his heart was broken by his friend's ordeal. Tomas looked devastated.

"I knew I had to give him something important, so the next day I told him about the prayer room. I was sure everyone would get away but I never thought about Yacov and his family." Rodrigo hung his head and breathed deeply. "I'm so sorry," he said. "Later, Perez asked me to watch you and Francesco, but I never said anything about either of you. Please believe me."

"Why did he ask about me and Francesco?" asked Gabriel.

"He never explained and I didn't ask. I didn't want to be with him any longer than necessary."

"How did you learn that Francesco was dead?"

"Perez told me. He said it was an accident. He seemed upset."

"Have you told him anything about the printing?"

"No. Nothing. He never asked. I don't think he knows anything."

"But he will find out, won't he?"

"Yes," said Rodrigo sadly. "Sooner or later."

Nobody spoke and the silence was frightening.

"What will happen now?" Rodrigo asked.

"You know the penalty for informing."

"Yes."

"We have men outside."

Rodrigo raised his head and stood a little taller. His look was one of infinite sorrow, but also pride.

"You won't need your men," he said. "I loved Francesco, and I love you, Gabriel." He looked straight into Gabriel's eyes. "I don't want to see Perez again. I don't want to hurt you any more."

"And I don't want you to die," Gabriel said. "One death among my closest friends is enough."

Pilar moved closer to him. Tomas didn't breathe. Rodrigo stood stock still. Gabriel agonized. How would I react if Perez threatened me like he had Rodrigo? What if Tomas had been taken? Or Pilar? Is there anything I wouldn't do to protect them?

"There's no choice," Gabriel said. "If you return to Seville, Perez will know everything."

Rodrigo nodded.

Gabriel continued, "Señora de Muyo will learn that you've died in an accident. Did you tell her where you were going? Does she know anything about the printing?"

"I never mentioned Arcos or the printing. Gabriel, please tell me you'll use my press to make the Hebrew books. Let something good come from this."

Gabriel had no more questions. He was already sick with himself for being so methodical. "We'll use your press. And I'll look after your sons," he said quietly.

They stood between the house and the cliff as the sun fell to the horizon.

"I wanted so much to be a Jew," said Rodrigo.

"You are a Jew," said Gabriel. "A flawed Jew, like all of us, but God will forgive you." He choked over his next words. "I forgive you, too. I know you didn't intend to do harm. Perez trapped you. It wasn't your fault. It could happen to any of us."

Gabriel stood between Rodrigo and Tomas. The sky was orange behind them. Tomas held out his hands to Rodrigo. He sobbed and Rodrigo enfolded the boy in his huge arms.

They recited the prayers of the afternoon *minchah* service. Pilar stood aside and Gabriel looked at her sadly. From the moment he had first worn his father's bloody *tallit*, she had insisted that it was madness to be a Jew. It led only to death, she said, and she was right.

When they reached the *Shema* prayer, Rodrigo left the others and walked slowly toward the edge of the cliff.

He recited in a clear bold voice.

"Hear O Israel. The Lord our God, the Lord is One. Blessed be the name of his glorious kingdom for ever and ever."

Then he stepped forward and plunged two hundred feet to the rocky banks of the Rio Guadalete.

12

Tomas had told her about the baby, but Pilar was not prepared for the blizzard of activity. She was glad, however. It kept her thoughts from Rodrigo.

Eventually, Pilar and Miriam found a quiet moment.

"Tomas told you what happened to us?" Miriam began, pain clear in her face.

"Yes." said Pilar.

"I felt dead. For months. I couldn't go near Yacov."

"I'm so sorry. And Esther?"

"Esther is better than I would have thought. She and Tomas ..."

"I know," said Pilar. "It'll be difficult for them."

"Impossible," said Miriam.

"Difficult ... but not impossible." Pilar surprised herself. She knew how Tomas felt about Esther, and her instincts told her it was something which must happen.

"What do you mean?" Miriam asked.

"Esther could convert." Despite her words, Pilar could not visualize Esther eating the wafer of Christ's body. Yet what other way was there?

"It would destroy Yacov," said Miriam. Pilar noticed that she did not include herself or Esther.

Judah squirmed in Pilar's arms. "He's alert," she said, "and strong." As she spoke, Pilar looked more closely at the baby, and then at Miriam. Something seemed odd. A thought came to her. She calculated the age of the baby, and the time when he must have been conceived. She looked at Judah's light hair, ruddy skin, thick bone structure. How could she have been so blind? None of this was Yacov. This was a child born of rape!

Judah started to cry and Pilar handed him to Miriam, expecting her to put him to her breast.

Esther had been in the front of the house, helping Yacov in the shop. Now she came back to where her mother sat. She took Judah and went off to the back bedroom. It was only then that Pilar noticed Esther's heavy breasts.

Miriam whispered, her voice laced with tears, "I wanted you to know, but I didn't know how to say it. We've kept it secret. Everyone thinks he's my baby. And Yacov's. Except for our family, and now you, only the midwife knows."

Yacov brought a complete copy of the *Shema* prayer from the synagogue, including all four biblical quotations. Using the smaller of the two Hebrew alphabets, Gabriel and Tomas were able to fit the text on a single page. Gabriel assembled the letters, and Tomas transferred each line of type to the tray. After several hours of concentrated work, the page of type was placed on the rails below the screw press.

They were about to apply the ink when Pilar arrived with Esther. Tomas and Esther exchanged a shy smile. Gabriel silently inquired and received a look from Pilar that said 'We'll talk later.'

Gabriel opened one of the jugs, vividly remembering the day he and Francesco had filled them, and poured black ink onto a flat metal tray. Tomas used a leather ball on a handle, a gift from Gutenberg, to spread it evenly across the type. The pungent oily smell of the ink filled the room.

Gabriel took a sheet of paper, Rodrigo's paper, fixed it securely in the holder, rotated it over the inked type, and slid the tray forward under the press. He motioned to Tomas, and hands intertwined, father and son pulled the lever to squeeze the paper against the inked type. After several seconds, they reversed the screw.

They looked in awe at the first page ever printed in the language of the children of Israel.

Gabriel opened his arms.

"Esther, will you help us pray?" he asked, taking her hand.

Tomas took Esther's other hand and reached for his mother with a pleading look. Gabriel couldn't believe his eyes as Pilar stepped forward to complete the circle and participated, for the first time ever, in Hebrew prayer.

They recited the *Shehekianu*, the Jew's simple thanks to God for allowing him to live to reach a special moment.

Blessed art thou, O Lord our God, King of the Universe, who hast kept us in life, and hast preserved us, and hast enabled us to reach this season.

"Esther," said Gabriel, "Would you tell us if you see any errors?"

Tomas held his breath as Esther read. She didn't look up until she was finished.

"Did you find a mistake?" Gabriel asked.

Shyly, Esther pointed to a word in the third line of the second full paragraph. "This should be an ע, not an א" she said, so softly that they could barely hear her.

"Thank you," said Gabriel.

Tomas beamed. He removed the א and replaced it with an ע, which stood out in shining contrast to the ink-blackened letters around it.

They produced another proof page, which Esther declared to be perfect, then several more pages. Esther interrupted. She pointed to a letter near the bottom of the last page they had printed. Only part of the letter was visible. The type had broken. Tomas replaced it and they went on.

Several pages later, Esther again stopped them. The lines of type were no longer even. Gabriel found that the type tray had loosened. He tightened it and they started up again.

They printed fifty copies in five hours. The first Hebrew press run was complete.

The Archbishop's palace occupied a corner of the square adjacent to the new Cathedral. It was a magnificent building, built by the first archbishop of Seville after the reconquest, enhanced and glorified by each of his successors. Marble floors, paneled walls, tapestries, decorative stucco, gold and silver ornaments. Convincing evidence of ecclesiastical prestige and power. They convened in a large paneled room on the first floor. The high ceilings were designed for Seville's summers, but even with the shutters open to a shaded courtyard, the heat was oppressive.

Don Alonso watched with seething hatred as Friar Perez entered the room and took the only unoccupied seat at the heavy oak table.

Perez looked around him for support, but none of the five men already seated rose or recognized him.

To Perez' right was a scribe. Next was Friar Menendez, who had been the scribe during the interrogations of Francesco Romo and who was to be a witness at this proceeding. Opposite Perez, at the head of the table, sat Archbishop Fonseca, looking tired and ill at ease.

Don Alonso was to the Archbishop's right. Between Don Alonso and Perez sat the papal legate, just arrived from Rome.

"This is a formal disciplinary hearing ordered by His Holiness Pope Calixtus, through his legate Cardinal Vicente Venezio, here present," the Archbishop began, speaking for the record. "I will be the hearing official. I am fully authorized to determine this matter, and there shall be no appeal from my decision. The defendant is Friar Ricardo Perez, of the Order of Preachers, assigned to the monastery of San Pablo. Friar Perez, you will hear the charges and you will be permitted to speak in your own defense. Do you understand?"

"Yes, your Eminence," Perez mumbled.

"You are accused of improperly causing the arrest of a Catholic citizen of this realm, and treating him in a manner which ultimately led to his death."

Don Alonso clenched his fists and slowly pounded the table. The charge did not include murder! They were going to let him live!

"Cardinal Venezio will tell us the position of the Holy Pontiff in this matter."

The papal legate opened a leather folder and ceremoniously removed a single sheet of parchment.

"The Order of Preachers," Venezio read, "shall go among the Jews, even into their houses of worship, and shall speak the way of Jesus Christ, and shall make every effort to convince those who hear to come to baptism and thus to the salvation of the Holy Church. They shall also seek out heresy among Christians who have faltered, and when they find evidence of such heresy, they shall present such matters to the Ecclesiastic Courts who shall conduct hearings, make findings and take such action as they shall deem necessary. These things the Order of Preachers is directed to do."

Cardinal Venezio finished reading. At a nod from the Archbishop, he went on, "The Holy Pontiff asked me to express his dismay at the actions of Friar Perez described in your letter, and to testify to this tribunal that no member of the Order of Preachers has authority to do as this man has done."

Fonseca spoke directly to Perez. "Friar Menendez recorded your interrogations of Señor Romo. We have read these appalling records, and will require only a brief recapitulation at this time." He gestured to the young scribe. "I understand you have prepared a summary?"

Menendez read without expression. "The prisoner was given little food, so he would be weak. He was shown the machines of torture, so he would be afraid. He was asked to confess, but was not told the charges. The first torture was on the rack. Naked, he was bound hand and foot, and stretched. When he screamed, the pressure was eased. When he didn't confess, he was racked again. Several times he collapsed, and at those times, the interrogation was officially suspended. The water torture was used once, but it didn't work correctly. The hoist was used when all else failed. He was dropped several times. His arms were ripped from his body, and he died. He never confessed."

Don Alonso covered his mouth and struggled not to vomit on the polished table. Even in his worst dreams, he could not have imagined such merciless treatment. How could a man of God be so loathsome and cruel? What kind of church encourages such behavior?

"Do you have any questions, Friar Perez?" Fonseca asked, his contempt obvious.

"No."

"Is this account accurate?"

Perez looked up, seemed about to offer a rebuttal, then simply said, "Yes."

"Do you have anything to say about why you arrested Señor Romo and treated him in this manner?"

"It is the task of the Dominican Order to seek out heresy," said Perez, showing animation for the first time. "The secret judaizing of Christians is a grave heresy and a threat to the unity of our beliefs. I had reason to believe that Señor Romo was a secret Jew, and I did my duty."

"No, you went far beyond your duty," Fonseca responded angrily. "You had no proof. You obtained no proof. You had no authority to arrest. No authority to use torture." Fonseca paused, struggling to keep his dignity. "What was the basis for your suspicion?"

Perez looked harshly at Don Alonso, then appeared to catch himself. He turned back to the Archbishop. Don Alonso tensed. What does he really know?

"I was informed that Señor Romo attended a secret prayer meeting and recited Jewish prayers."

"Who told you that?"

Perez did not respond.

"Who told you?" Fonseca responded angrily. "Answer my question!"

"It was a beggar. I don't know his name."

"You don't know his name?" Fonseca demanded. "Why did this beggar come to you?"

"He brought information before."

"Did you pay him?" Fonseca's disgust was clear.

"Yes."

"That was your only evidence?"

"Yes."

"Do you have anything else that you wish to say?"

"No."

"We will deliberate," Fonseca announced. "Take him away."

Perez was led from the room and the two scribes were also excused.

"Do you have the authority to execute?" asked Don Alonso.

"Yes," said Fonseca, "but that would be an extraordinary punishment. It would make things worse."

"He killed an innocent man — my friend, and yours," Don Alonso insisted. "He should be put to death."

"We don't want to make him a martyr," argued Fonseca.

"Don't let him live!" said Don Alonso, raising his voice. "Have you seen the cellars at San Pablo? Is this what our church has come to?"

Fonseca turned to the papal legate and Don Alonso knew he had lost.

"What do you recommend?" Fonseca asked.

"There is a monastery near the village of Hijar, in Aragon," Cardinal Venezio answered.

"That would be perfect, your Excellency," said Fonseca.

"We can sign the proclamation together," Venezio added. "Friar Perez will be exiled to the monastery at Hijar for three years."

Don Alonso rose angrily. As he spun to leave, he saw a painting hanging in the alcove behind him and stopped dead in his tracks.

Archbishop Fonseca stood quietly next to Don Alonso, and they stared at the painting together.

"It's Moses receiving the word of God at Mt. Sinai," Fonseca said.

"The techniques are copied from an Italian painter named Masaccio."

"Who ... ?"

"Francesco gave it to me ... the day he was arrested."

Perez was ecstatic. Three years was nothing! He would return, and he would not make the same mistakes again. He would find the judaizing *conversos* of Seville ... and he would see them burn.

Gabriel Catalan would be the first.

Gabriel and Don Alonso walked through the gardens adjoining the *Alcazar* in Seville. The late afternoon breeze drifting up from the river dispersed the muggy air. Palm trees swayed gently. Sounds of construction from the Cathedral were heard in the distance.

"I've lost my two best friends," Gabriel said.

"You took a great risk," said Don Alonso. "Suppose Rodrigo had not confessed."

"I had no choice. You weren't here, and I couldn't wait. I was sure he was the informer, and I couldn't let him return to Seville."

"How did you know?"

Gabriel envisioned the whore laying naked on the bed, legs spread. He shivered, and reached to rub the defilement from between his own legs.

"I learned that Rodrigo went regularly to confess to Friar Perez at San Pablo."

"You did well," said Don Alonso. "It took courage."

"It took fear," said Gabriel.

They reached the church of Santa Maria la Blanca and Gabriel looked for the three stars of David set high in the walls. These were the only remaining physical evidence that this church had once been a synagogue, before the recently sainted Vicente Ferrer had stolen it in 1412.

"We don't go away easily," he mused.

"God seems to have His uses for us," Don Alonso said with a wry smile. "You know that Perez has been exiled from Seville?"

"That bastard! I tried to kill him when he came to my shop. Where was he sent?"

"To a monastery in Aragon. But only for three years. I wanted him executed, but Fonseca wouldn't do it. He said the reaction against *conversos* would make things worse."

"It does give us some time," said Gabriel.

"So you've regained your interest in printing?"

"I have something to show you," said Gabriel with a smile.

Standing by the large desk in Don Alonso's study, Gabriel pictured Gutenberg in that same spot over a year ago. He unfolded four sheets of paper, spread them out, and looked up expectantly.

Don Alonso bent over and immediately caught his breath.

"This is incredible!" he whispered. "How many did you make?"

"Fifty."

"How long did it take?"

"Four hours to set the type. Five hours to print the pages."

"It works! You did it! You made Gutenberg's method work. Oh, Gabriel, you printed Hebrew!"

Gabriel did not respond to Don Alonso's enthusiasm.

"Aren't you excited?" Don Alonso asked.

"The price has been very great," Gabriel said sadly.

Don Alonso respected his mood for a moment, the erupted with a torrent of questions.

"Tell me all about it. What did you do? Where's the press? Who knows about it? Where did you get the *Shema* to copy from?"

Gabriel answered each question carefully. "Your cousin Isidro Lucero is guarding the press while we're gone," he concluded.

"Has Rabbi Modena seen this?"

"Not yet."

"He'll be thrilled. I'll go with you."

"What should we print next?"

"I have some ideas," Don Alonso said, "but let's ask the rabbi."

"We'll need more paper," Gabriel said, and again a look of dismay crossed his face. "Rodrigo ..."

Don Alonso came close to hold Gabriel's shoulders. After a moment, Gabriel continued, "... lead, ink, tools ... a way to bind the books ... a place to keep them safely ..."

"You'll have everything you need," Don Alonso said quietly, hugging him.

They walked to the courtyard near the front gate.

"Gabriel, I know the cost has been high, but you've more than fulfilled all of my hopes for you."

"Thank you."

"I have more in mind."

Gabriel snapped to attention.

"I'm getting older," Don Alonso said. "It's time to share my responsibilities."

"But Gonsalvo?" said Gabriel.

"My son has taken on much of the burden of our trading and other businesses. But farming the taxes, negotiating with the king, protecting the Jews and leading the *converso* community — these are not for Gonsalvo. We've discussed this, and we agree that we must find someone else. You are my choice. I want you to take my place in these things when I'm gone."

Gabriel flinched at the enormity of Don Alonso's proposal. It had taken all of his will power and effort to accomplish what little printing they had done, and he knew how close he had come to abandoning even that. How could he replace Don Alonso?

"I'm just a goldsmith," he said, shaking his head.

"And now a printer," said Don Alonso. "You displayed great courage with Rodrigo. You were strong enough to fight with me about Francesco and you were right. You care about our people and our heritage."

"What do I know about tax farming, or dealing with the king? I can't do what you do."

"Not now, perhaps. But as you see," Don Alonso said, smiling broadly, "I'm still here. When the time comes, you'll be ready."

"It's perfect! Every letter is perfect. When did you become a Hebrew scholar?"

"It was Esther," Gabriel said. "She found all the errors."

"Esther Ardit," repeated Rabbi Modena, nodding fondly. "That's very good. She's a good girl."

His attention returned to the printed pages. He compared them repeatedly, shaking his head in disbelief that they were identical. "I must show the other rabbis, in Cordoba and Burgos, even Barcelona. Can you make entire books? This will revitalize our synagogues and *yeshivas*."

"Rabbi, I'm afraid we can't do that," Don Alonso responded. "This printing must be kept completely secret. The important thing is to print these books and save the Jewish culture for future generations."

"So you would ignore this generation?" Modena said sharply. "There's no hope for them?"

Don Alonso was silent.

"You're only concerned with the future?" the Rabbi pressed, face jutted forward. Gabriel was moved by the Modena's defiance. He thought about Yacov Ardit and others like him, who simply refused to let Judaism die.

"You must print *Haggadahs*," said Modena. "God's rescue of the Jews enslaved in Egypt will encourage Jews who live in fear now. They must know that God has not forsaken them!"

"Even if I have?" Don Alonso said.

Modena was already reaching for the old illustrated Haggadah he had shown to Gabriel on the day Friar Perez had come to the synagogue.

Gabriel glanced quickly at Don Alonso and received a reluctant nod. "We can print *Haggadahs*," Gabriel said to Modena, "but you'll have to make sure the rabbis understand the need for secrecy."

Modena nodded in vague agreement and laid the large book on the table. He opened to the page containing the four questions which introduce the story of Passover. Gabriel and Don Alonso looked at the page while the Rabbi chanted softly:

מה נשתנה הלילה הזה
מכל הלילות

Why is this night
different from all other nights?

"Many Jews have never asked that question," said Modena, speaking to Gabriel. "You never asked Isaac, and Tomas has never asked you. Make copies of this book so every Jewish child can ask! No matter how hard the Church tries to squeeze every breath of Jewish consciousness from us, we can help Jews be Jews!"

Servants were bustling everywhere. It was a small dinner, but even for Don Alonso it wasn't every day that the Archbishop came to dine. The smell of roasting pig filled the air, as it often did when guests were present in the Viterbo home. Gabriel had come early, hoping to talk with Don Alonso before Fonseca arrived.

"Can you tell me more about the tax farming?" Gabriel began. "I'm not sure I'm ready to meet with the Archbishop about this."

"Don't worry. He has no idea of the details. Like the king, all he wants is his money."

"Do you have a contract with the church?"

"Yes. Very similar to the one with Enrique. It's for five years — the current agreement has three years remaining. There's a fixed payment each year. I give the Church three million *maravedis* each year, in advance. Then I collect the taxes from the people."

"And you keep what you collect?" Gabriel asked incredulously.

"Yes."

"Suppose you don't collect as much as you've paid?"

"Then I lose. But it's never happened. The profit has always been quite substantial."

"Couldn't the king and the Church collect their own taxes?"

Don Alonso smiled. "They don't know how. They wouldn't trust anyone who didn't pay in advance. And no one else has enough capital."

"So the people have one more reason to despise *conversos*," Gabriel said, realizing that he would soon be part of that hatred.

"No one likes the tax collector, especially if they're trying to cheat on their payments. And Old Christians are furious that *conversos* have replaced the Jews as tax farmers. Jews had all the business before they were excluded by law, and now converted Jews have it all again. There were riots in Toledo about this a few years ago." Don Alonso rose and walked several steps away before he continued. "Several good friends of mine were killed. They even passed laws to keep *conversos* out of tax farming. But the Pope objected — after all, we're Christians aren't we? — and the laws were repealed."

"And this is what you want me to do?"

"Is it more dangerous than anything else?" asked Don Alonso, smiling, as a servant entered the room to announce the arrival of Archbishop Fonseca.

13

'To require such a payment is despicable,' thought Rabbi Modena, unable to concentrate on the *Yom Kippur* service, 'when they know that even to touch money on the Holy Day is forbidden.'

The thirty *dinero* annual tax on all the Jewish communities had been restored after a hiatus of many years. Thirty *dineros* was an insignificant amount of money, but the emotions it spawned were frightening. Everyone knew it represented the thirty pieces of silver paid to Judas Iscariot in return for his betrayal of Jesus.

The Rabbi had agonized for weeks, and just before sundown on *Yom Kippur* eve, he had rushed to the synagogue. It was still a desecration, but it was the best solution he could devise.

With a start, he realized that the Torah service was reaching its conclusion. He had not prayed at all! Modena asked God to forgive this latest of his many sins.

Tomas Catalan took a position along the path from the synagogue to the *Alcazar*. He wore a cap pulled down over his face and tried to be as inconspicuous as possible in the midst of the unruly crowd. He wanted Rabbi Modena to see at least one friendly face along the route, but he became more nervous as the noon hour approached. Finally, ripples through the crowd signaled that the Jews had left the synagogue.

"Judas!"

"Jew devil!"

"Christ-killer!"

The individual shouts merged into a menacing roar.

Rabbi Modena came into view, head high, looking straight forward, walking at a stately pace. He held a Torah over his left shoulder, its silver breast plate and pointer resting on a richly embroidered red velvet cover. Sunlight glinted from the silver. Tomas raised his cap and inched forward, hoping the Rabbi would see him.

Behind Modena walked a group of old Jewish men, coarse black robes dragging on the cobblestones, scraggly white hair and beards untrimmed in accordance with Castilian law, faces grim against the terror around them.

"Filthy Jews!"

"Look at the silver. Stolen from Christians!"

A large melon exploded on the ground before the Rabbi's feet, splattering his robe. He continued without breaking stride. More rotten fruit and garbage followed, some of it hitting the men full on. They kept walking.

A man next to Tomas drew back a hand holding a large rock.

"No!" shouted Tomas, grabbing his arm and shaking the rock loose.

The man turned angrily toward him and Tomas tensed for a fight. But a line of mounted men in full armor appeared, trotting rapidly from the direction of the *Alcazar*, and the man backed off. The horsemen arranged themselves along both sides of the narrow street, sealing it off from the sullen crowd. Rabbi Modena and his congregation walked serenely between the horses. Tomas slipped away.

Modena led his procession into the square, around the fountain, past the Moorish tower, and toward the gate in the *Alcazar* wall. The horsemen spread out, blocking the crowds on the adjoining streets. The gate was open, the blue and white lion above its portals framing the series of courtyards beyond. The Jews passed through the first courtyard, under the ancient Roman arch, and into a second large space fronting the palace of Pedro the Cruel.

The heavy doors opened and Don Alonso emerged, followed by a small army of officials, witnesses, auditors and secretaries, Gabriel Catalan among them. It was his first official duty as tax collector.

Gabriel stood behind Don Alonso, ashamed to participate in the contemptible charade. But when he saw Rabbi Modena walking with thrilling dignity, Gabriel stood taller, ready to play his part. He even smiled inwardly at the irony of the moment. 'Let them do what they will,' he thought, 'they'll never destroy the Jewish spirit.'

Don Alonso adjusted his robes and solemnly read.

In the thirty-third year of our Lord, Jesus made ready to come to Jerusalem to observe the feast of the Passover. And he said to his disciples, 'You know that after two days the Passover will be here; and the Son of Man will be delivered up to be crucified.'

Gabriel was stunned by the explicit reference to Jesus' celebration of Passover. This was never mentioned in Church.

He entered the temple and a scribe of the Jews came to him and asked, Rabbi, which is the first commandment? And Jesus answered, The first commandment is "Hear, O Israel, the Lord our God is one God."

Gabriel caught his breath. Hear, O Israel, *Shema Yisroel*, spoken by Jesus in the Christian Bible! One God! He wondered if Don Alonso had added to the prescribed readings.

And Judas Iscariot, one of the Twelve, went to the chief priests to betray Jesus to them. And they were pleased, and gave him thirty pieces of silver. And when evening arrived, and they were at the Passover table together, Jesus said, 'One of you will betray me.'

"Rabbi David Modena, Chief Rabbi of Seville," said Don Alonso, "are you prepared to atone for the crime of Judas Iscariot?"

"I have the required payment," said the Rabbi, but he had a frantic look on his face that Gabriel did not understand.

"Then give it to me now," said Don Alonso quickly.

Modena did not give the payment to Don Alonso. Instead, he tilted the Torah from his shoulder and held it toward Don Alonso. There was an awkward pause, and nobody moved. Gabriel was as confused as Don Alonso seemed to be. What was Modena doing? Why didn't he present the payment?

Modena looked at Gabriel in silent despair. What was he trying to say? Then Gabriel saw the small leather pouch hanging from one of the Torah staves, and he understood. Modena did not want to touch the money on the Holy Day. Gabriel stepped forward and lifted the pouch from the Torah.

He carried it to a nearby table where three officials were seated, the chief of whom was the royal Treasurer of Seville. The Treasurer emptied the contents of the pouch into one of two golden trays. He counted the small silver coins, ceremoniously placing one after another into the second tray. When he reached thirty, the first tray was empty. Gabriel walked back to Don Alonso.

"The payment is in order."

Gabriel had never seen so much female flesh. Breasts exposed, dresses open to beneath their navels, legs painted suggestively well onto their thighs, Queen Juana's maidens paraded in the grand hall of the king's palace in Segovia, weaving in and out among the thirty four golden statues of the kings of Castile. They spread their legs on the knees of the seated monarchs of old and suggestively caressed their golden scepters. Courtiers and younger knights fondled the women in a continuous orgy of sexual play. Older men stood to one side, pretending to be horrified but missing nothing. There were no Spanish women in attendance. They would have nothing to do with Juana's "Portuguese nymphs."

The chaotic atmosphere was amplified by a constant din from the hammers of an army of workmen rushing to complete the huge oblong tower which guarded the southern end of the *alcazar*. Sweating masons walked incongruously among the naked flesh and foaming courtiers.

Gabriel and Don Alonso, with Tomas, had journeyed to Segovia to discuss with King Enrique the financing needed for the spring campaign against the Moors. Don Alonso was away at the king's nearby retreat arranging the details of their meeting, and Gabriel and Tomas stood wide-eyed at the never-ending display.

Gabriel spoke quietly to Tomas. "No Queen has ever behaved like this and no King before Enrique would have allowed it. It's a disgrace to Castile."

"Is it because the King prefers boys?" Tomas laughed.

"Even if he does, he should have some pride!"

"They're saying that the Queen has taken up with Beltran de la Cueva, and that Beltran has also seduced the King," said Tomas.

"Where do you hear such things?" Gabriel gulped.

"Everyone is talking." Tomas tilted his head, ready to repeat more lurid details. Gabriel, however, spotted Don Alonso coming toward them, and grabbed Tomas' arm.

"Here's Don Alonso," he said. "Maybe now we can do our business and leave this awful place."

"The King is busy today," Don Alonso said as he approached. "No one knows with what. He's certainly not at court."

"When can we see him?" asked Gabriel.

"I don't know. Maybe tomorrow. But now we'll see his Treasurer, Don Diego de Arias. Tomas, unfortunately this is a private meeting."

"Stay away from those whores!" Gabriel said as they walked away.

Tomas moved to the side of the large room, near the statue of El Cid, the legendary hero of the *Reconquesta*, then walked up the stairs to a portico which surrounded the main room. He chose a spot where he could watch quietly.

Just then the hammering ceased, replaced by the airy sound of a dozen lutes and an equal number of tambours forming a line at one end of the room. Silence. The erotic notes of a single flute. Queen Juana writhed slowly into view. Tomas' mouth dropped open. The queen's diaphanous gown revealed every curve in her voluptuous body. Tomas was shocked to see that she wore nothing under the thin pure white gown. Planting her feet, the queen bent her upper body backwards, thrust her pelvis forward, so that her dark pubic hair was visible to every eye. She stood stock still and the room was silent. The tambours resumed and grew in speed and volume until the pulsing beat assaulted every ear. The "nymphs" swayed around their still rigid queen, inviting, tempting, teasing, until she finally joined in their frenzied dance.

Tomas was transfixed by the swirling breasts and thighs. But as he glanced away for a second to catch his breath, a pretty girl on the far side of the portico caught his eye. She looked to be a year or two younger than he, and she was wearing a dark well-cut gown with a modest neckline that contrasted sharply with every other woman in the room. She was partially hidden behind a large pillar, glaring furiously at the sexual carnival between her and Tomas. Their eyes met and she held his gaze. When she looked away, Tomas walked around the edge of the portico to join her.

"You disapprove?" he asked, before she had seen him next to her.

She seemed surprised that he had spoken to her, but after a brief pause, she answered, "Yes. I disapprove. This is a disgrace to my country."

"Then why are you here?"

"For weeks, my maids have been telling me about these horrible things. I couldn't believe their stories, so I came to see for myself. It's worse than they said."

"I apologize for not introducing myself before speaking," said Tomas, removing his cap and bowing. "I am Tomas Catalan from Seville. I'm here with my father and Don Alonso de Viterbo, who have come to meet with the King."

"Welcome to Segovia, young Señor Catalan," the girl said with a glorious smile. "My name is Isabel, and it's my half-brother your father is here to see."

Tomas was aghast that he had approached Princess Isabel. He had no idea what to say next. Should he kneel? But Isabel turned to leave and his first royal audience was over. The Princess looked back and smiled again.

"You seem like a nice boy," she said. "Don't let our court change you."

With Don Alonso otherwise occupied, Gabriel and Tomas wandered through the twisted streets and hidden plazas of Segovia, inspected the enormous but damaged Roman aqueduct, and admired the views of the superb *alcazar*, constructed turret by turret by a long succession of Castilian kings.

Finally, after an interminable week, the time for the audience with Enrique arrived. Gabriel waited nervously next to Don Alonso. It was the closest he had ever been to Enrique, and the king was even more disgusting than Gabriel had imagined. His jerkin, a *quezote* in the Moorish style, was ripped, its velvet trim tattered and stained. He wore neither robe nor crown, and his brownish yellow hair was filthy and knotted.

Enrique sat awkwardly on the edge of his throne, one leg thrown over the other. His glance flitted unceasingly around the room, but made no contact with anyone. His long arms never stopped stretching, reaching, folding.

To Enrique's left stood his *converso* Treasurer, Don Diego de Arias, by now a familiar presence. To his right was a tall pale Dominican, straight as a ramrod, stiff and scowling. Gabriel was reminded of Friar Perez.

"Presenting Don Alonso de Viterbo, *Almoxarife* for the province of Andalusia, and Don Gabriel Catalan."

Gabriel started at the unexpected reference to himself as 'Don.' The room hushed as they walked slowly toward the king. Enrique raised his hand for them to stop, and turned to Don Diego.

"Why are there two? I expected only Don Alonso," the King asked in a high voice that surprised Gabriel. He saw derisory smiles on the faces behind the King, except for the expressionless monk.

"Don Alonso wants you to meet his new assistant," said Don Diego.

Enrique's large head bobbed its assent, and Don Diego motioned for Don Alonso and Gabriel to come closer. As they came near and knelt, the smell of the king's unwashed body was overwhelming. Enrique waved his hand in an unclear manner, but Gabriel saw Don Alonso rise, so he did the same.

"Your highness," said Don Alonso, "may I present Don Gabriel Catalan, who has already rendered great service to your majesty."

The King's brow furrowed. He did not speak for several minutes, then said, "Catalan. I've heard that name before."

Don Alonso answered. "When your majesty was last in Seville, Don Gabriel's son Tomas saved the life of the young son of Prince Hasan. You sent food and drink to express your thanks."

"And, Don Gabriel" said Enrique, "will you now provide the funds to destroy this same Prince Hasan?"

"Alliances change, your majesty," Gabriel answered. "I serve Your Highness and support your policies."

"Well spoken," said the King, displaying his thick teeth in an ugly smile. "It appears that you have chosen wisely, Don Alonso."

Tomas watched from a balcony, peering between huge golden pineapples which Enrique had inexplicably hung from every conceivable spot on the ceiling. He was amused by his father's clothes, new for the occasion, although he knew they were elegant and completely fashionable. Gabriel carried a black velvet cap lined with gold braid. He wore a sleeveless jerkin, known as a *sayo*, held tight at the waist, with a pleated skirt reaching to his knees. The billowing sleeves of his silk doublet, tied at the wrist and above the elbow, made Tomas laugh. Thank God he didn't make me wear anything like that! But he did like the bold crimson and black stripes. And the heavy gold chain, of Gabriel's own making, which hung around his neck.

Don Alonso and his father knelt again, then rose and backed away from the King. Tomas turned quickly, and bumped into Princess Isabel, almost knocking her down.

"I'm sorry, your Highness," he blurted as he caught her, embarrassed that his hand had touched her hip.

"It's not your fault," Isabel said, "I came up behind you. I've learned to move quietly in this palace." She smiled. "That way I can see more than they want me to."

"A Princess can't come and go as she pleases?"

"You have much to learn about my brother's court. Others may watch the King's audiences, but the Princess is forbidden."

"Well, I'm glad you came," said Tomas.

"So am I," said Isabel, looking down shyly.

There was an awkward pause, and then Isabel spoke, "So you were the one who saved Muhammad. I was there, in the procession. Everyone was talking about your bravery."

Tomas looked down, blushing.

"I know Muhammad," the Princess continued, "He was at Aravelo with his father. He's a terribly spoiled little boy. But I like Prince Hasan. I count him as my friend."

"So do I," said Tomas. He wanted to tell the story of the rescue on the way to Arcos, but thought better of it. "I'm sorry to hear that King Enrique is planning to destroy him."

"It has nothing to do with Prince Hasan personally. It's the sacred Christian destiny to reconquer all of Spain from the Moors. Of course, it's been over two hundred years since Seville and Cordoba were retaken, and not another *hectare* since. But don't worry about our friend. Enrique has no heart to make this war. Prince Hasan is quite safe, at least for the moment."

Suddenly, a frightened look spread over Isabel's face and she abruptly stopped speaking. She was looking over his shoulder. He turned, and not two feet from him stood the Dominican monk who had been next to Enrique. Tomas saw furious unsmiling eyes boring at him and he understood Isabel's distress.

"Come," the monk said, far more brusquely than Tomas thought anyone should speak to a Princess. But Isabel stood her ground.

Speaking to Tomas, she said, "May I introduce my confessor and sometime nurse maid. Tomas Catalan, this is Friar Tomas Torquemada. I will follow you, Friar, when my conversation is concluded."

Bursting with questions, Gabriel followed Don Alonso away from the King. When had he become 'Don' Gabriel? Why hadn't they talked about the taxes? Would there be another meeting?

A priest waited outside the entrance to the throne room. He addressed Don Alonso in a quiet voice.

"Follow me, please," he said. "The Archbishop wishes to speak with you."

"Fonseca?" Gabriel asked. "Is Fonseca here?"

"No," said Don Alonso. "Carrillo. The warrior priest, Archbishop of Toledo, hero of the battle of Olmedo."

The Cathedral at Segovia was across the drawbridge from the main gate of the *Alcazar*, and they were soon within its dark walls. They were led into a receiving room of much greater opulence and surely better taste than the one they had just left. A vaulted ceiling was decorated with frescoes depicting the life and passion of Christ. Dark wooden panels were broken by elaborate candelabras holding hundreds of blazing candles.

Archbishop Carrillo was resplendent as he came across the room to greet them. He had removed his mitre, but his brocaded cape was opulently lined in fur. He dismissed the messenger with an arrogant flick of his hand, and spoke to Don Alonso as if Gabriel was not there.

"He's gone too far. He raises money to fight the Moors and he gives it to his *creatures*." The Archbishop shuddered. "Unknowns! Persons of no standing and no character. Scum from the bottom of the barrel. Drunkards, bullfighters, pimps, unlettered louts. This is who he raises to positions of wealth and power!"

It was the first time Gabriel had seen the famous Carrillo and he was stunned by the Archbishop's angry talk in front of a stranger.

"Juan de Valenzuela, who paints his lips and eyes and goes in public dressed like a women becomes the Prior of San Juan! And that whore Catalina de Sandoral is made the Abbess of San Pedro de las Duenas! *My* nominations are ignored. King Juan never treated me like this!"

The Archbishop held up a scrolled document.

"We have written our demands," he said, and Gabriel heard a slight gasp from Don Alonso. It was one thing to speak sedition, but it was quite another to put things in writing. And who was 'we'?

Archbishop Carrillo unrolled the parchment and read aloud.

"Enrique IV is required to amend his life, to end his debaucheries and those of his Queen, and to comport himself in a manner befitting his station. There must be decency and decorum at the court. Further, he must rid himself of his Moorish guard."

Carrillo looked up and added, not from the document, "We must fight the Moors, not play with them!"

He resumed his reading. "There must be notable men in his Council ..."

"Those suggested by your Excellency, no doubt," interrupted Don Alonso. "Who joins you in these demands?"

Carrillo was not pleased by Don Alonso's manner. He struggled to answer in a controlled voice. "Santillo, chief of the Mendozas. The Count of Plascenia, head of the Stuniga family. The Admiral ..."

"What a mistake to allow him to return to Castile," said Don Alonso.

Gabriel inhaled sharply. It was widely known that Carrillo had been the one who insisted upon the Admiral's return.

"Enough of your sarcasm, Don Alonso," the Archbishop said. "Will you join us? We're going to present these demands to Enrique within the week."

"I'll have nothing to do with this treachery," said Don Alonso, and Gabriel was proud of his friend's forthright response.

"You're making a mistake," said Carrillo. "There are many Old Christians among us who hate *conversos*. Perhaps they would resent you less if you aided our cause."

"I will not join you," Don Alonso said adamantly.

"Do you think Enrique is such a wonderful ruler?"

"I'm aware of his deficiencies."

"Then why do you support him?"

"Because there's no better alternative."

"Prince Alfonso ..." Carrillo began

"... is a weak child," Don Alonso finished.

"He can be guided."

"That's what I fear."

Don Alonso paused, seeming to consider whether to say what he was thinking, and then added, "But his sister. If it were Isabel you were promoting ..."

"No woman will ever rule Castile!" Carrillo snorted, ending the interview.

It didn't take Friar Perez long to discover that the kingdom of Aragon was very different from the southern provinces of Castile. King Juan was incomparably stronger than Enrique and the nobles were weaker. Daily life was not armed chaos.

Then he found the library.

It far exceeded the Dominican resources in Seville, or even the library at Salamanca, and it transformed his exile into an obsession of study. He spent every daylight hour within its cool stone walls, scouring the heavy wooden shelves and cabinets. Thousands of manuscripts contained secular as well as religious works. The monastery of Hijar had become the official repository of the kings of Aragon, and copies of laws, proclamations, and letters of kings had been mixed in glorious confusion in the two hundred years since the library was established by King James. The texts were in Greek, Latin, Arabic, and even Hebrew.

Every anti-Jewish document ever written by or for the Church was now at Perez' fingertips: Chrysostom, Tertullian, Maximinis, Justin Martyr, Augustine. He indulged himself in an orgy of reading which fed his fury against the Jews, and his anxiety about their threat to the Church. His anger over *converso* heresies intensified, and in a burst of inspiration, he realized that he could more easily destroy men like Don Alonso and Gabriel Catalan by first attacking the Jews who were their brothers.

No one read these old church writings anymore, dull masses of virtually impenetrable Greek and Latin. But if certain phrases were extracted, and presented in clear forceful language that common people could understand, their hatred could be focused. This was what St. Vincent Ferrer had done many years before, and he would do it better.

Perez began to copy.

"This *Haggadah* is my most precious manuscript," said Rabbi Modena. "The Barcelona rabbis made a magnificent book. They even included some of Rabbi Shlomo's commentaries on the book of Exodus that I have never read anywhere else. The art is priceless."

"Maybe I shouldn't take it to Arcos," said Tomas. "It might get damaged."

"No. It's too valuable to leave here. You take it, print your copies, then hide it."

Tomas turned the pages of the old Haggadah as the Rabbi joyfully explained the stages of the Passover service and showed how the story of the Exodus was portrayed in many small paintings interspersed with the text.

"I want you to make me a promise," said Modena, suddenly serious.

"Of course. What?"

"It's the obligation of every Jewish father to tell his children how God brought us out of Egypt. In your family, the chain was broken. Isaac couldn't tell your father, and Gabriel couldn't tell you. I want you to re-establish that chain."

"If I ever have children, I promise I'll read these words to them."

"May it be God's will."

Pilar Catalan watched with growing apprehension the increased scope of her husband's activities under Don Alonso's tutelage. Gabriel diligently studied tax records, organized an army of collectors, and personally carried out all the tasks of tax farming in and near Seville. He was preparing to take responsibility for tax farming throughout the entire Andalusia province.

On this night, however, she was more concerned about her son. Tomas would soon return to Arcos to resume the printing, and there were things he must know before he went. She stood before the huge fireplace, turning a spit that held several choice pieces of meat, pausing from time to time to keep the fire hot with a hand bellows propped nearby, wondering how to raise the topics she wanted to discuss with Tomas.

"The lamb smells great!" Tomas called, approaching the kitchen.

"Did you close the shop?" Pilar asked.

"Yes."

Pilar looked at her son, opened her lips to speak, and stopped.

"Is something wrong?" he asked.

"No. I'm just looking at you, how you've filled out, gotten taller." She didn't add how handsome she thought he was, and how his eyes sparkled with a zest for life. "I'll miss you when you go to Arcos."

Tomas took his mother's hand. "It's only three days ride. I'll come home to visit."

"You must be looking forward to seeing Esther."

"I can't wait."

Pilar had spent many sleepless nights debating with herself whether to tell Tomas the truth about Judah Ardit. Part of her felt that it should be Esther's decision what to tell him, and when. But what if he didn't know, and Esther surprised him with the information, and he reacted badly? Pilar wanted their relationship to grow, and thought it would be better if Tomas was prepared for what had to be disturbing news.

"She's a good girl," Pilar said. "Have you thought about the problems because she's Jewish?"

"What do you mean?" Tomas asked.

"You can never marry Esther as long as she's a Jew. She would have to be baptized. She would have to leave her family, perhaps never see them again."

Pilar waited for this to sink in.

"It doesn't mean that it can't be done. Only that the price is very high. Esther understands, and so must you."

"How do you know that Esther understands? Did you talk with her? We've never spoken of such things."

"I spoke with Señora Ardit, and I believe that Miriam would support her daughter in this. It might be different with Señor Ardit. Of course, we're getting ahead of ourselves. First, it's up to you and Esther."

"I think we have a long way to go."

"Yes, but I want you to know the path ahead of you."

"Thank you, mother."

"Will you turn the meat for a moment," Pilar asked, reaching to ladle dark sauce from a pot standing on the hearth. As Tomas rotated the spit, she dripped the sauce over the roasting lamb, and they shared the familiar spicy aroma and the memories it evoked. But finally, knowing that Gabriel would be home soon, she could wait no longer.

"There's something else I want to tell you," she said.

"Yes."

"I don't know how to say it. It's difficult."

Tomas gazed directly at her, eyes sad and intent. "Do you mean about the baby?"

"You know?" she exclaimed. "How do you know? Did Esther tell you?"

"She didn't say anything. But it's the only thing that makes sense. That's why they didn't want us to come to Arcos. Besides, Esther looked different ..." Tomas fumbled with his hands and looked down.

"Her breasts?" said Pilar.

"Yes," Tomas answered, blushing furiously.

"And the baby doesn't matter to you?"

"It means that she needs me even more," he said in a determined voice.

"I'm so proud of you," Pilar said, reaching out to hug her son. "You didn't tell her that you know?"

"She'll tell me when she's ready."

14

Tomas threw back the shutters and the dark room blazed with light. Gradually his eyes adjusted.

"Everything seems to be as we left it," he said.

"I came by every day," Esther said. "No one else was ever here."

Tomas was pleased that Esther had watched over the shop. He smiled his thanks and received a dazzling look in return. A flush came to Esther's cheeks, and Tomas suspected to his own as well.

"We have a great deal to do," he said.

"I'm going to help you. Father and mother have agreed. The printing will be my occupation."

"I couldn't have a better partner," said Tomas, causing another blush.

"Look what I've brought," he said, removing the *Haggadah* from his pack. "Rabbi Modena said it's very valuable."

"It's beautiful!" Esther said as she looked through it. "We have a *Haggadah* but it's nothing like this."

"Will you read it to me? Teach me the Hebrew words?"

"I'd like that. Are we going to print it?"

"One hundred copies!" said Tomas.

"Do we have enough paper?"

"We don't have enough of anything. My father'll bring more supplies. We'll do as much as we can until he gets here."

They puttered around the shop, touching the press, the trays of type, the tools. It had been exciting when they printed the *Shema*, and Tomas hoped it would soon be like that again.

He was thinking about making new type when he raised his head and saw Esther silhouetted against the open window. His erection was immediate.

He turned away to hide himself. 'How can I think of such things?' A vision of Talavero, poised over her, ready to plunge, flashed through his mind. He was sure she would be revolted by his crude desires. Even so, his eyes strayed back to her.

Desperate to force his mind in different directions, he remembered his trip to Segovia.

"I met Princess Isabel," he said.

"Oh? Where?"

"In Segovia."

"What's she like?"

"She's nice, but not very happy. The King keeps her under very tight control. And she has a confessor, a monk named Torquemada, who looks quite fierce."

"Is she pretty?"

"In a way."

The town of Montoro appeared on the horizon, and Gabriel Catalan, *almoxarife* of Andalusia, on his first trip through his new territory, felt fear. Every stop had brought problems and difficulties. Life was infinitely simpler as a goldsmith. Even the printing now seemed relatively straightforward. 'Why did I ever let Don Alonso convince me to do this?'

He knew the answers well, having discussed them endlessly with Pilar. The travel enabled him to assemble supplies for the printing and bring them to Arcos. It was a perfect cover, and his wagons already bulged with the fruits of his endeavors. Then there was his growing relationship with the King and his advisors. By achieving stature and influence, Gabriel hoped he could affect policies, especially those concerning Jews and *conversos*. The proof and value of that lay in the future, if at all. He would also get rich, and that would happen immediately.

Of course, he might not live to enjoy his new wealth. He took an armed guard with him everywhere he went, ten men on this trip, but attacks on tax collectors were more frequent than ever and he never felt secure.

He also missed Pilar. His greatest pleasure in life was simply to lie down with her at night and awaken with her in the morning. It had been six weeks. Soon. This town. Then a visit with Tomas in Arcos. Then home.

Chain mail bulky under their crimson cloaks, swords slapping against their horses flanks, Gabriel's small troop did not exude a friendly visage, and they received surly looks in return. The farmers knew that visits from the *almoxarife* never brought good tidings. Soon they would learn the price for their evasion of the king's taxes.

There was no wall around Montoro. It was too far from the Moorish border to allow raiding parties easy access, and had too few resources to justify a powerful defense. Only the municipal building, repository of the records Gabriel needed, was well fortified.

"Why should we pay so much, when the people of Baeza pay almost nothing."

"What does the King do with this money? He doesn't fight the Moors. He gives it to those disgusting friends of his."

These and many similar objections beat constantly against Gabriel's resolve as he conducted hearings in Montoro's municipal palace. It was clear that there had been pervasive cheating to avoid taxes. But he had to admit, to himself at least, that if some other towns, including Baeza, had not been favored unfairly by the king, and if the purpose of the tax levy was more popular, compliance might have been greater. Later, he would discuss this with Don Alonso, and maybe even with Enrique. Meanwhile, he had his job to do.

"You will bring to this palace, and pay to the treasurer, within three days, the amount of one thousand *maravedis*," he proclaimed to one unhappy farmer.

"Should you fail to do so, you will be arrested and taken to Seville to face trial. Furthermore, in that event, the allocation for the entire town of Montoro will be raised by one quarter as a result of your obstinance."

Gabriel directed town officials to post a notice of this decree, so that public pressure would be brought to bear on the unfortunate farmer. There were many such notices already posted.

He was tired, and the process was repetitive. Gabriel decided to spend some time among the people, taking further measure of their discontent, before he proceeded. "Hearings are suspended for today and tomorrow," he announced.

Besides, Andujar was but two hours' ride, and Friar Perez' family farm was near that town. He remembered vividly the *Yom Kippur* day when he had asked Perez about his family and was sure there was something Perez did not want him to know.

Andujar was identical to a hundred other dusty enclaves that served the communal needs of surrounding farmers. Gabriel and his armed entourage approached from the north, through fields of grain and occasional groves of olive trees. They saw a church steeple with scaffolding surrounding the tower. A rundown castle. An abandoned monastery.

They approached the town itself, horses stepping carefully as the ruts deepened. Two inns competed on opposite sides of the road, the smell of stale wine and cooking meat announcing their presence. Four old men played cards in front of one, and a servant girl wearing a low cut blouse looked up hopefully as they passed. The square was a welter of wooden wheeled carts, farmers, pigs, and chickens. Sounds of the blacksmith and the smell of fresh bread and human waste permeated the air. Beside the church stood the small stone house of the local priest and a fenced in garden. Next was the dilapidated structure that housed the municipal records.

Any direct approach to the information he sought would probably not succeed, and it might be dangerous. But the king's *almoxarife* had other options.

"We've paid all of our taxes, Don Gabriel. Why have you come to Andujar?"

"I want to know the details of your compliance, so I can cite this town as an example to others."

Books were piled high on an oak table. Gabriel was careful to look first at pages in which he had no interest at all. Eventually, he was left alone.

There was nothing in the current generation of the Perez family to explain their youngest son's apparent embarrassment. Maybe it was my imagination, Gabriel thought. Taxes had been paid. Marriages, births and deaths were duly recorded.

The generation before that, however, yielded an intriguing clue. He didn't catch it at first, but when it hit him, the omission was glaring. He closed the book.

"Where's the synagogue?" he asked. "I'll see if the Jews have paid their taxes as faithfully as the Christians."

It took less than fifteen minutes. Gabriel had only to mention the name to the old rabbi, who went to a dusty volume with a cracked leather binding. The ink was faded, but the rabbi read in a firm clear voice. His eyes crinkled when he reached the relevant name, and Gabriel knew that no one would ever be told about the question he had asked.

"Rebecca de Barrientos, daughter of Abraham de Barrientos, married Cristobal Perez on May 15, 1399."

Perez' grandmother was a Jewess!

Gabriel glared at the ruined paper. Weeks of difficult and dangerous work had been wasted. He had found suppliers, carefully inventing plausible stories. He had carried the heavy weight from town to town. Now over half of it was wet and rotted.

"We need a better way," he said to Tomas. "Let's unpack the rest, and see what else has happened."

They worked silently, carrying packages from the wagons to the print shop. There were no other disasters. Ink, lead, and tools were fine.

As Gabriel worked, he saw piles of printed pages arrayed around the room. When they had unloaded everything, he waited for Tomas to show him the results of his labors.

"We did four pages," Tomas said. "One hundred copies of each. Then we ran out of paper."

Gabriel studied the pages, his emotions surging, and then he opened his arms to hug his son.

"This is wonderful."

"We've improved," Tomas said. "Our first pages were a mess."

"Tell me. What did you change?"

Before Tomas could answer, Esther came into the shop, a new confidence complementing her astonishing beauty.

"Good morning, Señor Catalan. It's good to have you back," she said.

"How are you? And your family?"

"Everyone's fine. Mother's preparing for Passover."

"Father wants to know what we've learned," said Tomas. "Shall we tell him how bad we were when we started?"

"We made many mistakes," Esther laughed.

"It took a long time to get just the right amount of ink," said Tomas.

"But now he gets it perfect every time," said Esther. "Then we didn't let the paper dry long enough and the pages smeared. I'm afraid we wasted a lot of paper that way."

"You should see how quickly Esther sets the type. And she never makes a mistake," said Tomas.

Gabriel was charmed by the way Tomas and Esther praised each other. It reminded him of his relationship with Pilar. As they talked, Gabriel looked at the pages piled around the room. He calculated quickly. Fifty pages. Four pages per sheet. One hundred copies. Even these little Haggadahs would take more than a thousand sheets of paper.

Tomas followed his father's gaze, "What are we going to do with all this paper?"

"They'll have to be bound," said Gabriel. "Then stored. Somewhere safe from the weather and the Christians."

"I have an idea," said Tomas, bouncing excitedly on his toes. "The Moors make paper. Señor de Muya told me it was the Moors who first brought paper-making to Castile. They also bind books. Don Alonso was selling their books at the fair."

Gabriel smiled. It was brilliant. He let Tomas say it.

"We could ask Prince Hasan for help."

"What's *hametz*?" asked Tomas.

"Mostly it's bread, or any grain which has begun to rise into bread," Esther answered.

"And why are we going to burn bread?"

"The *Torah* says we must get rid of all the *hametz* before Passover."

"Why?"

"When God brought the Jews out of Egypt, they were in a hurry, and they didn't have time to let their bread rise. They took the un-leavened bread ... *matzah* ... and they left. By not eating *hametz* on Passover, we remember what God did for us. Now come, help me search."

Miriam had already gathered almost every speck of forbidden food, but she left two small pieces of bread for Tomas and Esther to find. They added these last morsels to the pile, and Yacov lit the fire. All this was done before midday, in strict accordance with the ancient *Torah* law. In case they had missed anything, Yacov repeated the formula of annulment: *May any hametz in my possession, which*

I have neither seen nor removed, be annulled and considered as the dust of the earth.

Tomas sat next to Esther, facing his father across a Seder table for the first time in their lives. His eyes and heart were filled with the sights and emotions of the Passover holiday. He had never felt more Jewish.

"What's that?" he whispered to Esther, pointing to a delicious-looking mixture, one of several unusual items on the large plate in the center of the table.

"It's called *haroset*. It's made with apples and chopped walnuts. It's to remind us of the material used to make bricks when our ancestors were slaves in Egypt."

"Do we eat it? Does it taste like bricks?"

Tomas had more questions, but it was time to begin. Yacov gave him a prayer cap, and Miriam, her face beaming, filled the cups with wine. Yacov rose and even Judah stopped squirming.

"This is a very special Seder. We welcome Gabriel and Tomas as our guests, and we're pleased that their first Seder can be with us. Also, instead of just one *Haggadah*, tonight we have this treasure that Tomas brought from Rabbi Modena. And we have something even more precious."

In front of Yacov was a pile of the printed pages. He took the top set and gave it to Gabriel.

"Our honored guest receives the first copy," he said. "The work of Tomas and Esther. Only a few pages now, but next year the whole Haggadah."

Tomas looked at his father, absorbed as he paged through the printed *Haggadah*. It was the first time he had seen him in a prayer cap. He looked handsome, and happy. Their eyes met and he felt Gabriel's pride in him. He was thrilled that he had so pleased his father.

"Now, Miriam, my dear wife, a *Haggadah* of your own." Yacov also gave printed sets to Tomas, Esther, and Ruyo. He put aside the Barcelona *Haggadah*, and took up the worn manuscript which had been in the Ardit family for generations.

"My grandfather read from this *Haggadah* at the first Seder I remember," Yacov said. He closed his eyes and quietly recited the blessing of the wine.

"Everyone lean to the left and drink the wine of freedom," Yacov said. Tomas didn't understand this instruction, but he imitated the others. Several other prayers followed in quick succession, and then Yacov raised a plate containing three pieces of matzah, and said: *This is the bread of affliction which our ancestors ate in Egypt. This year we observe the Passover here. Next year may we be in the Land of Israel.*

Yacov took a flagon of wine and refilled all of the glasses. This done, he looked at Judah in Miriam's arms. "Our youngest son," he said, "is not yet ready. Ruyo, will you stand in for your brother?"

As Ruyo rose, Tomas' excitement grew. His turn was next. This was his surprise. He listened carefully to Ruyo, grateful for one more chance to rehearse. When Ruyo finished, Yacov looked at the unsuspecting Gabriel.

"We have another youngest son and his father with us today. Tomas, you too should ask your father the four questions."

"But I can't answer them," said Gabriel, looking sadly at Yacov and then at Tomas.

"I'll answer," said Yacov. "Tomas, read from your new book."

Tomas smiled back at Esther's beaming face. He remembered his promise to Rabbi Modena, and hoped that one day his son - Esther's son - would ask him these same questions. He blushed furiously. Then he stood and his chant was pure and strong.

מה נשתנה הלילה הזה מכל הלילות

Why is this night different
from all other nights?

As Tomas sang the ancient questions, a tear trickled down Gabriel's cheek. When Tomas finished, never having faltered, the table erupted with congratulations.

"Esther taught me," Tomas told his father, blissfully proud.

"This night is truly different from all other nights. I'll never forget it," Gabriel said. "Thank you, Esther."

"Now we must answer," said Yacov. "God has commanded us to tell of the Exodus from Egypt, and our tradition is that the Holy One Himself comes to hear His children recite the story."

Tomas felt the presence of God so strongly in his heart that he almost expected to see Him at the table. Out of the corner of his eye, he saw Esther looking at him, and he prayed silently, "Thank you, God, for bringing this dear girl into my life. Please make me worthy."

Yacov read from the family *Haggadah: In every generation they rise up to destroy us, but the Holy One, blessed be He, saves us from their hand. We were slaves to Pharaoh in Egypt and the Lord our God brought us out from there with a strong hand and an outstretched arm.*

The others followed in their books until they reached the end of the printed *Haggadahs*, and then they listened as Yacov read how God asked Moses to tell Pharaoh to let the Jewish people go, and how Pharaoh said he would but then kept changing his mind.

Miriam gave Judah to Esther to hold, and she in turn gave the baby to Tomas. When he had first returned to Arcos, Tomas had been uncomfortable with Judah, but soon Tomas was captured and now he played with him regularly. Yacov continued: *These then are the ten plagues which the Holy One, blessed be He, brought upon the Egyptians in Egypt: Blood, Frogs, Lice, Wild beasts, Pestilence, Boils, Hail, Locusts, Darkness, Slaying of the first-born.*

As each plague was mentioned, Yacov poured several drops of wine from his cup. When they were done, he explained, "Even though the plagues were the work of God and for the benefit of the Jewish people, we cannot rejoice at the pain of our enemy. All men are God's creation, and we pour off a portion of our joy as we say each plague."

Yacov carefully and tenderly displayed the items on the Seder plate. "This shank bone of a lamb represents the sacrifice made by the Israelites on their last night in Egypt, when they smeared the blood of the lamb on their doorposts so the Angel of Death would pass over their homes and not smite their first-born. This bitter herb we eat to remind us how the Egyptians made our lives bitter with hard labor."

There was much more, and Tomas could see why a printed *Haggadah* would be needed so that Jews could remember all of the customs and prayers. Finally, they reached the time to eat.

"No matter how bad our times may be," said Yacov, "the Passover meal is eaten in a festive spirit, in appreciation for the kindness God has bestowed upon us."

"Rabbi Modena was right when he asked us to print *Haggadahs*," said Gabriel. "Passover is a holiday of hope. Our lives today are not worse than those of our ancestors in Egypt. The Jewish people survived then, and we'll survive now."

"With God's blessing," added Yacov.

After the meal, there were more prayers, and songs of freedom and joy, some written by the great poet and philosopher Solomon Ibn Gabirol, who had lived in Saragossa four hundred years before when Jewish life flourished under the Moors. Yacov discussed several fine points of the commentary on the Exodus by Rabbi Solomon ben Isaac of France, known as *Rashi*.

When it was finally time to leave, Esther accompanied Tomas and Gabriel outside and was speaking quietly with them when a woman came walking by.

"Hello, Esther," she said.

Tomas saw panic on Esther's face.

"Hello, Señora Sanchez," Esther said, and the woman walked on.

"Who was that?" Tomas asked.

"Just a friend," Esther said quickly.

15

These Jews are gathering choruses of effeminates and a great rubbish heap of harlots. Their synagogues are brothels and theaters, dens of robbers and lodgings for wild beasts. Jews know but one thing: to fill their bellies and be drunk. Their condition is no better than that of pigs or goats. Refusing to accept Christ, they have made themselves fit for slaughter.

Perez was repeatedly drawn to the writings of St. John Chrysostom, where he found the earliest expression of attitudes that had since become commonplace in the sermons and minds of Christians. Chrysostom had delivered eight homilies to his congregation in Antioch in the years 386 and 387, and these were the source of the countless diatribes against Jews that had been repeated in the rural churches of Perez' youth. *You did slay Christ. You did lift violent hands against the Master. You did spill his precious blood, thus forfeiting any chance for atonement, excuse, or defense. You read the sacred writings but reject their witness. This is why I hate the Jews.*

Perez grew most excited when Chrysostom linked the Jews to the devil. *The synagogue is a dwelling of demons, and the Jews who pray there are themselves demons. If the Jews are acting against God, must they not be serving demons? For they did sacrifice their sons and daughters to demons. Jewish mothers ate their own children and the hands of Jewish women boiled their own children. Their synagogues are fortresses of the devil, and the pit of all perdition. The devil is a murderer, and the Jew demons who serve him are murderers, too.*

Perez' fury rose as he imagined Satan's evil Jewish army arrayed against the shining truth and grace of Christ the Savior. He copied the words of Jesus according to the Gospel of John, condemning the Jews as devils. *And Jesus said unto them, If God were your Father, you would love me, for I come from God. Why do you not understand my speech? Even because you cannot hear my word. You are of your father the devil, and the lusts of your father you will do. ... He that is of God heareth God's words. You hear them not, because you are not of God.*

'You are not of God!' How could Jews claim that they were still God's Chosen People when they had been so clearly rejected by the Lord Jesus and sentenced to wander the earth as slaves to Christians?

"I understand you're from Castile."

The unexpected voice shattered his concentration. He shook his head in confusion and looked angrily to see who had disturbed the silence. But something in the young boy's appearance kept him from expressing the irritation he felt. The skirt on his military style *sayo*, hemmed in ermine, hung only to mid-thigh, revealing powerful legs in rich black hose. The brim of his rakishly slanted hat was turned up in front. The handle of an exquisitely filigreed sword rose from a scabbard hanging low on his left hip, and a jeweled purse decorated the right side. His wide set eyes were frank and quite serene. And he wasn't the least bit apologetic about the interruption.

"Most recently from Seville," Perez heard himself answer.

"Have you seen the Princess Isabel?"

"Yes."

"Is she beautiful?"

"I suppose so. Why do you ask? Who are you?"

"You don't know me?" the boy said with a smile that didn't quite offset the chill in his voice.

"No."

"My name is Fernando. My father is Juan, King of Aragon."

"I'm sorry, your Grace," said Perez, rising and bowing in the same motion.

Fernando peered at the book Perez was copying from, and picked up the latest page of the friar's notes. He read for awhile without comment and put the page back on the table. He started to walk away, but Perez asked, "Is it true that you will marry Isabel?"

"Arrangements may be made," Fernando said with a shrug.

"I feel sorry for you if you're depending on Enrique."

"What do you mean?"

"He never makes a decision. And even if he does, he'll change his mind the next day. Surely you know that Castile is in chaos."

"I've heard."

"We need a strong ruler to control the nobles and defeat the Moors."

"Would there be support for such a ruler?" asked Fernando, and Perez was astonished to see his entire aspect change. Raw power and ambition drove all vestiges of adolescent charm from his demeanor. The Friar sensed an opportunity.

"Yes. Castile would welcome such a leader. A strong king would unite the country and rid it of those who suck its life blood, starting with the Jews and lying *conversos* who pretend to believe in Christ."

"I thought the *conversos* were actually quite helpful to the crown," said the young prince.

"They're not worth the price," said Perez.

"And what is the price?" queried Fernando.

Perez waited before he answered. He stood rigidly straight, his face frozen in ecclesiastic certainty. "Every minute of their filthy lives is a denial of our Lord Jesus. They undermine our faith. And without the rock of faith, Castile can never be unified."

"Nor Spain," said Fernando quietly, a distant look in his eye.

After two months away from Seville, Gabriel held Pilar's hands and gloried in the sight of her. The love of a woman, he thought, is the closest any man can get to God. Perhaps it's God's way of teaching us how we may love Him.

"Tomas is well?" she asked for the third time.

"He's more than well. He's flourishing in Arcos. He and Esther are remarkable together. Tomas is so happy to be with her. I think they really love each other."

"Did Tomas say anything?" Pilar asked.

"He didn't have to. You just have to see them together. Even without touching, it's as if they were locked in a passionate embrace." He smiled knowingly at Pilar. "You know what I mean." Just as quickly, the smile faded. "But I hope they have enough strength to face what lies ahead."

"They will. Just consider their parents." Pilar took Gabriel's hand. "How's Miriam?"

"She's lonely. And the baby takes a lot of her energy. At her age, it's not easy to have a little one. But other than that, she seemed well."

"Gabriel ...," Pilar stopped.

"What?"

Pilar looked away. "Nothing," she finally said. "I was just thinking of Miriam and Judah." Facing him again, a forced smile on her face, she asked, "How's the printing?"

"It's breathtaking," Gabriel answered, wondering what had bothered Pilar. "We used the pages they printed. Tomas and I went to Seder with the Ardits. Tomas asked the four questions. Esther taught him."

"That must have been wonderful for both of you," Pilar said, with a touch of both jealousy and sarcasm.

"It was," he said. "But I wish you had been a part of it, too."

She looked at him without expression and didn't respond. Gabriel didn't know what else he could do to convince her to be more accepting of Judaism. Since the day they printed the *Shema,* she had not joined them in prayer again.. He was afraid that if she kept herself isolated it would sooner or later drive a terrible wedge between them.

"How was your trip?" she finally said. "How were you received?"

"Not well. The people hate Enrique and these new taxes. They wouldn't mind if Enrique actually fought the Moors, but they think he takes their money and wastes it. It's not easy to collect taxes for such a king."

"Is it dangerous?"

"I won't lie to you. Even with all my guards, I didn't feel safe. It's easier to attack the tax collector than the king."

"*Converso* tax collectors especially," Pilar added.

"The people think of me as a Jew. They make no distinction between Jews and *conversos.*"

"At least Perez isn't here," Pilar said.

"You just reminded me of something unbelievable."

"What?"

"When I was with Perez on Yom Kippur, he told me he was born in Andujar. I was close by, so I went. I thought he was hiding something from me when he didn't want to talk about his grandparents, and I found out why. His grandmother was a Jew!"

"Well, well, well. So the *converso*-fighter is really one of us."

"Maybe that's why he wants to destroy us. To prove what a good Christian he is."

"What are you going to do? Did you tell Don Alonso?"

"Yes, of course. We didn't decide. For now, nothing. Also, for now, we've talked long enough."

"And?"

Gabriel offered his hand, and they rose. He ran his hands tenderly from her shoulders to her waist, then cupped her hips. He pulled her against his own rising passion and they rocked together.

Memory rudely intruded ... the whore spread disgustingly before him ... the taste of retching filled his mouth. Go away! Sadly, he knew he would never be rid of that awful day when he had betrayed the woman he loved.

Never.

"Quick! Come watch! It's a race of life and death!"

A rush of people ran past the print shop windows. Esther closed the shutters.

"Why did you do that?" Tomas asked from the other side of the room. "I need the light."

"Don't you hear the crowd outside?"

"What's happening?"

Reluctantly, Tomas joined Esther and they followed the others toward the edge of the cliff. Tomas never went there, never even looked at it, although it was within sight of the shop. The memories of Rodrigo and that terrible afternoon over a year ago were still too painful.

They found a place where they could see without being jostled, and below them, far across the fields, they saw several farmers desperately running toward the safety of the town walls. They were being chased by Moors on horseback.

"It's the first time they've come this far," said a man standing near them.

"Where are Enrique's troops?"

"They don't fight. They just provoke the Moors, who then come and kill us."

It appeared that several of the farmers had indeed been killed. Some had reached the river and would soon be inside the walls. All attention was now focused on a race between three farmers and two Moors on horseback. The farmers initially had a long lead, but the horses gained rapidly.

Tomas wondered if Esther was thinking about the chase they had lost to Talavero and his men. She seemed intent on the events of this day.

The men on the plains were close enough to recognize.

"That's my husband," a woman screamed. "Pavito!"

The horsemen closed on the farmers. Swords were drawn and one of the farmers was struck. He remained motionless on the ground. The other two were quickly tied. Ropes were attached to their necks, and they were led in a sad procession toward the Moor's camp which could be seen on the far horizon.

"They're stealing my Pavito!"

"At least he's not dead."

"Maybe Prince Hasan will trade him for one of Enrique's prisoners."

"Enrique doesn't have any prisoners."

"Did you say Hasan?" Tomas asked. "Is Prince Hasan with those men?"

"I saw him yesterday. He rode an enormous black stallion. I was hiding in a gully when he rode past."

Tomas grabbed Esther's arm and led her back into the shop.

"Did you hear?" he said. "Hasan is out there. I can go to him. I'll ask him to help with the printing."

Esther was quiet, and Tomas sensed her fear.

"It'll be all right. Hasan wouldn't hurt me."

"No. Not him. But there are others, and they may kill you before they learn who you are. Or suppose that man was wrong and the Prince is not there? Then you'll be a prisoner just like the others. They'll take you away and I'll never see you again."

"I have to take the chance," Tomas said. "Father and I agreed that we need Hasan. You know what the shop looks like. There's no more room. We have no more paper. We can't do this without his help." He paused for a moment. "But there's another problem. The gates will be locked. How will I get out?"

Esther sighed. "I know a way," she said.

Stars filled the sky and the moon was bright in the southern sky. Fires from the Moors' camp could be seen across the plains. Mounted patrols slowly circled the cluster of white tents.

Esther led Tomas along the edge of the cliff, far beyond the point where they had stood that afternoon. When she stopped, the towers of the Duke's castle were barely visible behind them.

"The entrance is here," she said.

"I don't see anything," said Tomas.

"It's over the side. Follow me."

Esther dropped to her knees, and as a horrified Tomas watched, she slid her legs over the edge and disappeared.

"There are two steps here," he heard her say. "I'm on the lower one. When you come over, I'll guide your feet. Come slowly."

Tomas knelt down, his heart in his throat.

"Don't look. Just put one foot down. I'm right here."

He did as instructed. Esther grabbed his ankle and placed it on a solid platform.

"Now the other one," she said.

He stood facing the cliff side, pressed hard against it, his head still above the top. His fingers clawed the ground above. Behind him was nothing. He was terrified.

"Now slide to your right and step down with your right foot."

Her hand circled his calf and guided him.

"Now duck your head and step forward. Into the mountain."

He was in a small room, a cave large enough for several people.

"What is this? How did you find it?" he gasped.

He could barely see Esther's face in the faint moonlight, but he could see that she was struggling with her answer.

"It was that night," she said, and he had no need to ask which night she meant. 'That night' had never been mentioned between them.

"When we rode here with the Moors," she said in a halting voice, "I overheard them talking. Many years ago, Arcos was a Moorish town, which the Christians couldn't capture despite many attacks. But a beautiful Moorish princess came down to the river one night to bathe, and a Christian knight watched her go into the cliff and emerge at the top where we are now. Soon after, he led a group of soldiers into the town and the Christians took Arcos from the Moors."

Esther paused, gathering the strength to continue.

"I saw them point to the bottom of the cliff and then to the top. Later, I found the entrance at the bottom and came up."

"That night ... ," Tomas whispered, anguish in his voice.

"Not now," said Esther. "We'll talk. I want to. But not now."

She put her arms around his neck and buried her head in his chest.

He had thought every night of holding her like this, never daring to think when his dream might come true. He would never have touched her first. But now he stretched his arms and squeezed her close. She looked up at him, lips parted, and he kissed her. His head was ablaze. They stood pressed together, kissing until they could no longer breathe. He wanted to hold her forever.

"Oh Tomas, I love you so."

"I love you, too, Esther."

"But let's keep our wits about us now," she said. "We've got a long trip down."

At some points, the passage was open to the sky above; elsewhere it was completely covered. It could not be seen from the ground below. At the most difficult places, someone, perhaps many centuries ago, had placed large rocks for footholds.

They climbed down, holding hands, for perhaps twenty minutes. Their bodies touched, and they made no effort to avoid contact. Tomas remembered his embarrassment when he had been aroused just watching Esther in the shop. He was aroused now, but not embarrassed. He suspected that Esther felt the same way.

They reached the bottom.

Esther peeked out. "There's no one here."

They stepped onto the river bank at a desolate spot covered with wild brush, the cliff rising behind them and the broad plain in front. At this level, they could no longer see the tents of the Moors, only a faint light far off on the plain.

"I'm afraid," said Esther. "I don't want to lose you."

"I'll be back," Tomas said, hugging her.

He stepped into the shallow river. Looking back from the other side, he saw Esther wave and watched as she disappeared into the mountain.

Esther scrambled up the passage at breakneck speed, scraping her knees and elbows. She reached the top, climbed the narrow steps to the cliff, and looked out. But the moon had gone behind the clouds and she couldn't see.

The clouds broke, and there was Tomas striding toward the Moor's camp. She relaxed. Then several shadowy figures appeared behind him. They must have been hidden in a gully. She opened her mouth to scream but he was too far away. All she could do was watch in petrified silence, her lips moving in silent prayer. "Please, God, let him live."

Another Moor appeared in front of Tomas. It looked like they were talking. Those behind him crept in closer and then one rose and struck Tomas in the head. He crumpled to the ground and didn't move. Two men picked him up and carried him back toward the camp.

When Tomas woke, he was lying in a dark tent, tightly shackled and gagged. He could smell others near him. He rolled over and tried to speak, but his unintelligible moan was met with a sharp smack to his head.

In the gathering light of dawn, he saw others in the tent. Several prisoners, at least one seriously wounded, and two guards, huge men with daggers and swords at the ready. From the noise outside the tent, Tomas realized that the Moors were breaking camp. Where were they going? What were they going to do with him? Where was Hasan?

Esther returned to the cliff before dawn, after a sleepless night. She too saw the tents coming down.

She raced to the house of Isidro Lucero, convinced him to give her a donkey, and rushed to the town gate, which was still locked against the threat on the plains. She argued with the guard until he opened the small door.

She headed straight toward the rapidly disappearing camp of the Moors. A lone girl, riding slowly on a small donkey, carrying a white banner on a stick. Several riders came out to meet her. She could see them laughing as they approached.

"Prince Hasan," she said. "Take me to Prince Hasan."

"Who wants to see his Excellency?"

"A friend of Tomas Catalan, who saved the life of the Prince's son in Seville. The Prince will want to see me and he will deal harshly with you if you refuse my request."

"This little girl threatens us?" said one of the Moors.

"I was in Seville with the Prince," another voice said, "and I remember Tomas Catalan. I also remember that all of the men who were supposed to be guarding the Prince's son were beheaded. We'll take this girl to his Highness."

All of the tents were down by the time Esther was brought to the camp. She strained to see Tomas, but to no avail. Then she saw Hasan, wearing his helmet, horse at the ready. She had arrived just in time.

One of her escorts, the one who had made the decision to take her to Hasan, approached the Prince. She could see them talking, and then Hasan was walking toward her, looking irritated.

"What is your name?" he asked.

"Esther Ardit."

"Have we met?"

"Yes, your Highness," she said. "You gave me a blanket."

Her tension eased as Hasan's face softened. He remembered. "Why are you here?" he asked.

"Last night Tomas Catalan came to see you."

"No. He didn't come here."

"Your guards attacked him on the plain. I don't know if he's alive or dead."

Hasan whirled to the man behind him. "Where are the prisoners? Take me to them." And to Esther he said, "Please wait here."

Esther watched Hasan stride off but she lost sight of him among the throng of men and horses. Then she saw the crowd opening before the Prince as he returned. There was Tomas walking beside him.

She ran to Tomas and embraced him.

"Thank you, Prince Hasan," she said between her tears.

A horde of attendants re-established the prince's tent in a matter of minutes. Center pole adorned with pennant, large billowing vertically striped canvas held out and down by a hundred stakes, a dozen carpets, soft cushions, a brazier heating tea. Hasan had removed his helmet, but still wore chain-mail armor. He looked fierce, but his manner was gentle.

"You have a brave friend," said Hasan to Tomas, who had not let go of Esther's hand.

"Yes. A wonderful friend," he said.

Sweet cakes, honey and moist orange slices arrived, brought by servants who moved so quietly as to be almost invisible.

"Perhaps someday we'll meet in a normal manner," said Hasan.

"I hope so," said Tomas, laughing and shaking his head.

"Why did you take such a great risk?" Hasan asked. "You could have been killed."

"It will take a while to explain," Tomas said.

"Take all the time you need," said Hasan, laughing. "They won't leave without me."

"We've learned a new way to make books. It must be done in secret, and we need help. I came to ask your help."

"You risked your life for books?"

"There's more." Tomas hesitated, suddenly uncertain. This was even more dangerous than his adventure the night before. He was about to trust the prince with their most important and possibly deadly secrets. He hoped it was not a huge mistake.

"We're Jews," he said. "Secret Jews. The books we're making are the product of our culture here in Spain. We're trying to make copies before the Hebrew manuscripts are burned by the monks."

Hasan stared at Tomas, and then at Esther. Several minutes went by before he spoke.

"We are both people of the book," Hasan said, "children of the same God. Your patriarch Abraham is also the father of Ishmael and thus of all the Arab people. The culture you are trying to save was one that we developed together, Jews and Moors, for almost five hundred years before the Christians returned. They are our enemy as much as they are yours." He smiled. "Tell me what you need."

An hour later, the Prince's tent was once more taken down, and a strange procession prepared to leave the camp. Tomas and Esther, and two other prisoners were mounted on Arabian mares. Four Moors were with them, also mounted. One of the Moors held the reins to Esther's donkey.

Prince Hasan walked out to say goodbye.

"Please tell the citizens of Arcos that there will be no more raids on their fields. As long as Tomas Catalan and those dear to him live in Arcos, we will make no war on this city." Hasan smiled and added, "There are many other places where we can bother King Enrique."

Coming closer so that the others could not hear, Hasan spoke quietly to Tomas. "Bring your materials to my palace in Granada. I will arrange for binding and secure storage. I will also provide paper. Perhaps when you come you can teach our people how to make books."

Hasan walked to Esther's side. "Thank you, dear one, for the courage to come here. I would have been distraught beyond measure had Tomas been injured."

"And so would I," said Esther.

"When you come to the *Alhambra*, Tomas, please do not neglect to bring this wonderful young lady with you."

They attracted a crowd. Again, the cliffs were teeming with onlookers, and many more gathered at the gate.

Three hundred yards from the hill leading up to the gate, the escort of Moors stopped. Tomas took the reins of the donkey. The Moors turned with a flourish and galloped back to the main group, which by now was moving rapidly away from Arcos. Tomas, Esther, and the others continued toward the town.

The gate opened before them and the crowds cheered.

"Pavito. You've brought back my Pavito."

It was only then that Tomas realized that being a hero in Arcos meant the end of the anonymity he had so far enjoyed. It would make their work harder. But of course it would also make it possible.

Off to the side of the crowd stood Marguerita Sanchez. Next to her was Hernando Talavero, her lover, in Arcos on one of his increasingly frequent visits.

Marguerita watched Talavero closely as he stared at Tomas and Esther. He seemed surprised and angry. She had never told him what she knew about that night on the plains. Never a word about the baby boy she had delivered.

The look in his eyes sent chills through her. She was afraid and she didn't know what to do.

16

"You've done exceedingly well, Don Gabriel."

Gabriel luxuriated in the king's smile, although he was distracted, as always, by the huge teeth and bobbing head. Since it was obvious that Enrique was pleased with his tax collection results, he decided to advance the idea he and Don Alonso had carefully rehearsed.

"If your Highness permits," he began, "there's another matter I'd like to bring to your attention."

"Proceed," Enrique said, but concern and uncertainty returned to his face.

"With your leave, I'll speak honestly, reporting what I've seen and heard. Then I have a suggestion for your Highness to consider." Gabriel paused, received no sign of any kind from the king, and continued. "Many of your subjects are not pleased with the war against the Moors. And there are those who would use this dissent to cause problems for your Highness."

"This is your report, Don Gabriel? I've heard this many times before. What is your suggestion?"

"Accept an offer of truce and use the time to consolidate your position."

"There is no offer to accept."

"There could be."

"Go on."

"You may recall that my son saved the life of Prince Hasan's son."

"Yes. In Seville."

"The Prince is very grateful. He would receive us. Perhaps we could suggest to him that a proposal for peace would not fall on deaf ears."

King Enrique's face broke into a broad smile. His teeth were grotesque.

"If your plan doesn't work, I'll deny that this conversation ever took place."

"Of course, your Highness."

"What are the rules of *Shabbat*?" Tomas asked as soon as Esther arrived.

"There are many rules, it's true, but it's the joy of *Shabbat* that's most important. *Shabbat* is God's greatest gift to the Jewish people."

Esther had a gloriously peaceful look about her. She had just joined Tomas after praying in the small synagogue of Arcos, a place where Tomas, of course, could not go.

"You're filled with that joy right now," he said. "Tell me about it."

They sat near the edge of the cliff, not far from the entrance to the secret passage. Tomas had been thinking about Rodrigo and the great forces loose in Spain. It made him want to hurry to complete the *Haggadah*. There was so much more to print when that was done, but Esther had asked him not to work on the day of rest.

She spoke softly, but with fervor. "*Shabbat* is the time to be closest to God. We put aside our work, and we give thanks. We enjoy our family and the company of other Jews. We think about what God wants us to do."

Esther stopped, questioning by her expression whether Tomas wanted her to continue.

"Please go on," he said.

"It's a time of holiness," said Esther. "We're invited to share God's holiness. '*And God blessed the seventh day and made it holy.*' It's a special period of time created for us by God. In a way, we imitate God. We rest just like He did. It's a good time to think about Creation, and Eternity, to look around us and be conscious of God's miracles."

"You are God's miracle," said Tomas, touching her hair.

Esther blushed. "And you, dear Tomas. You, too."

"It's a commandment to rest?"

"Yes. '*Six days shalt thou labor and do all thy work; but the seventh day is Sabbath unto the Lord thy God.*' But once you do it, really do it, you look forward to the opportunity to obey because it brings so much pleasure. All week I look forward to sundown on Friday night."

"I would like to have that feeling," said Tomas, and he took Esther's hand, but he was troubled.

Esther leaned over to kiss his forehead. "It's a sin to be sad on the *Shabbat* day. What's bothering you?"

Tomas shook his head, his tongue unwilling to yield to his heart. Esther did not press him. He took both of her hands and cupped them together in his.

"I want you to know," he whispered. "About that night. It doesn't matter. I love you. And when the time comes, I'll love you in every way."

Tears rolled down Esther's cheeks, and Tomas held her to him as he gently dried her face with his fingers. Esther looked at him in a way he had long dreamed she would. She stepped back, still holding his hands.

"We have so much to be thankful for. Even the bad things have brought good with them."

She stopped abruptly, and Tomas knew she was referring to Judah. He waited, but she went no further.

"Let's say the afternoon prayers together," she said distractedly, "I'll help you."

"Prince Hasan has agreed to help us."

Gabriel had just returned to Arcos, and, after Tomas and Esther had said hello, these were Tomas' next words. Gabriel's mouth dropped.

"How ... ?"

"He was here, down on the plains. It was a raid. Esther showed me a secret way down the cliff and I went at night to see him."

"That was dangerous."

"Yes. In fact, I was captured, and the Prince didn't know it."

A fearful tightness spread through Gabriel's body as he envisioned Tomas killed or enslaved.

"Esther rode out the next morning and told the Prince. Then everything was fine."

"Esther rode out ... ?" Gabriel repeated, dumbfounded.

"She borrowed a donkey from Señor Lucero and rode out to the camp."

"This is unbelievable," Gabriel said, looking at Esther.

"Prince Hasan said he would bind our books and hide them for us. Also supply paper."

"You told them we were secret Jews?" Gabriel asked.

"He said he was pleased to help us against our common Christian enemy."

Gabriel's fear was replaced by pride in what his son had done, and he realized how perfectly Tomas' actions fit with his own plans.

"This is excellent," he said. "I too want to see Prince Hasan. I met with King Enrique and offered to try to arrange a truce in this useless war. I wanted you to come with me when I met with Hasan."

"I'm ready. We've printed all the pages for the hundred *Haggadahs*. They're folded into the eight page sections, set for binding."

"Good," said Gabriel. "We'll load the wagons today and leave for the *Alhambra* tomorrow."

"There's one more thing, father," said Tomas, and he had that look that Gabriel had come to recognize as the forerunner of something audacious.

"Oh?"

"Esther must come with us. The Prince insisted."

The small group of riders and wagons settled into its long distance pace, and the cliffs of Arcos disappeared behind them. Tomas and Esther, wrapped in their cloaks and riding close together, never stopped talking. Gabriel rode nearby, quietly, thinking about the enormous changes his life had absorbed since Don Alonso had summoned him to meet Johann Gutenberg. No longer just a simple goldsmith, he was now a printer and a royal tax farmer, on his way to wealth he had never imagined, and an ambassador of the king on a diplomatic mission. No longer a secret Jew living every day passively in fear, he was now actively committed to the dangerous task of preserving his endangered heritage.

And he had begun to fulfill his obligation as a Jewish parent to teach the words of God to his son. 'God, are you pleased with me?' he thought, looking up at the cloudless sky. 'And am I pleased with you? Was it part of Your plan that Francesco and Rodrigo should die, and Perez should live? What kind of a plan is that? Who else will yet die for this plan?' No answer. He lowered his eyes.

The sight of Tomas riding beside him made his heart swell with pride. His son, brave, impetuous, yet able to master a complex new trade and stay with it, day after day. They had printed more *Haggadahs* than had been hand-copied in Spain in the past fifty years. This same son, remarkably a friend of both Prince Hasan and Princess Isabel. And a friend of Esther Ardit.

Esther rode easily next to Tomas, face proudly forward, body straight in the saddle. 'What a force she is!' Gabriel thought. After all that's happened to her, she carried on, became a valuable partner. Gabriel smiled as he imagined her riding, by herself, to the camp of the Moors. And it was she who was teaching Tomas to read Hebrew and to pray as a Jew.

On the third day, a large troop of Moors appeared on the horizon, riding ferociously toward them. As instructed, Gabriel's advance riders fell back and allowed Gabriel, with Tomas and Esther, to take the lead.

At a quarter of a mile, the Moors slowed. Gabriel and Esther stopped and Tomas, unarmed, rode slowly forward. At one hundred yards, the Moors reined in. Their leader rode toward Tomas, threatening, his face a mask of fury.

"Who are you?" he called harshly.

"I am Tomas Catalan, and I come to see Prince Hasan."

A broad smile broke across the warrior's face. "The Prince is expecting you. We will be your escort."

Gabriel saw the *Alhambra* when they were still several miles away on the plains, and caught his breath in anticipation. At the top of a hill to the east of Granada, the golden red walls studded with towers reflected the soft light of the late afternoon sun. Behind the palace, off in the distance, rose the snow covered peaks of the Sierra Nevada. Tomas and Esther came up even with him, and they rode together in silent awe.

"It's very rare that any Christian visits the Moor's capital," Gabriel said, "but Jews are always welcome."

When they reached the city, they rode through narrow streets which reminded Gabriel of Seville. They rounded a sharp turn and started up a steep tree-lined road which led to the palace.

The quiet was broken by a cavalcade of riders charging furiously down at them. Gabriel was amazed that they could keep their saddles in such a headlong rush. Tomas, thrilled, punched his hand into the air and cheered. The riders, wearing striped tunics and chain mail helmets, held brightly colored leather shields and waved curved scimitars. They pulled up sharply just a few feet from certain collision, dirt and dust flying. Still as statues for a long moment, they parted crisply to form a path through which the visitors continued up the hill. The road ahead glistened with the armor of more mounted warriors.

Huge rectangular blocks of the severe outer walls of the fortress loomed thirty feet high on their right as they rode up the hill, enormous guardians of the treasures within. The main gate, a large horseshoe arch set in a square tower, was open. They passed within the walls to a large open space, lined with troops, where they dismounted and gave their horses to waiting hands. Facing them was a long building, the royal palace, a construction of perfect symmetry. A dozen delicate double columns connected by arches, topped with a massive wood lintel, supporting a slanted red tile roof. Still higher, a large portico centered in the roof, other levels set back, the snow covered peaks of the Sierra Nevada.

From the center arch, the palace door swung smoothly on hidden pivots, and Prince Hasan strode out, accompanied by his son Muhammad. Father and son were dressed in matching silk robes and turbans. The little boy ran toward Tomas, stopped suddenly, and made a formal bow. Then he gave a loud whoop and leaped into Tomas' arms. Tomas held him high as cheers resounded.

Gabriel followed the sound of the cheering and saw thousands of warriors assembled in every corner of the courtyard, on the thick walls, on the roofs of nearby buildings.

What a welcome! And what a message! Feeble Enrique could never conquer this!

"It is a pleasure to meet you, Don Gabriel Catalan," the Prince said. "Tomas and Esther have told me about the printing, and I am eager to help. Neither Moors nor Jews can ever feel comfortable with the Christians."

"We need your help. We can't do this alone."

They walked through a series of colonnaded terraces. Fountains bubbled, and small pools reflected the structures around them. Marble columns supported vaulted ceilings. Ornate designs in gilded stucco and brightly colored tiles in precise patterns adorned the walls. Large arches afforded sudden, breathtaking views of the city below or the mountains beyond. Flowers were everywhere.

"Tomas said you would like to learn about the printing," said Gabriel.

"Yes. Books are very important to us."

"We'll be happy to teach you. Do you have a skilled goldsmith to make type?"

"I'll send our finest to you," the Prince said.

They reached a long courtyard with marble benches set around a glimmering pool. The open sky was golden as the sun set behind a crenellated tower. Hasan led Gabriel to a grouping of pillows near a small fountain whose waters ran through a channel and spilled into the pool.

When they were comfortable, the prince snapped his finger and serving girls brought food and drink. Gabriel gulped at the naked legs and breasts. He remembered the whore in Seville and felt shame.

"Father," a voice interrupted, "this palace is amazing."

Tomas, with Esther and the Prince's son, was standing before him. "Muhammad has shown us everything," he said. "Gardens, pools, fountains, arches, domes. It's fantastic!"

Esther stared at the harem girls, mouth agape. Gabriel watched as Tomas followed her gaze. Their eyes met and they giggled.

"Let's go," said Muhammad, "I want to show you the lions."

Gabriel looked up, startled, and Hasan said, "Statues of lions."

Alone again, Gabriel broached the subject he had come to discuss.

"I have other business," he began. The Prince's eyebrows rose and Gabriel continued.

"I've traveled greatly, farming the king's taxes, and I've seen the effects of this war. No one seems to gain from it."

He paused, but Hasan remained silent, so he went on.

"Perhaps it is not different with you. Perhaps ..."

"Do you speak for yourself?" Hasan interjected softly.

"I've met with King Enrique."

"Do you speak for him?"

"I have reason to believe that certain proposals would be well received by his Excellency."

Hasan looked impressed and pleased. "I will discuss this with my father the king," he said.

Esther was given a place of honor among the wives and concubines of Prince Hasan. Draperies surrounded her, but there were gaps. She heard the low murmur of women speaking. She removed her own clothing and wrapped herself in a light wool gown which had been left for her. It was soft and luxurious next to her skin. She tied the neck with a delicate twisted cord of spun gold and sat on a pile of pillows, wondering what to do next. Then she realized it had become quiet. Whispers. Giggling. A face in the opening.

"My name is Zorayda. Will you join us?" It was a girl of about her own age, struggling to speak in Spanish.

"Yes, of course," said Esther. Through the draperies, she saw at least two dozen women looking at her.

"We're going to the baths," the girl said, and Esther knew she had made a mistake. But it was too late, and she followed.

They passed through a series of rooms, across an internal balcony, and down a short flight of marble stairs. Esther smelled the delicately perfumed water ahead of her. She saw the mist and felt the heat.

Several older women stood near the entrance. Esther wondered if they were posted there to keep the men away. She turned a corner and came into a large room with many alcoves. Rich wool carpets covered the marble floor. A high vaulted ceiling was punctured by dozens of star-shaped skylights. Steam rose from a pool of water and passed upward through the skylights into the night. Several naked women were immersed in the pool. Others, equally naked, sat or lay on nearby marble benches. Legs, buttocks and breasts were everywhere.

Esther's entrance caused a commotion. Everyone was speaking, but in a language Esther did not understand.

"Everyone is curious about you," said Zorayda. "Stories have been told about how you rode to the Prince's camp. You were very brave."

Esther smiled, but she wasn't sure what she should do or say.

Zorayda began to disrobe, and the other women seemed quite relaxed to be naked together. Esther was terrified.

"Are you shy?" the girl asked. "It's not your custom to bathe together?"

"No. Only in the ritual bath, but it's not like this."

"You need not do anything which makes you uncomfortable," Zorayda said, but Esther could see her disappointment. They were trying to make her welcome, and now they were embarrassed. There was only one solution.

Esther walked over to the side of the room, next to one of the marble benches, and unfastened the gold cord. She let the gown fall on the bench. Zorayda gave her a large towel of the softest cotton, and she placed it around her shoulders as the others had done. But it didn't cover her, and she was naked in front of strangers for the first time in her life.

No! Jagged memories attacked her and she felt faint.

Zorayda took her hand and led her into the steaming pool. The bubbling water rose to her thighs, and then over her breasts and back as she sat on a submerged platform. A wonderful peaceful feeling flowed through her. She smiled her appreciation, and saw looks of approval all around her.

Gabriel and Tomas had joined Prince Hasan in another part of the palace, far from the baths. Dozens of candles flickered as they relaxed on soft cushions. Courses of lamb and fish were succeeded by figs and dates and long slivers of watermelon chilled with ice from the mountains. The gentle sway of the serving girls, accompanied by the soft sound of a harp, accented the mellow glow that permeated the room.

Crack! Gabriel jumped and looked around in alarm, but Hasan motioned that it was all right.

Another crack, then a rapid series. Violent strumming. Soft and bewitching rhythms.

Two women and a man strode purposefully into the room, followed by two more men carrying *chitarras* and castanets. Soft clapping, louder, men singing. Gabriel didn't need to understand the words to feel the message of pain and suffering. The melody reminded him of the chant of Hebrew prayers.

Crack! One of the women stamped her foot. Again. Her no longer young face was angry, defiant. Arms moving sinuously, naked white flesh stark against her dark dress and long black hair. Feet driving faster and faster. The clapping was deafening. The whirlwind froze. Crack! The other woman dancing. Singing and *chitarras* even more intense. Sweat glistening on her body. Gabriel out of breath just watching them.

The man had not moved a muscle. Lean, dangerous, dressed all in black. He took a single step. Quietly. Another. Then a flurry of cracks faster than Gabriel could imagine any human feet could produce. Slow controlled movements. Wild impassioned crashes. Raw speed and power, never flagging. A concluding crescendo. Cracking sounds rebounding throughout the room after he was still.

Total quiet. The man walking backwards, joining the others, bowing to the prince. They were gone.

"Gypsies," said Hasan. "The pain of their lives is clear in their dance."

Tomas and Esther were led through the winding streets of Granada by two of the Prince's palace guard. Their eyes feasted on the colorful shops and stalls, and vendors who simply spread their wares on the ground. When they reached their destination, the guards remained on the street while they entered through a doorway without a door.

Peering into the dark space, Tomas called out, "Hello."

"Back here," a voice responded, "Come back here."

Tomas took Esther's hand and they walked toward the voice. They emerged from the darkness into a brilliantly lit courtyard.

Tables were covered with papers. Tomas recognized the pages of the *Haggadahs*.

"I have assembled the folios into several complete books."

Tomas heard the voice but had not yet seen its source. A small man popped up. He had been leaning over a table, hidden behind mounds of paper.

"My name is Yusef," the man said, advancing toward them.

"I am Tomas Catalan, and this is Esther Ardit," Tomas said.

"Everyone in Granada knows who you are, but no one must know what I am doing here. The Prince himself told me it was worth my life to keep my work a complete secret. Even the guards do not enter."

Tomas walked to the piles of pages, awestruck that he was about to see them become bound books.

"Please look to see that I have done it correctly. Before I sew, make certain that the folios are in the correct order."

Esther stood next to Tomas and they read together. From time to time, they looked at each other and smiled.

"This is good," Tomas said when they had finished. "What happens now?"

"Watch," Yusef answered.

He took the pages and went to an open workplace where his tools were spread out. With exact precision he squared up the pile of folios. He laid a heavy weight on top, and made a series of marks across the folded backs of the pages. He opened each folded set and, with an awl, punched holes through the folds in the places he had marked. He laid each of the refolded sections into a form on which three linen strips were held in place. These lined up exactly across the marks on the folded backs.

Yusef expertly sewed the pages together, working through the punched holes, back and forth around the linen strips. He tied off the thread, lifted the now firmly attached package, and pulled gently on the linen strips to smooth them. He arranged the package in a vertical form, and pasted a piece of cloth along the back of the pages, over the linen strips. Next came the cover boards. They were made of parchment, pasted together to form a stiff whole, and Tomas was surprised to see writing on the parchment. Yusef was using old pages from some other book to cover the *Haggadahs*. Both the strips and the cloth were pasted to the boards. Removed from the form, the book was closed and placed under heavy weights.

"Now we eat," said Yusef.

A veiled woman brought one covered platter after another ... rice cooked with delicate herbs, cakes of corn sweetened with honey, figs from Malaga, sliced bananas.

"The glue has dried," Yusef said when they were finished eating. He selected a piece of supple red leather. Applying paste to the back of the leather and the covers, he pressed them together. Working quickly, he brought the edges of the leather over the cover and finished the pasting inside. Then, opening the book, he pasted the first page of the book to the inside of the front cover and the last page to the inside of the back cover. He was done.

"Take this one with you. By tomorrow, it will be completely dry and you can handle it."

Tomas caressed the small leather bound book, both proud and humble. Esther took his hand. They thanked God that He had given them life to reach this moment.

The delicacy of Arabic letters had always fascinated Gabriel. He had often copied those curves and shapes in his jewelry.

The goldsmith chosen by the Prince rapidly absorbed the ideas and techniques of printing. Gabriel showed him a punch and matrix, and explained how the type was made. He described how the type was used in a press.

As Gabriel saw how easy it was to teach the Moor, it occurred to him that the time had come to establish more Hebrew presses. Not only could they print more, but it would also spread the risk, so that if one press was discovered, there would still be others.

The wagons were much heavier on the return trip, loaded with tens of thousands of sheets of paper from Prince Hasan. The Moors would again provide an escort to the Castilian border.

"I'm certain that King Enrique will accept your proposal," Gabriel said to Hasan as they prepared to leave.

"He would be a fool not too," said the Prince, smiling. Gabriel started to say that Enrique *was* a fool, but held his tongue.

"We'll be back with more printed pages," said Tomas, "but I'd like to leave something else with you, if I may." He removed the Barcelona *Haggadah* from his saddlebag.

"This is a priceless manuscript," he said. "Rabbi Modena believes it will be safer away from Seville. Will you keep it for me?"

As Hasan took the manuscript, they were interrupted, as they had been so many times during their two week visit, by the exuberant cries of little Muhammad.

"Tomas! Tomas! Here I come!"

He flew up into Tomas' arms.

Tomas hugged him and, reminiscent of their first meeting, handed him to his father. He mounted his horse, stood tall in the stirrups for a long goodbye look, then joined the others.

"Come back soon," Muhammad hollered.

A week later, nearing Arcos, it was evident to Gabriel that something was very wrong. No farmers worked in the fields. No other travelers were on the road. Columns of smoke rose from the town up above.

The plague always came mysteriously.

One day everything was fine, and then people started to die. It struck some places and spared others, for no apparent reason. There had never been a total catastrophe like that first time in 1348, when almost one in three had perished, but it kept coming back. Andalusia had been spared for almost a decade.

Gabriel listened to Esther, chatting happily with Tomas, and feared for her family locked in the town ahead. He forced the words out.

"There's a problem in Arcos."

The gates were barred. Guards waved them away. No one was allowed in or out.

Esther, silent for the past hour, said only, "The passage."

They rode along the river bank, around the bend and out of sight. Leaving their horses with Gabriel's men, they climbed the ancient pathway and emerged at the top of the cliff.

The stench was awful. A few nervous people flitted by, but the streets were mostly empty. A large wagon passed, pulled by two tired horses, filled with jumbled bodies of men, women, and children. Limbs grotesquely awry. Mostly naked, on their way to join hundreds more in unmarked pits at the edge of town.

Bed clothes, bloody, covered with pus, burning slowly in front of infected homes. Smoke rising, obscuring, choking.

They ran toward the Ardit home. Esther, in the lead, stopped suddenly, and was almost bowled over by Tomas and Gabriel.

She stared at a pack of rats calmly eating two dead bodies crumpled in a doorway. She started to collapse but Tomas caught her. She tore from his grasp with a howl and ran on.

Isidro Lucero stepped from the Ardit house. "Thank God you've arrived," he said.

"My family! My baby!" Esther screamed.

"Your mother is very sick but she's still alive," he said, "and Judah is not sick. He's at my home."

Esther ran into the house, and Lucero turned to Gabriel. His look was downcast and haggard.

"I did what I could to make them comfortable. It came so fast. It seems to be over now. There's been no new sickness for at least three days. But many are dead. Burning clothes, disposing of bodies. I'm exhausted."

"Yacov?"

"Dead. I buried him four days ago. Ruyo, too. Miriam can't last much longer."

Tomas started to rush after Esther, but Gabriel restrained him. "Let her have some time alone. It's all she'll have."

Lucero nodded. "Come get the baby whenever you're ready."

Gabriel and Tomas went slowly to the house.

Miriam opened her eyes when she heard Esther's voice. The woman Lucero had left to care for her wiped her forehead and backed out of the room.

"Judah will live," Miriam said in a voice husky with pain.

"I shouldn't have gone," Esther said.

"I'm so glad you weren't here. God was good to keep you away from this horror."

Esther knelt on the floor next to her mother, then raised up to hug her. She barely recognized the distorted and discolored face staring back at her, and she sobbed uncontrollably.

Miriam placed her emaciated hand on Esther's head and patted her until she became quiet.

"Go with Tomas," said Miriam. "Go to Pilar. She'll be your mother now. Tell her I love her. "

"You're my mother."

"For a little while longer."

"Forever. I love you, mama. Please don't die."

"Tell Tomas about the baby. He'll understand."

"No. I can never tell him. You said no one would marry me if they knew about the baby. I heard you tell Marguerita. He'll hate me if he knows."

As she spoke, Tomas appeared behind her and placed a hand gently on her shoulder. Startled, Esther looked up in panic.

"Tomas, is it you?" asked Miriam, her voice weakening.

"Yes, Señora, it's me."

"Tell him," she said to her daughter, whose lips quivered. "Esther, you must."

"She doesn't have to tell me," Tomas said softly, looking sadly at Miriam. "I know." He touched Esther's cheek. "It doesn't matter. I love you and I want you to be my wife. Judah will be our son."

Miriam reached feebly for Esther's hand, and Tomas covered them both with his. A moment later, Miriam's hand fell away.

Judah Ardit screamed through the entire ceremony. Perhaps it was drafty. Maybe the water was cold. Archbishop Fonseca might have considered those reasons, but not Gabriel. He heard the voice of the Almighty, objecting to the desecration of a Jewish soul in the Holy Cathedral of Seville.

'A Jew has to become a Catholic in order to be a secret Jew. This, God, is a complicated plan You have.' Gabriel had to smile, and hope that Judah's howls did not mean that God lacked a sense of humor.

The ceremony took place in a small dark chamber near the cavernous main nave. Gabriel and Pilar were the godparents. The presumed parents, Yacov and Miriam Ardit, were of course dead of the plague, and as unbaptized Jews, would not have been welcome anyway.

It had not been frequent of late to accept a Hebrew baby into Christ. The Cathedral priests were excited, and so was the *converso* community, which appeared in large numbers to witness the event, and that of the baptism of the baby's sister which was to follow.

A red-robed priest pronounced the exorcisms, liberating Judah from sin and its instigator the devil. His forehead was anointed with oil. The priest laid his hands on the baby's chest and renounced Satan.

Gabriel held Judah. His amusement had turned to fury and he

struggled to hide his raging emotions. Why, God, are you doing this? Will Judah ever be a Jew again? He thought of Perez, who would soon be back, and his fingers tightened enough to make Judah shriek. Gabriel came back to the present. He kissed the child and carried him toward the baptismal font.

The priest dipped the golden cup, and holy water was poured over the baby's head.

May the power of the Holy Spirit be sent through his Son upon the water that this baby may be born of the water and of the spirit.

The pouring was repeated twice more to symbolize the three days of Christ's death in the tomb. Judah was anointed with the sacred chrism, perfumed oil consecrated by the Archbishop himself, and his name was irrevocably changed.

Judah Ardit is dead in Christ, Jose Ardit is risen.

The food of the new life, the body and blood of Christ, was forced into the baby's mouth, a candle was held high and finally it was over. Pilar immediately took him from the Cathedral.

Then it was Esther's turn.

Gabriel prayed that she would endure the ordeal. It had been but a week since they had arrived in Seville, thankful that the plague, in its mysterious ways, had overlooked the large city.

Esther had been devastated to see the streets of her youth, where her family would never walk again. Pilar did her best, thank God for Pilar. After several days, Esther was able to respond to conversation, although she did not initiate any. She and Tomas sat for hours, holding hands in silence. The need to care for the baby was a blessing.

She knew, of course, that baptism was necessary, and soon. She could not even live with the Catalans if she remained a Jew, let alone marry Tomas.

Marry Tomas!

Even the words sparkled. There had never actually been a time when he had asked and she had answered. But from the moment Miriam died, they had known there could be no other course. One day they began to talk about a wedding. The thought of receiving the sacrament of marriage from a priest revolted her, but she knew it had to be. She was in the Cathedral to take the first necessary step. Having already lost so much, today she would lose her name.

They had struggled to choose a new one. Nothing seemed right, because nothing *was* right. Maria had been Tomas' idea. Mary, mother of Jesus, was a Jewess, he insisted. Take her name, he said, and think of the baby Jesus and not the perversion his church has made of his teachings. Esther told him she would take the name, but to honor her own mother. Miriam was the Hebrew name by which the mother of Jesus was known in her lifetime.

Dressed simply in a green woolen robe covering her white baptismal gown, Esther walked past the small font used by her son and approached the dark pool. The priest spoke the words Tomas had prepared her to hear. She gave the robe to Gabriel and stepped into the water, her face without expression. She sunk to her knees, the gown clinging to her. Once, twice, three times she bent forward and plunged her body and head beneath the water, hair swirling at the surface.

Maria Ardit ate the body of Christ and drank of his blood, but her heart screamed a silent protest, and her head echoed with the Jewish prayer of mourning.

יתגדל ויתקדש שמה רבא
Yisgadal v'yiskadash sh'mei rabba

Again and again she prayed for the dead … for Yacov and Miriam and Ruyo … for Judah … and for Esther.

Don Alonso had insisted on a great party. He said that Gabriel's rising prominence required it, and that anything less would be an insult, impossible under the circumstances. So they gathered at his palace, the powerful and wealthy of Seville.

Judges, *alcades mayores*, members of the municipal council, the governor of the *alcazar*, the vice chancellor of the University of Seville — almost all of them *conversos*, and their ladies. The room a flurry of gowns and robes, turbans, flowered and feathered hats, flowing and braided hair, fur linings, contrasting satin sleeves, brocade, jewels, black, crimson, green, mulberry, tawny and white leather belts with jeweled pouches.

Archbishop Fonseca, dressed as richly as permitted when not serving in the Cathedral, led the entire diocesan delegation. They were joined by the Bishop of Cartage, the Master of the Sacred Palace of Ciudad Real, and an unending collection of archdeacons, deacons, abbots, canons, chaplains. When Gabriel saw them assembled, even he was amazed at how many of the churchmen were *conversos*.

So also among the royal officials. The *regidore* of Seville, *corregidores* from all parts of Andalusia, treasurers, *mayordomos*, ambassadors, the Grand Master of the military Order of Calatrava, an admiral of the royal navy — every one of them a *converso*. And, the most prominent *converso* of all, Don Diego Arias de Avila, *Contador Mayor*, the chief treasurer of the kingdom of Enrique IV.

"The people are not happy with the new taxes," Gabriel said in response to a question.

"Nor with the war?" asked another.

"No. The war with the Moors is not popular."

"If Enrique would only fight, really fight, the people would support him."

"But he won't."

"It would be better to stop the pretense of war. Do you agree, Gabriel? We've heard rumors that you may have discussed this with the king."

"Ah," said Gabriel, "you can't believe everything you hear. But I will say that in my travels, I've not found much reason to continue the current policy."

"I'm sorry about Francesco," said an archdeacon whose name Gabriel could not recall.

"It was awful," said Gabriel, not happy to discuss his friend in this room full of *conversos* who hated the idea of secret Jews jeopardizing their hard won success.

"Was he a secret Jew?"

"No, he was not," said Gabriel, annoyed.

"Was he tortured?"

"Did he admit anything?"

Don Alonso came to Gabriel's rescue. "Francesco Romo was unjustly accused and tortured for things he never did. And the real criminal, Friar Ricardo Perez, did not get what he deserved!"

"Which was?"

"Death!" said Don Alonso.

There were no more questions about Francesco. Conversation and food intermixed, and eventually they reached the topic of the contract for farming the taxes of the district of Cordoba.

"You're going to bid, Gabriel?"

"Yes." Gabriel answered. "For the first time on my own account."

"Congratulations. I hope you get it."

"I hear that a group of Old Christians is going to put in a serious bid."

"How ridiculous. None of the Old Christians I know could do the job."

"You might be surprised. I hear that Alvar Sanchez has accumulated a substantial amount of capital. He may have enough to give you some real competition."

"Well, that's his right," said Gabriel. "But my bid will be difficult to top."

Pilar was at home with Esther. Would she ever call her Maria? She objected to everything Jewish that her husband and son had adopted, but she was most infuriated by the idea that Esther's Judaism had been stolen from her, all the more so because conversion had been her own suggestion, so long ago in Arcos. She sobbed at the memory of Miriam, dear Miriam, who did not object but said it would destroy Yacov. Now Yacov and Miriam were dead, Esther was baptized, and it was she who was devastated.

She heard Esther praying and waited at her door, not wishing to intrude. When Esther was quiet, Pilar sat on the bed next to her and cradled her head in her lap.

"What were you saying?" she asked.

"I was praising God," Esther answered.

"Tell me the words."

Esther spoke softly, first in Hebrew and then in Spanish:

יתגדל ויתקדש שמה רבא
May His great Name
grow exalted and sanctified.
in the world He created as He willed.

"Our prayers of mourning don't mention the dead," Esther said, "and don't speak of sorrow. We sanctify God. I guess we hope He cares, and that whatever He has done, there is a reason for it. Even if we don't understand."

Her last words faded into a terrible sobbing, and the two women held each other as darkness fell.

18

Four centuries after the birth of Jesus, Christianity became the official religion of the Roman Empire, and the Church influenced the passage of laws which severely limited the civil and political rights of Jews. Ten centuries later, Friar Ricardo Perez carefully traced the repetition of these laws from their first appearance in Rome to the most recent Spanish codes.

From the Laws of Theodosius, adopted in 439 A.D.: *No Jew shall obtain offices and dignities; to none shall the administration of city services be permitted. We forbid that any synagogue shall rise as a new building.*

The 7th century Code of the Christian Visigoths, who had supplanted the Romans in Spain: *All Jews of Spain must accept baptism within one year, or else be subject to expulsion. Circumcision is forbidden, under penalty of amputation of the genitals. Jews are forbidden to work as officials in the public service.*

Perez copied from the official decrees of the Fourth Lateran Council, held in Rome in 1215 under the auspices of Pope Innocent III: *It happens at times that through error Christians have relations with the women of the Jews, and Jews with Christian women. Therefore, that they may not excuse themselves in the future for the excesses of such prohibited intercourse, we decree that Jews of both sexes in every Christian province and at all times shall be marked off in the eyes of the public from other peoples through the character of their dress.*

Thus arose the yellow badge.

And from the Castilian Code of 1371: *The Jews, brazen and evil people, enemies of God and of all Christians, perpetrate many wrongs*

189

and briberies, so that all our kingdoms are being destroyed and driven by Jews to a state of desperation. Jews must be marked and separated from Christians, wear signs, and have no office in the court of any lord, nor serve as farmers of royal taxes.

Thus what began as Christian anti-Jewish rhetoric reached full implementation in the civil code of Castile. But despite all these laws, thought Perez angrily, *conversos,* full of the blood and stink of Jews, continue to dominate true Christians in every aspect of our lives.

He thought of Francesco Romo, broken and bleeding, hanging near death from the hoist. He was sure that Romo was a judaizer, but he had failed to prove it. That's why he was in exile. But he would learn from his mistakes. He would study the manual of Bernard Gui, the leading papal inquisitor of the 13th century, and next time, he would succeed.

"I've never seen you work as a goldsmith," Esther said.

"It's good to get back to it," Tomas said, stepping away so she could get a closer look.

Standing on four dark wooden legs, perfectly milled, the main body of the miniature casket was eighteen inches long, ten inches deep, six inches high. The lid tapered to a proportionally smaller rectangle almost as high as the box under it. Both were elaborately decorated with pairs of figures, carved in ivory. Each pair was a musician, with varying instruments, and a nobleman, either eating or drinking. The figures were circled by an interlocking border, in silver filigree, reaching in uninterrupted grace around the entire box and lid. Topping the lid at each corner were silver knobs. "They look like *torah* staves," Esther laughed. The finishing touch was a carefully wrought clasp and lock.

"It's stunning," she said. "Who's it for?"

"A very wealthy customer," Tomas answered, thrilled at her praise, and even more pleased to see a look in her eyes that had been missing since they had reached Arcos on that dreadful day. "Are you feeling better?" he asked. "You sound better."

Esther lowered her eyes. "I've been very selfish. It must be a bother for you and your mother."

"There's nothing you could do that would ever be a bother," Tomas said. "I hope I haven't made you feel that way."

"Oh no. Not you, or Señora Catalan either. You've all been wonderful. Your father, too. It's just that I've ... "

"Don't apologize. We understand."

Pilar started to come into the room, but seeing them together, she stopped.

"Please stay," said Esther. "I was coming to see you. Now that I'm Maria, I need instruction in how to be a Christian."

Tomas remembered his conversation with Esther on their very first trip to Arcos, when she had asked him how he kept everything straight.

"Some things are obvious," said Pilar. "You can't observe the Sabbath, or eat kosher food, or cook in oil."

"Cook in oil?" asked Esther, twisting her face in disbelief. "What does cooking in oil have to do with being Jewish?"

"It means that you avoid cooking meat in butter," said Pilar, "and it's one of the signs that Christians are taught to look for to identify secret Jews."

A profound sadness came over Esther's face. Only a few minutes before, she had been almost cheerful. Tomas wanted to hold her, but he was afraid she wouldn't let him.

"As far as being a Christian," he said, "there's really very little to do, but much to believe, or at least to say you believe. You must accept the Holy Trinity — God the Father, Jesus the Son, and the Holy Spirit. Three that are really one. I've never understood it. Also the Virgin Birth and the resurrection of Jesus after his death. And finally that Jesus is the Jewish Messiah, and not, as the Jews believe, that the Messiah is yet to come."

Esther was not as upset as he had thought she would be. Then a puzzled look came to her face and she asked, "Isn't the Christian God the same as the God of Israel?"

"They took Him from us," Tomas said, arching his eyebrows in mock disbelief. "It's the same God, but they say He rejected us and now loves only Christians."

"What an awful thought," Pilar said quietly.

"When can I pray?" Esther asked.

"Do you mean Jewish prayer?" said Tomas.

"That's the only praying I'll do. The rest will just be words. Don't worry. I'll learn them perfectly, but they'll have no meaning for me."

Pilar went to Esther and put her arms around her. "You must pray, my dear. You must never forget your Jewish prayers."

Tomas was surprised. His mother had always opposed Gabriel's secret Jewish life. She had fought any Jewish involvement by Tomas, and she had objected, at least at first, to the printing of Hebrew books. Was she changing her view? He hoped so. He stretched his strong arms around both Esther and his mother.

"Will I ever be able to go to the synagogue?" Esther asked.

"Not for a prayer service," said Tomas. "But my father and I go there. We repair things." Tomas could not resist a grin. "You'll come with us. Rabbi Modena will be happy to see you."

"Everything is in order," Alvar Sanchez began. "All the bribes have been paid. We'll be told what Catalan's bid is, and ours will be just a few thousand maravedis greater. We're going to get this contract."

Sanchez was talking with a large group of Old Christian men who had banded together in a desperate attempt to win the same Cordoba tax farming contract that Gabriel Catalan sought. Twenty families had scraped together in order to pay the bribes which they believed would assure their success and make them rich.

"Can we trust ... ?" one of the men began to ask.

"Everybody knows what happened in Toledo," Sanchez interrupted. "They don't want that kind of violence here, and they know we'll fight if we're cheated."

"What if Catalan is paying the same people?" another asked.

"Listen," Sanchez insisted. "It's going to work. We're going to return to the tax farming business for the first time in over fifty years. The conversos think they have it all. This is going to be a big shock to them."

"Conversos. Devil Jews," said one of the older men. "They never let go. For three hundred years, only Jews collected taxes, ingratiating them-selves with the royal families. Good Christians never had a chance."

"Jews have been forbidden since the Cortes of 1412."

"Yes. But they converted. Sly ones. They pretend to be Christians and the same families still have all the tax farming contracts."

"The church teaches that Jews must be subjugated to Christians, pun-ished forever because they killed Christ. It's blasphemy that they're so rich and powerful"

"This time we'll beat them!"

"Yes we will!"

"When we win the bid, are we certain that we have the three million maravedis to advance to the king?"

"The Italians are committed," said Sanchez. "They want the Jews out

as much as we do. Señor Benavenista has pledged that the Pazzi will deliver. His word is good."

"It better be. If anything goes wrong, I'm ruined."

Gabriel and King Enrique were alone in the king's hunting lodge in the forest of Balsain near Segovia, its thick walls protected by huge Ethiopian guards and hideous dwarfs. Roughnecks and effeminate boys caroused through the halls and gardens. No women were present.

Enrique was admiring his fierce fighting bull when Gabriel arrived. Lions were caged nearby. In this impossible setting, Gabriel reported to the king.

"Prince Hasan and King Sa'd have accepted the truce terms, your Excellency."

A great smile came to Enrique's face, and he slapped his thigh lustily, drawing a snort from the bull. "I will have a worthy reward for you, Don Gabriel Catalan."

The throne room in Segovia was crowded. Bids would soon be made for the lucrative contract to farm the taxes of Cordoba.

Gabriel had done his calculations carefully, with help from Don Alonso, but his mentor was neither present nor a party to the bid. This was Gabriel's moment. His bid, written down and sealed in the paper he would soon hand to the king, was four million five hundred thousand *maravedis*.

He would have no competition from his peers in the *converso* community, who knew this was Gabriel's time. There would, however, be a competitive bid, and this was the cause of the excitement. Old Christians led by Alvar Sanchez had apparently assembled the resources for a serious bid.

But even the prospect of hot competition was not enough to displace court gossip. Queen Juana was pregnant! After many barren years, this being Enrique's second wife without children, the queen was with child.

But whose child?

Few believed Enrique was the father. Not from lack of effort. Bizarre stories circulated. The most insane, but believable because no one could make up such a thing, involved a special golden tube. Certain courtiers swore they were present when it was used.

Queen Juana, still a beautiful vivacious woman, had been placed on a low bed surrounded by a curtain. Her gown was parted, and one end of the golden tube was placed far into her vagina.

With the queen thus readied, the king was brought forth. He sat on a raised platform outside the curtain near the other end of the golden tube.

Here the stories differ. Some said Enrique masturbated himself. Others said one of his Segovian freaks did it for him. The idea, of course, was to catch his ejaculate in the tube and let it pour into the queen.

Of course it didn't work. First of all, nothing happened. Then when it finally did, what was wrenched from his distorted member was thin and watery and utterly useless.

If it was this disgusting incident which drove the lascivious queen to the arms of the dashing Beltran de la Cueva, there were few who would blame her. It was generally assumed that Beltran was the father of the unborn child.

Trumpets blared.

"Rise for Enrique IV, son of the House of Trastamara and King of Castile."

Enrique strode purposefully into the throne room, wearing his gold crown and looking more dignified than usual in a purple robe. His two half-siblings followed, Prince Alfonso and Princess Isabel, the younger children of Enrique's father King Juan by Juan's second wife. It was said that they had been brought to Segovia so Enrique could control their movements and assure that they were not used in a plot to overthrow him. Behind Isabel stood the scowling Friar Torquemada, whom Gabriel knew to be her confessor.

"I have wonderful news to announce today," Enrique began as soon as he was seated in his simple throne.

Gabriel was confused, and one glance at his competitor let him know they were equally surprised.

"We have brought the Moors to their knees," Enrique continued proudly. "They have sued for peace. A truce for five years."

The hall erupted in loud cheering. Enrique smiled and his large head bobbed happily in response.

"This truce is the work of one man who was my agent on a very dangerous mission. His skillful negotiations led to the truce."

Gabriel's heart sank.

"This man is here today," Enrique continued. "Don Gabriel Catalan, come forward."

Gabriel moved as if in a trance. This was all wrong. He knelt before the king.

"The crown of Castile appreciates and rewards those who serve it. It is not fitting that someone who has done such service to the king should have to compete for the crown's business."

Enrique searched the room for reaction but everyone was still. Gabriel watched the King pathetically seeking approval, and he was filled with sorrow. Enrique meant well.

"There will be no bidding today for the contract to farm the taxes of Cordoba. This contract is awarded to Don Gabriel Catalan, for a price of two million *maravedis*."

Gabriel's gasp was lost in the outpouring that filled the hall. This was much lower than he was prepared to bid, and he was sure it was also lower than the bid assembled with such great effort by the Old Christians.

Alvar Sanchez scowled furiously at him. 'Don't blame me,' Gabriel thought. But what else could Sanchez believe but that he had made a secret evil deal with the king?

Gabriel saw stupid glee on the faces of his fellow *conversos*, and he wanted to scream at them. Looking up at Enrique's toothy smile, however, he said the only thing he could.

"Thank you, Your Excellency."

Gabriel curtailed his plans for the wedding. Instead of a great celebration attended by hundreds, there would be a small private ceremony in a Cathedral chapel far removed from the main vaulted space originally reserved. Archbishop Fonseca would officiate, but Don Alonso would be the only guest. Fonseca was disappointed, but he knew the reason. And Gabriel made a huge donation.

The change was caused by King Enrique's award of the tax farming contract to Gabriel without a bid. The Old Christians were furious. Led by Alvar Sanchez, they complained loudly and drew angry crowds. It wasn't hard to incite people against *conversos*, and the mood got uglier every day. "They're taking over," was the cry. "We have nothing. They must be stopped."

In the two weeks since Gabriel had returned from Segovia, he had been accosted on the street several times, barely avoiding violence. Don Alonso warned him not to go out alone, and provided guards to be with him at all times. Another small army watched the Catalan house.

The morning of the wedding was sunny and problem free. Gabriel escorted his family to the Cathedral. Pilar and Maria, for today of all days she must be Maria, walked first, and he and Tomas followed. Guards went before and after.

Gabriel wore the same clothes he had worn when he first met the king. Tomas wore the finest outfit his parents could convince him to put on. But if there had been the largest audience ever to attend a wedding in Seville, they would not have noticed the groom and his father.

Esther's gown was of white crushed velvet, trimmed in white brocade. A white satin skirt hung to her feet. The neckline would have been scandalously low but for the fluted partlet in white taffeta which continued up into a high beaded collar. Her hair was braided and wound around her head, forming a crown which no queen could outdo. Her shoes were of white deerskin, trimmed in silk bows. Her bearing was regal, and it bothered her not at all that almost no one would see her and that she would never again wear these clothes.

Walking next to her in a gown of green velvet, Pilar was equally elegant, and Gabriel could not help noticing how slim his wife still was. There weren't many like her. Nor like Esther.

"You couldn't have chosen a finer wife," he said to his son. "The circumstances are tragic, but God will surely permit something wonderful to flourish."

"She's still not herself," said Tomas.

"Be patient. She's had so much pain. How could she not be frightened about the future."

"I love her. I can wait."

They reached the enormous Cathedral, still in the midst of endless construction. It was the largest Cathedral in Christendom, huge, dark, ominous.

The Church did awful things in buildings such as this, Gabriel thought. But Archbishop Fonseca was not one of the awful ones. He was kind, and when he spoke he made sense. It was amazing that he had risen so high, but although he aspired to the red cap, it was said that he had reached his limit. He greeted them at the great door, extending the honor of his position to the approaching family. Don Alonso stood behind him.

"There's no trouble today?" Fonseca asked as Gabriel approached.

"No," said Gabriel.

"It's very quiet all over the city," said Don Alonso. "The *converso* haters have taken a day off."

"*The church teaches infallibly that the seven sacraments of the New Law were each personally instituted by Jesus Christ as visible signs, that the grace of God might be known by man. Marriage was instituted by God in the book of Genesis and elevated by Christ to the level of sacramental dignity. And thus our Savior encounters every Christian spouse through the sacrament of Marriage.*"

Fonseca, after this brief introduction, summoned Tomas and Maria to kneel before him at the altar.

"Tomas, will you take Maria, here present, for your lawful wife, according to the rite of our Holy Mother, the Church?"

"I will," said Tomas.

"Maria, will you take Tomas, here present, for your lawful husband, according to the rite of our Holy Mother, the Church?"

"I will," Maria repeated.

"Join your right hands, and repeat after me. I ... take you ... for my lawful wedded ... to have and to hold from this day forward, for better, for worse, for richer, for poorer, in sickness and in health, till death do us part."

Tomas and Maria having done as requested, Fonseca pronounced, "I unite you in marriage, in the name of the father, and of the Son, and of the Holy Ghost, Amen."

The Archbishop sprinkled them with holy water. "May I have the ring?" he asked Tomas. Fonseca sprinkled the ring with holy water and gave it back to Tomas, who placed it on the ring finger of Maria's right hand, saying, "With this ring, I thee wed, and promise thee my fidelity."

Maria ate the body of Christ for the second time in her life. When Mass was concluded, the Archbishop turned again to Tomas and Maria.

"*May the God of Abraham, of Isaac, and of Jacob be with you, and may He bless you greatly in every way, that you may see your children's children unto the third and fourth generation, and thereafter enjoy without end the blessed life of heaven, with the help of Jesus Christ our Lord, who with the Father and the Holy Ghost, lives and reigns, God through all eternity. Amen.*"

Gabriel was surprised by the mention of the three Jewish patriarchs. It made him think once again just how closely related Christians and Jews were. We're the black sheep in their family, he thought, but it really is a Jewish family at its roots.

They shared a rather sad cup of wine with the Archbishop and Don Alonso, and then the Catalan family walked home, exchanged their fine clothes for everyday dress, and waited.

Later that same day, they went for another walk. Again the guards went with them. This time, Tomas and Esther went first, holding hands, followed by Gabriel and Pilar, also holding hands. There was, however, great tension in what they wanted to appear as a casual afternoon outing.

They wandered, seemingly without purpose, until they were certain they were not being followed. Then they edged toward the *juderia*, and eventually, to the synagogue.

Rabbi Modena had initially resisted Gabriel's request.

"They can't be married as Christians, eat the body of Christ, then come on the same day to the synagogue to be married as Jews."

"These are strange times," Gabriel had responded. Then he made the argument that convinced the Rabbi.

"Do you want them to have children?" he asked. "Children who might someday be Jews?"

"Of course," Modena answered.

"Then you must marry them under a *chupah*."

"I don't understand," said the Rabbi.

"Esther won't consummate a Christian marriage. If you want the possibility of Jewish babies, you must do as they wish."

"Esther Ardit is the strongest young women I've ever met. What a match for your Tomas! So … they must have babies!"

The subterfuge was easy to arrange, especially with Friar Perez still in exile far from Seville. Guards were positioned on the street outside, and they entered the darkened sanctuary. They pretended to work on yet another piece of synagogue silver, with the women along to assist.

Gabriel remembered his first visit to the synagogue, and then that horrible *Yom Kippur* day with Friar Perez.. He thought of his father, Isaac Catalan, who would have loved what was about to happen … his grandson Tomas, a Jewish wedding, hope for a Jewish future. They were about to sanctify one small moment from the chaos around them to dedicate a new Jewish family to the glory of the God of Israel.

Gabriel had been reluctant to suggest the second wedding to Pilar. But when Tomas told him that she had encouraged Esther to pray, he had taken the risk. 'Of course,' she said. 'Of course I'll come.'

The *chupah* stood before the Holy Ark, a canopy of white velvet, supported by four staves. They passed it in awe, all of them, and went to the rabbi's study, where a smiling Modena awaited them.

"I have the gowns," the rabbi said, indicating two robes of pure white silk, one for Esther and one for Tomas. A large square prayer cap sat on the table. Gabriel lifted it to Tomas' head and helped him with the robe. Pilar held Esther's robe, and then helped her fasten her veil. They moved quickly.

Modena stood before Esther: *"May God make you like Sarah, Rebecca, Rachel and Leah. The Lord bless you and keep you. The Lord make His face to shine upon you, and be gracious unto you. The Lord lift up His countenance upon you, and give you peace."*

All this done in the study to minimize the more dangerous time they would spend in the sanctuary, where detection was more possible, even with the guards posted. But now it was time, and the small procession went into the dark sanctuary. Gabriel was shocked to see a group of men standing near the *bema*.

"Who are they?" he asked Modena.

"There must be a *minyan*, ten men to give public witness to the marriage."

"But ..."

"There is no problem," said the rabbi. "They will never speak of this. Each of them would die first."

They faced Modena under the *chupah*, Esther to Tomas' right, Pilar next to her, and Gabriel next to Tomas. Esther and Tomas held hands.

"There are two benedictions of betrothal," said Modena. "First is the blessing over wine, for there is no joy without wine." He raised a silver cup: *"Blessed art thou, O Lord our God, King of the universe, who createst the fruit of the vine."*

Modena's hand shook as he sipped and passed the cup to Gabriel. Pilar lifted Esther's veil, and she took the cup from Gabriel and sipped. Then it was Tomas' turn.

"The second benediction," said Modena, wasting not a moment, his voice beginning to fail, "expresses the divine character of marriage: *Blessed art Thou, O Lord our God, King of the Universe, who sanctifies His people Israel by means of the chupah.*

"Tomas, do you have the ring?"

Esther could wear only one ring. Tomas had made it himself, and it had been used in the service at the Cathedral. Esther removed it from her finger and gave it to Tomas. He in turn placed it on the forefinger of her right hand.

"Behold, Esther Ardit, daughter of Yacov and Miriam of blessed memory, you are consecrated to me with this ring, according to the Law of Moses and of Israel."

Modena held up a parchment document, his hands trembling. "This is the *ketubah*, the contract stating the obligations Tomas has assumed for the care of his bride. I will read it aloud.

"Be thou my wife according to the law of Moses and Israel, and I will work for you, honor, support, and maintain you in accordance with the custom of Jewish husbands. All my property shall be mortgaged for the security of this contract."

There had been considerable discussion about the wording of this *ketubah*. Most such documents made reference to the virginity of the bride and the dowry she brought from her father's house, neither applicable in this case. After Modena finished reading, he gave the *ketubah* to Tomas, who formally presented it to Esther. Then Modena produced a glass. Tomas crushed it with his foot, and Modena said, "Serve the Lord with fear, and rejoice with trembling. In a place of rejoicing there shall also be trembling."

"We have no absence of that," said Gabriel, looking nervously at the door to the synagogue.

"We conclude," said Modena, "with Psalm 137.

If I forget you, O Jerusalem, let my right hand wither. Let my tongue cleave to the roof of my mouth, if I remember thee not, if I set not Jerusalem above even my happiest hour."

Gabriel was disturbed by the Rabbi's frailness. His arms were thin sticks, his robe hung loosely. He shuffled about, barely able to lift his feet. Several times he had stumbled over the words. How much longer would he live? What would they do when he was gone?

Tomas and Esther removed their robes, and for the second time that day, the Catalan family walked home from a wedding ceremony.

Their new room in the southeastern corner of the Catalan house was private, but Tomas was unsure, in a way that surprised and dismayed him. He had dreamed of this moment. He had longed to make love with this woman. He had forced himself to suppress those longings, convincing himself they were impure, not worthy of her. Now she was here with him, naked in their marriage bed, and he was afraid.

Her only sexual experience was a brutal rape. Would she find his approaches revolting? Would the act of making love destroy the tenderness they had experienced for the past two years?

He had no erection.

He couldn't even touch her. He considered the terrifying possibility that maybe he loved her too much. He thought of the impotent King Enrique. We were both married by Fonseca! Does he put a spell on certain men? His panic spilled out in a quiet moan. He turned his head, unwilling to let her see his disgrace.

Her fingers touched his shoulder, played with the curls at the back of his neck, traced a gentle pattern on his chest. She cupped the powerful muscles of his arm, and slid her hand along his forearm.

Her fingers brushed against his bare leg and Tomas' world changed forever.

Chills ran through his body and tears came to his eyes. She was astride him. He had no thoughts, none at all, and when he exploded into her, she shuddered but never stopped, laughing and crying, holding him tightly inside her body. They moved more slowly, conscious of their closeness, glorying in the smooth wetness of their union. Finally, they collapsed, arms squeezed tight, oblivious.

Later, Tomas would remember hearing noises from the street.

Gabriel left the house as darkness was falling. Pilar had gone to their room, and he rushed to leave so that Tomas and Esther could be alone without the need to excuse themselves.

Not that he didn't have urgent business. The mobs grew more threatening every day. This day of weddings had been quiet, but he was sure the troubles were not over. He wanted Don Alonso to convince Archbishop Fonseca to speak out against the violence.

As he walked, the presence of the guards allowed him to relax, and he let his mind wander. He didn't blame Alvar Sanchez for being angry. The Old Christians had worked for years to prepare a bid, and their chance had been stolen from them by Enrique's well-meaning but stupid gesture. Gabriel had tried to seek him out after the chaos in the throne room, but Sanchez had refused to meet. He would have offered to share the contract with them, but they never knew that. He was sorry that he had not tried harder, found an intermediary, insisted on a meeting. Now it was too late.

It wasn't just this contract. The Old Christians refused to accept any responsibility for their prolonged failure. They blamed Jews. They blamed *conversos*. It was the work of the devil. Most of them couldn't even read, but they never admitted that anything was their own fault.

"There he is! It's that bastard Catalan! Get him!"

Shouts came from the dark street ahead. The guards circled him. Swords were drawn. This was the moment, Gabriel feared, when blood would flow. He wasn't afraid for himself, but rather that these ignorant people would be wounded or killed, and *conversos* would be blamed.

"In here," he shouted, pointing to a dark alcove. "We can defend ourselves easily there. Try not to wound them. Someone will come."

The men in the street were poorly armed. They had no leadership and no experience in fighting. Two of them came close, but a flourishing of the guards' swords sent them scurrying. No blood.

The welcome sound of horses hooves confirmed the wisdom of Gabriel's strategy. The mob melted into the surrounding streets.

Gabriel saw Don Alonso dismount and went to join him. Only friendly faces remained in the street. It was over.

He had just reached Don Alonso when he spotted a movement in the alley. A powerful cross-bow was raised. An arrow was loosened. Gabriel leaped to push Don Alonso out of its path.

The arrow ripped through Gabriel's flesh with searing pain. His right hand was pinned to Don Alonso. Locked together, they fell to the ground.

Someone broke off the end of the arrow and freed Gabriel's hand. He was bleeding profusely, but he ignored his own injury when he saw the arrow lodged dead center in Don Alonso's chest. His friend lay on the ground, eyes closed, breathing weakly.

Gabriel knelt beside him. Don Alonso opened his eyes and motioned for Gabriel to come close.

"I told Tomas never to relax," Don Alonso said with an ironic smile. "That's when it happens."

A horrible cough racked his body, and blood trickled from his lips. Gabriel saw his friend passing away before his eyes. 'I need you,' he thought. 'Don't go.'

"We've made a beginning, Gabriel," Don Alonso whispered, "but there is much more to do. You must be the leader. You are ready. Be brave and don't be afraid to act boldly."

Don Alonso shuddered and closed his eyes. Then he was quiet and Gabriel knew he was gone. Francesco. Rodrigo. Now Don Alonso. He had never felt so alone.

Gabriel was restless in his darkened bedroom. His wounded hand throbbed. Pilar would soon change the bandage, as she had every three hours for the past six days.

After the murder of Don Alonso, an uneasy quiet lay over Seville. Gabriel's visitors reported that the city was embarrassed. The murderer had been caught and was held for trial in the Triano fortress along the Rio Guadalquivir. Archbishop Fonseca had spoken from the Cathedral pulpit, severely chastising those who committed violence against the *converso* community. Even Alvar Sanchez pleaded for a cessation of the bloodshed he had provoked.

"Sanchez wants to see you," one of his visitors had said. "He wants to apologize."

Don Alonso's death cannot be undone, Gabriel thought, stifling a sob as he remembered his friend. But there is the future. I'll see him. Maybe I should still offer him a piece of my contract.

His visitors did not come simply to offer condolences or see how he felt. Repeatedly, they said that Don Gabriel should take Don Alonso's place. He was the powerful tax farmer and the great diplomat. He was the only one of their number with access to King Enrique. He must accept the fact that he was Don Alonso's logical successor. At the same time, they began to ask his favor for appointments as tax collectors, treasurers, and other positions now within Gabriel's growing influence.

Of course, the *conversos* didn't know that he was a judaizer, or about the Hebrew printing. But neither did they know these aspects of Don Alonso's life.

He was flattered by their entreaties, although he harbored a queasy feeling that he didn't deserve their praise. Four years before, when he was just a goldsmith, he was unknown to most of them. How quickly he had risen. How easily he could fall.

Despite Don Alonso's dying words that he was ready, Gabriel knew that he was not. There were so many important aspects of Don

Alonso's life that he knew nothing about. Where did all the money come from? Who could be trusted? Don Alonso had spoken of men from Toledo and Barcelona, from other cities in Spain, and from other countries, but he had never met them. How could he take Don Alonso's place in their sphere? They would laugh at his lack of experience. He would be embarrassed. He would fail.

Gonsalvo de Viterbo came to visit, after observing, secretly of course, the traditional *shiva*, the seven day Jewish period of mourning. Gabriel compared Gonsalvo's loss to his own when his father Isaac had been brutally beaten to death by the same forces that took Don Alonso, and his heart went out to the younger man. In the end, they'll kill us all, he thought. As long as there are fanatical Christians, Jews will be hated and attacked. The tinder box stands ever ready. Perez, and others like him, will always strike the spark.

"I wish the arrow had taken me and spared your father," Gabriel said to Gonsalvo.

"You tried hard to make that happen. How's your wound?"

Gabriel held up his bandaged hand. "It'll heal. But I'll never be a goldsmith again."

"I don't think you would have much time for that anyway," said Gonsalvo. "You have much to do."

Again, Gabriel thought, the same unrelenting message.

"My father spoke about you often," Gonsalvo said. "He wanted you to take his place. It just happened a little sooner than he had planned."

"How can I do that?" said Gabriel, shaking his head. "Don Alonso was involved in so many things that I know nothing about."

"I'll help you," said Gonsalvo. "I already run most of the businesses. But you know the tax farming, which I don't. You've succeeded diplomatically where I, and perhaps even Don Alonso, would have failed. And you're the only one who can carry on the printing, you and Tomas. That was dearest to my father. The printing must not stop!"

Gabriel looked at Gonsalvo, then looked away. He was not convinced that he could do it, but he thought of the words of Rabbi Hillel in the Talmud, 'if not now, when?' and applied them to himself. If not Gabriel Catalan, who?

Gonsalvo was still speaking. "You do your part. I'll do the rest. But you must be the one in front. I'll be in the shadows."

"This is what you want?"

"I pleaded with my father to have it so. I know my weaknesses."

"And also your strengths?"

"And also my strengths," Gonsalvo repeated. "This is my will as much as my father's."

"Then I'll do it," said Gabriel, giving voice to the decision that had been growing within him. "May God give me the wisdom and the strength."

Gonsalvo smiled his approval, then said, "There's something else."

"I've heard that expression many times," said Gabriel, a smile creasing his face for the first time in days. "You are your father's son." He was pleased to see just a hint of a smile on Gonsalvo's face.

"Well? What is it?" Gabriel asked gently.

"Don Alonso wanted you and your family to have his house."

"What?" Gabriel exclaimed. "What about you? Don't you want to live there? It's your home."

"I haven't lived there for years, and I would feel very uncomfortable returning now. That palace is a symbol as much as it's a home. It announces the position of the person living in it. It's a place for meetings, dinners, great parties of state. The Archbishop will come, the king's ministers, perhaps even the King. It's not for me. It's for you, Gabriel. That's what my father wanted."

"How will I pay for such a house?" Gabriel asked. "Servants? Supplies? Repairs?"

Gonsalvo laughed. "You have no idea how profitable the tax farming is, especially with your contract. You'll be an enormously wealthy man. But until money starts to flow, I'll advance what you need. I'll even manage the household staff for awhile, until you and Pilar are comfortable with everything."

"All right," said Gabriel, unable to think of any further objections.

"What's troubling you now?" said Pilar, gently manipulating his injured hand. She had been standing next to him, ignored, for several minutes.

"How are Tomas and Esther?" he responded, avoiding the topic he was not quite ready to face.

"Say Maria," Pilar cautioned. "Be careful."

"Even here?"

"Yes. Even here. Can we trust every one who works in this house?"

"Soon there will be many more," he said, plunging in.

"What do you mean?"

"All week, people have begged me to take on Don Alonso's role as leader of the *conversos*."

"What exactly does that mean?" Pilar asked.

"You always get to the heart of the matter," Gabriel answered with a smile. "I'm not sure. Don Alonso was involved in everything. I can't begin to replace him."

He took a deep breath and exhaled slowly. "I'm so alone ... so afraid. Sometimes I can hardly breathe." He took Pilar's hand. "I'll surely do something stupid. I've relied on Don Alonso in every emergency."

Pilar smiled and waited. She understood her husband's habit of understating what he knew and what he could do. "Esther's been teaching me," she said. "In the Talmud, there's a book called *Pirke Abot*, Sayings of the Fathers. Just yesterday, Esther read 'in a place where there are no leaders, strive to be a leader.'"

"All right," he said. Another long pause. "There's no one else. I'll do the best I can."

Pilar hugged his face to her chest.

"My friends are gone," he said weakly. "Thank God for my family. This is such an ugly time."

"It will pass," she whispered.

"No. It'll get worse. Perez will soon be back. Fonseca is a lonely and ineffective voice in the Church. Of course he's sickened by what Perez did to Francesco, and he detests the violence of the mobs. But he's not the one they'll listen to. Jews and *conversos* have no future in Spain. I'll be the leader of a dying group, presiding over funerals."

"But you'll be able to influence Enrique."

"He does seem to like me, thanks to Tomas and Prince Hasan, but look what that brought. Even when Enrique tries to be helpful, he can't do the right thing. At least he still needs us. Without *conversos*, he has no money."

"And there's the printing," said Pilar. "So many books to print."

"And the children," said Gabriel.

"They must not die here." said Pilar.

"The final chapter of the Catalan family must not be written in Spain," said Gabriel softly.

He noticed that the burning in his gut had gone away. When Pilar was with him, and they were in harmony, he could face anything.

"By the way," he mumbled, his face still buried in her chest, "We're going to move to Don Alonso's palace."

"What?" she cried, pulling back. "What did you say?"

Gabriel's face broke into a great smile. "Later. I'll tell you later."

The fingers of his good hand traced their way up her leg with unmistakable intent.

"We're going to move where?" Esther screamed.

"We're going to live in the palace of Don Alonso," Pilar repeated. "You and Tomas will have as much room there as if you had this entire house to yourselves."

"We don't need so much," Esther said. "We're very happy here."

Pilar smiled. She had watched the young couple and she knew that Esther spoke the truth. She was amazed at her resilience. There was a joy to the new marriage that seemed to overcome everything. Pilar knew this joy with Gabriel, and was thrilled to see it repeated in her son and his bride.

"I'm very proud of you," she said to Esther. "You're so strong. You're very good for Tomas. He's such a dare-devil, but you and Judah, I mean Jose, are a healthy restraint for him."

"Tomas loves Judah as if he were the real father," Esther said, a distant look passing briefly through her eyes.

She'll never forget that awful night, Pilar thought, quickly changing the subject. "I'm happy that you're helping us make a Jewish home," she said. "I never wanted that before, but now I do."

"It's odd, isn't it," said Esther, "becoming a Christian and then teaching you to be a Jew."

"In a way, it's like having your mother with us. I miss Miriam so much, and every Jewish thing we do reminds me of her."

"I feel the same way," said Esther. "She would be happy to know it."

"It can't last, though," said Pilar with a frown.

"What do you mean?" Esther asked.

"Castile is not a place to raise your family. Some day soon, you and Tomas will have to leave."

"Where would we go? And won't you and Don Gabriel come, too?"

"We will never leave Spain," Pilar said solemnly. "But you, I think, will go to Italy."

19

Friar Perez copied furiously from the New Testament, the writings of the Church Fathers, the pronouncements of the popes. The official poison of Christianity against the Jews.

The Gospel of Matthew. The words of Jesus: *The kingdom of God will be taken from you. You are the sons of those who killed the prophets. Serpents, brood of vipers, how are you to escape the judgment of hell?*

Jesus according to Luke: *And they will be led away as captives to all the nations. Jerusalem will be trodden down.*

The epistle of Paul to the Romans: *The Jews are hateful to God, haughty, plotters of evil. Although they have known the ordinance of God, they have not understood, and they are deserving of death.*

Of course, the most damning words of all were their own, in Matthew: *The Jews said unto Pilate, 'let Jesus be crucified.' And Pilate saying, 'I am innocent of the blood of this just person.' Then answered all the people, and said, 'His blood be on us, and on our children.'*

This eternal damnation of the generations, echoed by Pope Innocent III twelve hundred years later: *The blood of Christ calls out against the Jews. They must be made to wander the earth and forced into servitude of which they made themselves deserving when they raised sacrilegious hands upon Him, thus calling down His blood upon themselves and upon their children.*

Finally he found a manuscript containing words of Peter the Venerable which he found personally comforting: *Really I doubt whether a Jew can be human.*

Francesco Romo was thus less than a human being, not entitled to the mercy of Christ. Ricardo Perez could not be guilty of his murder.

Thus the message of the Church, clear and unchanging for an entire millennium and half of another. The Jews who killed Christ, and their equally guilty and less than human descendants, deserved any calamity which could possibly be brought against them. The incontestable will of God demanded that they be persecuted forever for their rejection and murder of His only begotten Son.

"Jews pray three times every day," said Rabbi Modena. "The Talmud says we must sanctify each period of time by recognizing God who gave it to us. But so many forget the prayers. The old prayer books fall apart and there are no scribes to write more."

"So we should print prayer books?" said Gabriel.

"Just the essential prayers."

"Which are?" asked Gabriel.

"The *Shema*, of course, and the *Shemoneh Esrei*, the eighteen benedictions. Only now it's nineteen."

"The nineteenth blessing is the curse against heretics, including Christians?" said Gabriel.

"Yes," answered the Rabbi.

"This is why the Christians accuse us of cursing them three times each day?"

Rabbi Modena sighed and said, "It was added to the original prayers after the destruction of the second temple. There were many heretical sects … Sadducees, Essenes … and the followers of the Nazarene. Rabbi Gamliel *ha nasi*, the prince, thought we needed protection, so he wrote the added blessing."

Gabriel shook his head in frustration. "Why should Jews call God's curse against those who believe differently than us? When we say these words, we're no better than the Christians who curse us." Slowly, his disgust evident, Gabriel repeated the Jewish curse against heretics.

May all heretics perish in an instant;and may all the enemies of Your people be cut down speedily. Blessed are you, Lord, Who breaks enemies and humbles wanton sinners.

"How can we expect Christians to tolerate us if we say such a prayer?" Gabriel asked.

"They won't tolerate us whether we say this benediction or not," the Rabbi said sadly. "Their liturgy is filled with anti-Jewish hatred. This is the only hint of such a thought in ours. Anyway, those are the words. They come down through the centuries."

"I won't print them," Gabriel said suddenly.

"What? *You* will change the ritual? You're not a rabbi. Even a rabbi can't do that."

Gabriel stared straight at Modena as he repeated, "I won't print those words."

"You're the strangest Jew I know," Modena said with another sigh.

"Jews have always had many different views," said Gabriel. "It was Jews, after all, who embraced the Nazarene as God's Messiah."

"They were wrong," Modena said quietly.

"So we think," said Gabriel. "But that's not a good reason for asking God to destroy them. They're His children as much as we are."

"Even if they would destroy us?"

"Even so."

Modena shoulders drooped and his frail body seemed on the verge of collapse. "Do as you will," he said.

The old Rabbi shuffled slowly around the study, peering at his shelves. When he faced Gabriel again, he was fully composed.

"We have other business to discuss. What will you print next ... that is, after this abridged prayer book of yours?" Modena could not totally suppress a smile, although he tried.

"What do you suggest?" asked Gabriel, his small rebellion over.

Modena looked thoughtfully at a leather bound volume and started to bring it to Gabriel, but changed his mind and placed it back on the shelf. He did this several times.

"There are too many choices," he said.

"You must decide. Who else is there?" asked Gabriel gently.

"Not me alone," said Modena. "There's an assembly of rabbis next month in Valladolid. All the leading rabbis of Castile will be there. You'll explain the printing, and we'll ask them what to print next."

"They'll allow a *converso* to attend their meeting?"

"They'll make an exception."

"Will you go?" Gabriel asked, wondering how Modena could possibly survive such a trip.

"You can't go yourself," Modena laughed. "They'll never listen to you."

"Rabbi," said Gabriel, "there's something else. One press isn't enough. We need more. They should be in small towns, no more than four or five days travel from Seville, and they should be operated by Jews."

"I know just the places," Modena responded, "and the people."

"You're always so deep in thought when I come here."

The softly spoken words boomed in his head, and he spun around. It could only be Fernando. No one else ever came to see him. Only this boy, the strange and purposeful Prince of Aragon. Why did he return so often? Did he have such a deep interest in religion?

"Your friend from Seville has gained a great prize." Fernando said with a sly smile.

"What friend? What prize?" Perez asked.

"Why Don Gabriel Catalan of course," said Fernando. "A new force in Castile. King Enrique gave him the tax farming contract for Cordoba, and for far less than certain Old Christians were willing to pay. It raised quite a furor in Seville. There was fighting and one of the *conversos* was killed."

"Catalan?"

"No. Don Alonso de Viterbo. A very important man, I'm told."

"Why did Enrique ... ?"

"Because he's a fool," the prince interrupted angrily, his voice rising. "He gives power away instead of gathering it in. He makes enemies of the Old Christians and they cause violence and unrest that he is powerless to stop. His stupidity weakens royal authority."

Regaining his composure, Fernando spoke in more measured tones, "Enrique said he was rewarding Catalan for negotiating a truce with the Moors."

"Did he?"

"Somebody did. They stopped fighting."

"Enrique has no more heart to fight Moors than he does the Jews," said Perez. "He doesn't understand the threat of Jews and the *conversos*."

"But you do?" asked Fernando, mocking.

"It's very serious," said Perez.

"Why?"

"Because they're evil. They refuse to accept Christ."

"Do better than that, good friar, if you expect the ear of kings and princes."

"They threaten the unity of the Church ... and Spain."

"How?"

"All Christians think alike, as they're instructed, but Jews introduce doubt. There can be no doubt. All people must accept that Christ is God."

"And that the king is king?"

"Yes. Exactly," said Perez, amazed at where he had been led by the young prince.

"What do you think of Enrique's half brother Alfonso? There are many, I hear, who would support him."

"I ... don't know," Perez answered honestly.

"He would be no better than Enrique," said Fernando with a contemptuous sneer. "But the sister! She's the one with *cajones*." He laughed loudly as he walked away.

"Isabel has the *cajones* to be king."

Gabriel let the feeling grow.

A memory took shape. It was Pilar, a young girl. They had walked here, and by that wall he held her hand for the first time.

He peeked around the corner. Yes, it was still there. A small tavern where they ate figs and dates on that magical day. His heart sang, as it had then.

It had been years since he strolled leisurely in this part of Seville, and he feared there would not be many more such opportunities. He savored every moment.

An oak tree, like hundreds of others. But this one told a story. He had lifted Tomas to its branches. When? He saw a four year old boy. Sixteen years ago! He remembered his alarm when Tomas had climbed out of reach, higher and higher. But he was surefooted and strong, even then, and he had scrambled safely back to Gabriel's arms.

Every narrow street and open square stirred his memory. There was his father Isaac, delivering a delicately worked gold plate to a family that had later become his own good customer. No more, he thought, staring ruefully at the useless fingers of his right hand.

He passed a place along the river where he and Francesco and Rodrigo had often gone swimming as young boys. He remembered a fisherman who had joked with them and sometimes given them a fish or two when the catch was good.

He stood in the marketplace where Isaac had first introduced him to the great Don Alonso de Viterbo. He had known of Don Alonso, of course, but this was the first time they had spoken. His proud father, the busy Don Alonso, a young man himself, taking time to be patient with a little boy. He felt the awe that stirred him then.

Now he, little Gabriel Catalan, was Don Gabriel, the new Don

Alonso. He shook his head in disbelief.

Perez methodically assembled material for each theme he intended to use in his book and sermons. Pages were headed Jews - Killers of Christ, Rejection of the Old Law, and Christ is the Jewish Messiah.

It was the Jewish atrocities, however, which would excite the people. The theology of Christianity would establish a necessary foundation, but Perez knew that the success of his sermons would depend on lurid tales of the devil, ritual murder, and the poisoning of wells.

From the report of the English monk Thomas of Monmouth, Perez copied every word of the gruesome murder by Jews of young William of Norwich, now a martyred saint.

From the Canterbury tales of Geoffrey Chaucer, he gathered the well-known tale of the Prioress, another story of ritual murder by Jews.

He copied clauses from Castilian Law, the *Las Siete Partidas*, accusing the Jews of celebrating Good Friday by stealing a Christian child and fastening him to a cross.

Perez was ready. He had everything he needed, all of it from unimpeachable sources, the accumulated doctrine of the Holy Catholic Church against the Jews. He leaned back to anticipate his destruction of the Jews and *conversos* of Spain. Cadences of speeches-to-be rocked in his mind as crowds cringed and roared.

Then Perez remembered the one line from all of John Chrysostom's writings that he wanted desperately to forget.

"Don't you see," Chrysostom wrote, *"if the Jewish rites are holy and venerable, our way of life is built on lies."*

Chrysostom's anguish penetrated Perez's soul over the span of more than a thousand years. He shivered and held his head as the questions he sought to avoid tormented him once again.

What if the Jews are still God's Chosen People?

What if Christ is not the Jewish Messiah?

What if the Old Law of Moses is not invalid?

If the Jews are right, then what is left to Christianity?

He sweat profusely and shook with fear. These unthinkable questions must never be spoken!

His grandmother's dying cackle: *Now you live with it, my grandson Hebrew priest!*

Gabriel and Tomas found the small house in the village of Olvera.

An ancient rabbi peered cautiously through the crack in the door.

"Rabbi David Modena of Seville sent us," Gabriel announced, and the door opened.

"There's a goldsmith here by the name of Israel Lucena?" Gabriel asked.

"Yes."

"We came to meet him. Let me explain."

The rabbi insisted that they eat, and as they did, Gabriel told the story of Gutenberg's method and their plans to print Hebrew books. Although the rabbi asked many questions, it was clear he did not understand. His respect for David Modena, however, was enough.

"Tomorrow," he said, "I'll bring Lucena and you will explain these things to him."

"Since you can't come to me, I come to you."

Perez was startled by the familiar voice. Torquemada at Hijar! Fear ripped through him. He jumped to his feet, knocking his chair to the floor.

"Your letters were encouraging," said Torquemada, ignoring the chair. "Show me what you've written."

Perez nodded at the stacks of paper arranged on the tables around him.

"It starts here," he said, pointing.

Torquemada read, turning the pages furiously. Hours passed without a word. Perez fretted nearby, forcing his pen to scratch away although nothing he wrote made any sense. He rose only to light new candles.

"It's time to pray," said Torquemada, striding off. Perez ran awkwardly in his wake.

The recitations of Vespers passed in a blur. They returned to the tables, fresh candles in place. Torquemada read for hours, expressionless.

"Time to sleep," Torquemada said, without looking at Perez, and he was gone.

Perez leaped to see if Torquemada had left any marks to indicate his thoughts. He reached out but just as quickly pulled his hands back. Torquemada had not given him permission to look, and he was afraid to touch his own work.

Perez spent the night in the library, fitful, sleepless. Torquemada arrived with the sunrise.

"You must make clear that St. Augustine held that Jews were being punished for killing Christ, and that today's Jews are equally guilty," Torquemada said as he walked into the room. "And that St. Tomas Aquinas wrote that the Jews knew Jesus was the Messiah but crucified him anyway. Aquinas agreed with Augustine that all Jews, not just those who lived at the time of Jesus, are guilty of his death and deserve to be punished. 'The blood of Christ binds the children of the Jews,' Aquinas said. 'They are imitators of their parents' malice and thus approve of Christ's killing.' They add to their sin every day by their continued denial of Christ and their perverse observance of the Law of Moses."

Perez wrote feverishly, scrambling papers, spilling ink. As soon as he completed a change, Torquemada dictated the next, and then another. They worked that way for hours.

Gradually, Perez realized that none of Torquemada's changes was major. He strengthened an argument, substituted a more violent word, corrected a reference. But he did not change the substance of Perez' writings. How could he remember? He had no notes.

"That's all," Torquemada said. "What are you going to do with it?"

Perez stared at him blankly. With a start, he remembered his plan. "I'm going to give sermons. All over Castile. Week after week, building hatred against Jews and *conversos*. When the pressure is great enough ... riots, Jews beaten in the streets. Then I'll demand that Enrique create an Inquisition to seek out the secret Jews among the *conversos*."

"Are there any secret Jews? You didn't find one last time. That's why you're here."

"This time there'll be evidence. After I prepare the people, they'll come forward. Once it begins, it'll feed on itself and everyone will rush to become an informer. No one will dare to deny me."

"Enrique won't have the strength to implement an Inquisition," said Torquemada.

"I'll force him to act," Perez responded.

"No, you won't. But go ahead anyway. Enrique won't be king forever. There's already talk of replacing him with his half-brother Alfonso."

"Fernando says he would be no better."

"You talk with the prince of Aragon?"

"He comes here often," Perez said. "And he always asks about *conversos*."

For the first time since he had arrived, Torquemada's dour face revealed interest. He almost smiled.

"That is one to know," he said. "It may seem far fetched now, but some day Fernando could marry Isabel and become the king we need."

"He thinks highly of Isabel," said Perez.

"So do I," said Torquemada. "Ricardo, in your travels, you must be sure to meet prominent Old Christians. They hate *conversos* as much as we do. Especially Alvar Sanchez, who lost the tax farming contract to Gabriel Catalan. Your speeches will give them the fuel. They will light the fires. Meanwhile, I'll prepare Isabel!"

There had been endless talking. The purpose of the meeting was to review the status of the *takkanot*, laws for the self-regulation of the Jewish communities, which had been drawn up under the leadership of Don Abraham Bienveniste, chief rabbi of Castile, some forty years before.

Gabriel could not follow the debates on instruction in the Torah, taxes for weddings, circumcision, death, houses of worship, and the powers of judges to decide internal Jewish matters. When the conversation turned to cases of Jews who denounced and informed on other Jews, he was saddened by his memories of Rodrigo. There was no mention of *conversos*. For these rabbis, *conversos* did not exist. *Conversos* were Christians, not Jews.

Gabriel sat quietly next to Rabbi Modena. It never occurred to him to speak, and it would have shocked the rabbis if he had. They knew he was not one of them. Not a scholar. Not a real Jew. He had seen Modena in soft conversation with some of them and noticed the skeptical looks directed his way.

But then there was a lull in the proceedings, and Gabriel was startled to see everyone looking at him. Rabbi Modena rose and walked unsteadily to the center of the room.

"I've spoken to all of you concerning my friend Don Gabriel Catalan," Modena said. "He has something to show you. Then we will seek your guidance."

Modena nodded to Gabriel, who reached into a bag at his feet and withdrew six printed *Haggadahs*. He gave them to the rabbis and took his seat, folding his hands politely, waiting for the excitement he thought would follow.

"So?" he heard. "These are *Haggadahs*. So?"

Gabriel shook his head. Why couldn't they see?

"Look more carefully," said Modena patiently. "Compare one with another."

Rabbi Halorka of Burgos was the first to see.

"These two volumes are identical," he said. "Give me another."

He looked rapidly at all six copies, laying out the same pages on each.

"They are the precisely the same. No variations of any kind. How is this possible?"

"Don Gabriel. We have their attention," said Modena.

Gabriel explained the printing process, showed them type, and told them how this had come to Don Alonso from Johann Gutenberg of Mainz.

"Where was this done?" asked Rabbi Halorka.

Gabriel hesitated, reluctant to reveal too much.

"The press is in a town not too far from Seville, well hidden. Two more presses will soon be in operation in different towns."

"Can you make other books?"

"Yes."

The rabbis shook their heads in disbelief.

"Which books will you make?"

"That's what we've come to ask you. Which are most important?" Gabriel smiled at Rabbi Modena. "We have begun a short prayer book. We'll print a thousand copies."

"That is impossible," said Rabbi Halorka. "No one can make a thousand copies!" He looked at the other rabbis, and they laughed at Gabriel's preposterous claim.

"It will take three months," Gabriel said without emotion. "No more." He was pleased by the gasps that filled the room. "But what shall we print after that? There's so much to choose from. And we must act quickly. We can't know how long we'll have before we're discovered."

A dozen rabbinical voices spoke, simultaneously and heatedly. Names of Jewish scholars and Jewish works filled the air. "Abraham Ibn Ezra. *Orhot Hayyim*. Torah commentary by Moses Nachmanides.

No, Maimonides. No, Bahya ben Asher. A book of psalms. *Pirke Abot.* The Babylonian Talmud. Yes, *Berakot.* No, *Ketubot.* It must be *Shabbat.*"

Gabriel recognized some of the names, but many were unknown to him. Each suggestion had supporters and opponents, and it soon became obvious there would be no consensus. The arguments were fierce, and no dominating figure could command the will of the assembled rabbis.

Modena pulled at Gabriel's cloak. "I'm afraid this was a mistake. Nothing will come from this."

Gabriel rose, and waited until the room became quiet. He touched the scar on his damaged hand, his constant reminder of Don Alonso, and recalled his friend's words the night they first met Gutenberg.

"Perhaps," he said, "we should try to save those truly important works for which the fewest copies remain, so they are not lost forever."

The rabbis looked at each other and nodded their bearded heads. "You have brought us a man of wisdom," Rabbi Halorka said to Rabbi Modena. "Let us approach the problem from the viewpoint Don Gabriel has suggested."

A very different discussion now ensued. Each manuscript was considered and estimates were made not only of their importance but of the number of copies remaining in Spain. Three hours later, the room was quiet.

"Don Gabriel, here is our decision," Rabbi Halorka announced. "We would like you to print Reb Schlomo's commentary on the five books of the Holy Torah, the *Arba'a Turim* of Rabbi Yacov ben Asher, the *Mahzor* for the Day of Atonement and also for *Rosh ha-Shanah,* the *Sefer Ha'Ikkarim* of Yosef Albo, the *Mibhar ha-Peninim* of Solomon ibn Gabirol, and, from the Babylonian Talmud, the *Pirke Abot, Berakot,* and *Ketubot.* Five hundred copies of each. How soon can you get started?"

20

The Viterbo palace would never really be home for the Catalan family. The presence of Don Alonso was with them constantly. This was true even in the luxurious suite of rooms in a remote wing of the mansion occupied by Tomas and Esther and Judah.

"Tomas, pay attention," Esther exclaimed, smiling coyly. "How will you ever learn to speak Hebrew if you don't listen to me?"

"Why must I speak Hebrew?" said Tomas, trying to tickle her as she avoided him. "Who will I speak it with?"

"It's a disgrace. You're the leading printer of Hebrew books ..."

" ... the only one."

" ... and you can't speak the language you print."

"I know some words. And I know lots of prayers. Besides, in a few days I go back to Arcos. I don't want to use all my time learning Hebrew words."

"I'll make it easy for you," she said with a sly smile. "Say שד."

"What does it mean?"

"Say it."

"שד," he said.

"It means breast," said Esther. "Do I have your attention?"

"What else do you want me to learn?"

"ירך," she said.

"ירך" Tomas repeated with alacrity.

"ירך means thigh."

"Say מאהב שכבה עמי."

"מאהב שכבה עמי."

She shaded her eyes, as she had seen dancers do at the *Alhambra*, and struck her hips playfully in a provocative pose. "It means," she whispered with a smile, "my lover, make love with me."

Tomas walked quietly across the room. He could hear Judah playing noisily downstairs. He closed the door and locked it.

"Tomas! In broad daylight!" Esther said, her clothes already a pile on the floor.

Later, they curled together, relaxed and spent. Suddenly, Esther sat up and said, "Your mother wants us to go to Italy."

"She's tired of us already?" Tomas asked.

"No. She's worried about us. She thinks it's going to be too dangerous for us to live here."

"In Seville? Why?" asked Tomas.

"In all of Castile. Because of the hatred of the Old Christians."

"But we have so much to do."

"She doesn't mean right now. But soon. Maybe in a few years."

"This is my home," said Tomas adamantly. "I don't want to leave. I like it right here." He reached his long arms around her and hugged her tightly.

When he heard her sigh, he knew the reason.

"Don't worry," he said. "When it's time for us to make a baby, then the baby will come."

"Maybe not. Marguerita said that when Judah was born, there was damage and I may not be able to have any more children."

"Then we will be content with Judah."

"But he's not your child."

"Don't say that. I couldn't love him more. And he is my child. We've adopted him. Remember?"

As if on cue, a furious pounding at the door caused both of them to jump for their clothes.

"Mama! Papa! I'm here."

Laughing, pulling at his hose, Tomas hollered, "I'm coming, Jose, don't knock the door down."

Looking back first to see that Esther was dressed, Tomas opened the door and gathered the boy in his arms. He lifted him high and swirled around in circles, both of them squealing.

"Are you hungry? How about a picnic?"

"Yea! Picnic! Boat?"

"Let's see if we can find some cakes. We'll pack a basket and go to the river. If there's a boat, we'll go for a sail."

During Lent that year, in the city of Jaen, not far from Seville, a religious procession wound its way through the narrow streets. A young girl carelessly tossed a bowl of water from her window. It splashed on an image of the Virgin. The house belonged to conversos. Someone shouted that it was slop from a chamber pot, and that it had been aimed purposely to defame the Holy Mother.

Such an insult must of course be avenged. Torches were lit and mobs ran through the streets, some later said with more greed to rob than zeal for the service of God. Many converso homes were burned to the ground. Several girls and women were raped. The spark of disorder spread.

It so happened that Princess Isabel came to Jaen shortly after these events had transpired. She saw the burned out homes and, inquiring as to the cause, was greatly disturbed. She was said to view such rioting as a grave threat to royal authority.

In Arcos, Marguerita Sanchez lay near death. She had been racked with fever for days, her breathing labored. She drifted in and out of consciousness.

Hernando Talavero hovered over her, although the Jewish doctor had told him that nothing could save her. He tried his best to make her last moments comfortable.

He knew that she had given him much more than he deserved. She had long been the only source of pleasure in his destroyed life. No longer a respected member of the king's guard, he had no other place to go. He earned an occasional fee by carrying a message to some distant town. Twice he had ridden when the Duke of Arcos needed extra swords against the Moors, and he seemed on the verge of a permanent position. Then came the truce and again he was no longer needed.

"Esther Ardit," Marguerita murmured from her stupor.

Talavero paused as he wiped his dying lover's brow. Esther Ardit? Why would Marguerita say that name? That Jewish cunt was the cause of his downfall. She and Prince Hasan had ruined his life.

"Stay away from the baby!" Marguerita said, with surprising ferocity and strength.

"What baby?" he asked sharply. "What are you talking about?"

Marguerita opened her lips as if to answer, but no words emerged. Her head turned to one side and Talavero held her, tears in his eyes, as she passed away. Marguerita had no more answers. He closed her eyes and kissed her gently on the forehead.

He sat there holding her for over an hour, overwhelmed by his loss of the one person who had ever really cared for him. Gradually, he returned to the last words she had mumbled. Esther Ardit. A baby. Did Esther Ardit have a baby? Marguerita was a midwife. If the Jew did have a baby, she would know. Maybe she even delivered it. But why mention it to him? Why tell him to stay away?

Then it dawned on him. If the Jew had a baby, it must be his. He was the only one who had fucked Esther that night. He searched his memory. Had he ever seen Esther in Arcos with a baby? He remembered seeing her with Tomas Catalan, coming across the plains with the Moors. Tomas was the reason that Hasan had humiliated him and taken him captive. He quaked at the thought of Prince Hasan, involuntarily reaching to cover his groin. He hated Tomas Catalan. But he had no recollection of a baby.

The idea that he might be a father began to excite him. It was something to grab onto now that Marguerita was gone. He had nothing else. In the days that followed, the thought became an obsession. He had to know.

Tomas Catalan had returned to Arcos.

Talavero knew this because he had watched the house for weeks. It was easy to learn where Tomas had lived. He was known by everyone as the hero who rescued the captives and made peace with Prince Hasan.

The house was not occupied, but great care had been taken to seal off the windows and doors, and strong locks were in place. It had the look of a place which contained something valuable. Someone was sure to return. He had nothing else to do. He would wait.

One night he saw a light. The shutters were still tightly closed, but the glimmer of light behind them was unmistakable. Someone was there.

He found a spot behind some trees where he could watch unobserved. He was still there when dawn broke. An hour later, the door opened and two men he had never seen before came out and hurried down the hill. But they didn't lock the door from the outside. Someone else was still inside.

Moments later Tomas Catalan emerged, squinted at the morning sun, and stretched his long body.

'He's strong,' thought Talavero, 'but next time he won't have Hasan to save him.'

It was Gabriel's first return to court since the infamous day he had received the tax farming contract from Enrique. Now that he was wealthy and powerful, everyone wanted a word with him, and those words inevitably led to a request for a position, a favor, or a business relationship. There were many invitations to dinners and parties. And many unsubtle looks from willing señoras.

The last group was easy for Gabriel and disappointing to the ladies. The recurring memory of the whore in Seville hardened him to thoughts of any further infidelity.

Business opportunities were another matter. He listened politely to each situation brought to him. There were schemes to buy ships from the Venetians, to establish new trade fairs in France, to provide or seek funds for particular trade voyages, even to form a new bank and compete with the Medici. Later, he would review these conversations with Gonsalvo de Viterbo, and they would decide whether to invest. They had engaged in several ventures already, and Gabriel had been impressed with Gonsalvo's acumen. He was pleased to have him for a partner.

Tensions continued to rise between *conversos* and Old Christians. There was plenty of fault to share. *Conversos* were everywhere at court, and they passed by the sullen Old Christians as if they were dirt on the road. Not that the Old Christians were approachable. Gabriel tried again to see Alvar Sanchez, but was rudely rebuffed. Apparently, Sanchez had no lasting remorse for his part in the death of Don Alonso.

Despite the growing hostility, most of the *conversos* seemed oblivious to the approaching danger. Whenever Gabriel tried to warn them, his fellow *conversos* laughed at him.

Everyone laughed at Enrique, who ignored court life as much as he could. The king was inattentive and inconsistent, changing his mind frequently for the most trivial of reasons.

Enrique's treatment of Jews was as inconsistent as his actions on other matters. Sometimes, referencing the actions of one or another of his predecessors, but never, Gabriel noted, his own father King Juan, Enrique would proclaim that "his" Jews must not be mistreated.

But at other times, perhaps at the urging of other advisers, he would complain about lax enforcement of the laws and would insist that Jews wear the yellow badge, let their beards and hair grow long, and stay in their *juderias*.

Conversos also never knew what to expect. The official position of both Church and king never wavered: converted Jews were full Christians with all enuring rights and obligations. Enrique sometimes forcefully articulated this position. But there were other times, more often of late, when he seemed to believe the increasingly frantic complaints of Old Christians that *conversos* were secretly practicing Jewish rites.

Enrique was never predictable. After listening to a charge that *conversos* were being circumcised, and to the incredible claim, made by a young Dominican monk, that he had in his possession dozens of the actual foreskins, Enrique bobbed his great head and solemnly asked to see the foreskins, along with precise evidence that they belonged to *conversos*. No foreskins appeared, and the matter ended. Enrique seemed amused.

One Dominican in Enrique's retinue terrified Gabriel. Gaunt, fierce looking, Torquemada more and more had the king's ear. It was rumored that he used these opportunities to press for an Inquisition in Castile to investigate and root out judaizing among the *conversos*. Torquemada reminded Gabriel of Friar Perez, and he feared them both.

Gabriel was uncomfortable at court, and as soon as his business was completed, he departed for home.

Two days later, Friar Perez arrived in Segovia. His exile was over, and his manuscript against the Jews was complete. He wanted one final meeting with his mentor before commencing his sermons in Castile.

But first, there was other business. Torquemada hid Perez behind the confessional booth.

"Bless me father, for I have sinned."

Her voice was small and surprisingly timid. Perez couldn't see the princess, but he could hear perfectly.

"Have you considered the matters we discussed last week?" Perez heard Torquemada ask.

"The integrity and unity of the Church are always at the center of my thoughts," Isabel answered firmly.

"Have you weighed the threat to the Church presented by Jews and *conversos*?"

"I have considered your words."

"And?"

"I understand the influence and power of the *conversos*. They do much that is good for the kingdom. But if they also spread Jewish perfidy which undermines faith in the Church, this would cause much harm." She paused, then spoke with great conviction. "I cannot tolerate heresy. I find it despicable and terrifying."

"Good ... ," said Torquemada, but Isabel interrupted him.

"But I see no evidence that such claims are true."

"And if there was evidence?" said Torquemada, undaunted.

"Then I would have reason to be concerned."

"And to act?"

"If I had the power to act."

"She's coming closer to our view," said Torquemada to Perez when they were alone.

"She'll never act without proof," said Perez.

"There are many ways to find evidence," said Torquemada.

"Will she ever have the power?" asked Perez.

"Perhaps," said Torquemada. "Things change quickly. Is your book ready?"

"Yes. Over one hundred pages. All of the Church's best arguments against the Jews. My sermons are also written. I came here to review them with you."

"When will you begin?"

"Next Sunday, here in Segovia. Then Avila, Toledo, Guadalupe, and to Cordoba, Ecija, Carmona, and Seville. While I'm gone, do you have scribes at the monastery who can make copies of the manuscript? I have only three copies."

"Yes. Leave it with me. But I learned something that will be of interest to you. My uncle in Italy wrote to me about some Germans who came to his monastery at Subiaco. They brought a new way to make books. Apparently, they can make many copies. Someone named Gutenberg worked out the method."

A fully assembled press and everything else he needed was waiting for Tomas in Olvera. Twenty complete sets of Hebrew type, and matrices and molds to make more, were laid out in orderly fashion, exactly as he had diagrammed. All this was from Gabriel. In the other room, stacked on wooden pallets, were ten thousand sheets of paper, delivered by a fierce-looking group of Moors who terrified the village until their peaceful purpose was clear.

A letter from Hasan lay on the table. "Print the words of God," he wrote, "so that men may study and question as He intended. Please also extend my condolences to the beautiful Esther for the loss of her parents and brother. Be well and visit soon. Muhammad asks for you often."

Tomas treasured his unique relationship with Hasan. The Prince was a strange man, sometimes harsh and violent. But to Tomas he was always thoughtful and gentle. Tomas knew he could never have a better friend.

This was the third time in less than two months that Tomas was trying to teach printing to novices. At Arcos and at Ecija, his students had been young men and they had learned quickly. Israel Lucena was much older, and Tomas wondered how he would take instruction from someone young enough to be his son.

After brief pleasantries, he plunged in. First he showed Señor Lucena how to set a row of type, then how to combine lines to make a page. They printed a proof sheet. All this in less than one hour.

"Now you practice," Tomas said. "I'll watch. Take your time."

Lucena made many errors, which Tomas corrected without comment on the proof pages. As the day went on, there were fewer markings, but nothing close to a perfect page.

The physical techniques of setting type, spreading ink, and squeezing the press were only the beginning. Handling the paper was crucial. Speed and endurance were required. And a printer needed constant mental alertness to spot mistakes before time and materials were lost.

As the instruction continued, Tomas began to doubt that Lucena would be able to achieve the required level of competence.

"I'm not doing so well, am I?" Lucena said at the end of the fourth day.

"We'll keep at it," said Tomas. "You'll get it."

"No, this is too important. I have an idea."

Lucena waited for Tomas to nod, and then said, "My wife would like to help. She reads Hebrew very well. May I bring her with me tomorrow?"

The next morning, Tomas was greeted not only by Israel Lucena and his wife, but by four daughters, standing in a precise line from oldest to youngest, looking shyly at their feet.

"With these helpers, I'll make many Hebrew books," said Lucena, introducing the women in his life to the stunned Tomas. There was his wife Leah, and daughters Rebecca, eighteen, Rachel, fifteen, Deborah, twelve, and Hannah, eight.

Lucena must have spent the entire evening organizing his work crew. It was as if they had been printing all their lives. Rebecca set type, Deborah assembled the lines of type into pages, and Rachel did the inking. Hannah, perched on a stool, hung each printed page to dry. Tomas smiled as he watched the little girl, so earnest in her task. Leah was the proof reader, and Lucena himself did the heavy work of turning the screw. The Lucena family worked quickly and efficiently. The press at Olvera was clearly in twelve good hands.

"You're doing well," Tomas said. "Soon it'll be time to print real pages." He saw excitement spread over their faces.

"What'll we print?" bubbled Hannah.

"Hush," said her mother. "Señor Tomas will explain when he's ready."

"I'm ready now, and so are you. There's a wonderful book of the Talmud, different from all the others. It contains no laws, but many say it offers more guidance about everyday life than all of the intricate discussions in all of the other books."

"Is it the *Pirke Abot*?" Señor Lucena asked. "I remember reading that when I was a boy, but it's been many years. No one in Olvera has a copy any more."

"Yes," answered Tomas. "I brought a copy from Rabbi Modena. It's not a long book, but I want you to make five hundred copies."

"So many?"

"Set the type for each page, make sure it's perfect, and make all the copies of that page. Then do the next page."

Tomas went to his pack and removed Modena's *Pirke Abot*. It was a luxurious book, bound in soft brown leather. Many pages were decorated with exquisite designs. The first letter of each section was enlarged and incorporated into an elegant and colorful composition. The girls gathered round as Tomas turned the pages.

"I don't like that," said Deborah, pointing to a line in the book. "It says '*Do not converse excessively with a woman.*'"

"What do you think it means?" Tomas asked, looking with some trepidation at the five women around him.

"I'm not sure, but it isn't nice to pick on women that way," Rebecca answered.

"It better not apply in this family," said Señor Lucena, "or I would have to be very quiet."

"I think the idea is that men should study Torah and not be diverted by talking with women," said Tomas, "but often it's the women who make Torah study possible. I would know nothing of Judaism if it wasn't for my wife."

"Here's another one," said Deborah. "*Be as scrupulous in performing a small mitzvah as in a great one, for you do not know the reward.*"

"Is it a *mitzvah* to make these books?" asked Hannah, her eyes wide.

"Anything that promotes study of God's word is a *mitzvah*," her father said. "Thank you for giving us this opportunity, Señor Tomas."

"No. You're the ones who deserve the thanks. This is hard work, and it could be dangerous. God will surely reward you."

They continued reading and talking for several more hours, until it was almost dark. Walking home in the cool evening air, Tomas talked quietly with Lucena.

"I'll be back in about two months," he said. "I know you may think you're not ready to be left alone, but that's really the best way to learn."

"When you return," said Lucena, "*Pirke Abot* will be completed, and it will be perfect. You bring our next assignment and more supplies. We'll be ready."

21

Gabriel was home from Segovia. A steady stream of men carried his leather bags and wooden trunks into the house, and, without thinking, Gabriel looked for Don Alonso. Pilar and Esther joined him in the courtyard, so beautiful with orange trees in blossom, but also a reminder that this was really someone else's home.

"You have a letter from Herr Gutenberg," Pilar said.

"Good. I'll take it to Gonsalvo to translate. Any word from Tomas?"

"He wrote from Arcos," said Pilar, "on the way to Olvera, and then Ecija. It'll be another month until he's home. The printing is going well, but he sounded lonely."

"Judah asks for him every hour," said Esther. "Papa home today?"

"Now," said Pilar with an expectant smile, "tell us all the court gossip. What are the ladies wearing?"

"Not much," said Gabriel. "The queen's maidens are still parading around practically naked." Suddenly, he jumped up and exclaimed, "But, how could I forget? We have a new heir! Queen Juana had a baby girl, also named Juana."

"And who's the father?" Pilar asked with a biting smile.

"They call the baby 'Juana *La Beltranega*.' Does that answer your question? Enrique made Beltran the Count of Ledesma, a reward, he said, for his 'many willing services.' He actually said that at the baptismal service."

"What will he do with Isabel?" Pilar asked, ever alert to the next move in the political chess game.

"He's going to wed her to King Alfonso of Portugal," Gabriel answered.

"Why, he's twice her age, and fat as a pig," Pilar said.

"He's also her cousin. Enrique wrote to the Pope for dispensation."

"That's disgusting," said Pilar. "What else?"

"It's ugly at court. The Old Christians complain that the Jews take everything."

"Jews? Jews have nothing," said Esther.

"When they say Jews, they mean *conversos*. To them, *conversos* are Jews."

"But most of the *conversos* have nothing Jewish about them," said Esther.

"Except their grandparents," said Gabriel. "The church says we're Christians, but the people say we're Jews."

"Where will it lead?" asked Pilar.

"Confrontation. Riots … burning," Gabriel said. "Like before."

"We can feel it here," said Pilar.

"Are you bothered on the street?" Gabriel asked.

"People are surly," said Pilar. "They look mean, and speak under their breath. We can no longer enjoy a quiet walk."

"There's open warfare in Mainz," Gonsalvo read from Gutenberg's letter. "Two bishops are fighting to become archbishop. Gutenberg says printers can't work in the middle of a war. Some have already gone to Italy, and one's coming here, to work with you. Gutenberg says he's a Jew, and he can be trusted."

"What will I do with a German printer in Seville?"

"Open a press."

"Surely not a Hebrew press. Do you mean books in Castilian?"

"And Latin," said Gonsalvo. "The Church will be your best customer."

"That's good," said Gabriel, impressed again with Gonsalvo's business sense. "That will help us hide our purchases for the Hebrew presses."

"And we can make money," said Gonsalvo. "Remember, our family has been in the book selling business for years. It can be quite profitable."

None of these farmers can read, thought Friar Perez, surveying the flock in the small church in Carmona. All they know are the stories they hear in Church. They love Jesus and the Virgin Mother, and they'll accept what I say without question. They expect a rousing speech, and they're going to get it.

This was the third time he had given his sermon. Already, he had removed some of the dry theological references and embellished the gory stories of Jewish atrocities. This time he would include a complete description of the death of poor William.

Next was Seville. Two Jews had been arrested there for poisoning a well, and he did not want to miss their trial.

Next also was Gabriel Catalan. He had plans for Don Gabriel ... whose fingers he could still feel around his throat.

"Papa! Papa!"

Judah had been playing in one of the upper rooms, near a window, and he was the first to see Tomas. He scurried around the broad balcony and came screaming down the stairs. By the time he reached bottom, Esther, Pilar and Gabriel were all there, and Tomas was at the door.

Judah jumped into his arms, and Esther hugged him as best she could, laughing and crying with joy. Gabriel and Pilar stood aside, patiently waiting their turn.

Tomas' things were behind him in the foyer. He carried Judah like a flying bird and reached into one of the bags. Out came a brightly painted wooden sword and a Moorish turban. Judah whooped and ran across the courtyard waving the sword, and Tomas finally had a chance to hug his parents.

"We weren't expecting you until tomorrow," said Pilar.

"I rode all night. I couldn't wait any longer," he said, looking at Esther.

"Here," Tomas added, lifting a bag, "I have more presents."

Gabriel untied the ribbons of a small package and removed the wrapping. He stared at the Hebrew letters and tears came to his eyes.

"What is it?" he asked in a whisper.

"It's a copy of Reb Schlomo's commentary on the book of Exodus. Rabbi Levi ben Shemtov in Ecija insisted that you have it. He said it was a fit present for Don Gabriel Catalan, the great Hebrew printer."

Tomas gave a gaily decorated vase to his mother, and a silk scarf to Esther.

"Let's sit," said Pilar, leading them to a table laden with heaping platters of fruit and cheese and breads.

"Are the presses running?" asked Gabriel, his eyes still glued to the lush Hebrew script.

"All three," said Tomas. "I thought Olvera would be a problem, but then Señor Lucena brought his wife and four daughters. What a team they make! They remind me of Arcos when we printed the first *Shema*."

"I miss the press," said Esther, "and working together."

"That was a good time, wasn't it?" Tomas said, taking her hand. "We're too busy now, and apart far too often."

They met in the same room where Don Alonso had first introduced Gutenberg. Gabriel could not get used to the idea that it was his home, especially with Gonsalvo there.

"It is good to meet you, Don Gabriel and Señor Tomas," the German said in painfully articulated Castilian.

"Welcome to Seville. Herr Gutenberg has written about you," said Gabriel in equally poor German.

Exhausted by their linguistic efforts, they reverted to their native languages with Gonsalvo taking his familiar role as translator. The German, whose name was Zedler, told them that Gutenberg had finally printed a Bible with thirty six lines to a page. He showed them several proof pages, which were indeed works of art.

Asked in turn to report on their own printing activities, Gabriel and Tomas were both enthusiastic and circumspect. They showed examples of their work, and described some of the improvements they had implemented. But they were careful not to say how many presses they had, where they were, or what happened to the books they printed.

Talk eventually turned to the plans for opening a press in Seville. Zedler was surprised to learn that Gabriel, since receiving Gutenberg's letter, had already purchased a shop and installed a press. Gabriel, in turn, was pleased that Zedler had brought several sets of Latin molds and matrices. They would begin immediately on the task of making Latin type.

As they spoke, testing Gonsalvo's skills to their limit, Pilar and Esther came into the room and stood quietly by.

"This is my wife Pilar," Gabriel said, "and the young lady is Maria, wife of Tomas. They'll both be working with you."

Zedler's face showed his astonishment.

"Is this unusual in Germany?" Gabriel asked, smiling.

They came to Jerusalem, and Jesus went into the temple, and began to cast out them that sold and bought in the temple, and overthrew the tables of the moneychangers, and the seats of them that sold doves. And he taught, saying unto them, Is it not written, My house shall be called of all nations the house of prayer? but ye have made it a den of thieves. And the scribes and chief priests heard it, and sought how they might destroy him, for they feared him, because all the people were astonished at his doctrine.

Archbishop Fonseca completed the Palm Sunday reading. There was a rustle among the congregation and Fonseca waited until all were again quiet.

"This year, for the first time in Seville, we will celebrate Holy Week with a cycle of plays depicting the Passion of Christ. On Tuesday night there will be a dramatic representation of the Lord's entrance to Jerusalem. On Wednesday, a portrayal of the Lord's Last Supper and the Betrayal of Judas. On Thursday, the Trials of Jesus, and on Friday the Lord's Crucifixion and Burial. Then on Easter Sunday, we will culminate Holy Week with the celebration in this Cathedral of the glory of the Resurrection."

As soon as they arrived, Gabriel saw her. She caught his eye and smiled. He turned away, frantic, hoping that Pilar hadn't noticed. His stomach rocked violently, and the taste of vomit rose in his mouth. But the whore from Taverna Lucas moved on, and Gabriel's stomach quieted. He took Pilar's hand, checked that Tomas and Esther were behind them, and that all eight bodyguards were alert.

The Cathedral square was packed. Faces peered from every opening in the Moorish tower. Boys stood precariously atop the Alcazar wall, a dizzying thirty feet off the ground. Surrounding the audience in the square were four platforms, built against the adjacent buildings. Rising behind three of the platforms were scaffolds from which hung backgrounds for the scenes to be enacted on them. A fourth platform contained the musicians: three trumpets, two cornets, two drums, and a chorus of singers.

Chains had been strung across the streets which bordered the square to prevent the entry of carts and pack animals, except for one guarded path leading to the central platform. Nevertheless, several people dragged in boxes and stood on them, in order to get a better view. Those whose view was obstructed pushed them down, and scuffles broke out. Soldiers dragged the offenders away.

A fanfare of horns.

A flamboyantly dressed man, in a red and gold cape, with a wide brimmed feathered cap, rose magically onto the platform to the right of the Catalans.

"I am the manager of the actors from Valencia," he announced with a great sense of self-importance. "Tonight, our company will present the two Trials of Jesus. First ... our Lord Jesus before the Jews ... and then Jesus before Pontius Pilate." He fumbled in his cloak and withdrew a small sheet of paper. "We are grateful for the sponsorship of the guild of goldsmiths, and particularly to Don Gabriel Catalan, for his generous support of our players, the costumes and properties and ..."

"Enough speeches! Begin!"

"One more announcement. Please pay attention. The characters you will see are actors. They are not the real people. The actors portraying Jews are not really Jews! Last night, some members of the audience attacked the actor who was playing Judas, and he was badly hurt. Do you understand? These are only actors! Please don't attack them."

Actors appear and take their places. Directly ahead of Gabriel are the chief priests of the Jews ... black robes, yellow Jew badges. To Gabriel's left stands Peter, stocky, gray hair, matching his portrait in the nearby Cathedral. With Peter are several servants, warming themselves at a fire. To the right, the third platform is empty.

A roll of drums.

A cart at the edge of the square, pulled by an ass. Jesus in the cart, held firmly by two soldiers ... tall and thin, long hair, long beard. The ass is led along the protected path to the Jews.

Those near the chains fall back, in awe of the Lord before them. It is very real to them and the crowd is already angry. Murmurs are heard. "Jews did this to our Lord!"

Jesus in the cart, facing the Jews.

One Jew steps forward, turns his back on Jesus, speaks.

"High Priest Joseph Caiaphas, assembled elders of the Jewish Sanhedrin, here is the prisoner. This man, Jesus of Nazareth, is accused of crimes against the Temple."

"Present the witnesses," says Caiaphas.

Jews come forward.

Caiaphas, "What is your testimony?"

The Jews speak rapidly, all at once.

"This man Jesus overturned the tables of the moneychangers."

"He refused to allow the sale of doves."

"He called the temple a den of thieves."

"He said he would destroy the temple and rebuild it in three days."

"Enough!" says Caiaphas, the High Priest.

Standing, he asks Jesus, "What do you say? Do these witnesses speak the truth?"

Jesus answers not and Caiaphas is confused.

A huge fanfare of horns and drums.

Behind the Jewish elders, the awesome figure of Satan ... clawed hands and feet, long hooked nose, tail curling from his cape, Jew badge on his chest.

The crowd reacts wildly to the appearance of Satan. "The Jews are devils," they scream, "and here is their leader. See the Jew badge!"

Satan walks to Caiaphas, whispers in his ear.

Caiaphas smiles confidently. He now knows what to do. Loudly, boldly, he shouts to Jesus, "Are you the Christ?"

Jesus, "I am the Christ." A pauses, he adds, "But though I tell you, you will not believe."

"Are you the Son of God?"

"You say that I am."

The high priest rents his cape, cries to the elders, "You've heard his blasphemy! What is your judgment?"

The crowd, anticipating the decree, "Save him! He is the Lord! Let him live!"

The Jews on stage, chanting, "Jesus must die! Jesus who blasphemes against the Jews must die!"

Several Jews come close to Jesus, spit on him, strike his face and body. Caiaphas directs the soldiers. "Bind him! Take him to Pilate."

Tomas leans to Gabriel as the actors leave, and asks, "Did this really happen?"

"What does it matter?" Gabriel responds. "It's happening now. This play is real for those who see it, and it will send them out to kill Jews!"

Intermission.
A cart, in it a huge sow, her large distended teats swaying. Pulled, not by an ass, but by six devils ... horns, tails, Jew badges.
Jews, elders from the prior scene, led by Satan to the platform. Directed by Satan, each in turn under the pig, sucking her teats.
Devils howling fiendishly, dancing around the cart.

Esther cringes.
Tomas hugs Esther's face to his chest so she cannot see.

Having sucked his fill, each Jew rising from the sow, joining the dance of the devils. They've grown horns! Tails protrude from their black robes. Satan places large Jew hats over their horns, smiles approvingly.
A heavyset Jewish woman on the platform next to Satan, screaming, in labor. Jews gather round.
Satan raising her skirt, leering.
Satan reaching between her legs, extracting a piglet, alive, squirming. Throwing it high. The crowd catching the pig, tossing it again.
The pig falling. Stomping, killing. The dead and bloody Jewish pig thrown from one to another until finally tiring of their sport.
The intermission is over.

Second Act.
Pontius Pilate, imperial governor of Jerusalem, marching with pomp and ceremony to the central platform.
Caiaphas speaking to Pilate.
"We found a man perverting the nation, forbidding Jews to give tribute to Caesar, saying that he himself is Christ the King and the Son of God. By the law of the Jews he must die, because he has made himself the Son of God."

"Bring this man to me," says Pilate.

The crowd is silent, afraid.

The cart rolling ominously into the square, pulled by soldiers. Jesus in the cart, hands bound. The Lord looks, expressionless, at the Roman governor.

Pilate to Caiaphas, "Proceed."

Caiaphas to Jesus, "You call yourself the Son of God."

Jesus answers not.

Pilate, surprised, "Do you answer not? Behold what the Jews witness against you."

Jesus answers not.

Pilate astounded, asking, "Are you the King of the Jews?"

Jesus, "You say it."

Pilate, "Are you a king?"

Jesus, "You say that I am."

Pilate to the Jews, "I find no fault in this man."

"Let him go!" The crowd cries for the life of the Lord. "Don't listen to the Jew devils. Let Jesus live!"

Satan whispering to Caiaphas.

Caiaphas fiercely to Pilate, "This man Jesus stirs up the people, teaching throughout all Jewry."

Pilate, shaking his head, "This man has committed no crime worthy of death. I will release him."

The crowd cheers wildly.

Caiaphas, "No! Jesus must die!"

Pilate does not give in easily, "You Jews have a custom, that I should release a prisoner to you at the Passover feast, which is indeed today. I release this King of the Jews."

Devils howling fiendishly, rousing the Jews.

"Release not Jesus! Release Barabbas in his stead."

The crowd, hysterical. "Not Barabbas! Release Jesus! Don't listen to the Jews!"

The Jews on the platform face the audience. The two groups scream directly at each other, arms raised in fury. Gabriel holds Pilar, fearing violence. Soldiers march between the crowd and the stage.

Pilate to Caiaphas, "What shall I do with this Jesus who is called Christ?"
Jews and devils scream, "Let him be crucified!"
Pilate, exasperated, "What evil has he done?"
Jews, louder, "Let him be crucified!"
Pilate washes his hands. "My hands are clean. I am innocent of the blood of this just person."
Jews chanting, "The blood of Jesus be on us, and on our children." Repeating. "On us! On our children!"

Gabriel shakes his head in disbelief. He knows that these words appear in the Gospel of Matthew, but what people would so stupidly condemn not only themselves, but all of their future generations? This could not have happened as Matthew reported it! He must have made it up. But why? Then he understands. Christ's early followers failed dismally in their effort to recruit other Jews to Christianity. So they gave up on Jews and bent their efforts to the pagan Romans. Since it was the Romans they sought, Pilate must be innocent. And for Pilate to be innocent, the Jews must be guilty.

Pilate placing a crown of thorns on the head of Jesus.
Soldiers dragging the cart bearing Jesus out of the square.

As the cart disappears, the angry crowd is still screaming. "Don't kill Jesus! Kill the Jews instead!"
Tomas touches his father's shoulder. Gabriel looks in the direction of his son's nod. There, on the highest Cathedral step, is Friar Perez, his black eyes riveted on Gabriel. Standing next to him is Alvar Sanchez.
Gabriel's face reddens and his breath comes in short gasps. He starts forward toward Perez. Pilar grabs his arm, and Tomas holds him from behind.
Perez' eyes narrow and his mouth curls. He and Sanchez step back into the darkness of the huge Cathedral.

"You can't let him do this to you," Pilar pleaded, still holding him tightly although they had returned home and Perez was nowhere near.
Gabriel stared straight ahead, unwilling to look into her eyes.

"Do you hear me?" she insisted. "Do you remember how Don Alonso acted when Perez gave that awful speech years ago? He stayed calm. He walked over to Perez and spoke with him, smiling. He never let him know he was upset."

"I want to kill him," said Gabriel.

"Of course you do. And he deserves it. But you won't. That's not the way to beat him."

"He can be beaten?"

"Print Hebrew books," said Pilar. "Allow Tomas and Esther to escape to Italy. Then you win."

"And being a Jew?"

"That too. But it's more important for our children to be Jews than it is for us."

"Us?" asked Gabriel with surprise.

It was Gabriel's transcending hope that Pilar would one day embrace the Jewish religion. He had watched with pleasure as she supported Esther's efforts to retain Judaism in her life, but he never dared hope any of it might be for Pilar herself. Was she about to take that step? He reached out to take her hand.

She spoke with great deliberation, as if she had rehearsed the words. "A church that tortures to make people believe its Faith, and murders them if they do not, cannot do the work of God," she said. "Archbishop Fonseca is a good man, but so many of them are hypocrites and liars. Perez must be opposed. We ... our family ... are among the few who can fight him, and I want to help you and Tomas as much as I can. Especially with Esther here, it's the right thing to do. I will be a Jew."

"Do you now believe as Jews do, and not as a Christian?" Gabriel asked, tempting fate.

"No," Pilar answered, and his heart sank. "In fact, there are some aspects of Christianity which I find very comforting. And there are some parts of Judaism which I think are nonsense."

Gabriel thought it best not to ask for specifics, but Pilar continued without prompting.

"There is more than one way to worship God. We are all His children, and who can really know? Yet the Catholic Church proclaims that to be a Christian, you must hate and destroy Jews. That is obscene. I don't know why they do it. It certainly was not the teaching of Jesus. But I will no longer be a part of a church which kill its enemies."

"Jews are not totally innocent," Gabriel said. "Joshua and his troops massacred everyone when they entered the promised land. They said it was God's will."

"That was wrong," Pilar responded. "To kill God's children and say it's God's will is stupid and arrogant. I hope Jews will never do that again."

"So I should not kill Perez?" Gabriel asked.

Pilar raised her arm as if to hit him, but she smiled and he took her hand and brought it behind his neck and hugged her tightly.

"I have something for you."

Archbishop Fonseca had invited Gabriel to his sumptuous palace near the Cathedral. They walked through elegant rooms, paneled and tapestried, to a private section of the house where Gabriel had never been. The archbishop stopped at a dark alcove where candles struggled to dispel the gloom.

In the alcove was a painting. Gabriel stared, mute, remembering the pungent smell of ink and the forever silenced gaiety of Francesco Romo's laughing voice.

Fonseca stood next to him, respecting his silence. After several minutes, he said softly, "It's magnificent, isn't it? Moses receiving the Ten Commandments. You know who painted it."

"I saw it at his studio. He said it was for you, but I didn't know what happened to it."

"He gave it to me the day he was arrested. I've never displayed it publicly. It carries too much pain. I want you to have it."

"No, your Excellency. He meant it for you."

"He was your friend," Fonseca insisted. "Now that Perez is back, there will be many awful memories for you. This, at least, may speak to better times, past and future. Please take it."

"Thank you," Gabriel said, embracing the archbishop. "I will treasure it."

"You saw Perez yesterday?" Fonseca said. "In the square?"

"Yes. I wanted to strangle him. Tomas and Pilar had to hold me back."

"Don't do anything stupid. I hate him as much as you do, but his support grows every day. Did you see Sanchez with him?"

"I've tried several times to approach Sanchez, to tell him that the tax contract was Enrique's idea."

"He'll never believe you," Fonseca said, "especially now that he's become so close to Perez. It's frightening that the two of them are together. Perez will rouse the people's hatred. Sanchez will organize and direct it."

"Can we stop them?"

"I don't know," Fonseca said, and his uncertainty made Gabriel even more despondent. "I'll do what I can within the church, but I have no influence with Enrique. You must remain as close to him as you can. Keep pressing him on behalf of *conversos* and even Jews. If you can provide a balance against Perez, then maybe Enrique won't act. And Gabriel, make sure that your *converso* friends don't ridicule him. He sees that and it hurts him deeply."

"Will that be enough?" Gabriel asked.

"I don't know," Fonseca concluded.

22

Welcome in Christ.

Five thousand eyes looked up in respectful silence as Friar Ricardo Perez, framed by the huge bulk of the Cathedral, raised his arms high above his head.

With faith in Christ, we rejoice in the celebration of the Passion and Resurrection of Jesus and the Salvation of His love. We dedicate our efforts and our very lives to join with Him in the fight against the forces of evil. It is this fight of which I speak today.

Anticipation of this sermon had spread through the populace like wildfire, and the square was filled to overflowing. Archbishop Fonseca sat off to the side, unnoticed. The Catalan family were far to the rear, still within easy reach of Perez' booming voice. The friar's presence dominated the square.

We are prepared to fight for our Lord Jesus. But who are the forces of evil? Who are the enemies assembled against the Lord?

Expectant faces waited for the friar to answer. Perez spoke slowly, each word a dagger.

The mortal enemies of Christ today ... are the Jews who murdered Him ... joined in perfidy with their master the Devil. It is the Jews who seek to destroy Christendom.

Perez allowed the crowd to absorb his fire. Gabriel was frightened by their faces, distorted with fury. Yet he had no choice but to stay. Every *converso* must attend to prove his devotion to Christ.

Jesus said unto the Jews. If God were your Father, you would love me. But you hear me not, because you are not of God. You are of your father the devil! You have forsaken God and taken up with Satan. Your hands are stained with the blood of the Lord.

Gabriel looked at his hands and saw no blood. It is you, Friar Perez, whose hands are red with the blood of Francesco Romo.

The synagogue is a lodging place for robbers and cheats, and for demons who live in the souls of Jews. When Jews act against God, must they not serve the Devil? Can we doubt that the Jews serve Satan now when they dared a deed much worse in slaying the Lord? The Devil is a murderer, and the Jew demons serving him are murderers, too ... stealing Christian children and nailing them to crosses. So said our great king Alonso the Wise many years ago.

The crowd screamed and Gabriel struggled to remember. King Alonso was remembered and beloved, and his word meant much to these people. Did he actually say that? Gabriel didn't know. But what did it matter? These ignorant people will believe anything they're told. They need no evidence. Not when the Church controls the sacraments and condemns the unfaithful to eternal damnation.

The Jews have a despicable book called the Talmud. They claim this Talmud helps them understand their Law of Moses. But Pope Gregory warned us that it contains unspeakable insults, blasphemies, and wickedness. The Talmud arouses shame in those who read it and horror in those who hear it! It is these books which allow the Jews to remain obstinate in their perfidy.

This at least is true, Gabriel thought. It is the books which encourage Jews to remain stubborn in their love for the God of Israel. I'm proud that I make such books!

Pope Gregory ordered that the Jews be forced to give up their Talmuds, and that these ancient Hebrew incantations be burned at the stake. But ... this has not happened. Would that our kings heed that call.

Perez stretched his great frame even higher, and his voice rose to an awesome level of intensity. Why, Gabriel thought, does he have this power? God in Heaven above, why did You give this man such mighty skills?

The Jew is the devil's creature!

The Jew is not human!

The Jew is a demon!

A diabolic Jewish beast fighting the forces of truth and salvation with Satan's weapons. Jesus is a mighty warrior pitted against the forces of Satan. Jews are the implacable enemies of Jesus.

The crowd cringed with palpable fear. Their world knew the devil as a real presence among them. The thought that Jews were in league with Satan terrified them. Here were dangerous enemies before their eyes.

One cannot love the crucified Jesus without hating those who crucified Him. True followers of Jesus must destroy the Jews, lest Satan inherit the earth and salvation be lost. All Christendom is summoned to a Holy war, not only in Jerusalem but right here in Seville. And you are the warriors summoned to defend Jesus against the Jews and their devils.

If Jesus is so powerful, Gabriel thought, why does he need this motley group to defend him? The answer of course is that they are not being mobilized for Jesus, who would be appalled by their hatred, but rather for the more temporal goals of the Church and the Old Christians.

Perez' fury inflamed his audience and focused their hate. All of their problems were the fault of the Jews. More reasonable people, like Fonseca, could never counter distortions and lies so powerfully portrayed. And again, Gabriel thought, why does God permit this? Does God really hate the Jewish people?

The Jews changed the truth of God into a lie. For this evil, God abandoned them. God rejected the Jews, took away their promised land, and scattered them to the ends of the earth. These remnant Jews are consumed with envy. They hate God, they are implacable, and they are unmerciful murderers.

These Jews are worthy of death!

He would kill us all, Gabriel thought. All Jews, all *conversos*. Christianity cannot sustain itself so long as a single Jew lives to testify that Jesus Christ is not the Jewish messiah. They must silence every one of us or their religion will collapse.

But, he felt, with a sudden surge of emotion, they will fail! We will survive! Our books will live and we will remember the word of God! God may want us to struggle, but he will not forget those who worship His Name.

The Talmud demands that Jews must shed human blood, in order to obtain their freedom and return to the land of Israel that they lost by the murder of the Lord. Every year, in some part of the world, they must sacrifice a Christian child to the devil. I will tell you the story of William of Norwich.

What insanity, Gabriel thought. Even animal sacrifice was now prohibited by Jewish law. What Jew would ever consider the atrocity of human sacrifice? But the truth has no chance when lies are cloaked in the great majesty and authority of the Holy Catholic Church.

Each year, the chief Jews and Rabbis secretly assemble. They cast lots to determine which country must carry out murder to fulfill the duty imposed by their Talmud. Many years ago, they chose the Kingdom of England, and the exact place was the city of Norwich. At the beginning of Lent in that year, the Jews of Norwich chose one Christian child to be put to death. This was William, a boy only 12 years old and of unusual innocence.

At first, he was treated kindly by the Jews, and was ignorant of what was being prepared for him. Then they led poor William, like an innocent lamb, to the slaughter. Some held him hard from behind, while others opened his mouth and stuffed into it a large and painful wooden block. They fixed it by straps through both jaws to the back of his neck, and fastened it with a knot as tightly as it could be drawn. Taking a short piece of rope and tying three knots at certain distances, as precisely specified in their holy books, they bound it round William's innocent head, forcing the middle knot into his forehead and the other two into his temples, the ends of the rope being most tightly stretched at the back of his head and fastened in a very tight knot. The rope was passed round his neck and carried round his throat under his chin, and there they finished off this dreadful engine of torture in a fifth knot.

The crowd stood silent, mouths agape, straining to hear every word.

They shaved poor William's head, and stabbed it with thorn-points, so that blood come flowing from many wounds. They sang and danced as they mutilated this boy William, saying: "Even as we crucified the Christ, so let us crucify this Christian William and all Christians, uniting this Lord and his servants in a like punishment, so that our pain may be eased."

They fastened William with heavy nails upon the cross. They inflicted a frightful wound in his left side, reaching even to his inmost heart, and many streams of blood ran down from all parts of his sorely wounded body. They poured boiling water over him.

At long last, the glorious boy and martyr of Christ, William of Norwich, expired, dying the death of time in reproach of the Lord's death, but crowned with the blood of a glorious martyrdom. William entered the kingdom of glory to live forever. And many go to his place of death even unto this day, and worship there.

Perez paused, and the people, who had been shocked into silence by the story of William, became sullen and restless. But Perez was not done. He raised his hand to regain their attention, and continued in a quiet foreboding manner which forced everyone to listen again with great care.

There is a huge plot of the Jews to destroy the entire Christian population. When Jews pray, their most fervent prayers are for the destruction of Christians.

Gabriel recognized the reference to the 19th benediction, about which he had argued with Rabbi Modena, and which he had refused to print. He wished that Rabbi Gamliel had not given such a weapon to the Christians.

A terrible, mysterious horde of Jews is hidden in the east, waiting only for Satan's signal to pour out upon Christendom and annihilate it. I will tell you the plan by which the Jews hope to kill all Christians. It is prescribed in their Talmud. This Talmud teaches the Jews to make a poison from human blood and urine, and three kinds of herbs. They blend the heads of adder with the legs of toads and the hair of women from their private places. To this they add the hearts of Christians, sliced thin with sharp knives, and the body of Jesus obtained from sacred hosts which they steal from our churches.

The silent crowd held its breath as Perez lowered his voice to its most conspiratorial level.

Messengers carry the poison in narrow stitched leather bags to all parts of the world, even to the very gates of Seville. They pour it into wells where Christians drink. You know the effect of the Jew's poison. First the black swellings in the armpits and groin, oozing blood and pus. Followed by boils, black blotches on the skin, and bleeding within the body, causing the most intense pain. Everything that issues from the body, be it breath or sweat or blood or urine or black excrement, smells foul with the stench of the Jews.

Several women fainted. Even strong men wavered. Gabriel's legs shook and his heart pounded. Perez can excite this mob to any violence, he thought. And he will.

Be not afraid. The church will not abandon you. The church will not allow Jews to destroy the way of Christ. The Jewish assassins have been intercepted and arrested here in Seville.

Guided by our Lord, I am here.

I will personally take charge of their trial. Your children are safe from this evil conspiracy. The Jews have deserted God, and God has deserted them. We who carry God's mission on earth will assure that Jews do not triumph here. These Jews will be persecuted to the death!

With that, Perez turned on his heels and disappeared into the Cathedral, leaving a palpable void on the platform. The crowd continued to stare, as if expecting some apparition to appear in his place.

Perez had spoken not a single word about *conversos*, but Gabriel knew that it was judaizing *conversos* who were his true target. He would fan hatred against the Jews to fever pitch. Then he would claim that *conversos* were really Jews, only more powerful and wealthy, even more perfidious, even more worthy of persecution to the death. There was no question that the people would believe him.

The trial was held, of course, on the Jewish Sabbath. The room which had been set aside was far too small for the mob, and the proceedings were moved to the courtyard of the monastery at San Pablo. The only witness was a poor old man who had been cleaned up and given new clothes for the occasion.

"I saw two Jews near the well. It was night but there was a full moon. One of them removed a pouch from inside his cloak, and poured a white powder into the well"

"They killed Christ and now they want to kill all of us," a man hollered.

"Lord Jesus, save our children!" cried a woman.

Friar Perez, seated next to the municipal trial judge, raised his hand and the crowd quieted instantly.

"Even Jews must be allowed to testify on their own behalf," Perez said, but his ill-concealed malevolent smile let everyone know that this was just a formality.

"Come, Jews," he said, speaking to the defendants. "Tell the judge your story."

One of the Jews hesitatingly moved forward. Gabriel knew both of the accused. They had been good friends of Yacov Ardit, and their children had played with Esther and her brother. He cried in his heart for them, furious to be so helpless.

"We were walking home ... ," the old man began.

"From where?" Perez interrupted rudely.

"From synagogue."

The crowd gasped knowingly, wagging their heads.

"Did you get the powder from the synagogue?" Perez asked.

"No."

"Did you receive instructions from Rebbe Isaac ben Abraham from the Eastern kingdom? Did they meet in Constantinople? Is that where they decided to kill Christians in Seville this year?" Perez asked the questions so rapidly that the poor Jew could not answer. Since Perez never paused, it seemed that he didn't expect any response.

"What were you doing at the well?" This time Perez waited.

"We stopped to get a drink of water."

The crowd hooted its disbelief, and Perez did nothing to stop them. He leaned over and whispered in the judge's ear. The judge addressed the old Jew.

"Do you have anything further to say?" he asked, and hearing no answer, continued, "This trial is completed. A decision will be announced in two days. Until then the prisoners will be held in the back room of the inn of Pancho Lopez, along the Rio Guadalquivir near the *Torre de Oro*."

Although the result was as expected, Gabriel was crushed by a feeling of hopelessness. What chance did the Jews have in a trial like this? The arrest was made six weeks before. Many people had taken water from that same well every day since then. He had seen people drinking from the well this very morning. No one had gotten sick, and surely no one had died. Of course, none of that mattered.

On the day after the trial, Easter Sunday, Archbishop Fonseca spoke from the Cathedral pulpit.

"I urge the judge to consider the evidence," he said in his dry earnest manner. "No one has become ill by drinking from the well. Jews as well as Christians drink from it every day. We must not convict innocent people."

Gabriel wondered if the well-intentioned Archbishop knew how little impression he made on those who heard him. The rowdies who were fodder for Perez and Sanchez were not in Church. Nevertheless, Fonseca continued and his words were the essence of common sense and Christian good will.

"We cannot condemn Jews simply because they are Jews. Many Jews, including the Apostles themselves, have come eagerly to Christ, who was himself an observing Jew during His days on earth. Even as regards the crucifixion of our Lord, we must not condemn all Jews at the time of Christ's death, for only a few participated in that crime.

And surely no Jews living today had anything to do with our Lord's death."

These are the right words, thought Gabriel. A pity no one will listen.

As Archbishop Fonseca spoke, six men walked stealthily along the Rio Guadalquivir until they found the inn of Pancho Lopez, such an inadequate prison that it could only have been chosen for that very reason. The guards disappeared with no show of resistance. The flimsy door was thrown open. The two Jews were dragged into the street, ropes were thrown over a sturdy tree, and they were hanged. They died quickly, two bodies swinging softly in the Easter breeze.

No one was ever charged with their murder.

"Have you seen enough? Will you finally agree to leave this awful place?"

"What would I do in Italy?" Tomas asked, and to Gabriel it was the most encouraging thing he had said after months of unyielding refusal to consider the idea.

"You would be a printer. We have more than enough resources to get you established. You could take presses and type and everything else you would need. There are ships from Malaga. Prince Hasan could arrange it."

"I would just sail to Italy and become a printer?"

"To Florence, where Lorenzo de' Medici is the most powerful man in all of Italy. We bank with the Medici in Bruges, and our representative there has already agreed to write to 'Il Magnifico'."

"That's what he's called?" Tomas laughed. "The 'Magnificent One?'"

"Be respectful. He can help you. He'll love the printing. You can make a life for you and Esther and Judah, and ... and maybe there'll be more. In Italy, it's not so bad for Jews."

"We can never live as Jews again," said Tomas. "The Church would never permit it."

"If anyone could make that happen, it would be Lorenzo de' Medici."

Tomas looked impressed, pursing his lips, although his smile remained skeptical.

"There's really no future here," Gabriel said quietly. "If there's to be a Catalan family in this world, a Jewish Catalan family, it must be someplace else."

"But you're so helpful to King Enrique. Surely he'll protect us," Tomas argued.

"He needs me, and the other *conversos*. But he's weak, and the Old Christian hatred is unrelenting. They hate me most of all, for my tax farming contract. Perez will turn that hatred into violence. And he's not the only one. I saw a monk in Segovia who may be even worse than Perez, and who seems to have influence over the king. His name is Torquemada."

"I met him," said Tomas. "He's Princess Isabel's confessor."

"And he'll convince her to turn against Jews and *conversos*. If she ever becomes queen, she'll be worse than Enrique."

"That's not true!" Tomas exclaimed. "Isabel is a fair person. She's too intelligent, and too strong, to be taken in by Torquemada and the Old Christians. Do you really think she could become queen?"

"Many things would have to happen. But it's possible."

"We should help her," said Tomas. "She wouldn't forget us."

"I'm not so sure," said Gabriel.

23

"I won't go! I won't meet with that murderer!"

"You have no choice," Pilar responded, in a tone of voice Gabriel knew he was powerless to oppose. "God will punish him, not you. We need more time here. Time to print books. Time for Tomas and Esther to prepare. Time to make arrangements with the Medici."

Gabriel shook his head, furious because he knew Pilar was right. He could not have open conflict with Friar Perez. Not yet. He would go to San Pablo to see him.

"He demands a meeting at the very place where he murdered Francesco," Gabriel said in a faltering voice. "The man is an evil despicable person."

"But he's shrewd, and he's your enemy. Be careful."

"I hear you're a printer now. You don't fix trinkets in the synagogue anymore?"

Inside San Pablo, surrounded by the Dominican walls which had been Francesco's last home on earth, Gabriel squeezed the muscles in his legs and arms, and, forgetting, contracted his fists. Excruciating pain from his injured hand shot up his arm. He repeated Pilar's warning. 'Control yourself! Don't strangle him! Listen!' He forced himself to smile, but before he could answer, Perez' next question drove a spike of tension through his body.

"How did you become a printer so quickly?"

He knows!

"I know," Perez continued, and the word jolted Gabriel, "that one of the German printers came here. But why here? And why to you?"

Gabriel, panicked, unable to answer, but after a long pause, Perez went on, "Actually, I'm pleased there's a printing press in Seville. I have something for you to print."

Perez pointed to a pile of papers, neatly tied with ribbons in small bundles. "I want fifty copies," he said. "Can you do this?"

Gabriel considered a fire. Maybe there would be an accident.

"How much will it cost?" asked Perez.

"I don't know. I'll have to buy supplies and calculate the cost."

"How long will it take?" Perez persisted, obviously pleased that he could force Gabriel to do his bidding.

"Six months."

"I'll pay you double if it's done in three."

Gabriel sat alone in the secluded room where Don Alonso had taught him to say the Jewish *kaddish* for his murdered father. For hours, he pored over Perez' Latin manuscript. His horror grew with every page. Citation after citation, many taken directly from the Hebrew scriptures, claimed that Christ was the Jewish Messiah. This wasn't just angry Christian rhetoric or obvious lies. This was Holy Torah, the Psalms of David, and the prophecy of Isaiah. Could it be true?

"Jews read, study, debate, and often argue fiercely. Christians do none of that. They don't read their own Gospels — it's not permitted — let alone our Bible which they now claim is theirs. All they know is what they're told by their priests."

Rabbi Modena paused for breath, coughing, shaking.

"Anyone who questions Church dogma is branded a heretic, and if he persists after they correct him, they burn him at the stake. That's been the history of the church since the Dominican Order was created two hundred years ago."

Gabriel had asked Modena about Perez' references to the Book of Isaiah, but the rabbi, once prompted, had much more to say. Gabriel listened.

"Jesus of Nazareth was apparently a real man who lived about when the Christians say he did," Modena said. "But even his followers never called him God during his lifetime. A small group of Jews did believe that he was the Messiah, sent by God to expel the Romans and establish the Kingdom of the Lord on earth. When the Nazarene died without fulfilling these expectations, they were thrown into despair and confusion. The Hebrew prophets had said nothing about the Messiah dying.

"They had two choices. They could give up their hopes, like many other sects before and after, or they could seek to explain the Nazarene's failures and unexpected death. So the early Christians scoured the Bible, grasped at straws, distorted, and eventually made the words of Isaiah and others fit what they already knew had happened, even if those words had absolutely nothing to do with a Messiah, let alone with the Nazarene."

"So they lied?" asked Gabriel.

"I don't know if they meant to lie, but in their zeal they said things that weren't true. Take an example from Amos. The prophet Amos warned that a terrible day was coming when God's wrath would be unleashed. 'On that day, says the Lord God, I will make the sun go down at noon.' So the Gospels were written to teach that it became dark during the crucifixion of Jesus. The Roman historians Josephus and Tacitus both refer to the execution of Jesus and neither one mentions any darkness at noon, but the Gospel writers later invented the darkness in order to appear to fulfill a prophecy and provide a link to the God of Israel.

"Knowledgeable Jews immediately rejected these explanations, and it became obvious that the followers of Christ would make no more headway converting Jews. So they changed their strategy. Following the lead of Paul, they sought out Gentiles who had never read the Bible and were thus unable to question their preposterous interpretations. But they continued to use the venerable Hebrew Bible to root their new religion and give it substance.

"Once they chose that path, they were forced to discredit Jews as witnesses to our own Bible, since Jewish views were incompatible with their own. They said that Jews read without understanding. They said that the God of Israel had rejected the Jews, that Christians were God's new Chosen People, and that only faith in the Nazarene could lead to eternal salvation. They said that all of this could be found in the Hebrew Bible if only you knew how to read it.

"This was relatively harmless as a religious debate, although it got quite vicious. Then Christendom gained the power of the Roman state. The Church forced the adoption of secular laws which implemented their religious dogma, and used torture and murder to enforce them. Eventually, they thought of Inquisitions, directed by the Pope through the Dominican Order, as the best means to assure compliance and eliminate incorrect thinking."

Modena looked up, and seemed startled to see Gabriel.

"I'm sorry," he said. "I've been talking on about many things. What was your question?"

"Perez makes many references to our Bible," Gabriel said, "but there's one which troubles me the most."

"Let me guess. The fourth servant song of Isaiah?"

"Yes."

"That's certainly the most important of all Christian interpretations that Christ was the Jewish Messiah. Isaiah's 'suffering servant', as they call it, is cited directly several times in the New Testament and alluded to many times more." Modena brought down two volumes from his shelves. Let's read it and see if you think it refers to Jesus of Nazareth or even to the Messiah. He found his place and read aloud:

Behold My servant shall prosper, He shall be exalted and raised to great heights; He was despised, shunned by men; A man of suffering, acquainted with disease; Yet it was our sickness that he was bearing, And our suffering that he endured.

He was wounded for our sins, Crushed for our iniquities; He bore the chastisement that made us whole, and by his bruises we were healed.

He was maltreated, yet he was submissive, He did not open his mouth; Like a sheep being led to slaughter, He opened not his mouth.

My righteous servant makes the many righteous, It is their punishment that he bears; Yet he bore the guilt of many, And made intercession for sinners.

Modena took the other book and read to himself for several minutes. "I read first from the Hebrew Bible," he said. "The words of the Catholic version of the Old Testament are much the same, except for the headings. There are four of them: *The Lord Jesus' humiliations, The Lord Jesus' satisfaction, The Lord Jesus' death and burial,* and *The Lord Jesus' glory and exaltation.* This is remarkable, because, as you heard, the Nazarene isn't mentioned in either text, nor does Isaiah refer to the Messiah. It's the headings which convey the Church's message."

"Who was the servant?" Gabriel asked.

"No one knows for certain. The Christians, of course, claim that

Isaiah's servant is the Nazarene. Perez has surely repeated these arguments in his book. Does he say that only the Messiah could have been so exalted as the servant described by Isaiah? Or that the Nazarene is the servant who bore, on the cross, the penalty for the sins of others?"

"How did you know that?" Gabriel asked, astonished. "You haven't read Perez' book."

"Those are not new arguments," said Modena. "They've echoed through the centuries. Do they sound plausible to you?"

"It might be possible," Gabriel said, reluctantly, not wanting to anger the rabbi.

"Jewish scholars disagree. Rashi, whose commentaries on the Five Books of the Torah you are printing, says the servant is Jacob, renamed by God Israel, by which is meant the entire Jewish people, or at least the righteous among them. Ibn Ezra and many others agree with this interpretation. They say it is the people of Israel who are despised and rejected by man, but who one day shall prosper. It's the Jewish people who are sacrificed that the world may survive."

"But Isaiah writes about a single person, not a people," Gabriel interrupted.

"It's possible to read it that way," said Modena, "although the Bible often writes of a person when meaning a people. Some of the early sages did think that Isaiah meant the Messiah. But Rashi's interpretation has overshadowed those which came before. *Ramban*, the same one Tomas criticized for insulting King James, knew about these earlier interpretations, but pointed out that there was not a single reference, in any book of the Hebrew Bible, or in all of the pages of the Talmud, that the Jewish Messiah, son of David, would be betrayed into the hands of his enemies, or slain, or buried among the wicked. Hence, even if Isaiah meant the Messiah, this could not possibly be the Nazarene. But Isaiah did not mean the Messiah."

"Rabbi, how can we be certain?" Gabriel asked. "If learned rabbis reached different conclusions, how can we really know what Isaiah meant?"

"Indeed!" said Modena, excited. "And how can the Christians? How can Friar Perez? How can they arrogantly declare that anyone who sees it differently is a heretic who must be burned alive for his errors?"

"All this persecution and murder," Gabriel mused, "to force allegiance to a certainty that is unknowable. Why?"

"To Christians, Jesus of Nazareth must be the Jewish Messiah," said Modena. "If not, Christianity falls into the abyss. Without the God of Israel, there's no Son or Holy Spirit. Nothing is more frightening to an honest Christian thinker.

"If the Catholic Church allows such questions to be asked, some who have the capacity and will to think for themselves may come to the wrong answers, and then the whole structure ... sacraments, priesthood, Pope, monasteries, Cathedrals and universities ... will come tumbling down.

"For this reason alone, the Church will never treat Jews with fairness and human decency. The Church has no choice but to ignore and deny the clear words of their Jewish Nazarene who proclaimed the eternal validity of the Law of Moses.

"You see, Gabriel, they live in mortal dread that Christianity will be deemed a fraud."

"How much did you pay for the ink," Gabriel asked.

"Close to what he was asking," Tomas said, "but I deducted for a small batch that was no good."

"Hasan provided paper?"

"For all three presses, exactly on schedule."

"Are the villagers curious?" asked Gabriel, raising one of his main concerns. "Do they know what we're doing?"

"Christian villagers stay away from Jews, just as the Church tells them. The printers have been instructed to say nothing and keep everything hidden."

"Eventually, word will leak out," said Gabriel. "We need to work quickly. When will we have books to bind?"

"By my next trip, I hope. I think *Pirke Abot* will be completed at Olvera. The *Rosh ha-Shanah mahzor* may be finished at Ecija. I don't think that Yosef Albo's *Sefer Ha'Ikkarim* will be finished. I'd be happy with the first two parts. Maybe that'll be enough to bind separately. I'll send word to Prince Hasan to bring more paper and pick up the printed pages for binding."

"We're really doing this," said Gabriel, still amazed at the extent of their success. "You've done a wonderful job, Tomas. I'm very proud of you."

Each time Gabriel went to the monastery for more money, it was immediately forthcoming. He could not resist overcharging for the work, double, triple his costs and an outrageous profit. But it only made him feel worse.

Perez' book, which he called *Defense of the Faith,* was the death knell for Jews in Spain. It would add intellectual support to his frightening sermons. Yet Zedler, with Esther and Pilar assisting, had no choice but to print page after page.

Perez would easily connect *conversos* with Jews. He would use his attack on Jews to get at the much more powerful *conversos*. It was a brilliant strategy, and Gabriel Catalan, Christian printer, was his accomplice.

When would he hear from the banker in Bruges? Would Lorenzo de' Medici agree to help? Would Tomas and Esther escape?

The throne room pulsed with excitement.

Gabriel pushed his way through the crowd and came face to face with his worst nightmare. Perez was addressing an attentive Enrique. Torquemada was next to the king, solemn and inscrutable.

Perez' spoke. "There is a conspiracy of Jews and *conversos* which is intent on destroying Christendom."

"Why *conversos*?" Enrique responded. "*Conversos* are Christians, and have been for generations."

"No!" shouted Perez, shocking the onlookers with his boldness. "Most *conversos* are really secret Jews. They only converted to trick us."

"Are you going to bring me foreskins?" Enrique bellowed, convulsing in a loud guffaw.

"Your Highness, it's not a joke," said Perez. "And I do have proof. The words of our Gospels, of Our Lord, of our popes and kings. I have compiled it all in three years of labor."

"Where is this proof?" demanded Enrique.

"It will soon be brought to Segovia by none other than Don Gabriel Catalan, who, besides being your tax collector, is also a printer. The moment he arrives, I will give Your Highness a copy of my *Defense of the Faith*, and you can read for yourself of the perfidy of the Jews."

Gabriel tried to back out of the room but a man standing next to him shouted, "He is here!" and the crowd opened a path from Gabriel to the king.

"Splendid," said Perez.

"Welcome, Don Gabriel," said Enrique, waving happily. "Come ... come."

Gabriel advanced to the king, cursing the day he had first seen Perez.

"Do you have this book that Friar Perez has told us about?" the king asked.

"I have fifty copies in my wagon," said Gabriel.

"Fifty copies! How ... ?" exclaimed Enrique.

"It's called printing. Invented by a German named Gutenberg. I've built a printing press like his in Seville. With Gutenberg's method, many copies can be made very quickly."

Perez was impatient with the explanation of printing, and finally he interrupted.

"Perhaps Don Gabriel might show us the books he has printed," Perez said, "and then we could understand better what he means."

"Yes, yes," said Enrique. "Bring in the books."

Gabriel returned to the throne room leading a procession of five men each carrying ten books. With a nod from Enrique, he had the men place the books in piles on the floor. The crowd gasped. No one had ever seen so many books together in one place.

Perez gave a copy to the king, took one himself, and hovered nervously near the rest, trying to keep anyone from approaching his precious supply. Nevertheless, several were taken before Perez frantically appealed to the king and the guards restored order.

"Will you have your men take the rest of the books to the library in the Cathedral?" Perez asked Gabriel.

Enrique nodded his assent, and the books were removed. Perez, still flustered, addressed the king.

"Here is my proof, Your Highness," he said. "Here is all the proof needed to justify an Inquisition in Castile to search out the Jewish conspiracy among *conversos*."

"I will determine what proof is needed," said Enrique testily.

"May I address Your Highness?" said Gabriel.

"Yes, Don Gabriel," said Enrique.

"I've read this book. It contains no proof at all about any secret Jews among the *conversos*. *Conversos* are not even mentioned. This book is about Jews." Gabriel wanted to add that even what Perez had written about Jews was not true, but this, he knew, would raise difficult questions about how he came to know so much about Jews. He had said enough.

Enrique's head lolled from side to side, as often happened when he was confused. Torquemada leaned over and whispered in his ear. "I'll read the book," said the king. "Then we'll speak more."

Perez, Torquemada and the ever-present Sanchez distributed copies of the book to Old Christians they could count on to speak out and influence the king.

Gabriel tried to organize the many powerful *conversos* who were in Segovia, but they didn't respond to his exhortations.

"But Don Gabriel," they said, "this book is about Jews. We're not Jews. What do we care about Jews? The king knows the difference between Jews and *conversos*. We have nothing to fear."

"The king is not even going to read the book," Gabriel pleaded. "Perez and Torquemada will argue that *conversos* are the same as Jews."

"You worry too much," Gabriel heard over and over, and he despaired. Don Alonso was wrong, Gabriel thought, when he said I was ready to take his place. Don Alonso could have roused these clods, but I can't. They'll believe they're still in power until the ax has fallen and it's too late.

Gabriel tried several times to get an audience with Enrique, but his requests were ignored.

They assembled to hear Enrique's decision. Alvar Sanchez stood near Perez, smiling and laughing. The king was late as usual, and when he did arrive, he was in a foul mood. Torquemada walked in with him.

"I have several matters to announce," Enrique said hurriedly, his voice even higher than usual.

"I have written to His Holiness Pope Sixtus IV seeking permission to institute an Inquisition in the kingdom of Castile."

Gabriel caught himself on a pillar, his head spinning. Enrique had made his awful decision without consulting him or any of the other *conversos*.

"Effective immediately, all *conversos* are dismissed from my royal service. This applies to all offices, including the tax farming contract I so mistakenly awarded last year," and with this, Enrique looked directly at Gabriel. "I hereby revoke that contract and award it instead to Don Alvar Sanchez. I'm sure that our Old Christians will serve their king well."

Enrique rose and left the room, Torquemada following. Gabriel watched in disbelief as they walked away. He had failed, not only himself, but all of the *conversos*, stupid as they were. Don Alonso would have known how to prevent it. Perez and Sanchez advanced triumphantly on Gabriel.

"So, Señor Catalan, we see who has won," Perez gloated. "Are your hands so quick to grab my throat now? We will have an Inquisition, and we will find many judaizers among the *conversos*. Perhaps even you, and your son who is married to a Jew."

"She converted," Gabriel said mechanically, "as did my father long ago. Even the Pope says we're Christians, entitled to ..."

"You're entitled to nothing!" Perez screamed. "You and your kind have stolen from good Christians for long enough. Your time is over."

For once, Gabriel thought, Perez is right.

"We've won," Perez exulted.

"Don't be a fool," said Torquemada.

"What do you mean? Enrique did everything we asked. What more could we want?"

"Don't you know that Enrique will never have an Inquisition? He's too lazy. And soon he'll re-appoint the *conversos*. Most of the Old Christians are incompetent fools, even lazier than their king. They'll never satisfy Enrique's needs. Even Gabriel Catalan, if he's patient, will regain his contract."

"Have we wasted our efforts?"

"No. Not at all. This is a good beginning. It's just not an end. You continue your sermons. The more who call for the blood of Jews and *conversos*, the better for us when Enrique is replaced."

"Isabel?"

"Yes, Isabel ... in time."

24

News of Enrique's catastrophic decisions reached Seville while Gabriel was still in Segovia. Tomas was also away. The captain of the Catalan guards told Pilar that trouble was expected and that their home would be a likely target.

The Catalan household was always in a state of readiness. They had moved into the home after Don Alonso's murder by anti-*converso* rioters, and, though there had been periods of relative quiet, they never relaxed their vigil. Food in huge quantities was always on hand in dry storage bins and deep cool cellars. Great barrels of pure water were constantly maintained. Pilar ordered the servants to take inventory of all supplies, and to purchase as much fresh fruits and vegetables as could be had.

She was beginning to feel secure when she realized that Esther and Judah were not home.

They had gone to the river, Judah's favorite playground. Two guards had gone with them, enough under normal circumstances, but not if there was a riot. Pilar sent eight armed men to bring them home.

Talavero had followed Tomas from Arcos to Olvera, to Ecija, and finally to Seville. He watched Gabriel and Tomas leave, and waited. Several times he saw Esther and the child, and he was now sure the boy was his son.

Mobs had been gathering for hours, and Talavero was surprised when Esther and the boy left the house. Maybe they didn't know.

They were accompanied by two guards, so Talavero could only follow and watch.

His chance came suddenly. Just as Esther and Judah reached the river bank near the *Torre de Oro* several dozen men with clubs and swords came running toward them. The guards jumped between Esther and the mob. Esther held Judah in her arms.

Talavero ran at Esther from behind. He smashed his shoulder into her back, knocking her to the ground, loosening her grip on Judah. He grabbed the boy and ran. Esther's screams alerted the guards, but when they turned to her, they were attacked from behind by the approaching mob.

From the ground, Esther saw Talavero running off with Judah just before the club smacked against her head.

Reinforcements reached Esther in time to fight off the mob. They carried her home, but she didn't move and they feared the worst. The two guards had also been seriously wounded. Judah was gone.

Pilar, frantic, had to be restrained from rushing out to find her grandson. "We can't protect you out there," the captain insisted, and when she saw hundreds of angry men outside the palace, she agreed. They were safe inside, with food and supplies to last for months. But they were prisoners in their own home.

Two days later, they were able to sneak a small group out of Seville. Four men went to Segovia, four more to Olvera.

Esther was alive, but still unconscious.

"Gabriel, we must act," said Archbishop Fonseca.

Fonseca, just arrived in Segovia, approached Gabriel as he was about to return to Seville.

"Enrique will destroy Castile," said Fonseca. "Without *conversos*, he can't govern. And he'll also destroy the church, perverting it to the sickness of men like Perez and Torquemada. He must be stopped."

"Who is with you?" Gabriel asked.

"There are many, some who will surprise you. Even Old Christians are disgusted with this king. Archbishop Carrillo, of course. But also the Bishop of Coria, the Count of Miranda, and of Santa Marta and Ribadeo, and many other knights. Troops are beginning to assemble. But we need more *conversos*. Will you help us bring them in?"

"I've tried to be loyal," said Gabriel, deciding as he spoke, "but Perez and Torquemada have won. There's no hope with Enrique. I'll join you."

"Our plan is to make Enrique's half-brother Prince Alfonso the king. He's with us at Avila. Will you gather as many as you can and join us there?"

"Yes."

Two days later, when Pilar's messengers reached Segovia, Gabriel was gone.

Tomas was disappointed that less than one part of Yosef Albo's treatise had been completed at Arcos. He did his best to organize a better result, and hurried on to the village of Olvera. Dusty and tired, he and his men arrived after dark. They wound their way through tiny streets to the shop.

Israel Lucena answered his knock, and Tomas was treated to a joyous welcome by Leah and the four girls. Hannah jumped into his arms and hugged him tightly.

"See, Señor Tomas, we did as we said," Hannah said. "The last page of *Pirke Abot* is being printed now."

Piles were neatly organized in every corner of the room. This little Jewish family had printed twice as much as either of the other presses. When Tomas inspected the pages, the print was crisp and clear.

"It's just beautiful," he said. The girls blushed furiously.

"It's also correct," said Señora Lucena. "I proofread every word until my eyes burned. You will not find a mistake."

"I'll send word to Prince Hasan to take these pages for binding, and to deliver more paper."

"What will be next?" asked Señor Lucena.

"I have more of the Babylonian Talmud for you. The tractate *Berakot*, which explains the hours during which the Shema may be recited, and also about prayers in the *Amidah*, the eighteen blessings."

"Nineteen," said Señor Lucena."

"You can argue with my father," Tomas said laughing. "He hates that extra blessing. If you know a good reason for it, tell me. My father and Rabbi Modena had quite a disagreement."

"Well, we still disagree with the warning not to talk with women," said Rebecca, ready for a good argument.

"You must be hungry after your long trip," Señora Lucena interrupted, shushing Rebecca away. "Come home and eat. Bring your men with you."

The girls and their mother ran ahead to prepare the meal, the debate about the corrupting influence of women thankfully postponed for the moment. Tomas helped Israel Lucena close the shop. Standing in the dark as they were ready to leave, Lucena put his hand on Tomas' shoulder.

"Wait," he said.

"What's the matter?" asked Tomas.

"Someone's outside."

"How do you know?"

"It's one of the village boys. I think he's in love with Rebecca. He hides outside every night."

"Does he know what you're doing?" asked Tomas, alarmed.

"I don't think so."

"Is he a *converso*?"

"No. Old Christian. I've known about him for a week, but I waited to ask you. What should we do?"

"He could get you all killed."

"I know. But if we ignore him, his curiosity may grow. He may bring others."

"If you invite him into your family, he'll learn that you're printing Hebrew books."

"He doesn't read. We'll tell him it's Latin."

"That may not work. Your lives will be in his hands."

"Our lives are in God's hands. But it should be your decision."

"He may betray you, and all of us." Tomas knew it would be better to get rid of this boy, but how? They would have to take the risk.

"What's his name?"

"Diego de Monbiel."

"So, let's invite this young man to dinner."

Dinner was interrupted by a knock at the door.

The Lucenas looked at each other, surprised and frightened. No one visited after dark.

"Who's there?" Señor Lucena said through the door.

"We have a message for Tomas Catalan."

A life sized wooden effigy of King Enrique, clad in black, was enthroned on a hastily assembled platform in Avila. A huge crowd had assembled. An orchestra of horns, bagpipes and lutes entertained them in the reddish blur of the late afternoon summer sun.

Archbishop Carrillo rose to read the charges.

"Enrique IV, King of Castile, has committed vulgar excesses, sins and crimes. His indecision has weakened our land. He has refused to fight the noble war to reconquer our favored lands from the infidel Moors."

The crowd roared as the Archbishop removed a silver crown from the head of the wooden dummy. The Count of Plasencia wrenched loose the fake sword, symbol of sovereign authority, and kicked the figure of the king from its seat. He howled the previously unutterable, "*Puto*! Fag! Queer! Be gone from us."

Young Prince Alfonso was rushed forward and seated on the empty throne. Carrillo placed the crown on Alfonso's head. A fanfare of trumpets, and the deed was done. Castile had two kings.

'May God help us,' thought Gabriel, wondering if his new allies were worse than his enemies.

Tomas rode almost non-stop for five days. His horses were ready to drop when the towers of the Sevillian *Alcazar* finally appeared on the horizon. He covered the last three miles at full gallop, did not pause at the gate, burst dirty and exhausted into his home.

The house was swarming with people, boxes, food, buckets of water. It looked like an army camp. Servants hurried for Pilar and she came running to meet him.

"Thank God they found you," she cried, hugging him.

"Esther? Judah?"

"She's alive. She opens her eyes, she eats, but she says nothing."

"Judah?"

"No trace. I've had men scouring Seville. We don't know where to look. We don't know who took him."

Tomas went to Esther, who lay in their darkened bedroom, wan, breathing weakly. He had never felt such pain and loss, and fury. He sat silently by her side for an hour.

Esther moved in her sleep and Tomas caressed her gently. Tears poured from his eyes.

"Tomas? Is it really you?" she whispered.

"Yes, Esther, it's me."

She touched his face, and he hugged her.

"It was Talavero," she whispered.

"This time I'll kill him," Tomas said, clenching his fists.

"Judah?"

"I'll bring him back."

"Oh, Tomas. Be careful. I don't want to lose you, too."

He knew he should sleep, but instead he walked the streets of Seville, especially the poorer districts, making inquiries everywhere. Many who saw his fury stayed out of his way. He learned nothing. Talavero had vanished.

Esther got stronger every day, sitting up and eating, even taking short walks in the house and courtyard. But her eyes fell each time Tomas returned without Judah, knowing that every passing day lessened the chances of ever seeing her son again.

"I know he's here," Tomas said. "I'll find him."

"Tomas Catalan is looking for you."

The whore eyed Talavero suspiciously. For two weeks she had fed him and kept him hidden in her dirty little room.

"Tomas Catalan inquires for you by name. He says Hernando Talavero stole his son. He says he will come and get him back."

Judah stared at them from the bed where he was tied and gagged.

The whore was afraid of Talavero, but she was angry too. He had bullied her to take him in. He said he would pay but never did. His story about the boy had never made sense. Why had she ever believed him?

"He's the one, isn't he?" She shook her head in disgust. She pointed at Judah. "That's the son of Tomas Catalan!"

"No!" Talavero screamed. "He's my son!"

He jumped at the whore and without warning plunged his knife deep into her chest. He wiped the knife on her dress as she lay crumpled and bleeding on the floor.

"I must speak to Tomas Catalan."

The ill kempt women was led into the Catalan house, and made comfortable until Tomas returned.

"I know who took your son. He murdered my friend."

Tomas grabbed her shoulders. "Where is he?"

"He left this morning. I can show you where he was."

Tomas had allies.

Every whore in Seville wanted Talavero dead. One came with news that Talavero had stolen a horse. They spoke to the gatekeepers, all of whom they knew intimately, and learned that Talavero had left by the *Puerta de Cordoba*, heading north. Tomas was mounted and on his trail instantly.

Seven miles north of Seville lay the ruined colony of Italica, in the days of Julius Caesar one of Roman Iberia's major cities, but now a jumbled landscape of broken stone and overturned pillars. Tomas had been there long ago, with his father on an outing, and he remembered the many crevices and partially destroyed underground rooms where one could hide and accumulate supplies for a long journey.

His suspicions were confirmed when he approached the crumbling walls of the ancient amphitheater and heard the whinny of a horse. He dismounted, tied his horse near Talavero's, took the Prince's dagger in his hand, and entered the fighting pit of the gladiators.

"Jose! Are you here?" he hollered. His voice echoed. He circled the outer perimeter of the pit, squinting in the bright sun where forty thousand spectators had once roared, peering into every opening.

A movement caught his eye. A small animal scurried across his line of vision.

He approached the wall from which the animal had run and looked up to see a large stone block plunging toward him. He jumped aside, reached the wall, and began to climb. Sounds above made him stop. He listened. Talavero was circling.

Tomas climbed down and positioned himself where he could see the horses and block the escape route. He heard a grunt and a smash, and spun to see Talavero rising from the hard ground. He had fallen and his left shoulder was limp. His right hand held a knife.

Tomas was encouraged that Talavero wanted to fight. If Judah was no longer alive, Talavero would have fled.

Tomas had barely slept for over a week. His head began to spin. He blinked and forced himself to focus on Talavero, stumbling toward him. Tomas shook his head to clear it and began circling, staying on the side of Talavero's bad left arm.

The Moors' lessons came to him. Keep moving, stay low, feint, hold the knife low, strike up.

Talavero's knees wobbled. He looked incapable of fight. Don't relax! Don Alonso had warned that the danger is greatest when you think it has passed. Move! Strike!

Talavero lunged, and his knife ripped along Tomas' side, drawing blood, but Tomas struck under the larger man's extended arm, upward into his belly, driving, twisting. The dagger entered to the hilt and the strength of his thrust lifted the larger Talavero off the ground.

Talavero crumpled to the ground. Tomas withdrew the dagger and sliced it quickly across Talavero's throat. His head lolled to the side in a pool of blood. Tomas sank to his knees.

"Thank you, God," he said, but his eyes were already scanning the rocks. He walked unsteadily to the large block that Talavero had thrown down at him, squeezing his arm against the wound in his side. He began to climb. At the top, where Talavero must have been, he looked for a sign. He inched to the left.

The end of a rope stuck out from between two rocks. He pried the rocks aside.

Judah looked at him, eyes wide with terror.

Tomas removed the gag from Judah's mouth and hugged his son. He cut the bonds holding his arms. Judah grabbed him with ferocious intensity. For a long while, they sat there, Judah quietly sobbing, Tomas comforting him. Finally, Judah spoke.

"Papa. That man hurt Mama. He said he's my father. He said I would never see you again."

"Your mother is all right, and he's not your father. I'm your father, and I've come to take you home."

25

Perez had an audience with Isabel in Segovia.

"Have you discovered any secret Jews yet, Friar, in your travels?"

"You must take this seriously, Princess, especially now that your brother is king," said Perez.

"*Both* of my brothers are king," replied Isabel, "and I do take it seriously. The Holy Church is the sole source of eternal salvation. Our good Christian people must not be denied the grace of Christ because they are confused by Jews, and certainly not by secret Jews pretending to be Christians. As you know, I am appalled by heresy." She paused. "But accusations without proof are also not to my liking. *Conversos* are very important to the royal family. And may I remind you, to the church."

Perez wanted to pursue his denunciation of *conversos*, but the edge of Isabel's temper was clearly visible.

"I have a message for you," he said, coming to the real purpose of his audience.

Isabel arched her eyebrows.

"I was recently in the village of Siguenza, near the border with Aragon. You may remember that I lived three years in the monastery at Hijar, and came to know Prince Fernando very well. The Prince has sent a message. Actually, it's from King Juan."

Perez withdrew a rolled document from a leather case slung over his shoulder. It was tied with a ribbon and sealed with the royal crown of Aragon.

"Aragon awaits your answer," he said as he gave it to the princess, sounding pompous even to himself.

Isabel broke the seal and read the document. Perez had not read it himself, but Fernando's messenger had implied that it was a proposal of marriage.

The princess rolled the parchment and tied it with the ribbon. She eyed Perez with a disdainful look.

"I shall respond in due time," she said, dismissing him.

They had instigated war with Enrique by their rash actions at Avila, but they had not prepared for what followed. Now, two months later, the *grandees* assembled before Archbishop Carrillo's tent, confused, in disarray, at the edge of panic.

Where were Enrique's troops? The wide plains were frightening in the red sunset. Every distant movement in the fading light could signal a massing for attack.

Smoky lanterns hung on poles, large fires blazed. Maps were spread on rickety tables. Alfonso, boy king and nominal leader of the forces, had been ill for several days. He lay in his tent at the other side of the camp and no one regretted his absence.

Carrillo reviewed the battle fought five days before. "We met on the plains of Olmedo. Enrique's forces outnumbered us three to one. But our leadership and fighting spirit were greater. Both I and young Alfonso bravely appeared on the field, while Enrique, the coward, chose to conceal himself. The fighting lasted three hours, until it was too dark to see."

A voice sang out. "Nobody won! Nobody's going to win. It's time to end this fighting." This reflected Gabriel's opinion, and, he thought, the majority of those present.

"Anarchy rules the kingdom," the man continued. "Everyone uses the war as an excuse to rob and pillage."

In Seville, Gabriel knew, neighbor fought neighbor in pitched battle. Many were killed; homes were burned.

"Families are split," the voice continued, and now Gabriel could see that it was the Count of Miranda, one of the few who made sense amidst the general confusion and indecision. "Ancient feuds are revived. The families of Guzman and Ponce de Leon fight openly, and the streets run with blood. Travelers are attacked. No man dares move beyond the walls of his city without an armed guard."

Carrillo glared at Miranda, and then at the others, daring them to challenge him. No one did, but no one denounced Miranda either. Other voices were heard.

"What are we going to do?"

"We should attack."

"Where?"

As the discussion wore on, Gabriel concluded that it was all far less complicated than he had thought. Nothing seemed to happen. Despite Carrillo's bluster, neither side had won the battle at Olmedo, and no one knew what to do next.

Plans were made to re-position troops and there was vague talk of strategic advantages, but no plans for new battles. The main thrust seemed to be to attract allies and prevent defections. Gabriel imagined the same pointless, leaderless conversations in Enrique's camp, less than ten miles away. They had reached a stalemate.

Meanwhile, the costs of feeding and equipping thousands of men was enormous. Money was more crucial than fighting skills. It dawned on Gabriel that he, in supplying money and food, was more important than most of the generals and *capitans*.

Their deliberations were interrupted by the sudden arrival of the chief of Alfonso's private guard, who pushed his way to the map laden table. He looked frightened.

"The king has died," he said, looking down.

"Enrique?" a voice said hopefully.

"No. Alfonso."

A shudder passed through the leaders. They had taken great risks, and now they had no champion.

"Alfonso took a hot brew and laid down to rest," the guard continued. "His orderly heard him call out, and went into the tent. But he was ... dead."

Again, no leadership. Gabriel hoped Carrillo would take charge, but everyone spoke and no one said anything.

"He wasn't injured."

"Was it poison?"

"He was listless for several days."

"His tongue turned black. Like the plague."

"It wasn't plague. No buboes."

"This settles it," said Miranda. "It's time to make peace with Enrique, if we can, and go home."

Miranda had said what the others were afraid to utter. Men shook their heads in silent assent.

"No!" Gabriel said, surprising even himself with his intense passion. It was the first word he had ever uttered in the war council. Archbishop Carrillo glared at him, furious that an outsider, a man without military standing, had spoken at such a critical juncture. But Gabriel was committed and he continued.

"If we give up now," he said, "we have no chance. We'll never regain our status with Enrique."

"What else can we do?" asked a voice from the crowd.

"Isabel," said Gabriel. "Isabel is our hope. I say we switch our allegiance to Isabel and continue to oppose Enrique."

"Can a woman command?"

"This woman can. She's far more able than her dead brother," Gabriel said.

"Will she?"

"With your permission, Archbishop, I'll ask her," said Gabriel. "Will you ride with me to Avila?"

"Could we defeat Enrique on the battle field?"

"Perhaps, your Highness," Gabriel answered, cutting off Carrillo, "but it would be neither easy nor quick."

"And we could lose?"

"Yes," said Gabriel.

"No," Carrillo said simultaneously. "You must accept the crown, so that we don't waste the forces we've assembled at such great cost."

"But even if we win a protracted war, the people will suffer," said Isabel. "Castile has seen enough chaos. Our resources are diminished. Our great families are killing each other. If we continue, our weakness may encourage a Portuguese attack. Or the French. Maybe both."

Gabriel was impressed with the breadth and clarity of the young Princess's thinking. Her long years of careful observation in Enrique's court had apparently been well spent. At seventeen, she sounded more "kingly" than anyone Castile had known for decades. Her brother Alfonso had been the puppet of Carrillo and the nobles. Isabel would be no man's puppet.

"I deeply appreciate the support of those who were loyal to Alfonso, especially you, my wonderful Archbishop and Don Gabriel," Isabel said, "but the time for my coronation has not yet arrived. While Enrique lives, none other has a right to the crown. It was wrong to proclaim Alfonso as king. My brother's untimely death is a clear sign from God that the country has been divided long enough. I will negotiate with the king. We will have peace. Will you help me?"

Only a few days before, Gabriel had argued that it would be fruitless to negotiate with Enrique. But then they did not have a leader. With Isabel, peace was possible.

"It would be my honor, your Grace," Gabriel said with a slight bow.

"Here's my proposal," Isabel said, obviously having prepared for their arrival. First, there must be full amnesty for Alfonso's supporters. Second, the *conversos* must be restored to their positions."

Gabriel looked up sharply. He had not expected this.

"All of them, including you, Don Gabriel," Isabel said, pausing for a moment to let her statement sink in before continuing.

"Third and last, Enrique must name me his successor over the claim of his daughter Juana, and must secure the approval of the *Cortes* to my succession. Upon Enrique's death, with God's will, I shall be Queen of Castile. In return, there will be no war, and Enrique will remain king as long as he lives."

It was breathtaking. Isabel would gain much more than could be achieved by war. The country would no longer be despoiled. The people would love her. Enrique, who hated to fight, would surely accept.

Gabriel knew that Archbishop Carrillo wanted Isabel to be crowned immediately so the war would continue. He suspected that Carrillo had hidden motives that were unknown even to the princess. But Isabel was asserting her independence from those who would manipulate her. There was a budding strength in her that might bring much good to Castile and, he hoped, to himself and the other *conversos*.

"I would be pleased to negotiate such terms on your behalf," Gabriel said.

Carrillo glared at him.

"So, you will once again serve the crown of Castile," said Enrique, after listening to Gabriel's message from Isabel. "It's just as well. The Old Christians who replaced you have been nothing but trouble. You always delivered the revenues you promised."

"Does this mean that you accept the Princess's proposal?" Gabriel asked.

"Of course I accept. It's very reasonable. The Queen's daughter means nothing to me."

Gabriel was surprised, not at his acceptance, but at Enrique's frank confirmation of the rumors about his daughter. The young girl was called Juana *la Beltranega* by everyone, after her assumed father Beltran de Cueva. But always out of Enrique's earshot. The king himself had never said anything on the matter.

There was another rumor, however, that Gabriel heard when he arrived at the king's camp. The report was that Queen Juana, living separately from Enrique at Alaejos, was pregnant by a young lover. She had tried to run away to have the baby secretly, but as she was being lowered in a basket from a high tower, the basket crashed and she was injured. The story was spreading rapidly, and Enrique was embarrassed and furious. By luck or design, Isabel's approach had come at precisely the time that he felt no loyalty toward his wife or her daughter.

"I shall report immediately to the princess," Gabriel said.

"There's one more condition," Enrique said, with an ugly little giggle. "Isabel must not marry without my permission. Her virgin cunt is one of Castile's great treasures."

The king and the princess met to seal their accord in a rocky glade in the mountains near Toros de Guisando, so named for the four stone bulls which had guarded the spot since before recorded history. Isabel had added one provision. To balance Enrique's request that she not marry without his permission, presented to her by Gabriel in far more decorous language than the king had used, she demanded Enrique's guarantee that she would not be forced into a marriage against her will. He acceded, although Gabriel was sure the king felt he could "convince" Isabel to do as he wished when the occasion arose. Gabriel expected that Enrique would be surprised and disappointed when that moment came.

On the appointed day, Enrique sat mounted with a thousand troops, lances glistening, pennons fluttering.

Isabel advanced with her less numerous forces, her white mule led by Archbishop Carrillo. Isabel's long paneled skirt lay full on either flank of her mount. Her riding boots were like a man's. A short satin cloak lined with ermine lay over her shoulders and she carried a garland of yellow roses. Don Gabriel Catalan rode beside her, his own armor glittering.

Carrillo, acting like the mule he led, had announced that he would not kiss Enrique's hand until after the king had sworn Isabel his heir. When they reached Enrique, Isabel dismounted, and with an ugly look at the Archbishop, approached her half brother.

"I am here to pledge my loyalty to your Highness, the true and rightful monarch of Castile," she said, bending to kiss his hand. Her words and action were repeated by all of the nobles, clergy, and commoners who accompanied her, save for Carrillo.

Enrique rose in his saddle, his large body towering over his half sister. How opposite from their true power, Gabriel thought. She's worth ten of him.

The king spoke as arranged. "We are eager for true peace and tranquility to return to Castile and that the kingdom should not remain without legitimate successors of the high and exalted Trastamara line. We proclaim our dear sister heir and Princess, and we command everyone present to follow our lead."

Carrillo moved forward as he had promised, but Enrique waved him off.

Archbishop Fonseca held a Missal, a crucifix laid across it. Isabel and Enrique each laid their right hand on the *santos evangelios*, and repeated the binding oath three times in succession. Fonseca gave their acts the apostolic blessing, trumpets blared, and the civil war was over.

Shortly thereafter, the *Cortes*, meeting at Ocana, ratified the succession of Isabel to the throne of Castile.

Almost a year passed and Castile was quiet. Farms and herds, left alone, thrived. Trade routes and carnivals were reinstituted.

And the secret Hebrew presses put forth a prodigious quantity of books.

The Sefer Ha'Ikkarim was finally finished at Arcos. Both the Rosh ha-Shanah Mahzor and the book of prayers for the Day of Atonement had been completed at Ecija. Berakot, and another tractate, Ketubot, dealing with the laws of marriage, were printed at Olveda. All of these had been taken by Prince Hasan for binding. The presses were now working on Reb Schlomo's commentary on the five books of the Holy Torah, at Ecija, the Arba'a Turim of Rabbi Jacov ben Asher at Arcos, and the Mibhar ha-Peninim of Solomon ibn Gabirol at Olveda. Tomas rotated among the three towns, supervising the printing and assuring the interaction with the Moors.

Gabriel traveled extensively to collect the king's taxes. The people seemed less resentful.

Perez spewed his message of hate, but not near Seville.

Isabel, however, was virtually imprisoned in the town of Ocana, where Enrique also spent most of his time. The king intended to enforce his demand that she not marry except at his pleasure. His spies and agents were everywhere, and the young Princess chafed under the scrutiny. She was doubly thwarted because Enrique did not release the revenues which had been part of the promise of Guisando.

Intrigue swirled around them. The Duke of Gloucester, brother to King Edward the Fourth of England, was presented as a suitor for Isabel. She rejected him. The Duke of Guienne, brother of Louis the Eleventh of France, was similarly proposed and rejected. Rumors abounded that Isabel favored her kinsman Fernando, prince of Aragon.

Ignoring her desires, Enrique initiated negotiations on Isabel's behalf but without her knowledge, with the widowed King Afonso of Portugal. Such a union would both prevent a marriage to Fernando, and get Isabel out of Castile. The Archbishop of Lisbon suddenly arrived in Ocana, at the head of a large embassy, bearing the formal proposal of the Portuguese king. Isabel politely but firmly refused his entreaties, and Enrique was once again humiliated.

King Juan in Aragon was at work no less diligently. To increase Fernando's legitimacy, he made him King of Sicily, the most distant part of the Aragonese empire. He also sent an ambassador to Enrique to formally ask Isabel's hand for his son. Enrique of course turned him down, but that did not prevent the real purpose of the visit, which was to talk secretly with Carrillo and Isabel, and to bribe everyone he could to join his plot.

The people of Ocana joined the intrigue. Boys paraded the streets waving banners upon which the arms of Aragon were emblazoned. They sang verses contrasting in vulgar and graphic language the feebleness of the fat Portuguese Afonso and the youthful vitality of Fernando.

Things took a more serious turn when several Andalusian towns, including Seville and Cordoba, began to agitate openly for the coronation of Isabel. Enrique, alarmed, decided to quell the uncooperative territories himself, and organized an army to march south.

The moment Enrique was gone, Isabel flared into action.

It was just a year since the death of her brother Alfonso, and a visit to his burial site provided the flimsy excuse she needed. She fled Ocana within two days of Enrique's departure, accompanied by Archbishop Carrillo and five hundred of his troops. Her political motives were no doubt enhanced by descriptions of the handsome and daring Fernando. She was, after all, a blossoming young woman of eighteen, and she would have the husband of her choice.

It was the race of her life!

Once she married Fernando, Enrique could not touch her, for then it would be war with Aragon. But if she failed, she might never have another opportunity.

From Madrigal, a small town on her route, Isabel sent urgent word to King Juan at Zaragosa in Aragon. "I am at liberty! I will send agents to collect the dower and to bring Fernando through. Hurry! You must hurry! There is little time! I will be in Valladolid."

She sent another message to Seville, urging both Gabriel and Tomas Catalan to join her in Valladolid. They set out immediately.

"But your Highness, you gave your word to the king that you wouldn't marry without his permission," said Gabriel, aghast at Isabel's intention to marry Fernando.

"He has broken every promise," she said. "And I heard how he described the required concession."

Gabriel was horrified that she might think he had repeated the word Enrique had used.

"I know it didn't come from you," Isabel added quickly. "The king has repeated his filthy expression to many, and more than one has been indelicate enough to tell me."

Gabriel did not feel that the king's indiscretion, however bad, justified breaking her commitment. He saw Carrillo's hand, and wondered how much King Juan of Aragon had paid to gain his complicity.

"You don't agree with me, do you?" Isabel asked.

"I deplore the king's inexcusable language," Gabriel said, "but I think breaking your promise is a serious matter.

"So is the future of Castile," the Princess replied. "Enrique has pursued marriage negotiations with the English, the French, and now the Portuguese. Any of these choices are disasters for Castile, but my brother is too stupid to understand."

A look of sober determination came over Isabel.

"I will marry Fernando and no other," she said. She waited to see if Gabriel objected, then continued.

"The only way I can save Castile's sovereignty is to buttress it with Aragon, under my control."

Isabel saw Gabriel's involuntary look of skepticism.

"You doubt that I can direct the headstrong Prince of Aragon and his wily father?" she said. "When you read the marriage contract, you will know differently. And they will sign it, he and his father Juan who has lusted after Castile for all of his long life."

"Once again, your Highness," Gabriel said, "you have shown your wisdom and resourcefulness." He stood proudly at military attention. "How can Tomas and I be of service?"

Gabriel went immediately to King Juan at Zaragosa in Aragon. His assignment was to present Isabel's demands for political concessions, dowry, and wedding gifts. Isabel wanted Gabriel, who was not in any way beholden to King Juan, and who had no independent objectives, to represent her in this final phase.

Tomas was to wait two weeks, then also go to Aragon, contact Prince Fernando, and bring him to Valladolid. It had to be done secretly. Enrique had deployed a network of troops and informants, and the capture of Fernando would be the end of Isabel's plans.

On the eve of his departure, Isabel summoned Tomas to a private meeting. They sat on a bench before a crackling fire. Isabel wore a warm hooded robe that covered her from head to foot.

"You've no doubt heard stories about the Prince of Aragon and his many women?" Isabel began.

Tomas was well aware of Fernando's sexual proclivities, but he could not bring himself to say so. Isabel responded to his muteness.

"You're a good person, Tomas Catalan. One of the best I know. We must be frank with each other. Fernando is well known for his exploits. I believe he has at least two children from these liaisons."

Tomas gulped and nodded in what he supposed might be interpreted as vague assent.

"I'm not as confident as I try to appear when it comes to our ... personal ... physical ..." Her voice trailed off, but she resumed. "You're the only man I can possibly talk with about this. You're married, I understand."

Again Tomas barely nodded. Isabel laughed, throwing back her hood to reveal her red hair.

"Don't be so shy," she said in a lively voice. "I'm the one who's embarrassed here, not you."

"I'm married," Tomas said.

"Your wife was a Jew?" Isabel asked.

"She was baptized before we married."

"Do you love her?"

"Beyond any measure," said Tomas.

Isabel looked at him intently. "And what did she do to achieve that enviable status?"

Tomas thought of his long talks with Esther, riding across the plains, the awful rapes, printing together at Arcos, the trip to the *Alhambra*, the death of Esther's family, and their shared Jewishness. None of this could he ever tell Isabel.

"Maria loves me without reservation," he said, thankful that he remembered to use her baptismal name, "and she lets me know that in a thousand ways. It is the overriding goal of my life to be worthy of that love."

"Your wife is a most fortunate woman," Isabel said very quietly.

She rose and stood close to Tomas, looking up at him. Stretching on her toes, she pulled his head to hers and kissed him full on the mouth.

"I love you, too, Tomas Catalan. Now go fetch my husband."

Diego de Monbiel timidly gained admission at the dusty monastery on the outskirts of Olvera. He was escorted through the cloistered walks until he stood awkwardly before the great Dominican friar.

"Since you spoke here almost a year ago," Diego began, "I have been greatly troubled. At first I didn't believe it could be true, but I watched carefully, and now I'm sure. The family I work for are Jews, and they are doing suspicious work. I think they're making copies of the very Hebrew books you said should be burned."

"How do you know this?" said Perez.

"At first I couldn't tell the language of the books they printed ..."

"They print books?" Perez interrupted, grabbing the boy's arms in his excitement. "They have a printing press?"

"Yes."

"Where did they get it?" Perez knew only one printer, and that was Gabriel Catalan.

"I think it came from Seville."

"What else do you know?"

"Everything is kept secret. Moors come to deliver paper and take printed pages away. I listened to you, friar, when you spoke at the Cathedral in Olvera, and I began to wonder about the things they did."

"You've done well."

"I brought a page with me."

"Show me," said Perez, jumping up.

Diego took a crumpled piece of paper from his pocket and gave it to Perez, who stared with glee at the Hebrew letters.

"Who taught the Lucena family how to do this?"

"There's a young man who comes to Olvera. He's the one who teaches them."

"Who is he?"

"They call him Tomas. I heard his full name only once, but I remember. It's Tomas Catalan."

26

"These are terms already agreed to. The Princess has asked me to clarify them."

Gabriel had taken an instant liking to King Juan of Aragon. The man was over seventy years old, blind in one eye and nearly so in the other, but he had the enthusiasm and energy of a young stallion. All his life, he had dreamed and schemed to regain his ancient family lands in Castile and restore the united power of the Trastamara line in the person of his son Fernando. He was within grasp of his goal.

"Go ahead," Juan said patiently, and Gabriel went through his list.

"Isabel will succeed to the crown of Castile upon the death of Enrique.

"Fernando will reign in Castile as king consort, not as king in his own right.

"The monarchs will sign all decrees jointly, but Isabel's rights shall supersede Fernando's in the event of any disagreements.

"Fernando will honor all of Isabel's appointments, and make no war or confederation in Castile without her counsel and consent."

Gabriel knew how hard it was for the old war horse to accept these terms, but King Juan had no choice. Isabel was firm, and this alliance was his life's objective. Perhaps he thought that future events would modify the great powers this contract ceded to Isabel.

"Fernando," Gabriel continued, "will conduct himself fittingly, obey King Enrique, observe the laws and customs of Castile, appoint only Castilians to office, and live within the borders of Castile."

"Yes, we have agreed to all of that," Juan responded with a smile, "but I would hope that an occasional visit to his old father would be permitted."

Gabriel responded as he and Isabel had planned. "The Princess has specifically asked me to amend the prior language to encourage such visits. She values your counsel and advice, both to Fernando and to herself."

Juan smiled as he always did when he gained a point, and Gabriel imagined him calculating how he could use this advantage to secure the next.

"There are some new provisions," Gabriel said. "Fernando will make no ecclesiastical appointments without Isabel's concurrence."

"I assume you do not include such appointments as may be necessary in Aragon?" said Juan with a twinkle in his better eye.

"No indeed. Only in Castile," said Gabriel. Isabel had not specifically instructed him on this point, but in Aragon, Fernando would of course have precedence.

"Fernando shall serve as Isabel's military defender.

"He agrees to wage war against the Moors and to re-conquer the ancient lands.

"If the treaties of Castile are broken, and Enrique's forces move against Isabel, he will provide four thousand lancers in her defense."

"You mean I will provide four thousand lancers," said Juan. "I agree. Is there more?"

"Only the matter of the marriage gifts, your Highness," Gabriel said.

Juan eyes narrowed, and Gabriel held his breath. He had questioned Isabel on these terms, and she had reduced her demands somewhat. But she was still asking for a dowry far in excess of that given to any previous queen of Aragon. Gabriel listed the towns, some in Aragon and others in Sicily, the revenues of which would be paid to Isabel. Juan did not respond.

Gabriel continued. "One hundred thousand gold florins payable four months after the marriage, and twenty thousand gold florins now, in recognition of the betrothal."

"And if we have difficulty raising such sums within the required time periods?"

"I will provide the funds," said Gabriel, "of course, with appropriate securities and interest."

"Of course," Juan nodded, and Gabriel exhaled gratefully.

"There is one more matter," he said quietly, praying that this would not prove the ruin of all that had gone before.

"There's a necklace, said to be heavy with rubies and emeralds and pearls, which you gave to Queen Juana Enriquez, may her memory be blessed. This symbol of Aragon, when worn by Isabel, will speak far more than mere words of the friendship and ultimate union of the great kingdoms of Iberia. Isabel has asked me to bring it to her when I return."

"And so you shall!" Juan exclaimed. "Did you fear to mention the necklace? I'm pleased that Isabel has remembered my dear Queen and wishes to honor her memory by wearing this most precious of mementos. It could not grace a more worthy beauty."

Tomas rode across the mountains from Valladolid and along the bank of the Rio Duero to Almazan, the last town in Castile, then across the border to Aragon. Everywhere, speculation was rampant. Many guessed that Fernando would try to enter Castile to marry Isabel. Enrique's agents were in place, but the people loved Isabel and spoke well of the Prince of Aragon. They would be no help to Enrique's spies. Tomas had a safe conduct, under his own name as a merchant in his father's service, and he had no trouble with border guards in either kingdom.

Nor did Tomas have trouble finding Fernando. Isabel's instructions, delivered by Gabriel, had been explicit, and were followed to the letter. Fernando was waiting in the village of Calatayud, less than twenty miles from the border.

"Enrique has responded quickly and more effectively than we thought he could," said Tomas, soon after meeting Fernando. "The Castilian towns near the border are teeming with soldiers and spies."

"We'll get in," the Prince said without hesitation. He glanced at the small group of men and mules Tomas had brought with him, laughed, and said, "You could use another muleteer! I can be as ragged as anyone in that group. I'll tell my father we're ready. As soon as he sends word that negotiations are completed, we'll leave."

Scribes were preparing copies of the final betrothal agreement for signature. Gabriel and the king sat on a shaded terrace overlooking a lush valley below. Gabriel's robe, a gift from King Juan, was the softest he had ever worn, made from the pure virgin wool of mountain sheep.

"I wonder if your Highness would permit me to offer a suggestion about a personal matter?" asked Gabriel.

"What is it, Don Gabriel?" Juan answered.

"I notice that your Highness has great difficulty with his sight," Gabriel said, wondering how sensitive the old man was and whether he might respond angrily.

"The left eye went years ago, and the right is almost gone," said Juan in a matter-of-fact tone.

"Have you considered surgery?" Gabriel asked.

"I did, but my wife feared I would panic when the knife was brought to my eye." Juan paused and Gabriel understood that this was often on his mind. "It would be a great pleasure to see Fernando again, and Isabel, and even, if God is kind to me, their children. Do you know about these things?"

"You cannot see because the lens of your eye is clouded over. The lens must be removed. A tiny cut is made in the eye, and the lens is pulled out with a small forceps. The eye is bandaged and you rest quietly, for at least two weeks. When the bandages are removed, you stay in a darkened room until your eye adjusts to the light. Then you look through a thick glass of a certain design, and you will see. It requires great courage, but your sight could be restored. Do the left eye first. You can't see anything, so you won't see the knife."

"Do you know someone?"

"Yes."

"A Jew?"

"A *converso*. He's done this many times."

"I'll consider it."

Their conversation was interrupted by a messenger with a letter from Fernando.

"Will you read it for me, Don Gabriel?"

Gabriel observed the strong clear hand and read aloud.

"My dearest father and Lord King. Señor Tomas Catalan has arrived and we are ready to go to Isabel. The roads and towns are filled with Enrique's spies, but we have a plan to get us through. I will not describe it here, since there must be no chance of disclosure, but be confident that it will work. I will reach my destination. I await only your permission. Your loving son. Fernando."

Gabriel shared the apprehension he saw on the king's face. The culmination of Juan's lifetime plan hung in the words he would now utter. But any dangers facing Fernando also threatened Tomas. For the next few days, their son's lives were inextricably linked.

"Don Gabriel, you know how I feel," Juan began. "Like you, I have no other son. The risks of the journey to Segovia fill me with fear so deep and cruel that it passes description." Juan rose and paced fitfully. "But Isabel's position allows no delay. There will never be a better opportunity."

Juan motioned for a scribe.

"My dearest Fernando," he dictated, "I have but one instruction for you. Go! Go with speed and purpose, and may God's fortune shine upon you. Know that I pray Christ will one day permit you to stand again before my eyes, unharmed and prospered. If Tomas Catalan is as good a man as his father, you could not be in better hands. Send word to me when the deed is done."

Gabriel left within the hour, anxious to be in Valladolid when Tomas and Fernando arrived.

They crossed the ridge line and passed into the kingdom of Castile. Tomas on horseback. Three walking. In the wagon, Fernando, Prince of Aragon, in the coarsest of clothes, holding the reins of the four-mule team.

Tomas was surprised at how relaxed Fernando was. He acted as if they were on a lark in the forest, with all the armed might of Aragon at his beck and call. Despite the Prince's arrogance, and despite Tomas' dislike of Fernando from his conversation with Isabel, he could not help being taken by the young man's charm and daring.

Fernando was even an accomplished muleteer.

"That barmaid has a great set of tits," Fernando leered, "and she leaned over to be sure I could see all the way to the nipples."

"I guess she likes the smell of mules," said Tomas, laughing.

The son of one of the wealthiest men in Castile and the crown prince of Aragon shared a small airless room and a single narrow bed in the inn where they had stopped on the third night of their journey.

"It's been six days," said Fernando.

"Since what?" Tomas asked.

"Since I fucked a woman," said the prince. "The longest time in over a year. I bet I could get that barmaid up here."

"No," said Tomas. "It's too risky."

"Oh, I could do it. Women don't turn me down. But I won't, not tonight."

Tomas wondered how hard these conquests were for a prince. He decided not to challenge Fernando to prove that he could succeed in disguise.

"What's Isabel like?" said Fernando, suddenly serious.

The uncertainty in his voice made Tomas look at Fernando in a new light. Suddenly he was not the supremely confident Prince, full of bravado. Could he actually fear his upcoming encounter with the Princess of Castile? So much depended on it, his own dreams as well as those of his father. And Isabel, after all, was not one of his tarts.

"She's strong," Tomas said, guarding his friend.

"She's certainly dictated strong terms for the marriage contract," said Fernando, surprising Tomas with his frankness. "But it'll be worth it," he continued, a glint in his eye.

'Don't ever underestimate this one,' Tomas thought. 'Isabel is going to find him a worthy match.'

"What does she look like?" Fernando said suddenly, and Tomas understood his real interest.

"Her hair is reddish. And she has a pleasant face, especially when she smiles. Her eyes are ..."

"Tell me about her body," Fernando interrupted.

"Athletic. Lean. She's an excellent horsewoman."

"I've been with many women," said Fernando, reflecting. "And you, Catalan, have you slept with many women?"

"Only one. My wife."

"I've never been in love," Fernando said, very quietly. "Is Isabel a woman who can be loved?"

They arrived in Valladolid in late afternoon, tired and dirty from the journey, and were immediately brought to Isabel's receiving room.

After a quick look at Tomas, who smiled reassuringly, Gabriel pointed to the Prince.

"That is he," Gabriel said, aware that he and Tomas were the only witnesses to a momentous meeting. He watched Isabel carefully, and thought he saw a smile of satisfaction. Even covered with the dirt of the road, Fernando cut a dashing figure, strong and athletic, already known as a bold military leader. He was a man to quicken any young girl's heart. His well-set eyes looked directly at the princess. Isabel, however, remained all business. She asked Gabriel to produce the betrothal contract.

"Are you, Gabriel Catalan, witness to the signature of King Juan of Aragon, intending to bind both himself and his son Prince Fernando to its contents?"

"I am, your Highness," Gabriel said.

Isabel eyed Fernando. He stood with his legs slightly spread, bouncing lightly on his toes, as if ready to pounce. Isabel brought her back ramrod straight.

"We must act quickly," she said. "The arrival of Prince Fernando in Valladolid cannot go unnoticed. Riders are certainly on their way to Enrique. Are you familiar with the terms?" Her face was expressionless.

"Yes, your Grace," said Fernando, with a seriousness to match hers.

Isabel asked Gabriel to show Fernando where to sign, next to his father's signature.

Fernando took the pen, but did not sign the document. He took one step toward Isabel, thought better of it, and spoke from where he was.

"Your Highness, Princess of Castile, it is with great pleasure and anticipation that I come here to join with you in marriage. We will build a united Spain and accomplish many great things together. But it is also my fervent hope that the love which kindled in my heart at the first sight of you will blossom and lead to bonds of affection as well as accomplishment."

Without waiting for a response, Fernando bent to sign the marriage contract. Gabriel glanced quickly at Isabel and saw the hint of a tear in her eye.

The prince was permitted to clean up and change his clothes, with a strict admonition that the wedding ceremony would take place within the hour, in Isabel's private chapel, during the Vespers service. There would be a public ceremony the next day.

Isabel dispatched a polite letter to Enrique, informing him that Fernando was in Valladolid, that they would be married by the time he received the letter, and assuring him of the most dutiful submission of both herself and the prince to the crown of Castile.

As Tomas washed and dressed, he recounted the adventures of his trip, and Gabriel told of the negotiations with King Juan.

"I'm sure Fernando has no idea what he signed," Gabriel said. "He left long before we were finished. His instructions must have been to sign any document that bore his father's signature."

Gabriel led Tomas to the dimly lit chapel. Stone walls reflected flickering candlelight. Fernando and Isabel stood together, looking far more at ease than during their first meeting.

Isabel was radiant, her gown of gold satin broken by wide slashes of black velvet. Two ribbons on her chest blazed with diamonds, pearls, and rubies. Her neck was adorned with the fabulous necklace of Fernando's mother. Large rubies gleamed in light cascading through stained glass windows, complementing her reddish hair.

Fernando, handsome and muscular, completed a stunning portrait of the new royal couple. Wavy brown hair hung thick over his shoulders. He wore a cap slanted to the right and adorned with a single large feather. His knee length jerkin was of black and gold brocaded velvet, with sleeves of rich crimson velvet. Soft leather shoes, cream colored. Well fitted gloves in the same leather, gauntlets extended past the wrists. But it was his long robe, floor length, hanging loosely from his wide shoulders, that most attracted the eye. Open in the front, it was lined with ermine and inset with pearls and large beads around the shoulders.

How much the future of Spain would be impacted by this union could only be guessed, but to Tomas, the prospects seemed awesome. His concern, however, was for Isabel's personal happiness. She wanted to love her husband, and probably already did. Tomas prayed that Fernando would return and honor that love.

A papal dispensation permitting the cousins to marry, which Gabriel had brought with him from King Juan, and which he was certain was a forgery, was read aloud. The young couple then faced the priest who would say the mass and formally asked him to perform the marriage. Tomas was stunned by a flash of recognition.

"It's Perez," Tomas whispered, but even as he spoke the words, he could see from the look of horror on Gabriel's face that he already knew.

The wedding ceremony, performed at breakneck speed, was identical to that of Tomas and Maria.

As soon as it ended, Perez rushed triumphantly from the altar. Gabriel turned away, but the friar followed. "So you see you are not the only one who helps our Princess," Perez said. "We shall know, in the end, whether her material interests or the needs of her soul will prevail. Do not think the bread and horses you provide will make any difference. Long after all of that is but a memory, her soul will still belong to Christ, and to the Church."

"But perhaps not to you," said Gabriel.

Tomas, meanwhile, stared pensively at the young couple walking hand in hand up the stone steps to their bedroom.

Despite the snickering of the maids, Tomas was unprepared for the sight which assaulted his eyes. Held high, spread wall to wall in the narrow corridor, was the bloody evidence of Isabel's wedding night. The bedsheet, earlier the subject of official investigation and certification, had become a plaything for maid's gossip.

Perez had been a member of the official inspection team. Tomas was haunted by the thought of Perez watching Fernando and the virgin Isabel complete their ceremonial coupling. He was profoundly sad for his friend who could not share even this most private of moments alone with her husband.

"I've never seen the king so angry. He brought the Queen and *La Beltranega* with him into the throne room. The little one wore a crown of some sort, and Enrique shouted, actually shouted, in that silly high pitched voice of his, that she was his rightful heir, not his sister who had broken her word and married the prince from Aragon. Many of the families, the Mendozas, the Velascos, even the Pimentels, switched their allegiance back to Juana. Only the house of Medina Sidonia remains loyal to your Grace."

Archbishop Fonseca said all this in a single breath, as if he was afraid to stop. Gabriel watched Isabel and Fernando as they absorbed the news. They seemed neither surprised nor upset.

"Has he approached the old Portuguese for Juana's hand?" Isabel asked, and Gabriel thought he saw a shudder of repulsion as she remembered her own rejected suitor. She took Fernando's hand and they exchanged a look of real affection.

They're brave, thought Gabriel, but I hope we've not all been foolish.

"Yes," answered Fonseca reluctantly, "and I'm afraid it means war. Afonso will surely invade Castile to eliminate his rivals as soon as he's married to Juana."

"How much time do we have?" asked Isabel calmly.

"Not more than a few months," said Fonseca.

"Will that be enough, my King?" she asked.

Turning to Gabriel, Fernando asked, "Will you be able to assemble what we need?"

"Yes," Gabriel said.

"Then I'll be ready to fight," said Fernando.

"And to win!" added Isabel.

"Oh yes. Only to win!" said Fernando, tilting his head with a confident smile.

King Juan of Aragon sat alone with the unopened letter. He knew the news was good. The messenger had seen Fernando in Valladolid, well, safe, and married.

He's done it, Juan exulted, and his heart soared with joy and pride. Fernando had made it. He wasn't dead in some lonely gulch or held in one of Enrique's dark prisons. Isabel would have Castile, and Fernando had Isabel! It was the happiest moment in Juan's long life.

Now he would allow himself the exquisite pleasure he had delayed so no one would see his emotion. He broke the seal and unrolled the heavy paper. Holding the thick glass as he had practiced for many frustrating hours, he saw his son's distinctive handwriting. He saw Fernando's hand!

Tears came to the old man's eyes. The fearful operation had been worth the pain. Encouraged by his conversation with Gabriel Catalan, Juan had brought a Jewish surgeon from Barcelona. The operation had been a brilliant success. He felt a joy he could not have dared imagine.

But there was a shadow. The French were massing troops on their side of the Pyrenees, preparing to launch yet another attack into the long-contested border counties of Cerdagne and Roussillon. If they succeeded, Aragon's northern flank would be seriously exposed.

Juan had only one able commander. No matter what the risk in Castile, he would have to ask Fernando to return to Aragon.

Isabel and Fernando went to Segovia to organize their forces. Men and materials arrived at a furious pace. Gabriel had a hundred agents scouring the countryside for a hundred miles in every direction.

Wagons clogged the roads. Herds of animals surrounded the town, and strayed into the city streets.

Troops were encamped among the cows, sheep and horses. Tents, flags, blacksmith's smoky fires, shouts of vendors, and the lusty entreaties of camp followers presented a lively, ever-changing panorama.

Fernando organized his burgeoning forces superbly. He held meetings to discuss strategy, drills to teach men to move and fight as a unit, tournaments to practice skills. The first army of Isabel and Fernando began to take shape.

It all stopped when King Juan's request arrived. Fernando was torn between his father's need in Aragon and his own responsibilities in Castile. But Isabel urged him to go, and indeed convinced Archbishop Carrillo to provide troops to go with him.

"I'll return as soon as I can," he said to Isabel.

"Hurry back," she said. "We don't want to lose Castile while you're saving Aragon."

27

Tomas was particularly taken with the youngest of the Lucena daughters. He had never had a sister, and little Hannah captured his heart. She was excited by the printing, and was utterly precise in her job of tending to the printed pages. She had learned to set type, and was now almost as fast and accurate as her older sister.

"I don't understand something," she told Tomas on his first night in Olvera. "Will you explain it to me?"

And so, at the end of the next day, Hannah curled up with Tomas, and as the candles dwindled, they talked.

"We printed the prayer books for *Rosh ha-Shanah* and *Yom Kippur*," Hannah began, "and they have the exact prayers that every Jew is supposed to say. We printed them so Jews can read from them on those days."

"Yes?" asked Tomas. "What is your question?"

"In the *Pirke Abot*, it says that you shouldn't make your prayer a set routine. But if praying isn't supposed to be the same each time, why do we print books of prayers?"

"How did you learn how to pray?" Tomas asked, amazed at the perception of the little girl.

"I go to synagogue with my mother. She reads to me, and now I can read myself."

"But do you talk to God?"

"No. I say the prayers."

"Are the prayers about God?"

"Yes, of course."

"Do you remember any of them? What do they say?"

"They praise God, and say how wonderful He is to have made the world and each of us, and thank God for giving us food and other things we need."

"Very good. Anything else?"

"Some prayers ask God for things, like rain for the crops ... and peace."

"Think about the prayers that thank God. Are there some things that you would like to thank God for that aren't in the prayers in the book?"

"I want to thank God that he sent you to us, and that you became my friend."

Tomas blushed and hugged her.

"And are there things you want to ask for that aren't in the book?"

Hannah thought for awhile. "I want to grow up and get married and have my own babies," she said.

"So if you thank God and ask God for things that aren't in the prayers, then you would be outside the routine of the prayers in the book."

"Then why do we need the book?"

"To remind you to thank God and ask him for His help. To give you some ideas about what to thank Him for, and what to ask. But you can always go beyond what's in the book, and that's what *Pirke Abot* tells us. You can speak directly to God, and Jews are encouraged to make their own prayers, not instead of those in the book, but in addition to them."

"You're so smart. I love you," Hannah said, and gave him a little kiss.

"I love you too," Tomas replied, "but the candles are low and it's time to sleep. We have much to do tomorrow." He carried her to bed and tucked her in.

Then he went back to the main room where he knew Israel Lucena was waiting patiently for him. They discussed shipments of paper and delivery of the printed pages for binding. The Moors came regularly and reliably, to Israel's continuing astonishment.

"Why are they so helpful when we're always at war with them?" Israel asked.

"We pay them well," said Tomas, smiling. "And Muslims and Jews are both persecuted by the Christians. And, of course we share a common patriarch in Abraham."

"There must be more than that," said Israel.

294 ∓ THE HERETIC

"Well, I did save the life of Prince Hasan's son," Tomas said with a hint of a smile, and told Lucena the story. Israel shook his head in amazement.

"Some day, Castile will take Granada back from the Moors," said Israel, somewhat sadly.

"Not Enrique," said Tomas.

"No. But Fernando, if he becomes the king."

"Yes," mused Tomas, "he and Isabel will put fire in our troops. It'll be a bad day for me when my friends Hasan and Isabel come to mortal conflict. But perhaps it's still many years away. Much can happen."

"You've noticed that Diego is gone?" Israel asked suddenly.

"I see he's not here, but I didn't realize he was gone. How long has he been away?"

"Almost a month," Israel said. "I looked everywhere. He's not in town or on any nearby farms." Israel's face darkened. "He acted oddly before he left."

"What do you mean?" Tomas asked.

"He asked questions about what we were printing, and why. He was never interested before. I think he knew we lied to him when we said it was Latin. He never said goodbye, not even to Rebecca. And when he left, he took several pages of the *Yom Kippur Mahzor* with him."

Leaving Olvera, Tomas went to Arcos, worried about Diego. Whatever it meant, it wasn't good. He was still deep in thought when he saw the high cliffs from which Rodrigo had plunged downward to his death. He re-lived the horrible climb up the secret passage to the plague stricken town that took the lives of Yacov and Miriam and Ruyo.

There were also pleasant memories. In the shop where he and Esther had worked together for so many months, his lips burned again with the heat of their first kiss.

He didn't stay long. He looked approvingly at what had been printed, checked the supplies, saw that there was enough work to keep the men occupied until his next visit, and left.

He hurried to Seville and the people he loved.

After every trip, he was amazed how much Judah had grown.

"But that's what children do," Pilar said smiling. "Do you expect him to stay the same?"

"I miss him, and all of you," said Tomas. "I want to see all of you more."

"You and your father travel more than anyone else in Seville. It'll be a big occasion next week when you're both here together."

"The last time that happened," said Tomas, "we were summoned by Isabel to help her bring Fernando to Castile."

"I wish I could summon you so easily," muttered Esther.

Tomas knew that Esther was jealous of Isabel, but this was the sharpest rebuke ever, and the first time she had spoken critically to him in front of Pilar. Perhaps they had discussed it in his absence. He could never decide whether he spoke too much or too little about Isabel, but whatever he did was wrong. It was true that he had a special relationship with the princess, and it was clear that Esther didn't like it.

"How much longer will this go on?" Esther asked.

"Until you go to Italy," Pilar said adamantly. "You'll never have the life you want here in Spain. Every day it gets more dangerous."

"Has anything been directed against *conversos*?" asked Tomas, alarmed.

"No. But it will," said Pilar. "Friar Perez gives sermons all over Castile. That farce of a trial and the hanging were just the beginning. His horrible book influences even those who don't read. Old Christians talk about it everywhere in Seville. People hate Jews."

"But *conversos* are back in official favor," said Tomas. "All the positions are restored."

"For the moment," Pilar said. "But now that Isabel has married, and you and your father are so strongly aligned with her, Enrique will certainly revoke the contract again. If he hasn't already done it. You know he's preparing for war."

"When Isabel is queen, we'll be safe," said Tomas.

Esther looked at him sharply, and he realized his error, but it was Pilar who spoke.

"Do you think you'll be safe if Perez finds out you print Hebrew books?" she snapped. "Do you think your Isabel will protect you then? Her religion is of great importance to her. She prays alone for hours every day. Perez and that other beast Torquemada are at her all the time, complaining that *conversos* pervert and threaten the precious church. One day she'll believe them."

"No!" said Tomas, jumping to Isabel's defense much too quickly, and without the certainty he tried to project.

"Has there been any word from Bruges," he asked, to change the topic.

"How would I know," Pilar snapped. "Your father hasn't been here in months."

It was clear that Esther and Pilar, alone for long periods of time, virtual prisoners in the great palace, were impatient and unhappy with both Tomas and Gabriel.

In bed next to Esther that night, Tomas found the tension between them impossible to dispel. He had been so eager to feel her warm body. But as he lay next to her restlessly all night, she gave no sign that she was awake. His fingers touched her, as if with a mind of their own, but she did not respond.

Gabriel brought news of the war preparations. Fernando had gone to Aragon, but Isabel took his place.

"She's a whirlwind," Gabriel enthused, his eyes shining. "She inspects troops, bargains for supplies, chastises those who don't deliver as promised. And wherever she goes, the people love her. More and more nobles have pledged their support."

"When will the fighting begin?" asked Pilar, and Gabriel could not miss her lack of enthusiasm.

"Not until Fernando returns," Gabriel said. "At least I hope not. It was such chaos and confusion when we fought for Alfonso. Fernando is a leader. He knows how to win.

"There's more. Our new Pope Sixtus has decided that the marriage of the cousins Isabel and Fernando should no longer be incestuous, so he sent the Valencian, Cardinal Rodrigo de Borgia, to deliver a real papal dispensation to replace the fraud that King Juan had arranged for their wedding."

"And Bruges?" asked Pilar impatiently. "Is there any word?"

"Yes. Lorenzo de' Medici will welcome Tomas and Esther, and Judah too, of course. I sent word to him about our printing, and he wants to build a press in Florence. He'll arrange for a Moorish ship to dock at Pisa. Finally, I asked him to accept Tomas and Esther as Jews, and he agreed. He'll assure that the church doesn't make trouble, and he has the power to do that. He's agreed to everything we asked."

"But do we want it?" Tomas blurted out.

"Yes, we want it!" Pilar said emphatically, shocking them all with her vehemence. "No matter if Isabel becomes queen, no matter how capable she is, and no matter how much you help her, we'll never be safe here. We can't be real Jews, and Perez will make sure, sooner or later, that we can't be secret Jews either. You *must* accept this! I don't want our family to separate, but there's no choice. I want you and my grandchildren to live!"

"Things are not good between you and Esther?" Gabriel asked as he and Tomas walked near the river, both glad to escape the tensions in the house.

"No," Tomas admitted. "I'm afraid we've grown apart. I'm never here."

"Is it because you haven't had a child?"

"It could be," Tomas said. "We don't talk about it, but I know she's disappointed."

"And you?"

"I love Judah, but it would be good to have another. A child with your blood, and grandfather's."

"Your mother is right about Isabel," Gabriel said quietly.

Tomas looked at him in disbelief. Gabriel continued.

"She wouldn't set out to hurt us, but if she thought it was necessary for Spain, or for the church, she would sacrifice us. Even you. If she learned of the Hebrew books, she would have no choice but to act. *Pirke Abot* warns us: *Beware of rulers, for they befriend someone for their own benefit. They act friendly when it benefits them, but they do not stand by someone in his time of need.* Helping Isabel is only a delaying action. You must go to Florence. The help of Lorenzo de' Medici is not to be squandered. There will never be a better chance."

"I can't leave you and mother."

"You must! We must know you're safe. And a Jew! That the Catalan family will survive, and that you'll teach the ways of God to your children."

Gabriel stopped walking, and faced Tomas, holding his strong shoulders.

"There's another problem," Tomas said. "Do you remember I told you about a boy named Diego, in Olvera? He disappeared, and Señor Lucena said he took some pages with him."

"What pages?"

"From the *Yom Kippur Mahzor*."

"That boy will get to Perez," said Gabriel, wringing his hands. "It's just a matter of time."

Gabriel paced along the river bank, shaking his head, looking back at his son. Would everything be lost? All their planning and hard work destroyed by one boy? Years of fear and anxiety suddenly come true?

"Promise me, Tomas," he said. "Go to Prince Hasan and make arrangements for a ship. Get everything ready. Do it soon. Please."

Gabriel hugged his son with all his strength, wondering how many more opportunities there would be to do this. They shared a look of anguish so intense that both looked away.

"I'll do it, father," Tomas said. "I promise."

Segovia was in chaos. The reports from Aragon were unclear. How long would Fernando be delayed? What if he were killed or captured by the French? Fernando's continued absence was a dangerous drain on the morale of nobles and soldiers alike.

Isabel was stretched to her limit, her energy sapped, her patience gone. She lost weight, appeared drawn, even haggard. The wonderful bloom in her face was a thing of the past. She went on, however, visiting the troops, trying to keep morale and alliances together.

Gabriel returned with provisions, money and commitments. But an army without a leader cannot fight, and everyone knew it. Troops and horses were kept ready, to fight if Fernando returned, but perhaps to flee if he did not.

Enrique's messengers raced back and forth to Portugal, negotiating a marriage contract between his once again favored daughter Juana and the Portuguese King Afonso. When this was accomplished, and no one doubted it would be, the Portuguese troops would join Enrique, and Isabel's forces would either flee or be crushed. The only hope was to destroy Enrique before the alliance could be concluded.

But there was no Fernando.

Late one afternoon, several days after Gabriel had returned to Segovia, Isabel's scouts galloped in from the south, sounding a panicked alarm. Enrique's troops were advancing! They were only a few miles away.

Isabel calmly changed to a red and green satin dress, and a necklace of large gems and pearls. Mounting her favorite horse, she summoned her commanders and directed them to form up behind her. Her voice was clear and brimming with authority, and if anyone was tempted to run, she gave them no possible opportunity. They would live or die with their princess. Isabel rode out of Segovia with three thousand fighting men behind her, Gabriel Catalan among them.

Silhouetted in the setting sun before them was an army at least six times their number. There was no sign of Enrique. Even his banners were missing. Six riders detached from the front lines, came toward them behind a white flag. Gabriel recognized Andres de Cabrera, Enrique's *mayordomo mayor*.

Isabel drew to a halt and waited. Cabrera continued forward. At ten yards, he dismounted and walked to Isabel. The tension was unbearable. He dropped to his knee. Gabriel held his breath.

Isabel held out her hand, signaling Cabrera to rise. He looked her square in the eye.

"Enrique is dead, Your Highness. You are the Queen of Castile."

Gabriel thought back over Isabel's improbable path to the crown. When she had languished behind her half-brother Enrique, behind Enrique's daughter Juana, and behind her own brother Alfonso, her chances had seemed remote.

Then Alfonso had died, under suspicious circumstances, and now, Enrique too was dead. Suddenly. Strangely. Had he been poisoned? There might be a dozen suspects.

Enrique's daughter Juana still lived. Not a threat in her own right, she would jeopardize Isabel's primacy if she married the Portuguese king.

Cabrera did not know the status of the marriage negotiations. It was possible, he said, that King Afonso was even now on his way to Castile to marry Juana and claim Enrique's vacant throne. The legalities were also unclear. Enrique had declared Isabel his successor, and the *Cortes* had approved that choice. But then Enrique had rejected Isabel and named Juana. The *Cortes* had never ratified this latest change. Gabriel believed that the people, at least most of them, would support Isabel.

If she were strong.

If she acted quickly.

In Gabriel's view, Isabel had but a short time to make her claim to the throne unassailable. The first critical step must be a formal coronation ceremony, proclaiming for all to see that she was the Queen of Castile. The people would be moved by an elaborate royal ceremony.

The problem was Fernando's absence. He would be enraged if he missed the greatest event of his life. After all, it was to be his coronation as well as Isabel's. Gabriel had seen the growth of real affection between them, and he knew that Isabel would not want to hurt him. Yet it was critical not to allow any time for an opposition to form around *la Beltraneja*, or for King Afonso and the Portuguese troops to arrive. Fernando would be his enemy for life, but Gabriel knew what he had to do.

"Your Highness, thank you for seeing me," Gabriel said, rising at her entrance.

"How could I refuse to see the man who has been, above all others, so helpful to me?" Isabel answered. "Besides, I know why you've come, and I want your counsel."

Isabel led him into her private quarters and he was surprised at how small and plain they were, far less luxurious than his own home. Isabel had long been kept without resources by Enrique, and Fernando had none to spare from Aragon. Soon all that would change.

"If Fernando were here," Gabriel said when they were settled, "there would be no question. Do you have word from him?"

"He's somewhere in the Pyrenees mountains at the northern extreme of Aragon. I understand it's quite rugged there, and I doubt that any of my messengers have even reached him."

"And, when they do, will he come immediately?" Gabriel asked

"If he can," said Isabel. "But his last letter said that the situation is still precarious, and he may not be able to leave."

"So it could be several weeks?"

"Perhaps longer."

"Where is King Afonso?" asked Gabriel.

"We know he's left Lisbon, but we don't know where he is. It's possible that he's already entered Castile by way of Estremadura. You know that we have few spies there to report to us."

"If he were known to be in Castile, and approaching, could a coronation be held?" Gabriel hated to ask this question but had no choice.

"No," said the queen, as distressed to answer as Gabriel had been to ask.

"The marriage contract is clear as to your rights as sovereign in Castile, and that Fernando is to be king-consort but not king in his own right?"

"You helped make it so, Don Gabriel."

"Then you know what you must do?"

"Yes," said Isabel, with a little twist of her lips that expressed both sadness and resignation. She knew the consequences of her action, but the risks of not acting were unacceptable, and she did not hesitate.

"I understand it was you, Don Gabriel, who convinced the Queen to hold the coronation ceremony without me."

Fernando spoke as soon as Gabriel entered the king's private chambers in the *Alcazar*. Fury flashed in his eyes.

"I among others," Gabriel said, without enthusiasm.

"You *first* among others," snarled Fernando.

"Yes," Gabriel admitted.

"And it turns out that haste was unnecessary," Fernando said, his eyes focused darkly on Gabriel. "I arrived three weeks later, and even now not a single Portuguese knight has been seen in Castile."

"We couldn't know then," Gabriel said quietly, wondering how much he dared provoke with the glowering young king. Of course, Fernando had been named King of Castile at the same time Isabel was crowned, but his absence from the ceremony had made it clear to all that he was merely king-consort. This was all in strict accord with the marriage agreement, as Gabriel well knew, but Fernando had been humiliated and he would never forget. No queen before Isabel had ever reigned without being linked to a king with his own independent authority.

"The Queen would not have acted without your urging," Fernando said ominously, and Gabriel bit his lip but did not respond.

Several moments passed in silence. Gabriel feared that Fernando would reject him entirely, banish him from court, revoke his royal grants. But then he realized that the impending war against the Portuguese made that impossible. He was still an irreplaceable source of supplies and materials without which the reign of the young monarchs might be measured in months instead of decades.

"Perhaps, sire," Gabriel said calmly, "we can discuss preparations to defeat the Portuguese when they do arrive."

Friar Perez rushed to Segovia as quickly as he could. He had missed the coronation, much to his frustration, but quickly learned that Fernando was furious with Gabriel. He requested an audience with the king.

"Your book against the Jews has been a great success," said Fernando. "Everyone talks of it. And I'm told that your sermons attract large and enthusiastic crowds." The king paused and his eyes prefigured the sarcasm. "But have you found any secret Jews? Or, as our dear departed cousin Enrique once asked, 'do you have the foreskins?'"

"I have no foreskins," Perez said flatly, "but I do have evidence."

"What evidence?" said Fernando.

"I have pages from a Hebrew prayer book."

"So?"

"The pages were not written," said Perez. "They were printed."

"By Jews?" Fernando asked, his interest piqued.

"With the help of *conversos*."

"You can prove this?"

"I have a witness who was there."

"What will he say?"

"That the printing was carried out by the Lucena family, Jews in Olvera, under the direction of Tomas Catalan. Gabriel Catalan, as you know, operates the only printing press in Seville." Perez studied Fernando's face but did not see the expected reaction. He went on, disappointed, "This is proof that Gabriel Catalan is a secret Jew, a heretic, an enemy of both the church and the state. He should be arrested, tried, and burned at the stake."

A small smile appeared at a corner of Fernando's mouth. "Not so fast," Fernando said. "Surely you know that I need Don Gabriel's help to defeat the Portuguese."

Perez had not counted on this. How had he been so stupid? He thought he had Catalan and now he was slipping away. Again.

"But don't lose your witness," Fernando continued, bringing his hand to his chin. "We'll soon defeat our cousins from the west, and then ..."

28

"Rabbi, it's been too long since we've talked."

Gabriel was in Seville, taking a brief respite from his never-ending tasks of collecting taxes, purchasing supplies, and supervising the logistics of moving men and materials wherever Fernando needed them. The Portuguese army, under the personal command of King Afonso, had crossed the border into Castile, and was advancing rapidly.

"You're so busy now," said Modena. "I'm honored to be visited by the chief advisor to the Queen and supplier for the army of Castile."

Gabriel was hurt by the old man's sarcasm, but he understood how Modena could feel the way he did. The rabbi looked more frail than he remembered. He was close to ninety, and his Jewish world in Seville had suffered one horrible blow after another. The trial of the accused well-poisoners, and their subsequent hanging, was followed by many other acts of violence. Jewish homes were splattered with garbage and rocks. Jewish women were subjected to vile insults in the markets. Old men were pushed down in the street and robbed.

"We need you here, Don Gabriel," Modena said. "Only you can stop these Jew haters."

"I wish I could," Gabriel said. "I've spoken to the *regidores* and they've promised to provide extra protection and make some arrests."

"They won't do anything," snorted Modena.

"I've paid them exorbitantly."

Modena dismissed Gabriel's efforts with a shrug. "In another month it will be Passover," he said, "the time when Jews everywhere try to remember that God did not forget them in Egypt, and hope he does not forget them now. I have a favor to ask you."

"Anything, Rabbi."

"I want you to give me some of those printed *Haggadahs*."

"Of course. But I didn't think the Jewish families of Seville needed any more *Haggadahs*."

"It's not for Jews. Several men have approached me. They want to have a Seder this year. They need books."

"What men?"

"Men like yourself, whose fathers and grandfathers were Jews."

"*Conversos*?"

"I prefer to call them *anusim*, forced ones. They've had enough of this church of Jesus Christ, which persecutes and tortures and blames all Jews alive today for the death of their supposed Son of God fourteen centuries ago!"

Modena had worked himself to a fever pitch that Gabriel had not seen in years. His face was red and his breath came in short bursts. He coughed loudly, and yellow phlegm came from his mouth. The rabbi caught most of it in a rag he took from his pocket, but some remained on his face. Gabriel reached over and gently cleaned his chin. It was all he could do for him, because he was going to turn down his request.

"It's far too risky," Gabriel said. "Perez is suspicious, and he has spies. If those books are found with *conversos*, it'll be the end of the printing. Our work is essential to the future of the Jewish people."

"Jews are essential to the future of the Jewish people!" Modena said angrily. "Jews are more important than books! What good is the future if there are no Jews today? Don Alonso once spoke like this, and you argued against him. Now that you're important and wealthy, you no longer care about men less fortunate. The Talmud warns us not to become too familiar with the government, and not to seek renown. You print *Pirke Abot* and other tractates, but you learn nothing. Why do you print books if not for Jews?"

Gabriel was stung. Was he just being careful, or was he selfish? What was his obligation?

"I can't do it, Rabbi," he said, looking away from Modena's baleful stare.

"You mean you won't."

Rabbi Modena, hacking and shaking, walked out of his study. Gabriel's shoulders slumped. Although he had no choice, he knew that Modena was right.

Pilar was furious, as he had expected.

"After Tomas leaves, then you can give Hebrew books to whomever you want. Give them to Friar Perez. Maybe our dear Queen would like some. But now? How can you think for a minute that you did the wrong thing? Modena was unfair to ask."

"I don't think so," Gabriel said, choosing his words with great care. Tension in the Catalan family had been growing for almost a year, and he and Pilar had several times come close to a major confrontation. He knew that Tomas and Esther were the same way. How simple things had been when he made beautiful jewelry for the wealthy of Seville and gloried in his love for Pilar. When he didn't spend his life scurrying to Valladolid and Segovia and Toledo, and soon, west with Fernando to meet the Portuguese.

"Men who are sick of pretending to be Christians want to read the words of God before they die. That can't be wrong. I have the books. Why should I keep them locked away when they can do so much for these people?"

"Because you want your son to live," Pilar said between clenched teeth. "Because you want a grandchild."

"Is there news?" Gabriel interrupted excitedly.

"Every day I pray, but God does not answer. Perhaps Esther can't conceive again, and we'll have to be satisfied with Judah."

But he's not our blood, thought Gabriel, and there will never be another Catalan. Pilar's voice had softened, and Gabriel reached for her hand. She gave it to him. He touched her chin with his other hand, and kissed her cheek, gently, tentatively. She looked at him with the eyes that could always melt him, and he embraced her.

"Why do we argue?" he said. "I love you. Our time together is too precious to fight. We may not have much more."

"If you give books to *conversos*, it will be less. That I promise you."

"I won't. I told Modena I wouldn't. But still ..."

"No 'but still.' Just don't do it."

That night there was a visitor to the Catalan home.

"Don Gabriel, I'm sorry to bother you, but Rabbi Modena is very ill. He sent me to get you."

Gabriel rushed through the night to the synagogue. Modena was at his table. His head lay on an open book. His breathing was labored. Hearing Gabriel enter, he painfully raised his head.

"Don't think this is your fault," he said, struggling to sit up. "I'm an old man who should have died years ago. There's nothing more for me to do here."

"There's no one to replace you."

"The Jews of Castile are a beaten people. They have no fight left. They don't need a rabbi."

"I need you," said Gabriel. "I'll miss you." He placed his hand gently on the rabbi's arm. It was thin and cold.

"Thank you," Modena said weakly. "I wanted to see you before I died. I didn't want you to think that I died with anger."

"You were right," Gabriel said. "God needs Jews today."

Modena smiled. His eyes scanned the shelves from which he had studied the words of God for seven decades, as if taking a final inventory in the flickering candlelight. His eyelids closed; he slumped back in his chair. His hand touched Gabriel's, then fell to his side. A few seconds later, he stopped breathing.

"No! Don't do it!"

Pilar screamed at him but he didn't look at her and he didn't pause. He wrapped four of the precious *Haggadahs* in heavy wool and put them in a sturdy wooden box. His fingers fumbled with the leather straps as if they were writhing snakes, but finally they were secure.

"I'll be back in an hour. I'll tell them to be careful."

The two kings, Afonso of Portugal and Fernando of Castile, faced each other across the open space near the village of Toro on the western plains of Castile. Lances were lowered in furious charges, horses screamed, drums and trumpets sang, men fought hand to hand. After three hours of fierce battle, the Castilian troops prevailed. The royal standard of Portugal was torn to shreds and the Portuguese army fled. Many drowned in the Rio Douro. Only the onset of night and a driving rainstorm saved the scattered remnants from total destruction. King Afonso, at first thought dead, was among those who escaped. Fernando, bursting with energy, stayed on the field of battle until well past midnight, unwilling to leave the scene of his magnificent triumph. When dawn broke, there was no remaining military challenge to the supremacy of the young monarchs.

The victory at Toro resounded throughout Castile. In Seville, the *converso* community treated Gabriel as a returning hero and rejoiced at the prospect of peace. They were certain that Isabel's ascendancy and Gabriel's prominence would result in a new era of brilliant success for them.

Gabriel was less sure. Pilar's distrust of Isabel gnawed at him. He had seen enough to know how quickly men passed in and out of favor. Fernando hated him because of his role in Isabel's coronation, and now that the Portuguese had been so gloriously defeated, Gabriel was no longer essential to the king's ambitions.

Perez had been less prominent during the war, but as soon as the fighting ended, he returned to his anti-Jewish sermons. His wake was always filled with riled-up mobs attacking Jews. Perez fed on the peasants' fear of Jewish demons and the Old Christians' hatred of their *converso* rivals. It was easy to blur the distinction between Jews and *conversos*. Although *conversos* were still too powerful to be attacked directly, Perez continued to agitate for an Inquisition to uncover those he claimed were judaizers.

"Isabel will be here in ten days," Gabriel announced.

Tomas smiled, but Pilar and Esther made no attempt to disguise their irritation.

"Why is she coming to Seville?" Pilar asked.

"She's disturbed with the lawlessness and fighting," Gabriel said, "and she's intent that the largest city in Castile should not remain in chaos. Fernando is going to Toledo for a similar purpose." He paused, then added, "The Queen is also with child, and she wants to have it here in the milder winter weather."

"Will she have her child without Fernando, as she had her crown?" Esther asked.

"Fernando will join her before the blessed event," Gabriel answered, sadly shaking his head.

"You shouldn't be envious of the Queen," Tomas pleaded, when he and Esther had retired for the night.

"I'm not envious, and it's horrible of you to say so," Esther said without looking at him.

"Isabel is my friend, but I love only you."

"You might be better with her. At least she can have children. What use am I?"

"We have Judah and we must accept what God gives us. You know that better than I. You're the one who teaches me."

Esther sat rigidly on the edge of the bed, wearing the woolen gown given to her long ago by her friends at the *Alhambra*. He could hardly bear to look at her, but at the same time couldn't tear his eyes away. She had become unattainable. How could he break through her icy exterior? He longed for their former easy caring relationship, now so remote.

"Do you remember the first time you kissed me?" he asked hopefully. "I was so afraid. I had been in Arcos for days but you hardly ever spoke to me. I thought you didn't like me, and I was miserable."

Esther looked at him. The soft wool clung to her. Tomas stood forlornly on the other side of the room.

"I was alone in the shop. I saw a flicker of movement." He turned his head quickly, imitating himself. "I started to speak, but you put your finger to your lips."

Esther slowly raised her finger to her lips.

Tomas didn't dare move as she walked deliberately toward him, exactly as she had that night a lifetime ago. She came close to him and rose up to bring her eyes even with his. Her lips burned as they had before.

But she didn't turn and leave as she had then. It wasn't a dream. His arms encircled her and pressed her to him. She touched his arms, his waist, his hips. His hands slid down to cup her buttocks through the wool, and they stood that way for a long time.

Tomas loosened her gown and she his shirt. Their clothes intermingled on the floor. Their naked bodies glowed in the candlelight. They stood stock still, ravishing each other with their eyes.

Tomas dropped to his knees and kissed her belly. He buried his face between her legs. His tongue sought her heat. She spread her knees ever so slightly. Each glanced at the bed, and then dove for it, covers and pillows flying in wild unleashed passion.

By the time they were ready to sleep, the sun was starting to rise.

"Don't ever go away again," Tomas said.

"I was afraid," Esther said, "and it made me stiff."

"It's not you who's stiff now," said Tomas, placing her hand yet again between his legs.

"I can't have babies," Esther said, the gloom briefly re-appearing on her face.

"I don't care. Being with you. Making love with you. That's what I want every day for the rest of my life."

Esther bent over to kiss what she had been holding.

The surprising announcement was posted everywhere. On Friday, Queen Isabel would hold court. Real court. Any person in Seville was permitted to bring any matter, civil or criminal, before the Queen, and she would personally dispense justice. It was unheard of.

The *Alcazar* of Seville occupies the site of the palace of the ancient Roman praetor, its name derived from the two Arabic words, *al Kazr*, meaning house of Caesar. Subsequently occupied by Visigoth kings and then Moors, it returned to Christian hands when Seville was reconquered in 1248. Years later, King Pedro, known as Pedro the Cruel for good reason, the last monarch before the current Trastamara line, borrowed thousands of Moorish artisans who had just completed the *Alhambra* palace in Granada, and constructed the sumptuous rooms now occupied by Isabel.

The outer courtyard, once used to display caged lions, was jammed with Old and New Christians, nobles, knights, craftsmen, merchants and peasants, Jews and Moors, all come to seek Isabel's justice. Before them rose the magnificent facade of Pedro's palace, brilliant white stucco fronted by a series of arches at the first level and red brick above. The words "Allah is God" were repeated on scroll-like blue and white tiles above the red brick, and, bordering the scroll, carved in monkish script, the inscription "The most high and noble and most powerful and most conquering Pedro, by Grace of God King of Castile had these *alcazares* built, which was done in the year one thousand three hundred and sixty four."

Those summoned to the palace passed through a long narrow vestibule lined halfway up its walls with dazzling interlaced patterns in blue, black and orange tile. If they could see the floor, they probably chose not to notice the repetitive patterns of Jewish stars formed by dark and white stones. They moved quickly into a two story waiting room open to the sky, graciously decorated by intricate Moorish patterns on the arches and upper walls, where they were carefully watched by guards posted in the overhanging balcony alcoves. Again, their eyes probably avoided the Stars of David prominent in the delicate iron gates of the exterior walls.

Finally, they reached the great room of Pedro's *alcazar*, already renamed *Sala de Justicia*. Those who had been there before knew that rich oriental rugs and cushions had been removed in anticipation of the crowds. A huge wall, covered from floor to ceiling with decorative mosaics and stucco in a variety of patterns, faced the supplicants. Set high in this wall, behind a wrought iron balcony, fierce looking archers stood at the ready. Oil lamps, hung from the ceiling, blazed with light.

Below the archers, on a raised platform, was the empty throne, flanked on either side with the municipal officials of Seville. The Queen's advisors, including Gabriel Catalan, waited patiently among them.

A flurry of excited conversation filled the room. What would happen? How would the Queen possibly know about their local disputes? Would plain citizens dare to bring before the Queen their misuse at the hands of nobles, particularly the Guzmans and Ponce de Leons who backed up their illegal actions with powerful force?

Their questions were answered within five minutes of Isabel's arrival. She strode in briskly, unannounced, still graceful even though large with child. Some who didn't see her kept speaking, but their number quickly dwindled, and the room became totally quiet.

From her comfortable seat, Isabel explained.

"I will be here every Friday, until it is no longer necessary. I will hear any matter that anyone chooses to bring before me. I want especially to hear from those who have been wronged by powerful interests. My intention is to right those wrongs, and to prevent them from happening again. Do not fear retribution. Only those who fail to obey my decisions will have reason to fear."

Heads turned. People looked at each other in amazement. No king of Castile had ever acted like this. Gabriel was proud of his role in bringing this Queen to power. Isabel continued.

"When I make a decision, there is no appeal. You will carry out my will without fail, promptly and completely. That applies to the highest noble and the most humble resident, equally. I hope I am clearly understood."

She turned to chief judge of the municipal court of Seville. "Please present the first case."

The weeks went by and Seville's amazement grew. The Queen heard an incredible number and variety of cases. No matter was too large or too small for her attention. There were endless disputes about the growing and selling of olives, figs, oranges, grapes and peppers. It seemed that no plot of land nor its produce was clearly owned by anyone. The grazing and passage of large herds of cattle and merino sheep were discussed almost as often. Isabel listened carefully, conferred with her advisers, and decided. Fairly. Completely. Without ambiguity.

Gradually, the cases most on the minds of Sevillians and the Queen began to appear on her docket. Rodrigo Ponce de Leon, the Marques of Cadiz, was charged with assessing levies of wine and bread for the royal armada and then using them for his own ships. Enrique Guzman, the Duke of Medina Sidonia, had revoked an agreement guaranteeing Cadiz' right to fish for tunny, and requested Isabel to uphold the revocation. Isabel ordered Ponce de Leon to return the wine and bread, and refused to allow Medina Sidonia's restriction of fishing rights to stand.

Her authority was accepted indisputably and it gradually became clear that this was Isabel's true purpose. The new monarchs intended to consolidate the power of the realm in their hands. For the monarchs to hold more power, the nobles had to have less. Knowledgeable observers saw that the queen would prevail.

A majority of the municipal officials of Seville were *conversos*, and they played a prominent role in all of Isabel's proceedings. Many of these *conversos* behaved arrogantly, looking down on the Old Christians as incompetent and their social inferiors.

In the north of Castile, where Isabel had lived all of her life, this situation had never been so blatant, and she was shocked and dismayed by the level of conflict. The queen expressed her disapproval of the *converso's* behavior in various ways, and this in turn encouraged a torrent of complaints from Old Christians who felt their rightful place had been taken by Jewish usurpers. One Friday afternoon, after Isabel's regular court session concluded, she asked Gabriel to stay.

The Queen was now in her seventh month of pregnancy, and quite large. Her athletic grace was, at least temporarily, a thing of the past. Gabriel helped her from the throne to a comfortable couch in her private apartments. It was the first time he had seen the rooms that Isabel had remodeled for her personal use and for the birth of her child. A long room had been divided into three connecting sections.

Sunlight streamed through large windows along the southern wall of the palace, looking out on gardens lush with palm and orange trees, fountains and reflecting pools. The walls were stark white, but the high arches and ceilings were covered with delicate and intricate scroll-work in cream colored stucco. Brilliantly colored carpets from Babylon and Marrakesh covered every square inch of the floor. Large cushions, two heavy wooden chairs, and several tables occupied the first space, and Gabriel could see a canopied bed in the room beyond. Many paintings of saints and Hebrew prophets hung on the walls, but their was no crucifix or altar. Gabriel suspected that the third section, which he could not see, was a private chapel.

Isabel sat in one of the chairs and directed Gabriel to the other. She was, as always, direct.

"Many of your *converso* colleagues behave in a way that I find reprehensible," she said. "They're entitled to equal status with Old Christians, but they seem to think they're better. This unwarranted manner does nothing to aid their cause when complaints are made against them."

"I apologize to Your Highness," Gabriel said.

"It's not you who should apologize. You don't act like that. But perhaps you should speak to your friends. There are forces in this land which can be quite harmful to *conversos*. Surely you know that Friar Perez, no friend of yours, is here in Seville.

"Many *conversos* are very valuable and dear to me," the queen continued. "But I do not make all decisions by myself. The king, who will be here soon, is not as patient as I am."

Tomas followed the familiar route, but it was different. He understood that he would never return to any of these towns again. As soon as he completed these final visits to each press, he would ride east and make arrangements with Prince Hasan to sail to Italy.

He and Gabriel had decided to give the presses to the printers in Ecija and Olvera. Tomas brought them Latin and Castilian type, so they could run an "open" press like that which Gabriel operated in Seville. The Arcos press, Rodrigo's press, was going to go with Tomas, first to the *Alhambra* and then to Italy. Also with Tomas was the painting of Moses by Francesco Romo, a gift from Gabriel. Francesco was inspired to paint this in Florence, Gabriel had said, so it's fitting to take it there.

The most difficult stop was the one that had become the most pleasant to him, with the Lucenas in Olvera.

"Will you leave the Hebrew type?" Israel Lucena asked. "I want to print Hebrew books."

"That wasn't our plan," said Tomas. "I was going to take all the Hebrew type with me. What will you do with it? The Moors won't continue to collect the books or bring fresh paper."

"Maybe some day things will change," Lucena said.

"They won't, but, if you like, you can keep the type," said Tomas.

He gathered the printed books and loaded them into waiting wagons, leaving one of each for the Lucena family.

Leah Lucena had prepared a sumptuous lamb stew for Tomas and the fourteen men with him. After dinner, the men went outside to sleep. Tomas and the Lucena family shared their final moments together.

"Why are you going away?" Hannah asked. "Don't you like us any more?"

"Of course I like you," Tomas said, gathering her in his arms. "I always want to come here." Tomas had thought for days about how to answer this question, but he never found the right words. How could he tell them that Castile was too dangerous? He was going to escape, but he was abandoning them to whatever fate the country had for its Jews and *conversos*. There was no way to make that sound right, because it wasn't. The guilt Tomas felt about leaving his own parents was repeated here, but in some ways it was even worse. He had asked these people to do dangerous work, and now he was going to leave them to their own devices while he sailed off to a luxurious and protected future with the most powerful man in Italy, Lorenzo de Medici. It wasn't fair.

"Will you ever come back?" Hannah insisted.

"I don't know," Tomas answered, as honestly as he dared, tears welling in his eyes. "I will if I can. Maybe a long time from now, when you're a big girl, all grown up."

"The best port is Malaga," Hasan said. "I'll move everything there and keep a ship in port waiting for you. Will your father be going with you?"

"No. He won't leave. Nor my mother. But Esther will come, and our son Judah."

"I'll miss you, my dear Tomas." Hasan said, laying an affectionate hand on Tomas' shoulder.

"There's no way I can ever thank you."

"There's no way I can ever do enough," replied the prince. "How is our friend Queen Isabel?"

"She's remarkable," said Tomas. "She's going to make great changes in Castile."

"She's going to make war on me," said Hasan without emotion. "She and Fernando won't rest until there are no Moors left anywhere in Spain. Or Jews. They think that only Christians can know God. Can you imagine such arrogance? How can intelligent people believe such nonsense?"

"It's drummed into them from the day they're born," said Tomas. "Christ is the only way to eternal salvation, and the Church is the only way to Christ."

"They won't have an easy time taking Granada from us," Hasan said. "But if they really want it and they keep coming, eventually we'll be overwhelmed."

"Then why fight? Why not leave?"

"It's our land. I'd rather die fighting for it."

"I feel the same way. But the books …" Tomas paused, "The books are so important for our future. Jews are nothing without books."

"I don't think it's the books," said Hasan.

"What? What else could it be?"

"It's you, Tomas. It's men like you who make Jewish families which last forever. That's why your father wants you to go. The books will help, but *you* are the future of the Jewish people. You and that wonderful brave wife of yours. My men still talk of her riding out all alone to save you. Take care of that woman. There aren't many like her."

"I'll leave for Seville tomorrow, and then, as soon as possible, we'll return."

"My ship will be ready."

"Everything is prepared," Tomas told his anxious parents.

"Not much remains to be done here. You can get ready to leave," Gabriel said.

"You know I don't want to go," Tomas said.

"We know," Pilar answered.

But later, when they were alone, Esther surprised Tomas, and new plans were necessary.

"Something has happened," she said, her back to him.

"What?" he answered, frightened by her earnestness.

"It's the most amazing thing," she said, turning to face him. "After all these years, I'm going to have another baby."

The smile on Tomas' face lit the room. They hugged and cried. They looked at each other with shy smiles and then burst into joyous laughter. Tomas ran his hand over Esther's belly, and between her legs.

"It must have been that night," Esther said, grinning at the memory.

"Which time?" Tomas asked.

Esther blushed, then asked, "What should we do? Should we leave or wait until the baby is born?"

"Do my parents know?"

"I wanted to tell you first," Esther said, "but if you hadn't gotten back soon, they would have guessed." She patted her belly, and Tomas saw that it was indeed beginning to grow.

"How long will it be?" he asked.

"Three, maybe four months."

"Then let's wait. Seville seems quiet enough for now, and I want my parents to see their new grandchild."

29

The quiet was misleading.

Amid much fanfare, the queen had given birth to a son, an heir, and Prince Juan seemed to be a healthy baby. The monarchs, victorious over the Portuguese, having subdued the nobles, and with a national police force in full operation, seemed to be in control of their kingdom.

Only the *converso* problem remained unsolved, but it was potentially explosive. Friar Perez left a trail of bloody violence as he crisscrossed the country preaching sermons of hate. As Gabriel had predicted, he had switched his focus from Jews to *conversos*, and was challenging the monarchs to root out judaizing heresy with an Inquisition. Within the past few months, there had been riots and serious attacks on *conversos* in Cordoba, Toledo, and Jaen.

Perez was often joined on the pulpits and in the squares by Alvar Sanchez. Sanchez had become the champion of Old Christian merchants and office holders. Together, Perez and Sanchez made a fearsome pair, and they both despised Gabriel.

Isabel and Fernando invited their most important advisors to a private meeting in Seville to discuss the question of an Inquisition in Castile. Perez and Sanchez would be there, along with Perez' mentor Tomas de Torquemada, Prior of Santa Cruz. Torquemada was even more dreaded, in Gabriel's view, than Perez. He made no public speeches, but his piercing intelligence was more likely to influence Isabel than Perez' inflammatory bluster.

Friar Filippo de Barberi, the Inquisitor of Sicily, in Seville reporting to Fernando, was also invited. Lastly, in the camp of those favoring an Inquisition, was the Papal legate, Nicolao Franco, Bishop of Trevisa.

Isabel had spoken to Gabriel shortly after the christening of Prince Juan. She emphasized the need for absolute discretion. Not only was the substance of their talks to be confidential, but even the fact that they were being held. Gabriel was the only *converso* invited.

Gabriel's ally would be Archbishop Fonseca, steadfast and fair as always, but an ineffective orator and not a favorite of Fernando, who regarded him as closer to Isabel. Fonseca had honored Isabel's request, over Perez' objection, to try to teach the New Christians of Seville the ways of their religion and the foolishness of Judaism. But this herculean effort, employing much of the clergy's energy for many months, had yielded little.

Gabriel understood that he had slight chance of convincing Fernando of anything. Despite Gabriel's well-recognized and indeed critical services during the war against the Portuguese, Fernando barely spoke with him.

Isabel was his only hope, but he wondered how vigorous she would be. It was only four weeks since she had delivered, and she had tired quickly at her few public appearances since then. A lesser woman wouldn't even have tried.

Gabriel passed through the massive outer gate of the *Alcazar*, through the great Courtyard of the Lions, and into the Palace of Pedro. He was directed to a room on the second floor, overlooking the *Sala de Justicia*.

The room was intimate in scale, but richly decorated. A table had been provided for the participants, and it was consistent with the style and civility of the monarchs that all of the advisors sat together. Gabriel sat silently, arms folded tightly around himself, hearing but not following the chatter of the mighty prelates. Perez was also quiet, and Sanchez, out of his league in such company, shrank down in his seat.

Fernando and Isabel entered without pomp, deep in conversation as they walked. Torquemada saw them first and jumped to his feet, quickly followed by the others. Fernando helped Isabel, who walked with difficulty, to her pillowed chair, and took his own beside her. Their floor length robes, of rich material but unadorned, projected a businesslike demeanor. Neither wore a crown. Fernando looked to his wife to begin, and it was immediately clear that in this, as in all other matters, they had planned every step with precision.

But had they already made up their minds? Was this a charade?

Gabriel suspected that Fernando was ready to proceed with an Inquisition, but that Isabel was not yet convinced, and it was she who had arranged this last deliberation.

"Thank you for joining us," Isabel began in a voice strained by fatigue. "We have a difficult choice to make, and we want your frank and honest counsel. You may speak your minds openly. When we reach a decision, some of you may be pleased and others not. There can be no other way when differing views are held so strongly. But even if we decide on a policy opposed to your own, we will not hold it against you for expressing a view here that does not ultimately prevail."

Isabel's voice faded with her last words, and she leaned back in her chair. Fernando carried on.

"We will hear first," he said, "from those who believe that an Inquisition should be established in Castile, and we will permit, indeed encourage, opposing views. Then we will hear arguments against the measure, again permitting comment from those who favor it. We expect to be here for two days, but if it takes longer, we'll continue to listen. You may never have such patient attention from us again," he smiled, "but this question is of paramount importance and we must do the right thing."

Gabriel felt as if he were living a nightmare. The very calm was terrifying. They would soon be discussing the advisability of establishing a system based on sudden arrest, torture of defendants and witnesses, and burning people alive. Yet both Fernando and Isabel were explaining the rules as pedantically as if this were a university debate where the prize was a nicely bound volume of St. Augustine's *Confessions*.

"After the deliberations are complete," Fernando continued, "the Queen and I will discuss the matter privately. We will reach our decision. What that decision will be, when it will be announced, and when it will be implemented, will be our affair. You will not reveal what is said at this meeting. Ever. You will not disclose that this meeting took place. Each of you will now swear your solemn oath."

"As you have spoken, Your Majesties, so it will be," said Franco, the Papal legate and highest ranking person at the table. Gabriel heard murmuring around him, and realized that each man was repeating his oath of silence. He opened his mouth to speak but no words came out. Since the others were all talking at the same time, no one noticed.

"Who will begin?" asked the king.

All eyes, including the monarchs, turned to Perez. The Friar stood, moved to the space between the table and the thrones, and launched into his oft-repeated diatribe that all but the king and queen had heard many times.

"It is well known," he began, "that many *conversos* maintain close ties to their Jewish relatives and friends. They eat Jewish foods, practice Jewish customs, and use the Hebrew language their parents taught them in childhood."

"How do you know these things?" interjected Archbishop Fonseca with uncharacteristic sharpness. Fernando chuckled at the sparring.

Perez ignored Fonseca.

"Even if they go to church," he continued, "they persist in practicing Judaism alongside their new Christianity. Like dogs returning to their vomit, they return to their Jewish rites. Behind closed doors, under the cover of night, they blaspheme our Lord and His Mother." Perez paced back and forth, stopping directly in front of the queen. "After their children are baptized, they sneak home as quickly as they can to wash away the holy water as if it was swill."

Isabel gasped audibly. Gabriel caught her eye, and spoke in a voice choked with anger. "You have no morals! You're a man of religion but you lie through your teeth! Do you care that you're telling lies to your King and Queen?" Gabriel couldn't spit the words out fast enough. "Do you know even one *converso* who has ever done anything like that? Who can you name?"

Again Perez proceeded as if there had been no interruption. "This ugly disease of *converso* duplicity is not unique to Seville," he said. "It pervades all of Castile." He walked away and then back, again stopping in front of Isabel, speaking directly to her. "If this intolerable behavior is left unpunished and encouraged to grow, it will proliferate so widely that our Holy Catholic Faith will be severely wounded."

"Where is your proof?" screamed Fonseca. "You make outrageous claims without the tiniest scrap of proof!"

This time Perez answered.

"That is precisely why we need an Inquisition," Perez said with a triumphant smirk, having elicited from Fonseca exactly the challenge he wanted. "The *conversos* are too powerful and wealthy. They bribe or threaten those who might testify against them in an ordinary forum. They have such power that they force their poor servants, even if they be Old Christians, to submit to the barbaric Hebrew custom of circumcision."

Fernando glanced at Isabel, and spoke as they had no doubt discussed in advance. "We will have no more talk of circumcision, Friar, unless you have proof. I have told you this before."

Perez, momentarily chastised, quickly regained his composure and the thread of his argument, "Only the power of the Holy Order can offset these evil men." Looking squarely at Fonseca, he added, "You know this yourself, do you not, my dear Archbishop?"

Fonseca's head snapped at the direct challenge, but Perez did not pause.

"Did you not, Your Excellency, compose a certain catechism, in conformity with the sacred canons, prescribing proper Christian behavior, practices and beliefs?"

Perez had quoted directly from Fonseca's instruction book.

"And did you not make this known in all the churches of this city, and post it on trees and walls in every parish? And did you not declare that all the curates and clerics should indoctrinate their congregants, especially the *conversos* among them? Did you not inform those false New Christians about the True Faith, both through public preaching and in private conversations, and instruct them and attempt to return them to true belief in our Lord Jesus Christ? Did you not admonish them and demand that they abandon the heretical performance of depraved Jewish rituals, and warn them that they would incur the perpetual damnation of their souls and the perdition of their bodies and worldly goods if they persisted in these desecrations? Tell me, sir, did you not do all these things?"

Fonseca's face reddened. He stared blackly at Perez, but his eyes were filled with sadness at the failure of his campaign.

"And what did all of this effort produce? Nothing! Not a thing! Because the shrewdness and pertinacity of these secret Jews, these agents of the Devil, is such that no matter how they deny and conceal their evil heresies, secretly they fall back into it and perform the Jewish rituals. They observe Jewish holidays and the Sabbath. They send oil to the synagogues, and they discuss their affairs with rabbis."

Perez drew himself up and smiled obsequiously toward Fernando and Isabel, "Give us the procedure of the Inquisition, Your Majesties, and all which is now secret will be known, and those who judaize will either repent or suffer the dire consequence."

"More lies," Gabriel said through clenched teeth. "There were no false Christians to teach. That's why none came forward to receive the Archbishop's message." He wanted to say how ridiculous it was to expect any secret Jew, if there were such, to present himself and admit it. But since Fonseca's catechism had been Isabel's idea, he restrained himself.

Perez raised his arms to heaven. "O savage and malicious beast of heresy," he cried, "deformed sin that nourishes faithlessness. The habits of these bad Christians are those of the stench-ridden Jews. Gluttons and drinkers, they eat their stewed meats with onions and garlic, fried in oil. Thus they have a very bad odor in their breathing, and an awful stink in their houses. These judaizing *conversos* have the odor of Jews."

Fernando laughed out loud, slapping his thigh. "Tell us, dear Friar, have you smelled this *converso* stink yourself?"

"I have smelled it," said Perez solemnly, falling for Fernando's trap.

"Then why," said Fernando, still smiling, "did you not quickly grab those smelly Christians and show everyone the terrible consequences of their judaizing?"

"There were many people close together and it could not be determined which of them smelled," Perez said lamely.

Fernando's eyebrows rose, but he said nothing more, evidently satisfied that he had made his point. Gabriel was not encouraged by Fernando's ridicule of Perez. The messenger might be a buffoon in the king's eyes, but his message had swept the country and roused terrible hatreds and violence.

Gabriel knew that Fernando and Isabel could not tolerate the level of disorder that Perez and others had instigated. The horror was that they were likely to punish the victims of the thuggery and not its perpetrators.

"Perhaps," said Isabel, "it would be good to hear from Don Alvar now."

Gabriel was calmed by the sound of the queen's voice.

Perez hesitated, apparently not ready to be seated. He wisely decided not to confront the queen, and Alvar Sanchez rose to take his place. His frilled shirt and tight tunic looked out of place.

"As Friar Perez has explained," Sanchez began, "the majority of the *conversos* of your dominions are judaizers, desecrating the grace of the holy oil and baptism they have been blessed to receive. The water of baptism has touched their skins, but not their hearts. They remain hostile to Christianity and enemies of all true believers.

"You might ask why they pretend to be Christians when they are not. The answer is that they have a most evil plan, your Majesties.

They conspire with Jews who live here in Castile, with their fellows in many other countries, and with the infidel Moors. It has long been the plan of these *conversos*, under the guise and protection of being Christians, to squeeze the souls and bodies and possessions of good Christians who are old in the Catholic faith. Thus the Jews plot to take control of Castile."

Gabriel jumped to his feet in exasperation. "There are no Jews plotting to take over anything," he said, "and Your Majesties know how loyal all *conversos* have been to you. Sanchez and other Old Christians are jealous, and they malign us to advance themselves. Surely Your Majesties can see this."

"We plead with Your Majesties," Sanchez continued, "that converts of Jewish descent should not be allowed to hold any offices by which they may mistreat Old Christians. Just as Jews are forbidden from such offices, so should those who are of Jews, even in the tenth generation of their conversion."

"Now we see what this is really about," said Gabriel. "It has to do with positions and money, not religion."

"It is about money as well as religion," Sanchez admitted. "The *conversos* have stolen large quantities of *maravedis* and silver from Your Majesties, and have brought devastation upon the estates of many noble ladies and *caballeros*, and have robbed most of the old houses and estates of the Old Christians, whose loyalty to you is unquestioned. They should be sought out and severely punished before they destroy the Catholic religion and with it the realms of Spain.

"He invents these stories with no evidence," said Gabriel, "just as Friar Perez does in his sermons. Lies! All lies!"

"Many *conversos* in your kingdom have made great fortunes and estates," Sanchez continued. "Why is this so? Are they better than Old Christians? Not at all. They succeed because they act without conscience, and by cunning and deceit that honorable Old Christians would not lower themselves to emulate. These *conversos* believe that in all the world there are none better than them. They have acquired honor, royal offices, and the favor of kings and lords. Many of them have intermarried with sons and daughters of Old Christian cavaliers.

"Their goal is clear. They would dominate Christianity, seizing all positions of power, and then exploit the Christian masses to the point of exhaustion. When the Christians collapse, Jews will rise triumphantly over the hated religion which replaced them in the eyes of God. Thus the Devil will defeat the Lord. Then they will make us all be Jews or slaves of Jews. This is their plan. Only Your Majesties stand in the way of this evil design."

Gabriel looked to Fonseca, who had remained silent throughout Sanchez' speech, his head buried in his hands. He would be no further help. But someone had to discredit these allegations of a massive Jewish-*converso* conspiracy. He looked at Isabel and received her nod.

"This tired story," Gabriel said, "has been heard in Castile for many years. It has no basis in fact. It is ridiculous to contemplate. In fact, thirty years ago, when the leaders of the Toledo rebellion passed laws based on these same charges, laws known as the *Sentencia-Estatuto*, they were excommunicated and denounced as heretics by Pope Nicholas.

"There is no place in Christianity for two classes of Christians. All Christians must be equal before God, in the eyes of the Church, and in the laws of the state. When Friar Perez and Don Alvar seek to upset what should be the rights of all Christians, it is they who are the true threat to your dominions, not *conversos* whom Your Majesties know are the most loyal of your subjects.

"It is true that many of our number have been successful since our ancestors converted to Christianity. But neither we nor our fathers and grandfathers have any secret plan to take over Castile or any other country, and it is preposterous to say that is why we converted.

"Everyone in Castile knows full well that our ancestors were forced to become Christians. My grandfather was slaughtered like an animal in 1391, and my grandmother was raped and murdered, in bloody riots perpetrated in the name of Jesus by Archdeacon Ferran Martinez, in this very city. My father, who was but a boy at that time, had no plan to take over anything. He was given a choice of accepting baptism or death, and he chose to live.

"But he, and many others like him, received no instruction in the Christian Faith. Nor do most Old Christians who know nothing of Holy Scriptures, either the Jewish Bible or the Gospel of Jesus. Such instruction is important. It is needed even for the supposedly learned friar in this very room who has spoken before Your Majesties and dared to distort the teachings of Jesus!"

Perez jumped to his feet to object, but Isabel motioned him back. He slammed his big body into his chair.

Gabriel continued. "Jesus of Nazareth never preached the message which Friar Perez has taken to every corner of this kingdom. Jesus of Nazareth preached love for one's fellow man ... charity, and peace. When did Jesus call for torture? When did Jesus teach that you should burn your enemies at the stake? The very idea of Inquisition is a perversion of the teachings of Jesus.

"You must wonder why you are asked to bring intolerable suffering to so many of your loyal subjects. Is it because great numbers of your New Christian subjects are secretly practicing Judaism? There is no evidence that this is true. Is it because there is a plot of *conversos* and Jews to enslave Old Christians and take over this country? That idea is so ridiculous as to deny serious consideration.

"But there is a reason, and it is this. Baptism removed the restrictions which then and now limit the activities of Jews. We *conversos* have worked hard, and have applied ourselves successfully in many professions and occupations from which our ancestors were excluded.

"Many Old Christians have not done so well, and their jealousy is why we are here now. This jealousy led to the adoption of the *Sentencia-Estatuto* in Toledo. Driven by greed and avarice, they seek to destroy *conversos* so they will have sole domain in the country's commerce and government.

"Of course they try to disguise their jealousy and hatred with a pretended zeal for the Faith. Thus comes Friar Perez with his evil lies and sacrilegious hypocrisy, repeated endlessly to ignorant gullible crowds.

"Let me tell you about Friar Perez. Many years ago, he murdered my best friend. Late at night, he came to the house of the artist Francesco Romo, dragged him away, and put him in a cell under the monastery of San Pablo. This man of God denied my friend even food and clothing. He allowed him to be eaten by rats. Finally, he raised him on a hoist and dropped him to rip his arms from their sockets. Francesco Romo died in unspeakable agony.

"Archbishop Fonseca brought Friar Perez to trial, and found him guilty of the acts I have just described. Perez should have been executed for committing murder, but he was not, and he stands here today ready to condemn more innocent Christians to an awful death. I plead with you. Don't let him do it."

Gabriel walked off to the side, struggling to control his emotions. When he was calm, he returned to his place and looked at Isabel. He was amazed to see her eyes wet with tears.

"Alvar Sanchez, this ally of Friar Perez, has a particular animosity towards me. Some years ago, we were the only two bidders for a contract to farm the taxes of the district of Cordoba. You were there that day, Your Highness. I was prepared to bid, but King Enrique, on his own initiative, awarded the contract to me without bidding. I did nothing to encourage the king."

"That's a lie!" shouted Sanchez. "You bribed the officials, especially the treasurer Don Diego Arias, a fellow *converso*. It was all part of your Jewish conspiracy. Your bribes were greater than ours, and ..."

"I didn't bribe anyone," said Gabriel. "If you did, that is your business and your crime. I was prepared to bid four million *maravedis* for the contract. What was your bid?"

Sanchez hung his head, admitting silently that his bid would have been lower. But Perez jumped in to rescue his confederate. "It doesn't matter what his bid would have been," Perez argued. "You Jews had it all arranged."

"You accuse me of being a Jew?" asked Gabriel. He took a threatening step toward Perez and the friar raised his arms to defend himself, but Gabriel stopped. "Do you have proof?" he said. "I demand that you withdraw your false accusation!"

Instead of answering, Perez glanced at the king, seeking guidance. Oh my God, Gabriel thought, Perez does have proof and Fernando knows it!

Fernando nodded, a barely perceptible signal, and Perez sat down, but not before sneering arrogantly at Gabriel. Isabel, who never missed anything, look quizzically at Fernando, but no words were exchanged.

"Your Majesties," said Gabriel, hastening to conclude so that he could consider this new and fearsome development, "I submit that there has been no reason presented here today that would justify the imposition of an Inquisition upon this land. It is true that there is disorder and violence against *conversos*. But the cause of that disorder and violence sits here before you. Friar Perez and Don Alvar Sanchez, and others like them, are the guilty ones. I implore you to discipline those who provoke the violence and not those who are its victims."

Fernando glanced toward Isabel, who looked exhausted. "That will be enough for today," he said. "We will resume tomorrow morning."

"He knows," Gabriel announced as soon as he and Pilar were alone.

"Who? What?"

"Perez, and Fernando, too. They have some proof that I'm a judaizer."

"What did they say?"

"Perez accused me. He included me as one of the Jews. They think we're all in a great conspiracy against them. I challenged him to offer proof of my judaizing or withdraw his accusation. Perez started to answer, but he looked at Fernando and got some sort of signal, and didn't finish. Isabel look puzzled. Whatever they know, it's between Perez and Fernando.

"Why didn't they just come right out and say whatever it is?"

"I don't know. Maybe they want to wait until the Holy Order begins."

"If that's so, how long do we have?"

"They'll have to ask the Pope for permission. Then appoint Inquisitors. I'd say four months at least."

"Esther will have her baby before that. Can we wait?"

"I think so," Gabriel said. "Dear God, don't let me be wrong!"

The next morning, Fernando asked Friar Filippo de Barberi to describe the operation of the Inquisition in Sicily, where it had been in effect for many years. Barberi, a Dominican like most other Inquisitors, spoke in a brisk, bureaucratic manner.

"I am pleased to report that the Inquisition in Sicily has not produced the horrors feared by Don Gabriel. Whenever there is a report of heresy, we conduct a full examination. If there is guilt, we seek to reconcile the sinner. Sometimes this is not possible, and then he is punished and we confiscate his property."

Fernando looked up with fresh interest. "What happens to the property?" he asked.

"Two thirds of the value, once it is sold, is sent to the Papal Holy Office, and the remaining third is retained by the Inquisition in Sicily. This offsets the expenses of our operation, which I must say are quite modest."

"Why does two thirds go to Rome?" Fernando persisted.

"This is, after all, a Papal Inquisition, and there are expenses in Rome that must also be met."

"Who directs your activities?" asked Isabel.

"His Excellency, the Bishop of Palermo."

Turning to the papal legate, Nicolao Franco, Isabel asked, "Will the Holy Pontiff support the establishment of an Inquisition in Castile?"

"With the level of heresy that has been reported in Castile, His Holiness Sixtus IV is eager to implement the Church's only means of assuring the uniformity of the Faith."

"Thank you, Your Excellency," Isabel said. "We will hear next from Friar Torquemada."

In his fifty eighth year, Friar Torquemada was tall and gaunt, stooping slightly at the shoulders. He brought with him an impeccable reputation for sanctity. He never ate meat, wore a hair shirt and never allowed linen to touch his body, slept on a bare board, and observed the monk's rule of poverty with unusual rigor.

Gabriel feared the influence of Isabel's former confessor. It was rumored that he had, when the queen was still a young girl, extracted a promise from her that she would eliminate heresy from her dominions when she became queen.

Torquemada spoke softly, as if pained by words he would prefer not to utter. "It is sad to realize, my dear Isabel and Fernando, that there are Christians in your lands who do not feel well about our Lord and our Church. I have come, at your request, to speak for the glory of God and the exaltation of the Catholic Faith. Religious laxity is widespread. In these kingdoms, there are many blasphemers and renegades from God, especially among those known as *conversos*.

Slowly, ominously, Torquemada continued. "These judaizers make a mockery of the Holy Church. They defile the sacraments. They perpetrate the most abominable sacrilege by pretending to accept the Christian Faith. They sow confusion and doubt among those who see their bad example.

"There is no stopping these evil people, joined in concert with others of their race in every country, unless Your Majesties establish a Holy Order of Inquisition to root them out and destroy them, before *they* destroy the Holy Church and this country. Their detestable judaizing is spreading and only you can stop it!"

Even Gabriel felt himself drawn by the power of Torquemada's eloquence and quiet energy. To Isabel, who had spent hours confessing her sins to him, his presence must be compelling.

"In the sight of the Church," Torquemada continued in his priestly manner of absolute knowledge and total conviction, "there is no sin so intolerable or so execrable as heresy. It is the Church's duty to stamp out this awful pestilence of the soul to prevent it from spreading. It is your duty as guardians of the Catholic Faith to assist the Church in this holy effort by providing the means of the Holy Office.

"I am sure that the Queen Our Lady will do what she ought to do, and as a most Christian queen is *obliged* to do. Her duty to God requires no less."

Archbishop Fonseca took the floor with a confident air that boosted Gabriel's spirits, and went straight to the attack. He presented his arguments concisely, as if reading from a legal document.

"*Conversos*, in their Jewish ancestry," Fonseca said, "are one with the lineage of our Lord Jesus Christ according to the flesh. The very first to know our Lord were Jews, all of His Apostles and St. Paul and many others. All Jews who converted to Christ.

"How can we honor our Lord, who came from that lineage, or His Jewish Mother, if at the same time we adhere to the absurd idea that converts from Judaism, solely because of their race, are to be treated with abuse? This is not anti-*converso*. This is anti-Christian.

"Is Mary, Mother of Christ, the daughter of an accursed race? Would God choose the saintliest of all humanity, the human form of His Son Jesus Christ, to emerge from an accursed race?

"St Paul asked 'Has God cast off His people?' And he answered 'Far from it! For I am also an Israelite, of the seed of Israel, of the tribe of Benjamin. God has not cast off His people, whom He has known.'

"It is the goal of the Church to bring all Jews into its bosom. If we persecute those who do convert, how will we attract others?

"I do not believe that many *conversos* are judaizers, and if there are some, they are easily cured by effective instruction applied gently and persuasively over time. There is no need for a vicious and cruel Holy Order which declares all *conversos* suspect and promotes false testimony and causes great pain and disruption."

Gabriel was pleased with Fonseca's words, but his manner had no fire or passion. As the Archbishop droned on, Gabriel feared that he made little impact on the monarchs.

"The Church holds that baptism creates a new man free from sin," Fonseca continued. "If we deny this in the case of baptism of Jews, we blaspheme our own beliefs. Can we allow these friars to claim they represent the Church's teachings when they so flagrantly disregard them?

"Friar Perez says that circumcision is barbaric. If this is so, why then was our Lord Jesus Christ circumcised on the eighth day according to the custom of the Law of Moses?

"Many nobles families in both Castile and Aragon have intermarried with *conversos*. Are all of these great lords, prelates, and knights, and even members of monastic orders, who thus are part of the Jewish lineage, to be subject to ignominy and vilification? This for the crime of being of the same race as our Lord?"

Surprisingly, Fonseca turned from the monarchs and addressed Torquemada directly.

"Friar Torquemada, you are of a noble family. Yet Juan de Torquemada, your distinguished uncle, was himself a *converso*, descendant from his New Christian mother. You yourself may have similar ancestry."

Torquemada smiled, unperturbed.

"But speaking now of your uncle, who was regarded before his recent passing as the most learned member of the Sacred College of Cardinals, surely you know that when news of anti-*converso* riots in Toledo reached Rome some years ago, he was asked by the Pope to examine the matter. What did your uncle, a man well known as a fighter of heresies, report to the Holy Pontiff?

"Your worthy uncle wrote from Subiaco that any distinction among Christians based on their racial history is a grave threat to Christianity itself. He correctly identified as agents of the Devil, not the *conversos*, but rather those who seek to divide the Church one part from the other.

"You and Friar Perez are the ones who speak heresy when you deny that certain converts are not freed by baptism from their previous sins. You are the heretics here, not those whom you slander with no evidence whatsoever.

"Every day the Church prays to God that He bring the remnant of the Jewish people to the Faith. Yet we kill, rob and defame these Jews in every imaginable way. And you propose that we should do the same to those of this race who have already been baptized and who are as worthy and dedicated to the faith as any other Christian. How do you dare designate as unreliable and suspect those converts who are children and grandchildren of Christians, who were born in Christ, and who know nothing about Judaism or its rites?

"Friar Perez says that all baptized Jews and those who come from their line are an abhorred, damned and detested group. He calls them adulterous, sons of infidelity, judaizers, conspirators who suck the blood and sweat of the poor Christian race, responsible for all of the calamities that affect Castile.

"Can your Majesties even listen to this without laughing, it is so absurd? And yet, if Friar Perez is right, who here is not part of this damned and detested group, when intermarriage between *conversos* and the old nobility of Spain has been so extensive that the two groups are inseparably intertwined?

Suddenly, Fonseca stopped.

"I ask permission to rest for a moment," he said. "Would Your Majesties allow Don Gabriel to add some very interesting information on this point?"

Fernando indicated that Gabriel might speak.

"I had occasion, Your Highnesses," Gabriel said, "to travel to the village of Andujar."

Behind him, Gabriel heard Perez gasp.

"While I was there ..."

"Stop him!" screamed Perez. "This has no relevance."

"We will decide that," Fernando answered angrily. "Continue, Don Gabriel."

"...I learned that a certain Rebecca de Barrientos, daughter of Abraham de Barrientos, a Jew, married Cristobal Perez on May 15, 1399. Cristobal Perez was the grandfather of this Ricardo Perez here before you. His grandmother was a Jewess! He is among the accursed race!"

Perez leaped to his feet, and Fernando smiled expectantly, as he did whenever Perez was goaded to excess. But before Perez could say a word, Torquemada was at his side, whispering in his ear, and Perez sat down without speaking.

Instead, it was Fonseca who spoke next. "So we see that many among us share a part of the lineage of Jesus and Mary. Even your own royal houses ..."

Fernando raised his hand sharply, and Fonseca froze, panic stricken. He had gone too far!

Isabel placed her hand gently on Fernando's, and, after a moment of indecision, the king shrugged and Fonseca exhaled with relief.

"Don Gabriel," said Isabel, "do you have other matters you wish to address?"

Gabriel nodded to the queen. This was his moment, but he was sure the monarchs did not want him to repeat Fonseca's arguments. What could he add?

"Your Highness," he began, "many of us, myself included, were loyal to your cause even before your marriage to our Lord King. We risked much to help you attain that noble matrimony which has brought so many benefits to Castile. We have supported you with our lives and our fortunes ever since. It is an affront to the justice you value so highly for us to be held unworthy solely because of our ancestry."

Gabriel paced along the space separating the advisors from the king and queen. What is she thinking? Will she overrule Fernando?

"The arguments in support of an Inquisition, despite their religious trappings, have nothing to do with heresy. We are here because the descendants of Jews forced seventy five years ago to convert to Christianity have since become rich and influential.

"The Old Christians dare not attribute this success to its true cause! Can they admit that it is the *converso's* industry, learning, ingenuity, driving force, and other talents which have led them to prosper? They cannot. To do so would demonstrate the abysmal absence of these same qualities among those Old Christians whom the *conversos* have passed by."

Gabriel walked to where Alvar Sanchez was seated and stared straight at him as he continued.

"Alvar Sanchez and the others cannot admit their own inferiority, so they desperately seek another explanation, and the Friars give them what they need. Perez and Torquemada say that the *conversos'* success is not due to their virtues, but rather to their vices. They are still secretly Jews! It is their Jewish falsehood and deception which enables them to gain by fraud what no honest man could attain by fair means. Thus they support an Inquisition to do by terror and the false use of the Church what they cannot accomplish themselves."

Gabriel hung his head. Have I said enough? He knew that Isabel was tired. He composed himself for a final burst and approached the queen. Isabel's eyes bore directly at him as he spoke.

"Your Highness, I plead with you. Do not do this! You will accomplish no good, and you will do great harm. *Conversos* who have committed no crime will be tortured and killed. Do not unleash hatred and persecution against your loyal subjects. Rather I urge you to enforce your laws and punish those who incite disorder and riots. Do not appease those who are the cause of the problem, even when they come before you in monastic habits and claim that they act in the name of Jesus. Make them know that their criminal purposes cannot be achieved, and you will achieve the peace you so rightly desire."

The Queen summoned Gabriel to her private quarters at the *Alcazar*. After days of numbing anxiety and fruitless speculation shared with Archbishop Fonseca, he would learn her will.

He had barely been seated when Isabel began.

"We have decided," she said, "to request authority for an Inquisition in the kingdom of Castile. I'm sure His Holiness will grant our wish."

"You will allow the Pope such power in your domains?"

"Of course not," Isabel said quickly. "This will not be an Inquisition run from Rome. We will make the appointments, and we will remove any who do not please us. And ... we will also control the expenditures and the receipts."

"His Holiness will agree to this?"

"Sixtus will do what we want. No bishop controlled from Rome will have the power of Inquisition in Castile."

"This will cause much suffering."

"I don't deny it. But I am responsible for the spiritual well-being of my subjects. It is my duty to ensure purity within the church. If I allow heresy to continue, if I deliberately avert my eyes, then it's as if I committed heresy myself."

Alone with the queen, Gabriel allowed himself to express the anger he had previously bottled up. "So instead you avert your eyes from the vicious lies of Perez and Torquemada, and the Old Christians who clamor for what they have not earned? Even now they're planning another assault against us in Toledo. You encourage such lawless behavior?"

"We establish an Inquisition to prevent lawlessness and disorder," Isabel responded. "We provide a means to find the truth, and if there is no heresy, there will be no burnings. But the Old Christians will know that we have investigated thoroughly, and there will be no riot in Toledo or anywhere else."

"No riots perhaps," said Gabriel sadly. "But many burnings."

"There are many heretics?" Isabel asked.

"Perez will invent them. As he did with Francesco Romo. He'll torture the accused until they say anything, just to have a sip of water. He'll torture witnesses until they testify as he wants. And it won't be long before he doesn't even have to use torture. Witnesses will come running to him with false tales, frantic to arrive before their neighbors who would tell the same tales about them. That is what you will bring to Castile."

"We will not permit such evil."

"You'll never know. You'll be in Segovia, or Valladolid. Perez will do his evil work, and you'll never know."

"We will be told," Isabel insisted.

"Those who might tell will be arrested and tortured themselves."

"But heresy must be exterminated!" Isabel spoke rapidly, as if to convince herself. "While the Inquisition may punish some who are innocent, the harm from ignoring sin and withholding punishment is greater."

"Don't you see," said Gabriel, "that those in the Church who seek power must embellish doctrine with legends that make men's flesh crawl. Fear is needed to bring power. Surely you know that the Church employs the cruelest tortures ever known. The flesh of its victims is torn with red hot pincers, and molten lead is poured into the wounds. Those who survive are burned alive at the stake. Thus the seed planted by gentle Jesus is wrapped in ignorant dogma and made an instrument of death. Is this what you wish for the land you cherish?

"I want peace in this land and purity of religious belief," Isabel said, her voice bordering on hysteria. "We must have law and order. If mass rioting against *conversos* erupts, how will we punish all the lawbreakers? If two or three cities rebel at the same time, it could lead to a widespread insurrection that we couldn't put down. Look what happened in Jaen. Some slop water spilled on a religious procession, probably by accident, led to a week of chaos. We are always at the edge of violent disorder."

Isabel breathed deeply. When she spoke, her voice was once more calm and controlled.

"An Inquisition will provide a means for us to channel this violence and keep it under control. An Inquisition won't require special laws against *conversos*. It will only empower investigations into allegations of heresy, and a determination of the facts. Such Inquisitions have existed for centuries. Why not in Castile? We don't claim that all *conversos* are judaizing, or conspiring against Christians. We only provide a mechanism to investigate, a forum to see if any of these allegations are true. If they are, in specific cases, then appropriate action will be taken. Those who are not heretics have nothing to fear."

"No, your Highness," said Gabriel, "I must respectfully disagree. Every *converso* has everything to fear when you let loose this monster."

"We can control the monster," Isabel said solemnly, "but we need God's help."

She rose and motioned for Gabriel to walk with her. "Come pray with me, Don Gabriel, before you leave."

Isabel led Gabriel through her bedroom to the small chapel beyond it. They knelt together on the marble floor before the Blessed Mother.

"Your triumph over the Portuguese was glorious," Perez said effusively to the king on his first private audience since Fernando had arrived in Seville.

Fernando scowled at Perez' fawning, and the Friar quickly switched tactics.

"Have you made a decision?"

"We have written to Pope Sixtus. I'm sure he will not object."

Perez was exultant. The power to ferret out secret Jews in Castile would soon exist. But would it be his? Would he be appointed Inquisitor?

"Are you afraid to ask what must be highest in your mind?" Fernando asked. "There will be the three Inquisitors. You will be Chief among them."

Perez' knees were weak. "Thank you, Your Grace. I won't fail you."

"I'm certain of that," Fernando said. "We want you to prove that we're not soft on *conversos*."

Fernando paused, and Perez had the feeling that the main reason for the meeting was yet to come. The king continued. "You told me some time ago that you had a witness who would bring testimony against a family of Jews he worked for, and against Gabriel Catalan. Do you still have the witness?"

"Diego Monbiel waits in a monastery near Olvera," Perez said breathlessly.

"Good," Fernando said, smiling. "Arrest the Jews and bring them and their Hebrew books to the same monastery. Hold them there until I give you further instructions. Do it secretly so that Catalan is not warned."

30

Gabriel regretted his impulsive gift of four *Haggadahs from* the moment he made it. The men were reliable, and not too prominent, but Gabriel was terrified that their Seder would be noticed and the books traced to him. He was further on edge because Tomas and Esther, whom he thought would already have left Seville, were still at home, and would be for at least another month.

The Catalans themselves would have a short, circumspect Seder. They would not have all of the special foods, but Gabriel had obtained a single piece of *matzah*, the unleavened bread which symbolized the hurried exodus of the Jewish people from Egypt.

Windows were shuttered and covered inside with heavy draperies. Servants were excused.

Gabriel sat at the head of the table, Pilar to his right with Judah, and Tomas and Esther to his left. The deep gentle voice of Yacov Ardit echoed in his mind. Esther, sitting well back from the table, her belly huge, must share these same poignant memories. In only a few weeks there would be another child in the Catalan family, a grandchild that Yacov and Miriam Ardit would never see.

Tomas asked the questions, as he had in Arcos.

מה נשתנה הלילה הזה מכל הלילות

Why is this night different
from all other nights?

Gabriel answered, reading from the printed *Haggadah*. The meal was served, and the night ended with a peaceful but sad glow.

335

They all knew there would never again be such a gathering of the Catalan family.

Elsewhere in Seville, a group of four families held their first Seder at the home of the *converso* Señor Antonio Franco. One man, the only one who could, read haltingly from the *Haggadah* Gabriel had provided, and translated the Hebrew into Castilian after each selection. It was awkward, but the *converso* families were thrilled. They were joined to their Jewish ancestors.

They concluded the Seder and ate the festive meal. The plates were removed, and they were joyously singing traditional songs when the pounding on the door began.

They moved quickly according to pre-arranged plan. The visiting families left quietly by a rear door. They took their *Haggadahs* with them, and they were not detected as they disappeared into the night. But no one noticed the fourth *Haggadah* laying on a side table in the dining room.

The escape took less than two minutes, after which Señor Franco went to answer the knock.

"Who is there?" he asked through the still closed door.

"Open now. What took so long?"

"Please identify yourself," Franco insisted.

"My name is Friar Ricardo Perez. Open!"

Franco unbolted the door and allowed Perez, accompanied by six soldiers, to enter.

"Why are you here?" Franco demanded.

"We've been informed that you are secret Jews, and that tonight you've been celebrating the Jewish Passover. Search the house!"

Perez' men disbursed. Almost immediately, one returned with the overlooked *Haggadah*. Perez knew immediately what it was and couldn't believe his luck.

"Take them," he said, pointing to Franco and his wife. "Put them in separate cells beneath the monastery."

Early the next morning, Gabriel was visited by one of the men who had escaped from the Seder the previous night. He hurriedly called his family together.

"You must leave immediately," he said, explaining what had

happened. Pilar glared, but never said a word.

Within the hour, Tomas, Esther and Judah had said goodbye. Accompanied by twelve armed men and a midwife, they slipped slowly through the Carmona gate and out of Seville. At the slow pace necessitated by Esther's condition, it would take four days to reach the border and pass into territory controlled by Prince Hasan, and then another three days to reach the Alhambra.

If they made it that far.

"We arrested the *converso* Antonio Franco and his wife," Perez reported.

"You found evidence of judaizing?" the king asked.

"Yes. We found a Hebrew book. A book used in the Passover Seder."

Perez could scarcely contain himself. He knew that the next piece of information was the one Fernando really wanted. He made the king ask.

"And?"

"It was printed. Gabriel Catalan is surely the printer." Perez stood tall, and declared in a voice of pride and self-satisfaction, "We have him, Your Majesty."

"Wait until the Queen and I leave Seville," Fernando directed, "then arrest the Catalan family. Do it quietly. Hold them until we get permission from His Holiness to begin the Inquisition."

Two days later, Friar Perez knocked at the Catalan mansion.

"Assemble your family," Perez demanded when Gabriel opened the door.

"Here is Pilar," Gabriel said, his arm around his wife's waist. "Tomas and Esther have taken Judah on an outing to the country. They'll be back in two or three days."

"Arrest these two," Perez ordered. "Take them to San Pablo."

"May I ask why we are being arrested," Gabriel said. "And may I be permitted to inform the Queen?"

Perez did not answer as Gabriel and Pilar were taken away.

Esther rode the gentlest mare in the Catalan stable, a huge beast with a broad back and an easy gait. Tomas never left her side. Judah trotted back and forth on a small pony. They went slowly, but even so, Esther struggled to keep her seat. Her eyes, under a hooded cape, were taut with pain.

At dusk, they made camp. They had gone only twelve miles.

The next morning, Tomas sent two men back to cover their trail. They were to ride several miles behind the main group and report immediately if they spotted anyone following them.

All day, they made slow but steady progress across the plains. Tomas rode near Esther but neither were inclined to talk. They were riding away from everything and everyone they loved.

Tomas watched helplessly as Esther fought to stay on the mare. She cried out once, but otherwise kept her suffering to herself.

That night, the midwife came to him.

"It's time."

The men put up a small tent on a grassy spot, and laid blankets down. Tomas held Esther's hand. The midwife tried to chase him out, but neither he nor Esther would permit it.

Judah was frightened, so he was allowed to see his mother. Then two of the men settled him in warm blankets near the fire.

"The last time it took so long," Esther said. "I'll try to hurry."

"There's no rush," Tomas lied. "No one is following us."

"They will," she said.

True to her promise, the baby came quickly. It was a boy, and he seemed healthy and strong. At the crack of dawn, they all re-mounted, including Esther. The midwife carried the infant, and they stopped every two hours so Esther could nurse him, but at Esther's urging, they actually increased their pace. Every man among them was amazed at her strength and determination.

They were within twenty miles of the Moorish border when the trailing riders came galloping into camp.

"Fifty men behind us," they shouted. "Only five miles back. Coming fast."

There was no chance to flee. They backed up to a small ridge and formed a half circle around Esther, Judah, the midwife, and the baby.

The riders approached. At one hundred yards, their leader came forward alone. Tomas recognized Enrique de Guzman, the Duke of Medina Sidonia. He was surprised that Perez could command such high level support. Then he realized it was the king, not Perez, who had dispatched the Duke. This was confirmed by Guzman's first words.

"We are here on the lawful business of his majesty King Fernando," he said. "We have come to arrest Tomas Catalan and his wife, and return them to Seville."

There was no answer from Tomas or any of his men.

"We'll use force if we have to," shouted the Duke. "If we do, then every one of you, except the Catalans, will die."

Still no answer.

Guzman returned to his forces, and they assembled in fighting order. He raised his hand to give the order to charge.

Tomas steeled himself. Perhaps they could fight off the superior force for awhile, but they could not expect to prevail. All of his father's dreams, and his own, would soon be over.

Then, unbelievably, Guzman lowered his arm, not in the signal to charge, but with frustration and resignation. Tomas followed Guzman's eyes, which were fixed, not on him, but beyond. There sat five hundred Moorish horsemen, armed to the teeth, lining the top of the ridge. At their head was the prince of *Al-Andulas*, Abu' l-Hasan Ali, a huge grin on his handsome face.

The Duke motioned to his men and they trotted slowly away.

Fernando took Isabel's hand as she slept. He had grown to love his wife, and was pleased and proud that she had given them a son. A messenger came and whispered to him.

"What was that about," Isabel mumbled groggily when the messenger had left.

"We're rounding up *conversos*. There's evidence of judaizing, and we're ready to use our new Holy Order of Inquisition to bring them to trial. But one of the suspects has escaped."

"You'll capture him, I'm sure," Isabel said, now fully awake. "Who is it?"

"We've arrested Gabriel Catalan and his wife."

Isabel gasped, and Fernando knew he had made a serious mistake in not telling her before.

"For what?" she said, her voice rising. "He's one of our most important allies. We would never have been married, nor defeated the Portuguese, without his help. Why did you do this?"

"He's a Jew, a corrupter of the church and of all good Christians.

He prints Hebrew books! It is for men such as he that we agreed to have an Inquisition."

"Do you have proof?" Isabel demanded.

"Yes. Friar Perez has a witness who will testify, and he's also captured *conversos* who were using Catalan's book to hold a Passover Seder."

"Perez has hated Don Gabriel for years. He would lie. Are you sure of the evidence? Have you spoken to the witness yourself?"

Fernando's silence was all the answer Isabel needed.

"My husband, I hope you have not made a foolish mistake. I will not permit Don Gabriel to be punished for something he didn't do. Bring the witnesses to Cordoba. I'll interview them myself." She paused. "You didn't mention Tomas. Did you arrest him as well?"

"We tried. He escaped."

"And you chased him?"

"Yes. But we failed. That was the message I just received. He and his Jewish wife have reached Prince Hasan."

Isabel turned away from the king. She pulled her hand from his and smiled to herself as she lay her head back on the pillow.

31

Gabriel sat alone in the cold damp cell where he had been held for three weeks. He had been separated from Pilar even before they reached the monastery, and he knew nothing of her condition, or whether Tomas and Esther had eluded Perez' grasp.

He wondered what role Isabel had played in his arrest. Probably none, he thought. But now that Fernando had acted, she would be trapped into going along. Any evidence of heresy would do.

And, of course, he was guilty. By the standards of both Church and state, he was a judaizing heretic, their mortal enemy. He said to himself, 'I am a Jew.' He was thrilled by the echo of the soundless words. Isaac would be proud of him. He was ready to die, and he knew that Pilar would willingly join him.

But where was Tomas? If Tomas did not survive, and if Esther lost the new baby, it would all be for naught. There would be no Catalans after all.

Perez came into his cell. It was the first time since the arrest.

"Where's my wife, you bastard?" Gabriel yelled, and Perez smacked him hard across the mouth, splitting his cracked lips.

"You have more spunk than your friend did," he said. "But we'll see how long that lasts."

"What friend? What are you talking about?"

"Look around you," Perez said. "These are the same walls that Francesco Romo saw before he died cursing you for informing on him."

Gabriel tried to lash out at Perez, but the chains on his arms held him back. Perez laughed and left.

Gabriel's outburst gave him no information about Pilar or Tomas. Then he realized that Perez had not mentioned Tomas. That was the answer! He would have been gloating if he had caught him. Tomas had escaped!

"I had scouts scouring every possible route," Hasan explained. "My men saw you several days ago, and we consolidated our forces. Then we spotted the troop following you."

"Why were you looking for us? Did you know we had left Seville?"

"Yes. I have a few men there. But not enough to follow you along the way. And if we put large forces too far from the border, we would attract more attention than we could handle. Fortunately, you got close enough that we could act."

"I don't think Esther could have taken much more fast travel," Tomas said. After their rescue by Hasan, they had waited a full day, then, moving at a leisurely pace, they crossed the border and came to the city of Granada and the *Alhambra* palace.

"She's comfortable now?"

"Oh, yes. Her old friends are taking care of her day and night. She wants for nothing. And Isaac is fine too."

"You named him Isaac," said Hasan. "After the son of Abraham?"

"Yes. But also after my grandfather. The one who was forced to convert and live his whole life hoping that someday his child or grandchild would return to Judaism."

"When did he die?"

"When I was a little boy. He went out into a mob screaming for the blood of Jews, covered himself with his *tallit*, and prayed in Hebrew."

"He was brave."

"They stoned him to death. My father came too late. I was a little boy, and I saw it all."

Hasan looked at Tomas and shared his sadness quietly.

"I have the *tallit*," Tomas said. "It still has my grandfather's blood on it. Some day I'll give it to my son."

"Will you have him circumcised? I believe it should be done on the eighth day."

"I forgot," Tomas said. "And I don't know how."

"There are Jews in Granada. It can be done."

It was surely the first time in its glorious history that the Great Hall of the *Alhambra* palace had been used as a Jewish place of worship. It was a large square room, four stories high, with vaulted ceilings of cedar wood, gilded and brilliant. Graceful windows and balconies cut through the thick walls at each level. Horseshoe arches at floor level looked down on the town and gardens below, and the Sierra Nevada mountains in the distance. A small ark and a Holy *Torah* stood at one end of the room. Two thousand Jews crowded into the elegant space.

Rabbi Judah ibn Verga conducted the morning service. Every man wore a *tallit* and *tefillin*, including Prince Hasan who insisted on participating. Tomas fingered his grandfather's blood-stained *tallit* as he followed along in an old leather-bound prayer book. Esther sat on a cushioned bench, with the rabbi's wife and daughter, in a curtained off section where she heard Jewish men praying for the first time since she had left Arcos.

When the service was over, Esther came out from behind the screen. Zorayda, Esther's friend from the bath, was given the honor of carrying Isaac to her. Tradition was that the child should be held, during the circumcision, by a *tzadik*, a righteous Jew. Tomas asked if Prince Hasan could have that honor, and after a brief consultation with the elders of his congregation, Rabbi Verga gave his permission.

Rabbi Verga also asked Tomas about his Hebrew name, which would be used in the ceremony. Then he began: *And God spoke to Abraham, saying 'This is my covenant which you shall keep between Me and you and thy seed after you. Every male child among you shall be circumcised.*

"Since the time of our forefather Abraham, the Jewish people have observed the ritual of circumcision as the fundamental sign of the covenant between God and Israel. Bring the child to Prince Hasan."

Zorayda proudly carried baby Isaac to Prince Hasan.

"Now, Tomas," said Rabbi Verga.

Tomas repeated the blessing he had been taught. *"I am ready to perform the affirmative precept to circumcise my child, even as the Creator, blessed be He, has commanded. As it is written in the Torah, he that is eight days old shall be circumcised among you, every male child throughout your generations."*

Rabbi Verga turned to a bearded man carrying a small bag. "Every ritual circumcision must be performed by a *mohel* who is formally trained in the proper techniques and in Jewish law and tradition. The *mohel* must be a person of great piety, an observant Jew, who performs the circumcision in accordance with the intentions as well as the letter of Jewish law. Rebbe Schmuel is the finest *mohel* in all of Granada."

The Rebbe offered a brief prayer and then began. With Hasan holding Isaac firmly on his lap, the mohel pulled the baby's foreskin forward and slid a silver shield between the foreskin and the body of the penis. He ran a scalpel smoothly and quickly around the face of the shield and removed a portion of the foreskin. He took a clean towel and covered the penis, and handed Isaac to Esther, who went behind the screen and put him to her breast.

Rabbi Verga prayed: *"Our God and God of our fathers, preserve this child to his father and to his mother, and let his name be called Isaac, the son of Benjamin.*

"Let Benjamin son of Gabriel rejoice in his offspring, and Esther be glad with the fruit of her body. Let Gabriel and Pilar Catalan, held far from here against their will, also know and rejoice in this new child of God, and may Yacov and Miriam Ardit, already with God in heaven, look down with pleasure.

"We give thanks unto the Lord, for He is good, and His loving kindness endureth forever. And may this child, even as he has entered into the covenant of Abraham, so may he enter into the Torah, the nuptial chupah, and into good deeds."

Tomas went to Esther and Isaac, full of pride and joy, but also sadness that none of their parents could share this day.

Esther looked up at him. "Isaac has his name, and you too. As I hoped and prayed so long ago, now you are Benjamin to me."

"This has been a wonderful day," Tomas said. "If only my parents could know."

"I'm sorry to spoil it, but I have information for you, and it's not good," Hasan said with a frown. "I learned yesterday, but I waited so you and Esther could have this day with as little pain as possible."

"What?"

"Your father and mother have been arrested. They are held in the monastery of San Pablo."

"We expected that," said Tomas. "But I don't think they'll be found guilty on the basis of the *converso* Seder. There's no proof that we printed the *Haggadahs*. Isabel will require proof."

"I'm afraid there is proof," said Hasan. "A family from Olvera has also been arrested and brought to Seville."

"The Lucenas?" Tomas said, dumbfounded and heartbroken. "The girls too? Hannah?"

Hasan nodded. "A boy will testify against them," he said.

"Diego," said Tomas. "He disappeared almost a year ago."

"He didn't disappear. Perez had him hidden, waiting for his chance."

Hasan waited for Tomas to digest this awful information. Then he added the final blow.

"Your parents will be tried by the Holy Order of the Inquisition. The monarchs have received the permission they sought from Pope Sixtus. Friar Perez has been named Chief Inquisitor. It couldn't be worse."

"But surely Isabel won't permit this!" Tomas said excitedly. "Without my father, she would never have been queen."

"The memories of kings and queens are notoriously short," Hasan said.

"I must go to her. I'm sure she'll free my parents if I ask her myself."

"I knew you would insist on going. I advise against it. She won't intervene. But I don't expect you to follow my advice. I'll provide an escort as far as Arcos. After that, you'll have to go disguised, but I will always have one man near you. The man will change, but you will never be alone. Each man will wear a ring that looks like this."

Hasan showed him the ring on the small finger of his left hand. It was plain gold, broad, with five tiny square cut rubies running in a line around the upper half.

"And if I don't return?" Tomas asked.

"Esther and your children will always have a home here. Isaac will be raised as a Jew."

"Do you think she'll listen to you?" Esther asked.

"She'll see me, and she'll listen. Maybe she doesn't even know that they've been arrested."

"Fernando wouldn't keep that knowledge from her," Esther said.

"Fernando will do whatever he thinks he can get away with. He has no honor."

A sadness hung between them like the heavy impenetrable fog that often drifted over the *Alhambra* palace. So many troubles, so many tragedies endured, so much joy together, and now it came to this. They both knew that Tomas' mission could easily end in disaster. Not only could he fail to save his parents, but he might also end up in prison, sharing their fate.

Yet Esther did not object.

She had never expected to live through the race from Seville. She had never expected to have the baby, or survive the childbirth. She was living on God's time, God who had given and taken so much. She felt blessed that Tomas had fallen in love with her, and that she had borne his child. She knew what his parents meant to him, and she knew that he must go to them now. He might not come back. But if she convinced him not to go, and his parents died without him trying to save them, their own lives would be forever poisoned by that memory.

So they had talked, and they cried, and then it was time for Tomas to leave.

"I have something for you to take to your parents," Esther said, with just a hint of a smile.

She gave him two small leather pouches. When he looked inside, more tears came to his eyes. Each pouch contained a small lock of Isaac's hair.

On the way out of Granada, Tomas stopped at the home of Rabbi Verga. There was some scurrying around. Several people came and went. Then Tomas remounted and rode toward Seville.

When Gabriel awoke, a monk was standing near him, waiting.

"I come from Archbishop Fonseca. My name is Friar Menendez."

"I'm surprised that I haven't heard from the Archbishop before," Gabriel said.

Menendez ignored the complaint, and Gabriel did not pursue it. After all, the monk was here now, and that was more than anyone else had done. Fonseca hated Perez and his methods, Gabriel knew, but now that the monarchs had decided, he had no more to say about it.

"I understand that Friar Perez has taunted you about Señor Romo, who occupied this very cell many years ago. Archbishop Fonseca wants me to set your mind at ease on that matter. I was the scribe when Friar Perez interrogated your friend. Later, I testified at the hearing when Perez was exiled. The archbishop wants you to know that Señor Romo never believed it was you who informed on him. He laughed when Perez said it was you."

Gabriel buried his head in his arms, relief flowing like a warm fluid through his parched body. The monk waited until Gabriel whispered, "The Archbishop was very kind to send you."

"There is more," said Menendez. "Pope Sixtus has answered the monarchs, and they've received permission for their Inquisition. Friar Perez will be the Chief Inquisitor.

"Perez found a printed Hebrew book at the home of a *converso* family. He will charge that you and your son printed it."

Gabriel started to speak, but the monk motioned him to silence.

"The Archbishop wants to believe that these charges are not true." Menendez raised his hand as Gabriel started to speak. "There's no need to say anything now."

Gabriel peered silently at Friar Menendez, and saw nothing but open acceptance on his face. The friar did not question. He did not condemn. He knew this would not be the case with others. Should he deny the accusations, or should he admit his guilt? Fonseca was giving him time to think.

Menendez continued. "There's a family of Jews from the town of Olvera. They've been arrested and brought to Seville. They are accused of printing Hebrew books. You and your son Tomas are accused of guiding them in this printing. A boy who worked with them will testify against you."

Gabriel was shaken by this new information. Tomas had told him about Diego de Monbiel and the stolen pages, and he had even predicted that they would get to Perez, but the combination of the Olvera printing and the *converso's Haggadah* was going to be damning. Perez would not have to invent evidence.

"Is my wife alive?" he asked, fearing the answer.

"She is well, or as well as anyone can be down here. The Archbishop has assured her sufficient food, and she has a cell which is much more comfortable than this."

"Can I see her?"

"It may not be possible. But I will take messages between you."

"And Tomas? Is there any word about Tomas?"

"He escaped. The Duke of Medina Sidonia followed him, but it appears that Prince Hasan brought out the entire Moorish army, and Guzman did not choose to die."

"Is his wife well? Did you learn anything about a baby?"

"I have no reports about a woman or a child."

"Thank you so much, Friar. Please thank the Archbishop for me."

"He loves you dearly, Don Gabriel."

"Will you also tell Pilar that Tomas is safe with Hasan."

"Yes. I'll do that right away."

"Tell her that I love her."

Tomas was intercepted by Hasan's messengers, before he had reached Seville, with news that Fernando and Isabel had already left. Immediately, he redirected his mount toward Cordoba. Arriving there, he met another man who wore the ring of five rubies, and was directed to a home in the Moorish section of the city.

"Is there a way to get a message to the Queen?" he asked.

"It can be done," was the reassuring but inscrutable reply from the turbaned Moor.

Tomas wrote: *I first saw you across a balcony at Segovia. Would Your Grace consent to meet again?*

He did not sign the letter. In two days, he had his answer.

"You will wait within the old mosque tomorrow morning," the Moor said. "The one you wish to see will meet you there."

"How do you do this?"

He received only an enigmatic smile.

"How will I get into the mosque? Isn't it heavily guarded?"

"The guards change at the hour before dawn. You will be one of the replacements. You will walk next to a man with the ring. He will show you where to wait. Later, he will get you out."

"This mosque is second in size only to the great mosque in Mecca. Of course, since the Christian reconquest, it has been used as a church, and no Moor is allowed to pray here. It is surrounded by over two thousand feet of thick wall. The entrance arches combine Roman, Visigoth, and Moorish traditions."

Tomas, early for his meeting, was dazzled by the size and symmetry and elegance of an endless succession of arches, ingeniously raised to double height, painted in broad alternating stripes of now faded red and yellow. From the center, the arches receded in every direction as far as he could see.

"There are 865 marble columns supporting the arches," his guide said, "in measured rows of absolute precision. Abd ar-Rahman brought those columns here from all over Andalusia, some even from

Constantinople. Look toward the courtyard. The orange trees are planted to continue the rows of columns."

Shortly before the appointed time, they walked to the *mihrab*, once the holy of holies, an octagonal chamber set into the east wall and covered by a stunning dome of interlocking arches. The entire chamber was decorated with geometrically arranged mosaics in brilliantly colored glass chips. Tomas, left alone, was absorbed by the incredible beauty and tranquility of the once sacred place of prayer.

"Why did you return? You were safe, and now ..."

He had not seen the queen enter, and he was surprised by the sound of her voice. The look on Isabel's face showed that she still cared. But would she help? Could she?

"My parents are in prison. They will be tried."

"And they will be found guilty," Isabel said without emotion.

Tomas was shocked. Isabel went on.

"Because they are guilty," she said. "Don Gabriel Catalan has been more help to me than any other person in Castile, but the evidence will show that he is secretly a Jew."

His face screwed in pain, Tomas answered, "My grandfather was forced to convert ..."

"I know," Isabel interrupted.

"You know?"

"Your father told us."

"Then is it a surprise that my grandfather, and his son, were less than sincere in their forced religious beliefs?"

"And the grandson?" asked Isabel.

"Yes, also the grandson." Tomas answered, feeling belligerent.

Isabel dropped her head sadly. "There are many occasions," she said, "when all of the entries do not rest on the same side of the ledger. This is one of them. Fernando and I must have peace in our lands. We must unify Castile. In order to have a unified country, we must have a unified Church. We cannot have people questioning the very basis of the Christian faith. Heresy is abhorrent to me. I hate it."

"So you will not help my parents."

"I cannot. I have spoken to the witness Diego de Monbiel and I believe he's telling the truth. I have seen the book that the *converso* family used in their Seder. The Hebrew letters are the same as those brought from Olvera. The same skilled goldsmith carved them both. Maybe it was you."

Isabel looked at Tomas with the saddest face he had ever seen. The weight of decision lay heavily on her.

"Where did we go wrong," she said, "that we lost men like Gabriel Catalan ... and you?

"You didn't believe your own message," said Tomas quietly.

"What do you mean? The Church believes its doctrine. I believe."

"If you really believed what you teach is true, you would have the patience to wait until everyone else, especially Jews, came to share that truth. You would not use force, and you would restrain those who urge it. Even now."

"It's too late," Isabel said sadly. "The forces are loose."

"May I ask then that you arrest me, and let me stand trial instead of my parents."

"Not instead of them, and not with them. I will not have it!"

"I'm just as guilty."

"But my pain will be less if you survive," Isabel said, her head falling to her chest, eyes closed. She looked up, blinking back tears. "I must maintain the integrity of the Church. I cannot do less. But I will not see you its victim. Please leave Seville, take your dear wife, and make your life wherever you can."

"A Jewish life?"

"If that's what you want," Isabel whispered.

Isabel reached her hand to Tomas. It was a touch between two people who cared deeply about each other.

"I wish you well, Tomas Catalan. You're the best friend I've ever had."

Tomas returned to Seville in time for the arrival of the inquisitors. It was an awesome procession. At its head marched a Dominican monk carrying the cross. Friar Perez and the other two inquisitors wore white robes with black hoods, the reverse of the normal Dominican habit. Hundreds of friars accompanied them. Their robes were coarse and they went barefoot on the cold ground.

Silently, they paraded past the Cathedral, past the *Alcazar*, and through the *juderia* where Jews hid behind shuttered windows, until they arrived at the monastery of San Pablo.

The first trial of the Spanish Inquisition would begin in three days.

32

The room was long and rectangular, free of ornamentation but for a stark wooden crucifix high on the wall at the far end. Four large windows, shutters open, revealed the monastery courtyard. Behind a huge oak table, under the crucifix, were three large chairs for the Inquisitors. Smaller chairs at either end for scribes and other functionaries.

Before the table, an open space for witnesses to stand and testify. The rest of the room was filled with benches, twenty rows with space for thirty men on each row. The first row was reserved for the accused. Tomas took a seat about half way back. He recognized many of the men seated in front of him, some *conversos*, and several prominent Old Christians, including Alvar Sanchez.

He was confident that he would not be recognized. His entire body, from head to foot, was covered with the habit of the Cistercian Order. He had chosen the Cistercians because they were sworn to silence when outside their monasteries, and because their closest monastery was in Ubada, twelve days away. The habit had been produced by his Moorish protectors within hours of his request. He asked no questions. He had grown a thick beard, and scraggly hair protruded from the edges of his cowl.

He sat still for over an hour, eyes half closed. The room filled; men stood packed along the walls. Those seated near him respected his vow and did not address him. There was surprisingly little chatter, none at all when a door at the front opened. The Inquisitors, led by Friar Perez, filed in. They took their seats with Perez, the Chief Inquisitor, in the center. Scribes followed, and then Archbishop Fonseca, slowly, almost reluctantly.

Standing, Fonseca read the proclamation establishing the Holy Tribunal: "*King Fernando and Queen Isabel have determined that there have been and are bad Christians, apostates, heretics, and conversos in the kingdom who have turned and converted, and do turn and convert, to the sect and superstition and perfidy of the Jews. Not only are such persons continuing in heresy themselves, but they are influencing others and infecting them with their perfidy.*

"*Therefore, We, the said King Fernando and Queen Isabel, with the great desire we have to elevate, honor and preserve our Catholic Faith, and wishing that our subjects and people born in our realms live in it and save their souls, and in order to avoid the great evils and harms that would occur if the aforementioned behavior went unpunished and uncorrected, and because, as monarchs and sovereign lords of these realms, we must provide the remedy for this, and because we want that such bad Christians be punished and the faithful and good Christians be free of all stain and infamy, we accept the commission and faculty to us granted by our most Holy Father Pope Sixtus IV, and do hereby establish the Holy Order of the Inquisition throughout our dominions of Castile.*

"*We name as Chief Inquisitor Friar Ricardo Perez of the monastery of San Pablo in Seville, and as Inquisitors Fray Miguel de Morillo, master of theology and vicar of the Dominican Order, and Fray Juan de San Martin, prior of the monastery of San Pablo in Burgos. We are confident that said appointees will carry out their duties faithfully and diligently until the achievement of the proper end, and if this not be so, we will dismiss said appointees and appoint others in their stead, in accordance with the rights granted to us by the Holy Pontiff.*

"*These Inquisitional examiners are to seek out diligently those who are judaizing heretics, so that through inquiry and accusation they can be corrected and reconciled to orthodox church doctrine through mercy. If, after a thorough investigation and proof of heresy, a sinner refuses to repent, he is to be condemned as a heretic, a crime, which being treason is punishable by death. Such as are so convicted shall be turned over to the secular authority for execution of the penalty in the appropriate manner.*

"Bring in the accused, that they and we may hear the testimony against them," Perez' thundered, as soon as Fonseca had finished.

Tomas cringed. A door at the front of the room opened inward, and all eyes strained to see the hopeless souls who would emerge.

Gabriel Catalan was first, and Tomas' gasp was lost among the others. His father was thin and looked very weak. He was coarsely dressed in an ill-fitting tunic, but he held his head high and defiance was clear in his eyes. He was taken to the first bench and directed to stand, facing the Inquisitors. Perez could not wipe the sneer of satisfaction from his face.

When Pilar came in next, Tomas fought to contain his tears. His mother, always meticulous in her appearance, was raggedly dressed and disheveled as he had never seen her. She blinked at the light, and then she saw Gabriel. A bright smile lit her face, and she stumbled toward him. She tried to hug him but was sharply restrained. She was, however, placed next to him, and Tomas could see that they were holding hands.

Tomas barely noticed as another *converso* couple was led in, one at a time. These were the ones who had hosted the Seder, at whose home was found a printed *Haggadah*.

The next defendant, however, was a shock. Had he not been tightly wedged into his seat, Tomas might have collapsed as he saw Israel Lucena, gaunt, terrified, barely able to walk, brought to a spot on the front row. His wife Leah soon joined him, and then Tomas was heartbroken to see the four Lucena daughters. He thought back to the last time in Olvera. He had promised to see them again, but not, dear God, like this! He closed his eyes and drew the coarse cowl tightly around his face.

The testimony was crisp and straightforward.

The soldier who had accompanied Perez to the *converso's* home told how he had found the *Haggadah*, and stated that the book he was shown this day was in fact the same one he had seen that night. Perez himself added that they had gone to that home on the evening of the first night of Passover, when Jews celebrate the Seder. A monk from the monastery, a scribe by profession, stated that the *Haggadah* had not been handwritten, that it had been printed by the new technique perfected in Seville by Don Gabriel Catalan. A learned Church scholar testified that the book was in Hebrew, and that it was the story of the Exodus of the children of Israel from Egypt, a story repeated by Jews on the Passover holiday.

"Antonio Franco, stand before this panel," Perez ordered, and the accused man took his place.

"Are you a Christian?" Perez asked.

"I am a Christian, true to the faith of Jesus Christ," Franco answered.

"Then why did you and your family celebrate the Jewish Passover?"

"We did not observe that holiday or any other Jewish rite."

"Why did you have in your home this Hebrew *Haggadah*, on the very night of the Passover Seder?"

"I don't know how it got there."

"Did you obtain this book from Don Gabriel Catalan?" Tomas jumped at the mention of his father's name.

"No. I did not receive that book from anyone ... unless it was you who brought it to my house."

"You do not repent of the sin of heresy occasioned by your judaizing activities?"

"There is nothing to repent. I have committed no sin."

Tomas handed a note to the monk outside the Archbishop's palatial residence, and was soon granted admittance. When he approached Fonseca, Tomas saw an old man, the vigor gone. It made him sad.

"If Perez finds out you're here, you'll be arrested," said Fonseca.

"He won't recognize me," said Tomas. "Do you like my disguise?" Despite everything, both men laughed.

"I saw you this morning," said the Archbishop, "and I wondered why a Cistercian monk was present, but I had no idea it was you." He sighed deeply. "This is all wrong. Your father isn't a heretic and this Inquisition is a dangerous travesty. Pope Sixtus authorized a Papal Inquisition, run by bishops who would be responsible to him. Responsible clerics. There are many whom I could recommend. But Fernando and Isabel ignored him and appointed only those, Perez and the others, whom they believe they can control. I was embarrassed to read the proclamation. I'm sure that Perez asked Fernando to assign that task to me, just to make sure all of Seville knows he's in charge."

"I want to see my parents," Tomas said. "There won't be another opportunity. Will you help me?"

Pilar did not look up when the Cistercian monk entered her cell. She sat on her hard bed, staring blankly ahead. Tomas sat down next to her. She didn't move.

"Mother," he said, "don't cry out."

He turned his face toward her and pulled back the cowl so she could see him. Recognition spread over her face. Pilar shook her head in disbelief. Tears ran down her cheeks.

"It's too dangerous for you to be here," she whispered. "We're going to die."

"I'm going to leave Seville tonight, but I wouldn't go without seeing you and Father."

"How did you get here?"

"Hasan, Isabel, Fonseca. They all helped."

"Isabel?"

"Yes. But I have other things to tell you. You have a new grandson. His name is Isaac."

Pilar buried her head in Tomas' chest and shook with silent sobs.

"Esther?"

"She waits in good health at the palace of the *Alhambra*. As soon as I return, we'll leave for Italy. Hasan keeps a ship waiting for us in Malaga."

"You must not linger. I don't want you to die."

"I'll leave soon, but first I have a present for you."

Tomas showed her two packets. "This is for father," he said, putting it back in his pocket. "This is for you."

Pilar held the lock of Isaac's hair. Her smile was radiant, and Tomas knew it was the last time he would see it.

Gabriel was pacing about when Tomas came through the cell door, finger to his lips. Gabriel grabbed his son, fingers digging into Tomas' well-muscled back.

"I saw you this morning," Gabriel said. "I knew it was you."

"How? I thought my disguise was perfect."

"I don't know. My eyes were drawn to you. I didn't dare keep looking, but I knew it was you."

"This is very bad, isn't it?" Tomas asked.

"We will die at the stake. But I'm not afraid."

"Neither is Mother."

"You saw her. Is she all right?"

"Yes."

"You must leave. How did you get here? Oh, Tomas, if you don't survive, what was it all worth?"

"I'll leave today. And I have much reason to live."

He gave his father the other lock of hair.

"His name is Isaac. He's a Jew. He's already been circumcised into the covenant of Abraham."

Gabriel held Tomas' shoulders, as he had so many times before.

"Isaac was the gift of God to Abraham and Sarah in order to assure the continuity of the Jewish people. Now God has given you and Esther the same gift for the same purpose. Your grandfather would be so happy."

His smile faded. He seemed bothered by a new thought.

"The most important obligation of a Jewish father is to circumcise his son," he said. "I never fulfilled my duty. *'He who nullifies the covenant of our forefather Abraham has no share in the World to Come.'*"

"It's not too late," Tomas said, just a trace of a smile peeking onto his face.

"What? How?"

"I have the knife and the other ... tools. I got them from the rabbi in Granada. I helped with Isaac. I want you to do it."

"But you have to travel. You'll be in pain."

"Just a little snip will do," said Tomas, laughing.

He gave the knife to his father. He leaned against the closed door, opened his habit, and raised his gown. Gabriel knelt before him.

"I don't know the prayer," Gabriel said.

"I do. First you say, *'Behold, I am prepared and ready to perform the commandment that the Creator, Blessed be He, has commanded me, to circumcise my son, and bring him into the covenant of Abraham.'*"

Gabriel repeated what Tomas had said.

"Now, one more," Tomas said, and this they said together in Hebrew, Gabriel repeating after Tomas.

ברוך אתה יהוה אלהינו מלך העולם
אשר קדשנו במצותיו וצונו על המילה

Blessed art thou, O Lord our God,
King of the Universe,
who has sanctified us
with His commandments,
and has commanded us regarding circumcision.

Gabriel reached forward, attached the clamp and raised the knife. It took only a second and it was done. Several drops of blood fell to the cell floor.

"I will be known from this day on as Benjamin ... Benjamin Catalan ... Jew. Thank you, Father."

"Your mother and I are going to die. You know that. We're ready. Our work is done. You and Esther and Judah and now Isaac. You're our work ... God's work. We go to God ... you to Lorenzo de' Medici. A Jew faithful to the covenant. You've made me very happy, Tomas Benjamin Catalan."

"I brought you something else," Tomas said. Reaching again into his monk's cloak, he withdrew a sheaf of pages. "These are from the *Rosh Ha-Shanah* prayer book we printed. I thought you might want to have these words with you in ..." Tomas couldn't continue. He handed the pages to his father.

"Goodbye, my son. Thank you."

He watched as Tomas walked away. At the end of the hallway, Tomas turned, their eyes met briefly, and he was gone.

Gabriel hid the *Rosh Ha-Shanah* pages under his thin mattress, and lay down, sobbing.

Later, he retrieved the pages, horrified that they had been printed at Olvera, and that the Lucena family would die as a result. He faced away from the door, and began to read, moving his lips silently.

This day of Rosh Ha-Shanah is holy unto the Lord your God. Mourn not nor weep. Grieve not, for the joy of the Lord is your strength. Prepare to meet thy God, O Israel.

I'm ready, God, Gabriel thought. I will not weep as I approach you. I will thank you for all of the blessings you have bestowed upon me, more than I deserved.

O God, cruel men are risen up against me, and a company of ruthless men have sought my life. I cry to Thee, for Thou, God, wilt answer me. Shelter me in the shadow of Thy wings from the wicked who would destroy me.

The *shofar*, the ram's horn, is blown on *Rosh Ha-Shanah*. Near the end of Tomas' pages, Gabriel reached the prayers of the *shofar* service.

O Lord, let Thy shofar with clarion call proclaim for us redemption, and gather in Thy scattered flock. In thunder and lightning Thou appeared to them in the sound of the Shofar, the Lord in the sound of the Shofar.

Gabriel entered the large room for the second day of the trial, looked for Tomas, relieved that he was not there. Pilar joined him on the first row, and they smiled at each other as if it was the happiest of occasions instead of the trial they both knew would lead to death. They had seen Tomas. They had a new grandchild. Their family was safe.

Diego de Monbiel was called to say what he knew about the Lucena family and their printing activities in Olvera. He told of the Hebrew books they printed, the Moors who took the books and brought fresh paper, and about Tomas Catalan.

"How do you know his name?" Perez asked.

"I often heard them call him Señor Tomas, and once, when messengers came to the door, they used his full name, Tomas Catalan."

Perez motioned to one of the men at the end of the table, who left and returned with a large pile of books. He placed them on the table before Perez.

"Are these the books?" the friar asked.

Diego came to the table and looked at the books. He peered at each one, opened it, and went on to the next, although it was obvious to everyone that he could not read them.

"Yes," he said. "These are the books printed by the Lucena family."

"Thank you very much for your help, young man," Perez said. "You're excused."

Perez and the other Inquisitors conferred among themselves for several moments, and then Perez announced, "There will be no more witnesses. We will now hear from the accused. Israel Lucena. Stand before me."

Other than in this room, Gabriel had seen Israel Lucena only once, the day he and Tomas had gone to the rabbi in Olvera, and Lucena had joined them briefly to talk about the printing. Israel and his family had been a spectacular success as printers. They had made more books than the other two presses combined. And Gabriel knew how much Tomas had come to love them and treasure his visits.

Gabriel looked at Israel's wife Leah, whom he had never met, and the four girls. Tomas had talked about them after each trip. They were so enthusiastic that they were doing God's work. Now they would die for it. Incredibly, they returned his look with smiles.

"Did you print these books?" Perez demanded.

"Yes," said Lucena, in a surprisingly strong voice.

"These are Hebrew books?"

"Yes."

"Tell me what they are."

Lucena took a book in his hands, smiled and said, "This is the tractate *Pirke Abot*, from the Babylonian Talmud. It tells us how we are to lead our lives. And how we are to die." He put it down and took up the others, one at a time. "These are prayer books to be used on the Days of Awe, when we plead for forgiveness. These are proverbs collected by Solomon ibn Gabirol, who lived in this land when Jews were not persecuted as they are today. These are commentaries on the Five Books of Moses by Abraham Ibn Ezra. Those books are also part of your religion, are they not?"

"Why did you print these books?" Perez asked, ignoring Lucena's question.

"I'm a Jew. This is not allowed? Jews are permitted to live in Castile. Where is it written that Jews are not allowed to make books? What authority does the church have over Jews?"

"You question the authority of this Inquisition?"

"I heard the proclamation. You have authority over Christians. You have no authority over Jews."

"Jews who aid *conversos* in their judaizing activities are under the authority of this body," said Perez with the full force of his great voice. But Lucena refused to be cowed.

"Has there been any witness to such activity by me or my family?" he asked.

"From whom did you learn about printing?"

"A printer, a man from Mainz in Germany, came to Toledo. We met, and he taught me how to print. He helped me build the press and make the letters."

"Where is this man?"

"He left Olvera. I don't know where he is now."

"What is his name?"

"He called himself Solomon ben Moses."

"Who arranged for Moors to come take books and bring paper?"

Lucena hesitated. He had seemed prepared for the other questions, but not for this one.

"Where did they take the books you worked so hard to print? Who were they printed for?"

Still Lucena remained silent. His confident air dissipated. He started to look around, but stopped.

"Were you looking for Don Gabriel to tell you the answer? You don't know where the books were taken, do you? But you do know they weren't for Jews. Did you ever give any books to the other Jews in Olvera?"

Lucena did not answer.

"Those books were not for Jews, at least not for Jews who openly profess their religion. They were for *conversos*, and you and your family are guilty of abetting heresy."

Lucena stood calmly facing Perez. Gabriel felt his strength and took pride in a fellow Jew who would not be cowed.

"The penalty for abetting heresy is the same as for committing it," said Perez. "A Jew who preaches to a Christian, who exalts his own belief and disparages ours, shall be put to death and lose all his property. You may help yourself and your family by confessing your sins. Do you confess?"

"I have committed no sins before the God of Israel."

"Put this liar and heretic back in his seat," Perez snarled. "Gabriel Catalan, stand before me!"

This is the moment, Gabriel thought, that Perez has dreamed about. When I first saw those eyes in Yacov Ardit's house, they struck me with fear. Perez didn't succeed that day, nor later with poor Francesco, but he never gave up. He made me print that awful book with every lie the Church ever told about Jews. He convinced Fernando, and even Isabel, to hold this vile Inquisition. He found the *Haggadah* that Pilar said I should never have given to Antonio Franco, he found the poor Lucenas, and now he has me. He thinks he has me. I'll burn, that's for sure. And so will Pilar. But Tomas will live, and Isaac. A new Jewish family will carry on the promise of the Jewish people to honor God and do His will.

"Are you a printer?"

"Yes."

"Did you print these books on the table?"

"No."

"Did you give this *Haggadah* to Antonio Franco?"

"No."

Gabriel was troubled by his answers. Is it right to lie like this? I *am* guilty of all that is charged. I do practice Jewish rites. Just yesterday, I circumcised my son! His heart soared at the thought and he must have smiled.

"What are you so pleased about?" Perez demanded. "You're going to die."

So close to the end, Gabriel at last enjoyed the confrontation that had bedeviled him since he had first seen Perez in the house of Yacov Ardit. Soon he would be with God, and he was no longer afraid.

"We're all going to die, even you, exalted Chief Inquisitor. I'm ready. Are you?"

"You trifle with me and with this Holy Inquisition?"

"What more can you do to me? You can't convict me on the evidence you've assembled. You have no proof of any of the charges. But you will convict anyway, because you and your Old Christian accomplices are jealous of the success I and other *conversos* have enjoyed. Will you take my worldly goods? Will you live in my house, which used to belong to the saintly Don Alonso de Viterbo, may he rest in peace?"

Perez jumped, and Gabriel thought he must have guessed the truth. He went on, surprised that he was given this much opportunity to speak but determined to take advantage of it.

"But what if you could prove everything? What then? Is it the way of Jesus to burn those who dare question the almighty Church? Where do the Scriptures teach such things?

"Jesus was a Jew," Gabriel continued. "He taught Jewish law and moral behavior, and he spoke the Hebrew language, just as it is printed in those books on the table. His Last Supper, as you know, was a Passover Seder. Jesus never taught that the Jewish Law was not to be observed. It was the Apostle Paul who changed this, years later, after the Church failed to convince most Jews that Jesus was the Jewish Messiah. Only then did Paul say that Christians did not have to obey the Law of Moses, which all followers of Jesus until that time had piously observed. Surely it made it easier to recruit among the gentiles if circumcision was not required. But Jesus, who was himself circumcised, never said any such thing.

"So Christianity went a new way, and Jews continued in their old way. Who then are the Old Christians and who are the New? Perhaps, Friar Perez, you have it reversed.

"Who created all these New Christians? Your Old Christian friends say it was a plot. The evil Jews are planning to take over the kingdom, they say, and enslave all of the Old Christians. What nonsense! What lies!

"My grandfather was a Jew. He was here, in Seville, in 1391, when

Archdeacon Ferran Martinez led mobs through the street and screamed 'Convert or die!' His father was beaten to death, and his mother raped and killed, but their son chose to live, and so he converted. He had no plan to conquer Christianity, nor did the thousands of others who converted with him. They just wanted to live.

"But your plan, the plan of the Church, did not work out as you had expected. When Jews were baptized, the Church said, quite rightly, that they had the same rights and privileges as any other Christian. So we worked hard and we succeeded. We did better than many Old Christians. Maybe they didn't work as hard. Maybe they weren't as smart, or as skilled. They became jealous. They tried to pass laws against *conversos*, like those in Toledo in 1449. But the Church would have none of it. Christians must be treated alike, the Pope said, and the laws were repealed.

"Now you have a new tactic. You cannot pass a single law against *conversos*. You cannot convince the Kings, or the Church, or even the city of Seville, to dismiss *conversos* and hire inferior Old Christians in their place. Right now, as this very tribunal takes place, the city of Seville has entrusted the gathering of its taxes to twenty one *converso* tax farmers and two *converso* treasurers, and not a single Old Christian!

"So you place all *conversos* under the suspicion of heresy, and you hold trials like this to convict without evidence, and thus you hope to eliminate the competition you cannot otherwise match. And the Church, or at least some of it, goes along with this terrible hypocrisy.

"Shame on you, Friar Ricardo Perez, you who are the grandchild of the Jewess Rebecca de Barrientos! Shame on all of you who are so uncertain of the message of the Jew Jesus Christ that you must burn alive any who challenge the Church's infallible positions. Such arrogance will not succeed! You will burn me in your fire. But you will never accomplish God's purpose by killing His children. This Church is one of arrogance, not love. Shame on you who pervert Jesus' message of God's love in this disgusting charade."

"Are you a Jew, Don Gabriel?" Perez asked quietly.

Such a simple question. It sent a chill through Gabriel. He could not speak.

Until that moment, Gabriel had planned to deny that he was a Jew. He did not want to leave any proof that any *converso* was really a secret Jew. So few were, but it was so easy to accuse.

But there were others who meant more to him than the despicable Dominican and his pitiful Church. Señor Franco and his wife, who would die for the first and only time they had sought the God of Israel. The Lucenas, who had worked so hard and willingly taken the risks so that others, his grandchild among them, would know how to be a Jew.

And Pilar. Pilar who said it was foolish to print the books. It will lead to death, she said. Pilar who never let Esther become Maria, who insisted that she remain a Jew, and in helping her, became a Jew herself. Pilar, who knew how stupid it was to give *Haggadahs* to the *conversos*, but who never said a word when she was proven correct. Pilar, who saw his father Isaac brutally murdered.

Isaac. Five minutes a Jew, and it meant everything. But for his bloody *tallit*, there would be no baby Isaac. His immortality, and Pilar's, soon safely sailing from Malaga.

Gabriel's tightly closed eyes saw others. Others he never knew. *Conversos* who accepted Christ, first to live, later to prosper. Like him. Could he be their Isaac?

Tomas, whose blood of the covenant was still fresh on his cell floor. Tomas, who offered his books and his flesh that the name of God might be known among His creatures.

He felt the presence of God. *I am He who is.* You shall love the Lord your God. Most exalted. Who chose Abraham to know Him, and the unworthy children of Israel to bring His name to the nations.

Jesus of Nazareth, one of those children. A Jew. A son of God like all the others. His Jewish message perverted by a fearful intolerant church. Yet even the Church needs Jews.

Suddenly it was clear to him that the Church must ultimately make peace with its Jewish roots, and must accept that the God of Israel will never reject the race they call accursed.

He stared directly at Perez. He smiled. He finally knew what his father Isaac felt so many years before.

"Yes," he said. "I am a Jew."

Archbishop Fonseca, once again forced into a role that Gabriel could see was abominable for him, advanced stiffly to the front of the room.

"The work of this Holy Tribunal is concluded," he said. "Don Gabriel Catalan, Pilar Catalan, Señor and Señora Franco, Israel Lucena, Leah Lucena, Rebecca Lucena, Rachel Lucena, and Deborah Lucena, are all judged guilty of heresy. Hannah Lucena is judged too young to have knowingly committed such heinous crimes, and she will be placed with a good Christian family that her soul may be saved through Faith in Christ."

Hannah would live! Gabriel hoped that Tomas would somehow learn that she had been spared.

"All of those convicted by this Holy Order are urged to confess their sins, that their souls may share the salvation of our Lord Jesus. Which among you will so confess?"

None rose in response to the Archbishop's offer.

Fonseca continued, "Each of the convicted shall participate in a final Mass, tomorrow in the Cathedral Square. They will then be burned in the fires their crimes have warranted until they pass from this life without hope of salvation."

Gabriel expected him. He had come to the cell only once before, but he would come today. This was his last chance. Tomorrow Gabriel would be with God, unavailable for Perez to torment.

Gabriel wanted to read again from the prayers that Tomas had left, but he waited. He would pray after Perez left.

As had happened so many times before, Perez simply appeared. One moment, Gabriel was alone, and the next, there he was, framed in the open doorway, his smirk and arrogant posture proclaiming his triumph.

"All these years you were lying," Perez said. "You went to church and you took the sacraments." He paused, truly upset. "You ate the sacred Host, and it meant nothing to you. You profaned the Church."

He came into the cell, close to Gabriel, not even bothering to close the door behind him.

"Jew!" he whispered. "You're a Jew!"

"It's amazing," Gabriel said with a smile. "All these years, and you couldn't smell my Jewish stench. Why was that, Friar?"

Perez backed off, and Gabriel jumped on his uncertainty.

"What choice did the Church give me?" Gabriel roared. "Most *conversos* are happy enough to be Christians. They've forgotten whatever they knew about Judaism. But for those few who remember, what can we do?"

"You're baptized," said Perez. "You have no right to be a Jew. It's heresy and you'll burn for your choice."

"By your rules. By the rules of a Church that cannot permit independent thought. Why are you so afraid? Are you really concerned for the souls of Jews who don't accept Jesus? Or are you terrified that your own faith will collapse if it's opened to question?"

"There … can …be …no … dissent!" said Perez, spitting out each word, the vein on his forehead throbbing.

"You're a fool," Gabriel said, "and you delude yourself. Tomorrow, you'll burn nine innocent people, guilty of no crime against another human being, no crime against the monarchs, and no crime against the teachings of Jesus. The only crimes any of us have committed are against the fanatical desire of the Catholic Church to preserve its power and wealth by forcibly preventing any Christian from questioning its stale dogma, none of which comes from Jesus anyway.

"But you won't eliminate dissent. You won't stop people from thinking. You surely won't do away with the Jews. Do you think God has abandoned His chosen people? Never! He tests us. He makes our lives difficult. But that's because He loves us. God will never permit the Jewish people to disappear from the earth, no matter how many you burn."

Surprisingly, Perez didn't respond. He seemed to be frightened.

"Tell me, Ricardo," Gabriel said, "your grandmother, the one who was a Jew, was she your mother's mother?"

Perez looked away, giving Gabriel the answer he already knew.

"So she was," he said. "You know that under Jewish Law, that makes you a Jew, the son of a Jewish mother."

Perez shook uncontrollably.

Gabriel pressed. "I guess you don't really believe that the Law of Moses was made invalid by Christ. If it was, you'd have no worry." Gabriel smiled.

"When you confess your sins, Ricardo, do you believe that you're really absolved? Tomorrow you're going to kill innocent people, and don't pretend that you avoid that responsibility by turning us over to the secular arm. God knows better.

"What if you're not absolved? Our Talmud teaches that 'He who influences the masses to sin will not be given the means to repent.' You will die with those sins on your head, out of grace because you haven't confessed, or because God refuses to accept your confession. You'll go to Hell, Ricardo! That will be a good joke, don't you think?"

Perez was aghast. He had come in triumph, and his victory had turned to dirt. Gabriel had never seen him so devastated. He backed away, but when he reached the door, Gabriel couldn't resist a final shot.

"Go in peace, Ricardo. *Shalom Aleichem.*"

The sound of nearby workmen building the stakes at which Gabriel and Pilar would soon burn mingled with the clang of the slamming door.

Gabriel waited until he was sure Perez was gone, then went to his mattress. He had remnants of two candles left, enough to last an hour.

He knew the full ecstasy of prayer for the first and only time in his life. The only time that mattered. He said the words again and again, and he knew that God heard him. Gabriel Catalan was known to Almighty God. The Lord of the universe cared about him. Waited for him.

"God, thank you that you have made me and given me life, that most incomprehensible gift, that I might pass your gift to Tomas and he to Isaac. You have blessed me with a woman who has shared my life and who will share my death. I am grateful for these things, Lord, and I thank you.

"But you have made man to seek, to wonder, to be unsatisfied. So I ask for more. Tomorrow I will give my life in Your honor, with words of praise for You on my lips. I ask that You give me a sign, O Lord, that You hear my prayer and that You know my name. Speak to me, O Lord, as I speak to you. Bless me, as I have blessed You."

Confident that his God would hear and answer, Gabriel Catalan slept untroubled on his last night on earth.

Before dawn, he was jostled awake. His first panicked thought was for the pages of prayers. *Where are they?* Then he remembered that he had tied them to his chest with a piece of his undershirt.

He was covered with an ugly yellow cloak, thankfully over his other clothing. On the cloak he saw his name, a crude Jewish star, and the word 'judaizer,' along with grotesque images of dragons and devils, in blood red.

One end of a rope was looped securely over his neck; the other end tied to his wrists. The prisoners were assembled in the still dark courtyard of San Pablo. Gabriel saw Pilar, dressed exactly as he was. He went to her. They were not prevented from standing next to each other, and when others moved away, they spoke.

"I should have listened to you about the *Haggadahs*," Gabriel said.

"It made no difference," Pilar answered. "If not that, something else. Perez has the power."

"We have a grandchild," Gabriel said with a smile.

Pilar returned his smile. "Yes, we do" she said.

"Are you all right," he asked.

"I'm ready," she said quietly. "We go to God."

"We should have left Castile years ago," Gabriel said. "You were always right."

"But you couldn't leave. I always knew that."

"What do you mean?" he asked.

"Your work wasn't done."

"It had better be now," said Gabriel, smiling through his tears.

They stood together, touching for as long as they could. I have loved this woman for my whole life, Gabriel thought. I can ask no more than to die with her, our children away and safe.

"Line up! Move!"

Dozens of Dominicans surrounded them. Two monks grabbed each of the prisoners and arranged the sequence according to their predetermined plan. Gabriel and Pilar were pulled apart.

A cacophony of sound proceeded from the Dominicans, each screaming to "their" prisoner the same maniacal message. "Confess! Confess! Admit your sins and the Mother Church will show its mercy." Gabriel ignored their insane noise. What mercy could any of them expect?

Ahead of him, Gabriel saw a strange cross, made of freshly cut wood, shrouded in a mourning veil of black crepe. Four soldiers beat slowly, ominously, on the deep voiced kettledrums. A canopy of brilliant scarlet and gold cloth was carried by four acolytes. Walking under the canopy, a priest, bearing the Host on a black velvet pillow.

The gates of the monastery swung open. In the gathering dawn, Gabriel saw mobs of people lining the street. The Cathedral bell kept somber pace with the kettledrums. When the crowds saw the Host, they fell flailing to the ground, prostrated in excitement and fear.

In this manner, the procession advanced from the convent of San Pablo through the *juderia* to the square before the Cathedral, its huge black stones rising out of the gloom, the Moorish tower incongruously graceful next to it. How much had transpired, Gabriel thought, since he had rushed through this square in response to Don Alonso's call to meet Johann Gutenberg.

The prisoners were led by their Dominican guards to a platform at one side of the square. Standing there, Gabriel saw for the first time the white mules in funereal trappings which had trailed behind him. Friar Perez and the other two Inquisitors, resplendent in their white habits, rode ramrod straight on their mules. The Inquisitors headed for a second platform, upon which an altar had been raised, and where they were soon joined by the priest carrying the Host. The wooden cross was placed behind the altar and a hundred long tapers were lit.

The priest offered the Mass. It seemed endless. Latin words rolled sonorously and pompously from his tongue. The Church, having captured its prey, was in no hurry for the kill. The priest pleaded with the prisoners to confess and repent, that their souls be saved by the Church's mercy.

Gabriel was able to get close to Pilar. Their shoulders touched. The Dominicans on the platform pushed them apart, but then the friars' attention drifted and they touched again.

Israel, and then Leah Lucena, refused to repent. Each was dragged back to join the other prisoners.

Rebecca Lucena, looking timorously at her parents who urged her on, said she would repent. Rachel and Deborah did the same.

But then all three girls were returned to the first platform, and Israel Lucena screamed that they had been misled. What did the promise of mercy mean if they were still to be burned at the stake? The priest explained that the mercy of the Church would be expressed by strangling them first so they would not feel the flames. Leah Lucena collapsed and had to be propped up by her two Dominican guards.

Pilar, and then Gabriel, declined the Church's kind offer.

The prisoners are marched to the Campo de Tablada where a special place of burning has been constructed. There they are incongruously greeted by huge statues of the Hebrew prophets Isaiah, Jeremiah, Ezekiel and Hosea, presiding over the sufferings of those among their descendants who dared to remain faithful to the God of Israel.

A huge white cross has been erected in the middle of the field, surrounded by nine stakes. Each prisoner is bound to one of the stakes. Dry firewood is stacked at their feet and up their legs. The Dominicans continue their exhortations, screaming "confess, repent, save your soul. Christi nomine invocato." All in the name of Christ. "Do not go to eternal damnation. It's not too late."

Soldiers march in, carrying lighted torches, two for each pyre. The fires are lit, the dry wood crackles. Nine human torches light the field. The Lucena girls scream. Reminded of the Church's promise of mercy, the closest soldiers drop their torches and garrote the three girls. Necks broken, their heads hang grotesquely.

Flames lick at Gabriel's feet. He feels the heat and readies himself for excruciating pain.

But instead, the drawn out sound of an exultant shofar fills the air.

It must be my imagination, he thinks. The sound changes to a repetition of powerful, shrill blasts, strident sounds in rapid succession. The kettledrummers drop their sticks, and Gabriel sees fear on the faces around him. They must hear what he hears.

He feels no pain. His clothes burn, he smells his own burning flesh, but there is no pain. He turns to Pilar, and her astonished smile tells him that she too feels nothing.

The flames burn through the cords holding Gabriel's hands and slowly he raises his arms. His sleeves are fully engulfed, but still there is no pain. Pilar raises her arms to mirror his. The crowd shrinks back, afraid. Some turn and run. Gabriel wants to look at Perez, to see his terror, but he cannot take his eyes from Pilar. There are only a few seconds left.

Gabriel Catalan sings out the prayer of a joyous Jew, accompanied by long, fervent, ear-splitting blasts from the unseen Shofar.

שמע ישראל
Hear, O Israel,
יי אלהינו יי אחד
the Lord our God, the Lord is One
ימלך יי לעולם
The Lord shall reign forever
יהא שמה רבא מברך
May his great name be blessed forever

The prayers tied to Gabriel's chest burst into flame. Those still close enough to see the eruption of light run frantically from the revealed power of the God of Israel.

Gabriel Catalan sees Pilar smile as her face is consumed in the flames.

EPILOGUE

Tomas's heart soared when he saw the Archbishop's great seal emblazoned in red wax. He had written several times to Fonseca, sending the letters by ship from Pisa, but was repeatedly disappointed when there was no answer. It had been almost a year.

He sat alone in the courtyard of the villa provided by Lorenzo de Medici, not far from *Il Magnifico's* palace. The familiar sounds and smells of printing emanated from a nearby building. Three presses were already operating, with four more in various stages of assembly. An army of assistants created Latin, Italian, and Hebrew type at a furious pace. With the Medici resources, he would print more in a few months than in all the years in Spain.

Esther's voice, singing gently to Isaac, wafted through an open window. Judah was no doubt close at the feet of his new friend, a young sculptor, who had been sent by Lorenzo after he had seen Francesco Romo's painting. Michelangelo Buonarroti knew immediately that the style was borrowed from Masaccio, whose work in the Church of the Carmelites was just a short distance away. He and Judah had become constant companions.

Staring at Fonseca's letter, he was both anxious and reluctant to break the seal. He saw his parents' cells, smelled the dank air, heard their last words. Fonseca had been there after he had left.

> *Dearest Tomas,*
> *Your letters were a blessing, the only I have had in Seville*
> *since this hell began. I regret that I have nothing but evil tid-*
> *ings to report. Every day there are arrests. Every week the*

carts go to the Campo de Tablada and more are burned. Almost two hundred so far and no one knows who will be next. I cannot believe that Queen Isabel intended this, but no one can stop the friars now.

The only thing that did stop the burning, for awhile, was the plague, which visited us in June. Friar Perez became sick, but recovered. Such is the imponderable will of the Lord. I am ashamed to say that Perez lives in your house, which is now the home of the Chief Inquisitor. Would that I had taken Don Alonso's advice so many years ago when it would have been possible to keep Friar Perez from gaining such influence.

I have tried many times to write, but my pen would not reveal my sadness. Now it is time. I have not much longer on this earth and I must answer the son of my dear friend Gabriel Catalan.

I say friend even though I now realize that your father was secretly a Jew for all the time I knew him. I put my own life in jeopardy if these words become known to the dark friars, but my respect and love for Gabriel Catalan outweighs my fear, and I will die soon anyway.

Your father was exultant at the time of his death. Likewise your mother. I don't understand it, but they felt no pain. There was a fearsome sound, the roar of a huge unseen wind, or horn, and a bright flash of light coming from your father. The crowds shrunk back, terrified. Perez was also terrified, but he held his ground. There were nine burned that day, your parents, Antonio Franco and his wife, the Lucenas and the three older daughters.

You wrote that you are a Jew in Florence. As a churchman, I cannot condone this. As a human being, I applaud you. Jesus never wanted men to be forced, upon pain of death, to follow Him. Each man must choose. This tragic hatred is the Church's doing, not our Lord's, and in my old age, I find the courage to say that the Church is wrong.

I wish you well, Tomas, and your dear wife Maria, who is now once again Esther. May the Lord bless your lives that you be a credit to His glory. May there be an end to the insanity that has gripped our land, that you may one day return.

I remain your friend, in love, and in Christ.

Alfonso de Fonseca

Tomas stared intently at the words of the old Archbishop, taking comfort in the joy his parents felt when they went to God. As he read again, he found another blessing in Fonseca's letter and he shivered with excitement.

Hannah was alive.

ACKNOWLEDGEMENTS

It took six years to write *The Heretic* — in the early morning hours, on weekends, and to and from work on the M104 bus in Manhattan. During that time, I was fortunate to have many professional associates, friends, and family members who read all or portions of the manuscript and offered comments, criticisms, and encouragement. Now I am trying to remember all of the people who were so helpful, and I am terrified that I will forget someone. If so, I apologize in advance, as I list, alphabetically: Rabbi Mark Angel, Mel Berger, Linda Bernstein, Shirley Chapin, Ann Cohen, Marissa Costello, Bernie Dishler, Julie Domonkos, David Dubnau, Herb & Marlene Feldhuhn, Jane Gerber, Francesca Giancotti, Tim Hanahan, Hank Hanahan, Msgr. Thomas Hartman, Chris Lenny, Kerry Lenny, Kevin Lenny, M. J. Lewin, Ruth Nathan, Susan Otradovec, Abraham Pinter, Rev. David H. C. Read, Gianni Riotta, Marlene Schwartz, Connie Smukler, Joe Speakman, Jon Weinstein, Josh Weinstein, and Janet Zimmerman. In addition, Mayapriya Long, Eric Kampmann and Gail Kump have been of invaluable assistance.

There are several people without whom it is unlikely that *The Heretic* would have been completed. Chronologically first among these is my high school English teacher, Mrs. Margaret McGinley, who told me I could write and said that I should. Thirty five years later, I took her advice. Next was Rabbi Harry B. Kellman, with whom I discussed the book when it was just a concept, and whose enthusiasm and insistence that "this book must be written" was often in my mind. When I had written the first three chapters, and it wasn't really clear that I would go on, I had the good fortune to meet Pamela Pearce, who became my "friendly reader" through the rest of the process, until this day. Richard Marek, my editor, offered both professional advice and friendly encouragement. And of course my wife Pat Lenny, who put up with countless hours of quiet time and postponement of many other activities, and to whom *The Heretic* is dedicated, may her Catholic family never read it too carefully.

And finally — to Benjamin, and the rest of the life he never had.

SOURCES AND FURTHER READING

I have made every effort to be consistent with the facts and with the spirit of the times about which I wrote. There were several instances where I did modify or compress the sequence of events to create a more smoothly flowing story, but I don't think this has done any serious damage to historical truth. For those who want to learn more about the events and themes which underly *The Heretic*, I recommend the following:

Baer, Yitzhak, *History of the Jews in Christian Spain*; Brantl, George, *Catholicism*; Bratton, Fred Gladstone, *The Crime of Christendom*; Burke, Peter, *Popular Culture in Early Modern Europe*; Burman, Edward,*The Inquisition: Hammer of Heresey*; Casazza, Ornella, *Masaccio*; Catholic Encyclopedia, *Tomas de Torquemada, St. William of Norwich, Judaism, Inquisition*; Chappell, Warren, *A Short History of the Printed Word*; Chaucer, Geoffrey, *Canterbury Tales*; Chavel, Charles B., *Ramban: Disputation at Barcelona*; Chilton, Bruce and Neusner, Jacob, *Judaism in the New Testament*; Christian, William A., *Apparitions in Late Medieval & Renaissance Spain*; Chrysostom, St. John, *Adversus Judaeos*;

Cohen, Jeremy, *The Friars and the Jews*; Crossan, John Dominic, *Who Killed Jesus?*; Deanesly, M., *A History of the Medieval Church: 590-1500*; Dolan, John D., *Catholicism*; Duby, George (editor), *History of Private Life, II, Medieval World*; Eisenstein, Elizabeth L., *The Printing Revolution in Early Modern Europe*; Eusebius, *The History of the Church*; Farrar, Frederic W., *Early Days of Christianity*; Fisher, Leonard Everett, *Gutenberg*; Fitzgerald, George F., *Handbook of the Mass*; Flannery, Edward H., *The Anguish of the Jews*; Fletcher, Richard, *Moorish Spain*; Fredricksen, Paula, *From Jesus to Christ*; Gerber, Jane S., *The Jews of Spain*; Gilmore, Myron P., *The World of Humanism*; Harvey, L. P., *Islamic Spain 1250 to 1500*;

Heschel, Abraham Joshua, *The Sabbath*; Hood, John Y. B., *Acquinas & the Jews*; Hope, Thomas, *Torquemada, Scourge of the Jews*; Ing, Janet, *Gutenberg and his Bible*; Irving, Washington, *Alhambra, Conquest of Granada*; Lea, Henry Charles, *A History of the Inquisition of Spain*; Lea, Henry Charles, *The Inquisition of the Middle Ages*; Liss, Peggy K., *Isabel the Queen*; Longhurst, John E., *The Age of Torquemada*; Maccoby, Hyam, *The Mythmaker* ; Maccoby, Hyam, *Judaism on Trial*; McMichael, Steven J., *Was Jesus the Messiah?* ; McMurtrie, Douglas C., *Wings for Words*; McMurtrie, Douglas C., *The Book, The Story of Printing & Book-making*; Medieval Sourcebook, *William of Norwich, Chrysostom - Homilies versus the Jews*; Miller, Townsend, *Henry IV of Castile; 1425-1474*; Millgram, Abraham E., *Anthology of Medieval Hebrew Literature*; Netanyahu, B., *The Origins of the Inquisition in 15th Century Spain*; Neuman, Abraham A., *Jews in Spain*; Nicholls, William, *Christian Antisemitism*; O'Callaghan, Joseph F., *A History of Medieval Spain*; Plaidy, Jean, *The Spanish Inquisition*; Poliakov, Leon, *History of AntiSemitism*;

Prager, Dennis and Telushkin, Joseph, Why the Jews?; Prescott, William H., Ferdinand and Isabella; Rice, Eugene F., Foundations of Early Modern Europe; Roth, Cecil, The Spanish Inquisition; Roth, Cecil, Jewish Printers of Non-Jewish Books in 15th and 16th Centuries; Rowland, Beryl, Medieval Woman's Guide to Health; Rubin, Nancy, Isabella of Castile; Ruether, Rosemary Rather, Faith and Fratricide; Sabatini, Rafael, Torquemada and the Spanish Inquisition; Sanders, E. P., The Historical Figure of Jesus; Schreck, Alan, Basics of the Faith: A Catholic Catechism; Scott, Anderson, Christianity According to St Paul; Segal, Alan F., Paul the Convert; Smith, James E.,What the Bible Teaches sbout the Promised Messiah; Soulen, R. Kendall, The God of Israel & Christian Theology; Trachtenberg, Joshua, The Devil and the Jews; Vermes, Geza, Jesus the Jew; Zeitlin, Irving M.; Jesus & the Judaism of His Time.